7.95

W9-ABM-893

THE SOD-HOUSE FRONTIER

THE COUNCIL BLUFFS CROSSING ON THE OVERLAND TRAIL

James Linforth, *Route from Liverpool to the Great Salt Lake Valley*, 1855.
Engraved after a drawing by Frederick Piercy.

THE
SOD-HOUSE FRONTIER
1854-1890

A Social History of the Northern Plains
from the Creation of Kansas & Nebraska
to the Admission of the Dakotas

BY

EVERETT DICK

UNIVERSITY OF NEBRASKA PRESS
LINCOLN AND LONDON

Copyright, 1937, 1954, by Everett Dick

First Bison Book printing: 1979

Most recent printing indicated by first digit below:
1   2   3   4   5   6   7   8   9   10

Library of Congress Cataloging in Publication Data

Dick, Everett Newfon, 1898–
    The sod-house frontier, 1854–1890.

Reprint of the ed. published by Appleton-Century Co., New York.
Bibliography: p. 519
Includes index.
    1. Great Plains—History. 2. Frontier and pioneer life—Great Plains. I. Title.
F591.D54   1979   978'.02   78-24204
ISBN 0–8032–6551–4

Published by arrangement with the author
Manufactured in the United States of America

DEDICATED

TO THE MEMORY OF MY MOTHER AND TO
MY FATHER WHO IN THEIR BRIDAL DAYS
LEFT AN OLDER STATE AND SETTLED IN
KANSAS DURING THE CLOSING YEARS OF
THE SOD-HOUSE EPOCH

PREFACE

KINGS have had their annalists; military men and statesmen have had their biographers; the Frontier in American history has had its general historians. In few instances, however, has the common life of the people been portrayed. The present volume is an attempt to depict the life of the common man on the cutting edge of the frontier immediately following the date when it leaped across the Missouri River into Kansas and Nebraska and across the Red River into the vast domain now known as North and South Dakota. My purpose has been to relate the story of how the residents of the settled regions to the East left their old homes, journeyed to the new land, and conquered the obstacles incident to making new homes. The struggle was a heroic one and brings into view the dominant characteristics of the race.

The sources are largely newspapers, biographies and autobiographies, diaries, personal interviews, monographs, and material such as historical society collections and local histories.

I gratefully acknowledge the many courtesies and the help rendered by a host of people interested in the undertaking. Mrs. Clarence S. Paine, Secretary of the Mississippi Valley Historical Association, has given valuable suggestions as well as rendered every courtesy in her capacity as Librarian of the Nebraska State Historical Society. Dr. Addison E. Sheldon and his associates at the Nebraska State Historical Society have given assistance and encouragement in the research that made this volume possible, and I am especially indebted to Miss Martha Turner for her valuable aid in assembling illustrations. Mr. L. K. Fox, Secretary of the South Dakota Historical Society, likewise extended every courtesy in connection with my investigation at the South Dakota Historical Society Library. Mr Kirke Mechem and his large staff at the Kansas

State Historical Society rendered efficient and courteous service on the author's numerous visits there. Special thanks are due Professor Edward Everett Dale, President of the Mississippi Valley Historical Association, for his valuable suggestions and encouragement. To my honored major professor of university days, Professor Frederic Logan Paxson, I express not only gratitude for the stimulus for the research embodied herein, but also grateful appreciation for reading the manuscript and making valuable suggestions. Professor James Lee Sellers of the University of Nebraska has also given counsel and encouragement. To my wife, Opal Wheeler-Dick, are due words of appreciation for her faith in the project through years of research and for her valuable assistance in arranging the material and putting it in final form.

Nearly twenty years have passed since the Sod-House Frontier was written. The cordial reception which the public accorded this volume has been very gratifying. After three printings the supply was exhausted and the work has now been out of print for several years. Continued calls for the book, however, have led to the belief that another printing is desirable.

Only as they are familiar with the life of the common man who conquered this raw untamed area, can the present residents intelligently interpret the present. This printing is offered with the hope that on this one hundredth anniversary of the formation of Kansas and Nebraska, the Sod-House Frontier may be made available to the largest possible number of readers in order that our generation may better understand its cultural heritage.

Lincoln, Nebraska
May 7, 1954

Everett Dick

CONTENTS

CHAPTER I

WESTWARD HO!

CHAPTER II

PREËMPTION DAYS

CHAPTER III

TOWN-BUILDING MANIA

CHAPTER IV

THE RIVER CITIES OF THE FIFTIES

CHAPTER V

LOG-CABIN DAYS

CONTENTS

CHAPTER VI

PIONEER FINANCE

CHAPTER VII

ROAD RANCHES

CHAPTER VIII

THE SOD HOUSE

CHAPTER IX

HOMESTEADING

CHAPTER X

VIGILANTE DAYS

CHAPTER XI

THE HOMESTEADER-CATTLEMAN WAR

CONTENTS

CHAPTER XII
HUNTING AND TRAPPING

CHAPTER XIII
WHITES AND INDIANS

CHAPTER XIV
COLONIES AND COLONIZING AGENCIES

CHAPTER XV
NATURE FROWNS ON MANKIND

CHAPTER XVI
WOMEN AND CHILDREN ON THE FRONTIER

CHAPTER XVII
HOMESTEADER DAYS AND WAYS

CONTENTS

CONTENTS

CHAPTER XXIV

THE CHURCH AND THE FRONTIER

CHAPTER XXV

THE COMING OF THE IRON HORSE

CHAPTER XXVI

PLEASURE AND PLAY

CHAPTER XXVII

THE PRAIRIE TOWN

CHAPTER XXVIII

ALONG MAIN STREET

CHAPTER XXIX

THE PIONEER NEWSPAPER

CHAPTER XXX

THE PIONEER DOCTOR

CHAPTER XXXI

LAWYERS AND LEGAL PROCEEDINGS

CHAPTER XXXII

TURBULENT DAYS IN COUNTY AFFAIRS

CHAPTER XXXIII

ITINERANTS

CONTENTS

CHAPTER XXXIV

PIONEER INDUSTRIES

CHAPTER XXXV

CRUDE FRONTIER CUSTOMS

ILLUSTRATIONS

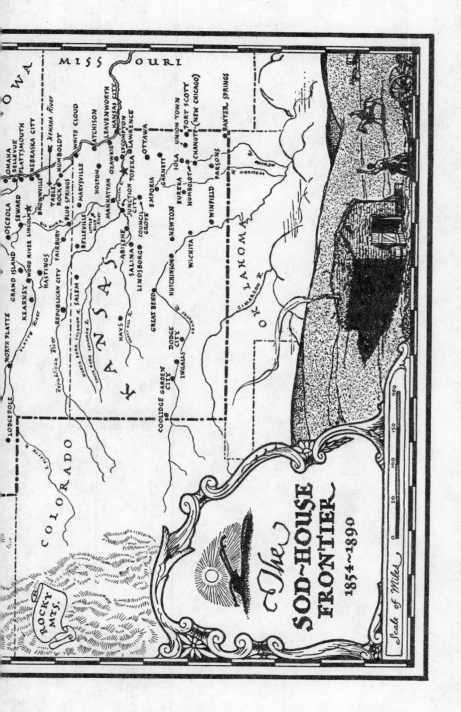

The
SOD~HOUSE
FRONTIER
1854~1890

Scale of Miles

THE SOD-HOUSE FRONTIER

INTRODUCTION

FROM THE TIME when the white man first stepped foot on the eastern coast of America, the course of settlement has been ever westward. By means of the decennial census maps the historian traces the steady advance of settlement and draws the frontier line a little farther to the west with each ten-year report until 1890, when the last land in the rain belt was removed from public to private ownership by land-office entry. Land hunger has been the principal motive for westward migration from the time when the early Virginians abandoned the idea of picking up jewels and gold from the ground and turned to the pursuits of husbandry. Although the frontier line moved westward by starts and jumps, its progress through the years was unremitting.

In the first decade of the nineteenth century, however, Zebulon M. Pike, in his report following a government exploration into the West, declared the immense prairies beyond the Missouri "incapable of cultivation"; and Major Stephen H. Long ten years later, in a report on his exploration of these prairies, said that they "bear a resemblance to the Desert of Siberia."

The United States maps of the middle of the nineteenth century bore a space, extending from Texas to the Canadian line and from the Missouri River to the Rocky Mountains, entitled the "Great American Desert." As late as 1861 a United States senator, in opposing the admission of Kansas into the Union as a state, declared that "after we pass west of the Missouri River, except upon a few streams, there is no territory fit for settlement or habitation. It is unproductive. It is like a barren waste." [1]

The movement across the prairies occasioned by the Santa Fe trade and later by the far more numerous trains of the Mormon migration and the white-topped wagons of the Argonauts of 1849, slowly lifted the plains region from the realm of conjecture to the light of reality. Men began to realize that a land where millions of buffalo and antelope thrived was habitable. The partial dispelling of the desert myth, together with the need for a railroad to span the uninhabited gulf between the settled areas on the Atlantic and the Pacific, brought about the organization of the territories which I have called in this volume "the Sod-House Frontier."

It seems particularly fitting that the states of Kansas, Nebraska, North Dakota, and South Dakota should be considered together. All four states are largely agricultural [2] and, with the exception of the Black Hills, form a vast plain from the Canadian border to the northern boundary of the land reserved for the Indians. The settlers in these four states faced the same problems and hardships. In point of time the peopling of this area was concentrated within the generation from the creation of Kansas and Nebraska, which through the clouds of the slavery struggle emerged to territorial status by the terms of the Kansas-Nebraska Act of 1854, to the admission to statehood of North and South Dakota thirty-five years later. The migration of this generation, together with its settling and its struggle for a livelihood, is the theme of this book.

[1] John Lee Webster, "The West: Its Place in American History," Kansas State Historical Society Collections, Vol. XII, pp. 26, 27.

[2] With the exception of western South Dakota and southeastern Kansas, which bear deposits of minerals.

CHAPTER I

WESTWARD HO!

IN MANY HOMES east of the Missouri River there was glad anticipation when it was decided to leave the old home for the promised land made possible by the persuasive powers of the "Little Giant." [1] As preparations were made, there were days and weeks of delightful dreams of the new home where life would take on a new meaning. Whole families lived in imagination on the frontier where land was cheap and opportunity beckoned to all. Some, perhaps, owned town shares in some commercial emporium that was sure to become the county-seat of a rich county if not the capital of the state itself. As the prospective emigrants sat by the hearth and discussed the possibilities of becoming wealthy and perhaps holding high office when the territory became a state, they could hardly wait until the day of departure. When the great day arrived, the emigrants, severing old ties, hopefully turned their faces toward the setting sun.

Many of those leaving for the newly opened territories went by water. Those who lived east of the Allegheny Mountains naturally chose this mode of travel. It was quite the usual thing for the emigrants to journey by train to some point on the Ohio or the Mississippi River and travel by way of St. Louis up the Missouri River to the chosen home. [2]

[1] Stephen A. Douglas was known as the "Little Giant." He was chairman of the Committee on Territories of the Senate and pushed through the Kansas-Nebraska Bill opening up these two territories.

[2] The parents of Thomas F. Doran traveled from their home at Bridgewater, New York, to St. Louis by rail and thence by steamer to St. Joseph, where they secured a prairie schooner for the journey into Kansas.

Samuel J. Crawford, later a gallant soldier and governor of Kansas, left his home in Indiana, traveled eight hours on the train to St. Louis, took the steamer

3

The time and price of the river journey from St. Louis to Kansas City or Omaha varied with the season. The rate was highest in the summer, when traffic was heaviest, and cheapest in the spring and fall. In 1856 a man and his wife left Dayton, Ohio, at 3 o'clock on June 23 and arrived in Brownville, Nebraska, on Sunday, June 29, making the trip in a little over five days. In April, 1860, the *Nebraska City News* announced that goods were in Nebraska City only four days after leaving St. Louis. This was stated to be the quickest time on record up to that date. Ordinarily the time from St. Louis to Omaha was about ten days, and from St. Louis to Kansas City about three or four days. On the other hand, it took some boats three weeks to make the trip from St. Louis to Omaha.

The Reverend Reuben Gaylord, in a letter to his wife, gave his fare from Omaha to New York in 1859 as $42.50, first class. In the fifties the *Herald of Freedom* [3] listed the fare from St. Louis to Kansas City as $12.00. In 1860 the fare from Nebraska City to St. Louis was $8.00. It seems reasonable to surmise that the downstream passage was cheaper than the upstream passage because the traffic was so much lighter.

Colonization agencies were able to arrange liberal terms for their emigrants. The New England Emigrant Aid Company arranged for a ten-dollar fare from Pittsburgh to St. Louis, ten dollars from St. Louis to Kansas City, and a dollar to a dollar and a half by vehicle from Kansas City to Lawrence. Freight rates were relatively much higher than passenger fares. On household goods the rates

for Kansas City, and thence with a companion walked to his future home at Garnett, Kansas.

J. Sterling Morton, famous Nebraskan who was Secretary of Agriculture in President Cleveland's administration and the father of Arbor Day, left Chicago by rail for St. Louis, traveled to St. Joseph by steamer, and thence to Council Bluffs by stage. This distance, now traversed in a few hours by airplane, required seven full days and nights of tedious riding.

Erastus Beadle left Buffalo, New York, for Detroit by train. He continued the journey by rail to Cincinnati, where he boarded a boat for St. Louis. Being a speculator, Mr. Beadle was in a hurry, and when the boat was delayed at Louisville, he went by train via St. Louis to Jefferson City, Missouri. There he boarded a boat for Omaha. The boat was too slow, however, and the last stretch of the journey was made by stage.

[3] Lawrence, Kansas.

were $1.21½ per hundredweight from Chicago to St. Louis and $1.00 per hundredweight from there to Omaha. Erastus Beadle remarked that the rate from Chicago to St. Louis was double what it ought to have been.

The years 1855, 1856, and 1857 were the epoch of a tremendous movement from the states. Mrs. Charles Robinson, wife of the first governor of Kansas, from her home on Mount Oread at Lawrence, observed in 1855:

The roads for many days have been full of wagons—white-covered, emigrant wagons. We cannot look out of the windows without seeing a number, either upon the road through the prairie east of us, which comes in from Kansas City, where most emigrants leave the boats and buy wagons and provisions for the journey, or going on the hill west, on their way to Topeka, or other settlements above

The Lexington, Missouri, *Express* stated in March, 1855: "Every steamer up the Missouri brings hundreds of abolition emigrants to Kansas."

This great wave of emigration reached its peak in 1857. The clerk of the *New Lucy*, the boat on which Mr. Beadle took passage, told him on March 26, that since the river opened, twelve thousand people had passed up the Missouri in boats for Kansas and Nebraska, and as many more had gone by land. Beadle himself makes the observation that

every ferry we came to was crowded from Morning to Night. Such a tide of emigration was never before known. They are pouring in one continual stream to every town and ferry on the east bank of the river and stand in large groops of men, women, children, waggons, horses and oxen awaiting their turn to cross into the promised land. They tell us they are only pioneers and have but to write home favorable to bring parties of from ten to twenty for every individual now entering the Territories. They are covering the territories like a swarm of locusts.

Other witnesses verify these observations. In May, 1857, the *Nebraska Advertiser* averred that it was common for not less than one hundred persons to arrive at Brownville in a day. During that spring every available public building was occupied. The church and the school-house were used to shelter newcomers, and many camped under the trees. Furthermore, the editor published a report well calculated to gladden the heart of the most ardent speculator or town-builder:

> During an absence of four or five weeks, we were in portions of Illinois, Indiana, Ohio, and Kentucky, and found everywhere the "Western fever" prevailing to an "alarming extent"—all eyes turned toward Nebraska. With a knowledge of prevalent Western notions, those in the States have no idea of the immense rush for this country. . . .
>
> When we left here, four weeks ago, claims could be had within three to five miles of town; now we are told claim hunters must go from twelve to fifteen miles back in the country. Our farming lands are all taken by actual settlers—160 acres to each head of a family. At the rate matters have commenced this spring, six months from now will not find a foot of unoccupied land in Nemaha county.

When Brownville was first laid out in 1855, there were only two or three regular boats. In 1856 there were thirteen, and the optimistic Brownville editor expected fifty the following year; he noted that on a Monday night there were five boats discharging passengers and freight at the wharf. Steamers brought as many as five hundred and fifty emigrants at one trip. Ordinarily about four hundred were carried. Of these, one hundred and fifty were state-room passengers, and two hundred and fifty slept on the deck; the deck price was five or six dollars. In addition to this human cargo they carried five to eight hundred tons of freight.

The Missouri River honestly merited its nickname "Old Muddy," because, according to Horace Greeley, it was so muddy that an egg dropped in a glass of its water became invisible. Senator Thomas Hart Benton facetiously described it as a little too thick to swim in, and not quite thick enough to walk on.

Although the water route was much more comfortable than other modes of travel to Kansas and Nebraska, it had its drawbacks. If there was a lack of passengers, the boat might lay at the wharf

THE MISSOURI AT KANSAS CITY IN THE FIFTIES

Charles A. Dana, *The United States Illustrated.*

several hours or even days after its scheduled departure waiting for more passengers. The Reverend Henry T. Davis paid his fare and went on board the steamer *Sioux City* at St. Louis on Monday. The captain said he would be off in a short time. Firemen were feeding the furnace, and smoke was rolling from the smoke stack. The boat stayed all day. Tuesday morning the firemen were busy again, and apparently the boat was ready to move. However, to the disgust of the minister, the boat did not leave St. Louis until five o'clock on Saturday afternoon.

Usually the steamers were well loaded. This was especially true in 1857 when every boat was crowded to suffocation. Erastus Beadle was obliged to take the train from St. Louis to Jefferson City in order to get passage.[4] Before the train stopped, everyone had his carpet bag in hand and was ready to spring from the train and dash for the ship. When the train did stop, the crowd rushed in a mass tumbling over each other in the dark. Alas, not one place on the boat was unoccupied. Beadle, who had a "pull" with the captain, got a place anyway. The others had to await another vessel.

Once the boat started, progress was slow and the trip was tedious. The flat-bottomed vessel, which proverbially drew so little water that it could float on a heavy dew, in practice frequently grounded on sand bars. There was little for the passengers to do except watch the ever-changing scenery, converse, read, or play cards.

Life in every phase could be found on a river boat. There were young married couples seeking new opportunities in the West and unmarried men, free lances, seeking their fortune; men who had left their wives behind while they went to spy out the land and wives and little children going to meet the husband in the new home; the speculator bound for the land sales and the exuberant agent of a new Kansas or Nebraska town;[5] the missionary and the gambler; the merchant with his stock and the well-to-do planter, a

---

[4] March, 1857. The "Lightning Line" ran in connection with the Missouri Pacific Railway west from Jefferson City; it carried the United States mail and express.

[5] The portion of eastern Dakota Territory settled before the Civil War received its settlers mainly through Iowa and Minnesota.

perfect gentleman of culture and refinement, traveling to his plantation in western Missouri;—all these and many others were confined in this little world.

The passengers became well acquainted during the trip and some of the associations were destined to change the careers of the travelers. In the spring of 1857 a steamer with three hundred passengers ran aground. To break the monotony of the long delay a colony was organized to settle in Nebraska. A constitution and by-laws were framed, and thirty-five men signed the agreement. This group founded Beatrice, Nebraska, naming the city after the daughter of one of the chief members of the company.

Gamblers were always on hand ready to take advantage of the unwary. At one end of the saloon a game of cards was constantly in progress. Women frequently played, and often for high stakes. At the other end, in sharp contrast with the noise and excitement of gambling, a small but serious group might hold a prayer meeting. Another type of gaming was dice. A gambler displayed gold and silver watches, ear-rings, other cheap articles, and pieces of money, each on little numbered squares of oilcloth. For fifty cents a person could throw the dice. Each throw brought something, but the really valuable articles were on numbers which could not appear on the dice. Occasionally the gambler bought back a trifling article at a sum in excess of the value, and so lured the money of the credulous. Some of these rascals, by means of liquor and crooked set-ups, secured all the money of an emigrant before he reached his destination. These gamblers played night and day.

Not infrequently while the boat was unloading freight at a wharf the passengers, glad of a little freedom, held contests of races and jumping, the cabin and steerage passengers competing for honors. Very often the boat voyage was enlivened by a band. Some had steam calliopes which played old plantation melodies when approaching or departing from a town. To hear "Swanee River," "Old Folks at Home," or "Susannah" reverberating from the hills on a calm summer evening was charming.

At night the boat tied up to a tree on the river bank or on a small island, because snags and sand bars endangered the run. It was necessary for the captain to refuel the boat occasionally. He might take a flat boat loaded with wood in tow and unload en route, or load directly from one of the wood yards found at various points along the shore in the timbered country. It was customary for the captain to dicker for wood. He and the manager of the wood yard sparred for the financial advantage until finally after much hard talk, a bargain was struck, only to be followed by another verbal explosion. The mate bellowed invectives accompanied by threats without number and occasional blows on the backs of the deck hands as they hastened to load the wood. The passengers, bored by the long monotonous journey, welcomed this opportunity to stretch their legs and help load. For the most part profane language and gambling accompanied a river trip, but now and then a captain was found who forbade these things.

The steamers differed widely. Some had bed bugs and poor food, but the majority were clean and the food was extremely good. It was to the advantage of the captain, especially when business was slack, to have a good reputation. Sometimes passengers who were well pleased with the service, met and passed resolutions recommending the steamer and its captain to their friends, publishing their resolutions in the newspapers of the river ports.

In the rush days of 1857 the crowded conditions on the boats caused considerable inconvenience. Hundreds slept on the floor, and many amusing incidents occurred. Beadle gives a good picture of his trip between Jefferson City, Missouri, and Wyandotte, Kansas. In the evening

the porters comenced turning down the chairs along the state room doors completely blocking up the entrance or exits through the door. This being done they brought in a lot of Mattresses arranging them along one end on the chair backs to serve as a pillow. I took the hint and made fast to one then came a general strife to see who should have a bed About one half were accommodated. Some had a mattress some a pillow others a blanket. Covering about two thirds of cabin floor, one would' laugh another sing and a third curse, those that could get no chance to sleep done all they could to prevent others from sleeping and kickt up a general uproar until they got exhausted and we at last got to sleep. I was soare from laughing at the vanity of disposition, one was for fun, another kept up a constant growl. those however who said least fared best. I have often heard people tell of a crowd, but this beat all.

Again he mentions the scramble for a place to sleep on the cabin floor. "At nine o'clock a dive was made for the mattress, claims taken, and in the general melee, in which some got kick and scratches we went to bed."

At 6:30 in the morning the first gong sounded; the beds were taken from the floor, and the tables were elongated and spread. The passengers emerged from their berths and rushed to the washrooms where they made their morning ablutions in dirty black river water. At seven the breakfast gong sounded and was followed by a rush for first places at the table. This table ran the entire length of the cabin. For dinner there were immense roasts, stews, and broils. The captain, in all the grandeur of his vested authority, stood at the head of the table with a long knife, cutting and carving as he pleased, politely asking what each one wanted. A darky steward stood behind him to assist him. A troop of twenty colored waiters, as well drilled as soldiers, trotted down the long table bearing heaping dishes of food. There were rich pastries, cakes, jellies, ices, fruit, and nuts to tempt the palate.[6] One man remarked, "Juicy! Fat! Those were dinners when you got at them once"! [7] The long wait for meals apparently caused some to resort to a ruse in order to get to the first table. Again Mr. Beadle, shrewd schemer that he was, made the best of the occasion. He wrote in his diary:

Sunday 22—This morning another amusing scene was enacted which will probably be repeted three times per day during the trip. There

   [6] Mrs. H. A. Ropes, *Six Months in Kansas* (Boston, 1856), p. 27.
   [7] John A. MacMurphy, "Part of the Making of a Great State," *Proceedings and Collections*, Nebraska State Historical Society, Series II, Vol. I, No. 1, p. 8.

are three hundred passengers on board and only table room for some Seventy five. Who was to be first at table was the all engrossing subject as soon as preparations were commenced for breakfast. It was with difficulty that the waiters could get around to put the dishes on the tables. I saw at once that those without ladies must of necessity fare slim I accordingly secured Mrs. Leavett for meal times which was for me very fortunate. The table had to be cleared and set again four times before all the passengers were served. The fare is of the poorest kind I ever saw on a steamboat even at the first tables. Females were in great demand at meal times, even little girls that went free were engaged for the trip in order to secure a seat at the first table. We have two large and very amusing men by the name of Martin from Flint Mich who are brothers they take girls of 11 and 9 years to the table as their ladies. We are all becoming acquainted and are anticipating a pleasant time.

In case a man did not care to drink the river water, which had been allowed to settle, he could find a stronger liquid at the ship's bar.

As the steamer neared the Kansas and Nebraska towns, it was flooded with circulars and pamphlets boosting the country. All were glad when the journey came to an end, and yet the trip on the water had its bright spots. Before the emigrants reached their destination they seemed like one big family. Friendships were made and business associations were sometimes formed which lasted a lifetime.

The steamboat, although probably the most comfortable manner of making the long journey, was by no means the only method employed. A stage line ran across Iowa with its western terminus at Council Bluffs; and another ran across northern Missouri from Hannibal to St. Joseph. Such a trip, although ordinarily quicker than the other modes, was very unsatisfactory as to comfort and expense. In addition to the constant jolting of the springless coaches, the mud, terrible roads, and poor hotel accommodations made the trip a nightmare.

One passenger who paid ten cents a mile for his passage on a stage coach said that they carried fence rails to pry the coaches out of the muddy ravines and then walked up the hills and rode down.

On the trip from St. Joseph to Rockport, Missouri, they arrived one or two days late.

A man who made the trip east by the Hannibal and St. Joseph stage line wrote back to the *Kansas Chief* at White Cloud:

Swim the Missouri, wade, work your passage, skate, roll around the world and come up on the other side, go to purgatory and spend a month, visit the devil and stay a fortnight, even go to Chicago and pass the night, but do not take this line of stages for the East.

In the late fifties the Hannibal and St. Joseph Railway was built between the two cities, giving a speedy, comfortable passage. Some steamer passengers who were anxious to reach Omaha traveled from St. Joseph to Council Bluffs by stage. The fare was ten dollars and the trip miserable. A speculator's story of an incident on his trip on this line will give the reader some idea of what stage travel in the fifties was like:

Night had set in by the time we had made six miles. At this point was a sluce some twenty feet wide and about as deep. The watter was out of the banks and overflowed a large space of the bottoms both sides of the bridge. In the midst of the water before reaching the bridge the horses got set and could not move the coach. We were all obliged to get out . . . and wade to dry land. The water was cold as ice. our boots were full and more was pattering down on our heads while a cold north wind sent its chilling blasts almost through us. We stood a few minutes in this condition while the driver tryed to make his horses draw out the empty coach, but without success. What was to be done! No house was near, and to stand still was not deemed safe, in our wet and chilling condition. The driver wished us to wade in and unfasten his horses, while he remained on the Coach, thus enabling him to get on one of the horses and get away without *his* getting in the watter We declined however as we think he might have went around another road and thus prevented this Catastrophe. Each man waded back to the coach and got his carpet sack and flounced along throug the water to the bridge. here we rested a few minutes and plunged in on the other side, and for near one hundred rods we waded knee deep and some of the way up to the seat of our pants. It was a trying time but the only alternative. The excitement kept the watter from chilling us through. Reaching the dry ground a ground as dry as could be during a rain we paddled on the best we could with our heavy Carpet Sacks boots filled with water, clothes wet and stif, and at every step our feet sticking like tar to the muddy prarie soil. We looked in vain for a farm house by the way. After a short walk we discovered a light across the prarie, glimmering faintly through the darkness of the night and the falling rain. One of our party said he thought it was at Council Bluffs, and if so it must be four miles. This information was rather discouraging. We consoled ourselves however with the belief that the light could not be over one and a half miles at the extent We draged ourselves along for one whole hour until it seemed we could go no farther. Still that deceptive light receded from us as fast as we traveled, and we could not discover that it was any nearer than when we started I could easily imagine how one be-night on the prarie in a snow storm would become disheartened and lay down and take his last sleep while the winter wind covered him with pure white sheet of snow. Another half hour and instead of one light we could discover some dozen or more. this animated us afresh at the same time we had another hundred *yards* to wade in mud and water above our knees. Our last half mile we paid no attention to the best part of the road so we made headway. At ten o'clock we reach the *Paciffic House* Council Bluffs. My head was dizzy and I could barely see while my arms seemed pulled down to the ground by my heavy satchel.

The covered wagon was the favorite method for those coming comparatively short distances or desiring to bring their possessions and travel more slowly and economically. Great preparations were made weeks and months before the start for the new home. It was no small job to decide upon what was most necessary to take and what could be eliminated. The general plan was to keep house along the road. A substantial wagon was covered with white canvas, and provision was made several weeks or months before starting. One family baked a large quantity of bread and dried it out so that it would not mold and would be lighter. Frequently a kettle of hot milk and some of this dried bread made the evening meal. In addition to bacon, beans, flour, salt, and other groceries, the essential tools and utensils for housekeeping and farming were brought. A cookstove was frequently set in the center of the wagon, the pipe running through the top. This made a traveling home where the family could live until they found a good location and had a house built. The women did the washing, baking, and churning at regular intervals. The cream was placed in a pail and hung on the wagon. By night the rocking motion of the wagon had churned the butter.

Cows and oxen were both brought. Sometimes one wagon was drawn by cows and another by oxen; but more often the cows were driven. Frequently these animals became footsore and both oxen and cows needed to be shod at a blacksmith shop. One pioneer told the names of the oxen he brought. These might be of interest in this age of gasoline: "Kip" and "Yuler," "Ball" and "Broad," "Dick" and "Darb," and "Rock" and "Paddy."

If two or three wagons were driven by the same family, one would be loaded with farming necessities such as a breaking plow, axes, saws, carpenter tools, and seed potatoes. Great numbers of these wagons collected on the east side of the Missouri River and waited patiently to cross that last muddy gulf between them and "Beulah Land." At certain points steam ferries operated. The emigrants were given numbers and took their turn at crossing. At times the whole river valley was covered with these "ships of the desert" but some had to wait a week.[8] Soon after crossing the river, these caravans joined with the newcomers who had arrived by steamboat, and had outfitted at the river towns; together they formed a mighty exodus.

On leaving the river towns the long lines of wagons with their countless home-seekers wound across the prairie like a huge white serpent on a vast carpet of green. Each unit in the long procession represented a home-seeking family pressing toward the setting sun in search of a new home on the boundless rolling prairie. The father drove the oxen while the mother rode in the sway-backed canvas-covered vehicle. The lumbering wagon was decked with a spade, hoe, axe, or other equipment. Now and then a coop of chick-

[8] A considerable portion of this traffic was bound for California.

AN EMIGRANT NIGHT ENCAMPMENT ON THE PLAINS

From a drawing by Theodore R. Davis, *Harper's Weekly*, 1869.

ens or a beehive adorned the overloaded conveyance; buckets and pails dangled under it. The faithful family dog trotted along behind. Boys of all ages, barefoot and shaggy-haired, trudged along; now and then a sun-bonneted girl drove the family cows; or shouting men and boys on horseback, more seldom a woman in a buggy or light rig, closed the scene so familiar to that thin line of settlement on the western side of the Missouri River. Soon after leaving the outskirts of civilization these pilgrims began to scatter and seek homes over the territories. The lonesome settler was glad to have these homemakers pass, and to have them camp nearby. They brought news to the isolated family, hungry for information from the states.

Organized colonization was a common mode of migration in the fifties. The New England Emigrant Aid Company was the best known of these organizations. Its benefits were numerous. Friends and neighbors went together and enjoyed each other's society and help in the new country. The company was able to secure a marked reduction in transportation fare and at hotels. Much worry was also saved in sending with each company a superintendent who "knew the ropes" and could render assistance in an emergency.

The rigors of raw frontier life were greatly softened upon the first arrival in the new country by the company's assistance in building hotels, providing steam mills, and other conveniences. Their trains left Boston at regular intervals with from twenty-five to two hundred emigrants, adding recruits by the way. The route was by way of Albany, Cleveland, Chicago, Alton, and thence by water via St. Louis to the Kansas towns. The Missourians closed the Missouri River to the emigrants because of their abolitionist sympathies and the route was changed to one crossing Iowa overland.

There were other colonizing agencies, but the majority of their colonies were small and of local origin. A minister occasionally led his flock to the new West; or several families became interested and migrated in a body. In some cases a linguistic group sought new homes on the plains.

The first settlers at Fremont, Nebraska, were of the first class. They were a group of old acquaintances and friends in Outagamie County, Wisconsin. Returned Forty-niners gave glowing accounts of the wonderful fertility of the Platte Valley. Accordingly a colony of thirty-three persons started for Nebraska in 1856.

One group started on May 1 by rail and steamer for Omaha and arrived there ten days later. They bought wagons and other necessary camp equipment in Iowa and proceeded up the Platte. The other group, detained by business in Wisconsin, left in prairie schooners on August 4 and, driving by easy stages, arrived at Omaha on September 25.

Grand Island, Nebraska, founded by the Germans, is an example of the scores of Kansas, Nebraska, and Dakota towns settled by linguistic groups.[9] Mr. A. H. Barrows of Davenport, Iowa, pushed this settlement, alleging that influential and wealthy parties, among whom were members of Congress, would back his enterprise. He expected that a railway would be built up the Platte Valley and that eventually the national capital would have to be moved to a more centrally located point. The object of the speculators was to locate a town as near the center of the continent as practicable and to attempt to have the national capital moved there. A large group of Germans elaborated the plan. At that time, in 1857, according to territorial laws, a settler could preëmpt 320 acres. The company hired the settlers to take full claims wherever their surveyor directed. The company was to furnish all the funds for the final purchase. In consideration of this the settlers were to deed one-half of their claims to the company, while the other half should remain their property. In addition to this, the settler was to receive ten town lots. Parties without money were to be provisioned for twelve months on loan. As a financial venture the plan was a decided failure; the company lost six thousand dollars. The territory between Yankton and Wanari, Dakota Territory, was settled by Scandinavians in the fifties.

[9] Most of these were established in the seventies and eighties, however.

Less frequently a queer sect or a society of reformers made up a colony and moved to the frontier where land was cheap and experimentation was tolerated. Such a colony was the vegetarian colony near Humboldt, Kansas.

In the emigrant trains of prairie schooners the stages of life from birth to death were exemplified along the trail. Many a mother gave birth to a babe under the canvas cover of a prairie schooner and nursed the baby on the long westward journey, while she suffered from the lack of the comforts essential to maternity. Many a maiden and youth awoke to the realization of love and plighted their troth. Marriage was not infrequently celebrated among the rude surroundings of the westward journey. Death in almost every form overtook the travelers.

On Sunday the emigrant train usually stopped for the day. The women spent most of the day washing clothes and cooking food in preparation for the first few days of the week, while the children played. The men made necessary repairs or took care of other details preparatory to a full week's travel.

In crossing streams every source of ingenuity was awakened. The heavy wagons were floated or hauled across, or in some places small bridges were built if it were convenient to do so. On the prairies storms blew into the tents or blew the tents completely down. As a result on stormy nights travelers slept in the wagons. Spring wagons or light rigs had to be picketed down to keep from blowing over.

Not a few of the early settlers of Kansas and Nebraska came from the West. Disappointed California gold seekers or Pike's Peak gold hunters, returned and located on the choicest bits of land. In May, 1859, D. C. Jenkins, disappointed in his search for gold in the Colorado gold rush, turned his face eastward. Pushing a wheelbarrow loaded with all his possessions, he wearily measured the distance back to eastern Nebraska where he established a ranch at Big Sandy in Jefferson County. There he found the fleeting prosperity which had eluded him in his search for the shining metal. Merrick County, Nebraska, was first settled by a number of these disappointed Pike's Peakers. Others, who were met by disappointed returning miners, were persuaded to stop and squat on a favorable location. Joel Helvey started with his family for Colorado in April, 1859, and met a long line of disheartened gold hunters. He stopped in May and located a ranch on the overland stage line.

Many travel-worn emigrants gathered in the evening around the prairie camp-fire. Seated on the skulls of buffalo killed long ago by Indians, they debated whether to turn back, to forge ahead, or to remain on the prairie. Some parents, compelled to tarry by the long sickness of a member of the family, learned the value of the country and decided to stay. Others, having buried a child on the lonesome prairie, could not bring themselves to the point of leaving the little one there, and decided to remain and make their home nearby.

It was no uncommon thing for a man to walk to his new home from an eastern state. Neither was it uncommon for a man to come West, spy out the land, and having made a home, send for his wife or sweetheart to follow him. Those first few years on the prairie were fraught with hardships and loneliness. All honor to these path-breakers!

CHAPTER II

PREËMPTION DAYS

ONE of the knottiest problems the government faced from the time of the first land law in Washington's administration until the public domain had melted away, was that of an equitable method of distributing the public land to private owners. The first policy called for the sale of large tracts to big interests. The succeeding land laws made land available for purchase at low prices by the actual settler. There were two main methods of securing land in the fifties. One was by means of soldiers' military bounty land warrants and the other was by preëmption. Since 1776 land warrants had been given as a reward to the nation's soldiers. They were intended to provide a home for those who had risked their lives on the battle-field. In the fifties Mexican War land warrants were used; they had a face value of $1.25 an acre. These bounty warrants were assignable and were often sold at a discount by the improvident soldiers who disposed of their land rights for a mess of pottage. In 1861 these warrants sold for as low as fifty cents an acre. Holders of these documents secured land at this price without residing on it. Land amounting to more than the entire area of Kansas was granted on Mexican War bounties. During the sales of 1859, land warrants were used in Nebraska forty times as frequently as was cash. Land bounties enabled speculators to buy a large number of warrants and trade this paper for blocks of country on the plains, which after the Civil War was sold to settlers for four to ten dollars an acre. The government received nothing for land sold to such speculators and the soldier received less than half the face value of his pension or bounty. The public domain melted away not only by the use of legitimate land warrants but also by means of forgeries; forged warrants to the amount of over a million acres were discovered to be outstanding at one time.

The land law of 1841, which is usually called the Preëmption Act,[1] provided that the head of a family, a widow, or a single man over twenty-one years of age could file a claim for 160 acres of the public domain. The claimant was required by this law to erect a dwelling on the claim, make proof of his settlement to the register and receiver at the land office for which that official received fifty cents from each claimant. The latter, in accord with the specifications laid down, was required to swear that:

1. He had never preëmpted before.
2. He was not the owner of 320 acres in any state or territory.
3. He had not settled on land for the purpose of selling it.
4. He had made no agreement or contract with anyone, directly or indirectly, to turn the land over to anyone else.

The intent of these last two was to guarantee that he was a bona fide settler.

The register and receiver made such regulations as he deemed necessary to safeguard against fraud. On taking the proper oath and making proof, the settler was allowed to purchase the claim at the minimum appraised price. This was in most places $1.25 per acre.

Persons swearing falsely were guilty of perjury according to the law, and the perjurer was penalized by the loss of both land and money.

Even before the Indian titles had been extinguished the greedy land-seekers had gathered along the eastern borders of Kansas and Nebraska and impatiently waited to cross into the land of promise.[2] A few, more anxious than the rest, crossed the border and, at the sufferance of the red man made possible by the payment of a small

---

[1] *United States Public Statutes at Large*, 27th Congress, 1841, Vol. V, pp. 453–458. This act became law September 4, 1841.
[2] The same thing to a lesser degree was true in Dakota.

sum,[3] staked out claims in the choicest spots. This little stream of settlers increased day by day until during the later fifties it formed a
surging flood of land-hungry home-seekers.

In the early stages of this occupation the land, of course, had not
been surveyed; indeed, it was still warm from the camp-fires of Indian occupation. Almost everyone made settlement upon a parcel
of land and laid claim to it. There was no office in the territories at
which the squatters could register their claims and warn or notify
second parties not to intrude.[4] For a variety of reasons it was imprac-
ticable for many of the bona fide settlers to remain continuously
upon their claims, so that they were exposed to second or third
comers.

Furthermore, disputes often arose over the boundaries of claims.
These first settlers, running ahead of the government and its paternal provisions, protected their own needs. Extra-legal organizations were formed to protect the settler in his possession of the land
and to act as an arbiter in the case of disputes. These popular tri-
bunals were not indigenous to the territory west of the Missouri
River but have always been found in new settlements. Those in
Kansas and Nebraska went under the general nomenclature of
"claim clubs." The actual names of the different clubs varied greatly,
however. At Bellevue, Nebraska, the organization was called "The
Bellevue Claim Association." Another in the same vicinity, really
a reorganization of The Bellevue Claim Association, was called

[3] At Nebraska City the amount secured by the Indians was anywhere between
five and forty dollars depending upon how easily scared the white men were. E. H.
Cowles, "Otoe County in Early Days," *Transactions and Reports*, Nebraska State
Historical Society, Series I, Vol. I, p. 42.

[4] Before a land office could be opened, the territory had to be surveyed. This
took up some two years, for the letting of contracts, surveying, and approving
surveys called for an immense amount of time and work. During this period of
waiting numerous claims were filed at the office of the Surveyor General which
assumed the duties of *ex officio* land office. Later there was no end of trouble when
these claims were transferred to the regular books, since the numbers were irregular
and often duplicated, not infrequently calling for land not even open to entry.
The first filings were made in Kansas at the Lecompton land office in May, 1856,
and the first in Nebraska at the Omaha land office in July of the same year.

"The Platte Valley Actual Settlers Club." At Brownville, Nebraska, the club was called "The Mutual Protection Society." In Kansas such organizations were sometimes informally called squatters clubs or squatters courts. They appeared generally over the prairie, springing up as readily as did the sunflowers wherever the prairie sod was broken. In the absence of law these courts dealt with matters other than land claims. These claim clubs, as a rule, extended over an area about equal to a township and were considered a township arrangement.

The organization of a claim club was ordinarily effected in the following manner: A mass meeting was called and a committee was named to draft a preamble, constitution, and by-laws. This constituent assembly might be held on the occasion of any public gathering. At Lawrence, Kansas, a temporary organization for a claim club was effected at a house raising on August 15, 1854. The report of this committee was adopted with the necessary changes, if any, at a following mass meeting. The articles provided for a full corps of officers. The number and names of these officers differed with the several sections, but they were similar. At Bellevue the officers consisted of a president, two vice-presidents, one register, and one marshal. There was also a committee of five whose duty it was to decide all disputed claims, subject, however, to an appeal to the association. The register kept the record and was allowed a fee of one dollar for each claim registered. It was the duty of the marshal to enforce the decisions of the committee and association and to preserve order at the meetings. A regular meeting was held once a month, and the president called special meetings when he deemed it necessary.[5] The proceedings were sometimes published in the nearby newspapers but not often for apparently some of their work would not bear scrutiny. Other clubs differed little in structure from the one at Bellevue; the general form and purpose was the same.

A later organization in the same community had a president, a vice-president, a marshal, and a treasurer as officers. It provided for

⁶ *Nebraska Palladium*, October 11, 1854.

all disputes about claims or other affairs to be settled by the president, but, upon the demand of either party, he was to summon a jury of six persons to be selected as follows: The president wrote down the names of eighteen members of the club. Each party crossed off one name alternately, the defendant marking first, until only six names remained. A smaller number could be agreed upon if desired by the disputants.[6] This organization also provided a salary of three dollars for every day or part of a day's service for the marshal. The president, when engaged in judicial duties, received the same amount. This was to be paid by the party obtaining redress.

As a rule new members were accepted on the vote of the club at a regular meeting. All lands were recorded at a meeting in full hearing of all the members. A member desiring to make a claim was required to hand the description to the recorder several days prior to the regular meeting. When the body convened, the claims were recorded in the order in which they were filed. These organizations conformed rather closely to the United States land office in so far that they had their "office" with regular times for filing and recording land claims.

In a few particulars the squatter association varied from the United States land office and consequently by illegal means enforced its will. First, the association occasionally protected minors in possession of claims. Furthermore, in many instances claimants were allowed to file on 320 acres of land in Kansas and Nebraska. This policy, actuated no doubt by land hunger, was enacted into law by the legislatures of both territories; but it was absolutely contrary to the statutes of the Federal Government. It was indeed possible, due to irregularities or to the lay of the land, for one person to hold nearly a section of land.[7] This was not only illegal but unjust. It resulted in many bitter quarrels and loss of life, and

[6] At Lawrence, Kansas, the number was six or twelve men.
[7] A. L. Child, *Centennial History of Plattsmouth and Cass County, Nebraska* (Plattsmouth, Nebraska, 1877), p. 18.

in general was a curse to the community. Men would come in, knowing the real United States law, and "jump" [8] the settler's odd 160 acres. In such cases the jumper was several times warned away by the club; if he did not quit his claim force was used.

Quickly all the land along the river was taken up by the new-comers who were not able to use a tenth of it but expected to sell at a handsome profit. This brought about much dissatisfaction on the part of later arrivals and prevented the country from being settled thickly and improved. In some communities where only 160 acres was allowed to a settler, it was pointed out that the country rapidly became populous, and improvements on every quarter section provided a rich trade for the cities. [9]

Little or nothing has been preserved in the way of records of the work of the claim clubs. Diligent inquiry among old settlers of Sarpy County, Nebraska, by Edward L. Sayre, failed to discover any trace of such records. Probably these were guarded carefully and duly destroyed on the theory that dead records incriminate no one. From meager information available from reminiscences, diaries, and other documents which throw incidental light on the work of the clubs, it seems that they enforced their decisions rigorously. Claim-jumping, like horse stealing, was regarded on the frontier as a crime of the highest order. When a man settled on a piece of land claimed by a club member, the latter immediately carried the matter to the club "court."

The decision, once handed down, was executed to the discomfort of the jumper. If he were wise, he left for parts unknown. If he were obstinate, he was warned several times and then, failing to heed the warning, was dealt with summarily. There was no machinery for assessing fines, no jails nor prisons, and hence there was

[8] The act of laying claim to a piece of land already claimed. This term was generally used on the frontier.

[9] The vicinity around Omaha followed the 320 acre rule. That around Nebraska City allowed only 160 acres. Nebraska City claimed it was a big advantage to follow the United States law. At Lawrence, Kansas, settlers attempted to hold forty acres of timber land in addition to the quarter section of prairie.

no attempt to grade the punishment according to the offense.[10] The offender was required to relinquish all claim to the land in question. Failing to heed the warning, he was beaten, "ducked," his property destroyed, or his life made miserable in various other ways. The penalty of obstinate and unyielding disobedience was "removal from the territory" or, in the language of the day, he was "put over the river." In extreme cases "over" did not mean to reach the other side. Few had the hardihood and persistence to resist judgment long, for it was well known that persistent offenders would be so effectually removed that they would cause no more trouble.[11] In Cass County, Nebraska, four men were started on their journey over the river; they were never seen or heard from again.[12]

It must be remembered that at this time no one owned a deed to his land. The claim-club member had only a squatter or claim "title" in the real estate, and, when transfers were made, the squatter merely gave a quit-claim deed. Ordinarily, the jumper signed a quit-claim deed without further ceremony or a second bidding. To refuse or to return after leaving was to court death. A trial might not last over ten minutes and the sentence was executed immediately. Some, however, chose to remain and defy the club. In Burt County, Nebraska, a certain man by the name of Miller was ordered by the club to leave his claim. He did not "scare" at all and lay behind a wall of logs with a rifle between the chinks defying the club. A compromise was finally arranged in this case. In carrying out the sentence of the court a group of claim-club men, armed with rifles and carrying a rope, rode on horseback or in a wagon. Near Plattsmouth the club had its rendezvous at a trader's store where the group took a final drink to bolster up their courage before they marched to dispossess some aspirant of 160 acres.

In the vicinity of Omaha, Nebraska, every claimant was holding

---

[10] A. L. Child, *op. cit.*, p. 7.
[11] *Ibid.*, p. 8.
[12] *Ibid.*

320 acres. One man held 160 acres for himself and then held 160 for his daughter. She did not live on it and made no improvements on it. The claim club protected 320 acres of land. Another man came into the territory with his two sons and built a cabin on the quarter section claimed by the daughter. The claim club forced the newcomers out and destroyed the cabin. When these claimants came back, there was a fight and the club started to tar and feather them. A woman tossed a pillow out of an upstairs window for use in this connection. Finally the club put the three across the Missouri River without tar and feathers. Even after the land office and surveyors had belatedly followed the impatient squatter, there was still work for these clubs to do.

When the newly arrived settler claimed the extra quarter section of the squatter and filed on it at the land office, the club used every means to coerce him into giving up his certificate of entry and signing it over to the squatter. The claim protected Thomas B. Cummin, acting governor of Nebraska, in the possession of his claim. Since he could not reside on it, he hired a man named Callahan to live in the cabin and paid him forty-five dollars a month to hold it for him until the land sales. Callahan, seeing an opportunity to advance his own pecuniary interests, decided like John Alden of old, to speak for himself and therefore went to the land office and filed on his employer's tract. The claim club acted immediately and demanded that Callahan surrender his certificate. On his refusal a committee took the hard-headed man to the Missouri River; a hole was cut in the ice and the obstinate son of Erin was ducked until he had a change of mind if not of heart. He turned over the certificate and afterward remarked to a friend that he "did not want that land very bad no how." [13]

Another incident well illustrates the methods employed. A jumper entered the land claimed by another at the land office and

---

[13] Alfred Sorenson, *The Story of Omaha* (Omaha, 1923), pp. 121–122. Another version of the story is that Callahan simply had the misfortune to claim a tract already claimed by a member of the club.

received the customary certificate. Soon afterward the club to which the first claimant belonged took the case in hand. The certified claimant was knocked down, tied, thrown into a wagon, and taken to a big cotton-wood tree. Here a rope was placed around his neck and he was told to say his last prayers. He was to be hanged at once unless he signed over the certificate. Inasmuch as he declined either to pray or to sign away his land, he was instantly suspended and allowed to hang for a time. He was then chopped down and as he still remained obstinate after regaining consciousness, the performance was repeated. He was still obdurate so that after a consultation the committee decided to lock him up, place a sentinel over him, and secure submission by starvation. After enduring extreme torment, the claimant sent for the captain of the club and signified his readiness to sign over the certificate which he had received from the land office and to sign a quit-claim deed.

Some of the more determined spirits, on hearing that the club members were searching for them, hid or fled the country, certificate in hand, and later returned, presented their cases at the land office and secured the prize. In one such case a man hid under a store counter for three days and then left, later returning and receiving his land.[14]

Probably if the full truth were known, not a little of the civil warfare and bloodshed in Kansas just prior to the Civil War was occasioned by the cupidity of men and their hunger for land, and many crimes, committed in the name of freeing the slaves or making Kansas a slave state, in reality merely covered the avarice of the land-hungry settler.

A colony of free state settlers located in Wabaunsee County, Kansas. They spread themselves all over that part of the state, holding as much land as possible. When a man drove a stake on a quarter section of land, the stake held it. A man from Missouri

[14] For further particulars concerning claim-club activities see A. Sorenson, *op. cit.*, and A. L. Child, "History of Cass County," *Transactions and Reports*, Nebraska State Historical Society, Series I, Vol. II, pp. 233–235.

built a cabin on a staked claim; he "wanted to be shown." One dark night some thirty of the colony came upon him, tied him to two logs pinned together, and set him afloat on the Kaw River. The crowd had attached a rope to the logs and pulled him in after he had been "shown" enough. They then administered an oath that he would leave the country never to return. He was marched off toward Missouri by men armed with Sharps rifles. The free state men burned his cabin and marched homeward in triumph.[15]

It must not be thought that public sentiment was entirely with the claim club. A number of the later immigrants were sure to sympathize with the jumper who was merely endeavoring to exercise his rights and preëmpt a quarter section of land. The claim-club member, on the other hand, was trying to reserve 320 acres of land, an illegal holding in the eyes of the United States Government, which deprived the late-comer of his rightful heritage. Sometimes certain members of the club itself sought to aid a jumper.

It was not unusual for two rival clubs to come into conflict on some boundary line. This might almost break up a community with its internecine warfare and neighborhood quarrels.

Claim clubs varied greatly. On the one extreme, self-interest ruled largely in most of the proceedings, while on the other, the general interest and welfare of the settlement was the ruling principle.[16] Some of the clubs along the Missouri River were composed largely of speculators and outlaws who congregated there only long enough to secure several claims, raise on them what cash they could, and then return home. These unprincipled individuals, devoid of honor and integrity, obtained titles to land by perjury and all manner of fraud. They had no interest in the country except what they could obtain in ill-gotten gains for their pockets. Many times these transients outnumbered the real homemakers in the clubs and ruled

[15] S. H. Fairfield, "Getting Married and the Ague," Kansas State Historical Society Collections, Vol. XI, pp. 610–611.
[16] A. L. Child, op. cit., p. 7.

its action to their own interest, thus bringing the claim club into disrepute.

Fifty or sixty bona fide settlers on the California road west of Lawrence called a meeting to perfect the organization of a claim club. One hundred and twenty-five Missourians who had heard of the meeting were encamped on the ground waiting for the assembly. The chairman, an actual settler, ruled that only those who could prove their residence by pointing to the smoke of their own chimneys, could be called legal residents or claim holders and participate in the meeting. The Missourians, many of whom were hardened Sante Fe trail bull whackers, plainsmen, and Missouri gamblers, had been drinking freely, and much oratory led to threats. Finally the partisans of each side lined up with guns in hands. While they stood thus facing each other, a fat widow, who was camped on the spot in her wagon, waddled to the midst of the mêlée just in time to avert bloodshed. Stamping her foot vigorously, she firmly declared that that spot was her claim and that she would allow no fighting there that day. Finally a drunken Missourian cried, "Bully for you, old gal," and burst into loud laughter. It was contagious and this company of laughing men dispersed without bloodshed. The interior settlements were less troubled by this class of transients.[17]

The records of the Bellevue Settlers' Club reveal that approximately one hundred and twenty-five persons became members. Among the names are found those of judges, lawyers, ministers, and other officials. In their rules they claimed the right to hold 320 acres of land against all comers.[18]

Squatters taking land before the survey was made were completely at sea in the matter of defining their boundaries. In view of this fact the settler was obliged to draw out a plot of land at ran-

---

[17] W. H. T. Wakefield, "Squatter Courts in Kansas," *Transactions*, Kansas State Historical Society, Vol. V, p. 71.

[18] J. Q. Goss, "Bellevue, Its Past and Present," *Proceedings and Collections*, Nebraska State Historical Society, Series II, Vol. II, No. 1, pp. 44–45.

dom and stake it out or blaze it if it were timber. Usually the "home-made" survey took the line of some Indian reservation mission or military reservation as a base line from which to measure, and drew up the land units from there. Members of the claim clubs agreed that, upon the survey of the territory, they would mutually deed and redeed to each other, so that as much as possible of the original claim would be left. This redrawing of boundary lines caused many disputes in which the clubs served well as arbiters. The description of some of these early claims were crude indeed. The following description in the Bellevue section of Nebraska is listed in the records of both the claim club and the county:

A-5 Charles A. Henry Claim.   *Recorded March 3, 1855.*

Commencing at an oak tree 75 rods north of the northeast corner of the southeast quarter of Mission Reserve; thence north 135 rods to northeast corner of Mission Reserve thence to low water mark of Missouri river; thence down the Missouri river 320 rods; thence west 180 rods to the southeast corner of William Hamilton's claim; thence north 185 rods to the northeast corner of William Hamilton's claim; thence west 140 rods to beginning, containing 320 acres, more or less.[19]

A-178. S. M. Pike's Claim.   *July 6, 1855.*

Commencing at a stake in prairie, southeast from the south end of what is known as Sailings Grove, 8 chains, and runs thence west 40 chains to stake in valley, thence south 40 chains to stake on side hill, thence east 80 chains, thence north 16 chains to Spring branch, and 40 chains, to John Sailings southeast corner, thence west 40 chains to beginning. Containing 320 acres. Situate in Bellevue district.[20]

B-37. John Butcher to B. F. Jones.   *Janry. 18, 1856.*

Beginning at J. N. Enoch's southeast corner, running due east along line to B. P. Rankin's west line, thence north along said line to a stake about 200 yards north of said Rankin's northwest corner, thence west a half mile, or to J. N. Enoch's northeast corner, thence south to the

[19] Edward L. Sayre, "Early Days in and About Bellevue," *Collections*, Nebraska State Historical Society (Lincoln, Nebraska, 1911), Vol. XVI, p. 80.
[20] *Ibid.*, p. 88.

place of beginning. Containing 320 acres more or less, or what I suppose to be.[21]

Quite frequently when the boundary lines of sections and subdivisions were run, two preëmption claimants were within the boundaries of the same half or quarter section, or, if the whole plot were not in dispute, some portion of the same tract would be claimed by each. These difficulties arose in spite of the agreements to deed and redeed land for the security of original claims. The Hon. James Humphrey says:

Conflicting claims of this character gave rise to many prolonged and bitter suits before the land offices, in some of which the costs and expenses involved in the litigation far exceeded the value of the land. . . . The neighborhood assumed sides in these controversies. . . . In some instances, where the rival claimants were men of local prominence, these contests were, in those days of partial isolation, events of no small importance. They formed the staple of neighborhood discussion as long as they lasted. The man among them who had seen a copy of Blackstone once or twice in his life, or who had heard a hint dropped by the lawyer on his side, was wont to discourse learnedly upon the legal aspects of the case, and he would be listened to with all the deference due to an oracle. Besides rescuing the rural population from social stagnation, these land contests gave profitable employment to young lawyers at a time when the courts had hardly got fairly under way.[22]

Claim-club government did not hold sway for more than two or three years. The land office came in, and with it the clubs disbanded and the law of the United States was observed. In some places, by local agreement, the organizations maintained jurisdiction over all crimes against person or property. A jury of six or twelve men acted as a court. This was the case with the claim club west of Lawrence, Kansas. This mode of government was, after all, very expensive because of the time required of each member.

The characteristic of exploitation, of rugged individualism, was

[21] *Ibid.*, p. 91.
[22] James Humphrey, "The Country West of Topeka Prior to 1865," *Transactions,* Kansas State Historical Society (Topeka, 1890), Vol. IV, pp. 290–291.

perhaps never better illustrated than in staking out preëmption claims in Kansas and Nebraska in the fifties. Even before these twin territories were opened to settlement, the voracious squatters were beginning to trespass on Indian land. In order to hasten the extinction of Indian title, runners were sent out in 1854 into Nebraska to convene the Otoe nation at a point near the mouth of the Platte. The Indians, after eating a dog supper and smoking the pipe of peace, drew up and signed treaties. The Indian agent escorted the chiefs to Washington to make the final arrangements. In the meantime, before the project had been confirmed, a number of settlers moved over and commenced a permanent settlement. The newly-arrived Indian agent ordered all whites to leave the west side of the Missouri River. The Indians, having come into possession of the facts, formed a painted and hideous war party, came upon the whites, and frightened men, women, and children. They threatened to drive the settlers off the territory but were appeased with a tribute of from five to forty dollars from each settler. In spite of threats from the war department and in spite of Indian scares, these early arrivals stayed until the country was opened.

There were several types of landless newcomers who were undesirable from the viewpoint of the permanent resident. First of all there was the professional squatter, a migratory type who lived without labor. He might be called a small-scale speculator. Squatting became a trade or business pursuit. This type would take a claim, sell, move on, select another tract, and sell again. He got control of the valuable points such as mill sites, fords, the best land, and then induced the real homemaker to buy. This the homemaker was obliged to do or leave the country, for the squatters organized for the protection of their mutual rights.

Horace Greeley, who visited Kansas in 1859, mentioned this class. He noted that there were many idle shiftless people in Kansas. These were not lawyers, speculators, and other non-producers which were in excess, but were squatters who would be farmers if they were anything, but who did not break the land, raise crops, or build houses fit to live in.[23]

Another exasperating thorn in the flesh was the absentee claimant. When the first party from New England arrived at Lawrence, Kansas, and camped on Mount Oread where the University now stands, they found the future university town site unoccupied but not unclaimed. On an area not including more than 320 acres, five original claimants for 160 acres each appeared. One man came after the city had become a reality and claimed 160 acres of the town site because he had visited it and put up a log pen some time before. All the timber and good bottom land along the river had been claimed by non-residents whose whereabouts was unknown and whose very existence was problematical.[24]

The *Kansas Free State* of Lawrence had this to say with regard to these claims: [25]

There are . . . quite a number *fictitious* [sic] claims, which have been marked out by visitors, or by those who have left the country without designing to return, and have entrusted them to agents to be sold on speculation. Actual settlers should not submit to such extortions. The bona fide resident and improver is the only person for whom the benefits of the pre-emption acts were designed, and he alone can hold a claim.

The editor of the *Herald of Freedom* at the same place stated that he knew men who traveled about making numerous claims in different localities and selling them to the bona fide settlers. Another witness asserted that he found hundreds of claims in Kansas and yet in riding twenty-five miles saw but one occupied house. A man who arrived at Yankton, South Dakota, in 1858 found that unclaimed land was equally scarce in that region. He said: "We soon began looking about for locations, but found that lands for a

---

[23] J. Sterling Morton testified to the same thing in Nebraska.
[24] W. H. T. Wakefield, *op. cit.*, p. 72.
[25] March 17, 1855.

long distance in all directions were claimed and foundations for log cabins already on the ground." [26]

The Preëmption Law was a hot-bed in which all sorts of graft, perjury, and misrepresentation flourished. No less an authority than J. Sterling Morton, later acting territorial governor of Nebraska, and an early settler, says that while there were many honest bona fide preëmptions, there were more which were perfected by professional perjurers who took the necessary oaths at the Federal land office with deliberate intention of violating them within the next twenty-four hours. Men with money and reputation hired men with neither to preëmpt and then deed the land over to them.

The custom in preëmption days was for the claimant to stake off his tract and then take his axe, cut logs, and begin a house. This indication that a building was in the process of construction held the claim temporarily while he went to town or back to the old home to get his wife or property. Preëmptors grew less careful, however, and it became the fashion to drag a few logs out of the woods, build a sort of pen three or four feet high, return to their former home, and leave these logs as a proof of ownership. A shingle was usually driven into the ground bearing the name of the architect and proprietor.

Even the formality of erecting a log pen became too rigorous for the anxious land grabber. It was quite the custom for one of these men to select a claim, drop a stone at each of the supposed four corners of a house, take a small stick and, splitting it, put a small bit of glass in it and place it on one side of the house for a window. He would then borrow a blanket or two and a plank from a neighbor, sleep a night within the confines of the imaginary walls, and, after giving all assurance that he would be back in a few days or weeks, go to the land office, swear he had built a dwelling with glass window and plank floor. He then pretended to go after his family. He had secured a fine piece of land for sixty to eighty cents

[26] Joseph R. Hanson, "Reminiscences of Yankton's Early Days," *The Monthly South Dakotan*, May, 1898, p. 16.

an acre [27] which he expected to sell for ten to fifty dollars an acre.[28]

As has been implied, some land offices were particular in requiring a house to have glass windows. The well-known correspondent, Albert D. Richardson, while visiting in Kansas, noticed a window sash without panes hanging upon a nail in a settler's cabin. He had seen similar frames in other cabins and asked what it was for.

"To preëmpt with," was the reply.

"How?"

"Why, don't you understand? To enable my witness to swear that there is *a window in my house*"!

Ordinarily the land office required a man to have a house at least twelve feet square. Witnesses could be secured to swear that a particular house in question was "twelve by fourteen" when actually the only building on the premises was one whittled out with a pen knife, twelve inches by fourteen inches. It was not an unheard-of thing for a half-dozen pieces of land to be proved up with the use of the same house which was moved from place to place. In Nebraska a little frame house was built for this purpose, mounted on wheels, and pulled by oxen. It enabled the preëmptor to swear that he had a bona fide residence on his claim. This structure was a real money-making enterprise since it rented at five dollars a day. Scores of preëmptions were proved with it.[29] A. D. Richardson says he never knew of a title to be invalidated because of such perjury. The young merchant, lawyer, or other speculator, rode into the interior, laid four poles on the ground, went to the land office and filed notice that he had started a foundation and had begun settlement for actual residence. If the man was relatively honest he returned, built a rough house at a cost of ten to twenty dollars, ate one meal in it, and slept there for a single night. More often, however,

[27] By land warrant.
[28] A. L. Child, *op. cit.*, pp. 9–10.
[29] Horace Greeley testified to the same thing. The settlers sold the land to speculators for $50 to $300. They in turn sold it to the bona fide settler for $250 to $1,500.

he never visited the place again. Then in thirty days with a witness he went to the land office and proved up, swearing that this tract of land was for his "own exclusive use and benefit." He further swore that he had erected a habitable dwelling and that he was still residing thereon. Sometimes he was questioned closely under oath, but he and his witness proved equal to the occasion. Having deposited a land warrant to cover the cost of the land, he left, and according to Richardson, in three out of four cases, he never visited the land again except for the purpose of selling it.

A woman could not preëmpt unless she was a widow or the head of a family. An ambitious and unscrupulous girl occasionally borrowed a child, signed adoption papers, swore she was the head of a family, preëmpted her claim, annulled the adoption papers, and returned her temporary family with an acceptable gift.[30]

People traded in claims and city lots as elsewhere they did in horses, slaves, and other chattels. Town shares and preëmption lands in Nebraska were widely traded over the river in Iowa for cattle, flour, and whiskey.

Early arrivals west of Leavenworth, Kansas, found that claimants had not even taken the time to erect log pens or to indicate the confines of a claim by corner stakes. Some claims on the prairie were held by one stake and a shingle alone. A stake was driven and a shingle stuck in the cleft. On this shingle or on the blazed side of the stake was written in pencil: "I claim 160 acres, of which this is the center stake."

Anyone locating a claim within one-half mile of another was looked upon as an intruder. Naturally conflicts over claims were numerous and caused much bloodshed. It was not at all unusual for claimants to fight until death. Sometimes several men barricaded themselves and fought a claim club or group helping an opposing faction. Reports of bloodshed and death from this cause constitute one of the principal items of news in the territorial newspapers.

[30] Albert D. Richardson, *Beyond the Mississippi* (Hartford, Connecticut, 1869), pp. 138–141.

A HABITABLE DWELLING

A HOUSE "TWELVE BY FOURTEEN"

A BONA FIDE RESIDENCE

TYPES OF PREËMPTION FRAUDS
Albert D. Richardson, *Beyond the Mississippi*, 1867.

Jim Lane, later senator from Kansas, had a quarrel with another man over a piece of land on which both lived. Lane killed the other man in the course of the friction while the case was pending in the courts at Washington; he did what the typical frontiersman would have done under the circumstances. The settlers readily forgave such an act, as is manifested by his election to the Senate when Kansas was admitted to the Union.

In due time the land sale came. This was an auction on an appointed day of land in certain districts which had been thrown on the market. Theoretically the land was to go to the highest bidder; but actually each quarter section was sold to its occupant at the appraised value. The squatters respected each other's rights and the first man who bid against one of them was shot down, thus concluding further opposition. In some places land was appraised from $1.50 to $10 per acre, but most of it was sold at the minimum price of $1.25 per acre. At Ozawkie, Kansas, 100,000 acres of public lands were sold in July, 1857. Two thousand people attended. A huge hotel had been erected and every building was crowded; hundreds of strangers lived in tents or in the open air. Gambling and drinking booths stood upon every corner. Sometimes these sales lasted as long as six weeks. The prairie around the sales town was converted into a huge camping ground, some prospective land owners living in tents, some in wagons, and some living out of doors with blankets and the leafy boughs of the trees as their covering; they cooked, ate, and slept while waiting to be called to stand before the dreaded judge and give an account of their stewardship of the acres they sought to own.

The manner of conducting the sale was to sell by townships, commencing at section one and disposing of it by quarter sections in regular order and then passing on to section number two. The forenoon was taken up by claimants making proof of settlement. In the afternoon those who had passed the morning ordeal made payment for their land at the appraised value and received their certificates of purchase. The man who could not furnish satisfactory

proof of his good intentions had his claim sold to the highest bidder. This was an extremely rare occurrence. A witness attending
one of these sales for four weeks, saw this happen but once.

If claimants were unable to decide their contest satisfactorily, the
dispute was carried to the commissioner of the sale. He appointed
a committee of two to hear the evidence. It was not an unheard-of
thing for corruption to determine these decisions. Prior to hearing
the case, the committee would evaluate the financial status of each
contestant. Before they would consent to hear the case, each member
of the committee would exact a sum varying usually from ten to
fifty dollars, according to the amount at which they thought the
claims were valued. They then heard the case with all the solemnity
and gravity of a regular court. Having assembled the evidence,
they took time to consult each other and then demanded another
fee before they rendered a decision. A man sometimes paid this
committee as high as one hundred dollars in fees.

Money was plentiful—currency was almost wholly gold and
silver—not that the squatters were rich, but the sale was largely attended by monied men, that is, men with money to lend. The man
who was unable to raise the money to pay for his land was obliged
to borrow from these money lenders at an interest rate of from $2\frac{1}{2}$
per cent to 5 per cent per month. These men took as security the
land for which their money paid. This was done by assigning the
squatter's certificate of purchase to the lender.

Few ladies attended the sales. While the great crowd was waiting, it contrived various kinds of amusements. These were generally constructed to bring in money to someone. All kinds of games
of chance and contrivances to part people from their money, from
the roulette wheel to throwing clubs at a mark, were in action at
all hours of the night or day. The camping ground was a scene of
confusion and noise. Occasionally a politician came to win the great
crowds to his support by fiery speeches. Perhaps the circuit rider
occasionally came to break the Bread of Life.

Some of the land bought at a low price was very valuable. Ten miles from Ozawkie, Kansas, lived a family of Missourians who had resided there eighteen months. Their claim had not yet been preempted and they had to pay the $1.25 an acre before they could receive a perfect title; yet they refused $4,000 for it. In the days of these land sales the vicinity was much more heavily populated, temporarily at least, than thirty or fifty years later. Visiting the drowsy little town of Ozawkie now one can hardly bring one's self to realize that such stirring scenes were enacted there nearly a century ago.

CHAPTER III

TOWN-BUILDING MANIA

THE LEGISLATION providing for the reservation of town sites was enacted by Congress May 23, 1844. It provided that three hundred and twenty acres could be held as a town site when it was occupied. Such a plot was not subject to entry at the land office under the preëmption act. The owners of the town site were given the privilege of buying the plot at the minimum price. The disposal of the lots and the proceeds of the sales thereof were to be in accordance with the regulations of the legislative authority of the state or territory in which the town was located.[1]

The great occupation of the few citizens of Kansas and Nebraska in the fifties and sixties was town-building. Owing to speculative activity merchants and towns preceded buyers and farmers in the settlement of the country. At the hotels in western Missouri and Iowa representatives of various towns in Kansas and Nebraska worked feverishly to interest people in the new towns across the river. Men were constantly coming and going, bearing in their hands rolls of foolscap paper covered with charcoal sketches of future cities. Some displayed copper ore or other products to induce prospective buyers. They offered shares in town stock at so much a share. It was the habit of those promoting various town sites to have an agent at the river landings to meet the new emigrant and verbally advertise his town site, crying out like the town crier of old "Hear ye me, come to my town; it is the best located."

A writer in the *Kansas Herald*, May 4, 1855, said:

[1] *United States Public Statutes at Large*, 28th Congress, First Session, Vol. V, p. 657.

. . . in some localities it has become almost a mania with many speculators in town stock. New towns are being laid off, and each one claiming some advantages over its predecessor either in *natural* location, timber, adjacent country, proximity to certain points, mineral resources, *the best location for the capitol* or some other as absurd desideratum as the last, when in fact none, or but very few of the advantages claimed are possessed.

Colonel Barnabas Bates recalled that so many came to Nebraska at that time feeling they were ordained to found some mighty city that it began to look as if the whole Missouri bottom would be laid off in town sites. In order to protect the agricultural interests, the Colonel introduced a bill in the Territorial Council, while a member of that body, which "reserved every tenth section for farming purposes." [2] It has been said that a steamboat captain was a fool to haul passengers when he could have made a fortune freighting town stakes. Of the fourteen Missouri River cities in Kansas in the fifties, only three—Leavenworth, Atchison, and Kansas City—were surviving in 1867.

The ordinary thing was for a group of speculators, three, or four, or half a dozen, to incorporate by a special act of the legislature, stake out the 320 acres which the government allowed, and then, in order to enlarge the site, engage settlers to preëmpt adjacent quarter sections. Title, of course, could be secured only by the settler's swearing that the land was to be used solely for his own use and that he had not contracted to sell it. This was easily taken care of by means of perjury, however, and the town company secured 500 to 1,000 acres of land which was cut up into building lots 125 feet by 25. Ten lots made a share. [3] A number of towns were chartered by the first General Assemblies in each state. These towns were almost without exception the so-called "kiting" towns. That is, the word "city" was appended like a kite's tail to the name of the place to make it sound important. For example, in Nebraska we

[2] A similar story has been told of how S. N. Wood of Kansas proposed to reserve certain lands in the territory for agricultural purposes by act of the legislature.

[3] A. D. Richardson, *Beyond the Mississippi*, p. 30.

find Omaha City, Wyoming City,[4] Kearney City, and Bellevue City. Nearly all the new western towns flew this tail in their infancy. Then they cut off the tail. Other places prefixed the word city on the title to impress people in the East: City of Plattsmouth, City of Fontenelle. Sometimes other impressive names were chosen with the view to advertising an infant metropolis. Emporia, Kansas, since famous as the home of William Allen White and Walt Mason, had its name chosen from ancient history. The well-known historian Rollins spoke of a country of the Carthagenians named Emporia which was most fruitful and wealthy. Eureka,[5] Kansas, indicated in its name the happiness of the founders in having secured such a desirable location.

It was a popular idea that great cities would grow up on the western side of the Missouri River and hence that such cities as St. Joseph, Sioux City, and Council Bluffs would *never amount to anything*.

Although the principal activity in town booming took place in Kansas and Nebraska, the fever touched eastern Dakota also. When Minnesota was about to become a state in 1857, the settlers in a strip of land between the present boundaries and the Big Sioux River were left outside any organized territory. The Indian title to this land had already been extinguished by the treaty of 1851. Accordingly the territory between the Minnesota line and the Big Sioux River, and only that part which later became Dakota Territory, was open to white settlement. As early as 1856 the first settlement was attempted at Sioux Falls by an organization known as the Western Town Company, of Dubuque, Iowa. They were ordered off the land by the Indians and returned to Sioux City, Iowa. In 1857, the same company returned and took possession of 320 acres around the falls. In the same year the Dakota Land Company, chartered by the Minnesota legislature, made a claim near the half section laid out by the other company at Sioux Falls. They named

[4] Extinct.
[5] From the Greek "I have found it."

the place Sioux Falls City and it became the first permanent settlement in South Dakota. At the beginning of winter in 1857 there were three dwellings, a store, and a saw mill; the population numbered sixteen men. After the Indian Treaty of 1858 which was carried out by August 1, 1859, settlers moved into eastern Dakota rapidly.

The Dakota Land Company was a newer development in town booming. It was the chain store idea in full bloom. The territorial governor of Minnesota was the president of the company and its aim was to seize every valuable town site that could be found on the James, Vermilion, and Wanari Rivers, and on the Missouri from the mouth of the Sioux to old Fort Lookout. The company was certain Sioux Falls City would be the capitol of the new territory and made the most of its opportunities there. A number of counties were organized and the *Dakota Democrat* of 1859 mentions six towns which had been laid out. A delegate was chosen to represent the new territory, called Dakota Territory by the land companies. Congress did not recognize the delegate since no Dakota Territory had been organized by the national government. Nevertheless the inhabitants elected a legislature, and officers were elected and functioned; but the national government, busy with the slavery question, did not take time before the Civil War to organize Dakota Territory. Town building, although not as extensive, was carried on with the same religious fervor that obtained in Kansas and Nebraska.[6]

After a town was laid out it was necessary to attract residents. Several methods were used. It was desirable, if possible, to secure a printing press and hire someone to print a newspaper or to persuade an editor, by word or subsidy, to locate in the town and throw his lot in with the citizens. Having secured a mouthpiece such as the *Bugle* or the *Herald*, it was then much easier for the little com-

[6] Doane Robinson, *History of South Dakota* (Indianapolis, Indiana, 1904), Vol. I, pp. 166–180; Effie Florence Putney, *In the South Dakota Country* (Mitchell, South Dakota, 1928), p. 40.

munity to sound its own praises. The company paid for a large number of papers to be sent East. If the town company did not do this, citizens clubbed together and sent copies to the eastern states.[7] In 1857, Dr. George W. Brown, editor of the *Herald of Freedom* at Lawrence, Kansas, had a subscription list of 7,000 in that little three-year-old town. Probably many of these were sent back to the home states for old neighbors and friends to read. It was also necessary to secure the requisite establishments for a new town. It was quite impossible to have a town without at least one store, a blacksmith shop, and perhaps a saloon or a livery stable.

Another method of booming the town was to build a hotel. This not only made a good impression on the readers of the paper in the states, but it provided a place of sojourn for the newcomer, particularly the more prosperous speculator, while he traded in town lots and claims. Many times the town company erected the hotel and rented it to a proprietor If this were impossible, the project sometimes became a community enterprise. At Brownville, Nebraska, a lottery scheme was devised for this municipal undertaking. Tickets were sold at five dollars each. The prizes, totaling 1,927 were valued at $11,000 and ranged from the first prize of $2,500 in land (147 acres adjoining the town) and a second of city lots worth $800, to a minimum prize of twenty-five cents cash.[8]

Still a third way in which to build a town was to give away lots. Lots were given to churches, lodges, and other organizations for building purposes. Business establishments were lured into the town by the promise of entire business blocks.[9] A lot was promptly given to the first child born, to the first woman resident, and to the first couple married. A certain number of lots were set apart as a sort of inducement fund, one lot to be given to anyone who would build

[7] In September, 1858, the citizens of Council Bluffs, Iowa, in order to aid immigration to their part of the country, subscribed to 2,000 copies of their city's newspapers for distribution in the eastern states. They were sent free to hotels, reading rooms, and other places.

[8] *Nebraska Advertiser*, September 3, 1857.

[9] At Tecumseh, Nebraska, W. P. Walker and Company were given all of block 37 with the understanding that they build and stock a store there.

a house worth a certain sum. Each house built according to specifications enhanced the value of the lots still held by the town company. Erastus Beadle was secretary of the town company of Saratoga, Nebraska; [10] one of the chief duties in his strenuous life was to give away lots. When towns in close proximity became rivals, their representatives stopped all comers and offered them lots. Sometimes the rivalry was so keen that one town bought out its neighbor in order to save itself.

It was customary for the town company to hold a huge celebration with outstanding attractions, and at the same time to auction lots; frequently it was arranged to occur on a holiday. For weeks these sales were advertised for miles around. On July 4, 1857, at a sale in White Cloud, Kansas, twenty thousand dollars' worth of property was sold; lots averaged $400 each. This, no doubt, was much higher than the usual sale prices.[11]

Towns, which really developed, sprang up like magic. It would take little imagination to believe that Aladdin himself had been on hand with his wonderful lamp in some places on the prairies during the fifties. In sixty days in 1855 fifty dwellings were built in the struggling little town of Lawrence, Kansas. Many large stone structures were quickly erected, and buildings of humbler pretensions arose overnight on the prairie.[12]

The *Kansas Herald*, proudly narrating the rapid growth of Leavenworth in eight months, mentioned that there had been erected one steam saw mill, two brick-yards, one three-story hotel, four boarding houses, five dry goods stores, five groceries, five saloons, two boot and shoe stores, two saddlery shops, one tin shop, two blacksmith shops, and one hundred tenanted houses, while twenty or thirty houses were still in the process of construction. There were

---

[10] Now a suburb of Omaha.

[11] The terms for town lots at Brownville, Nebraska, in 1856, were: "One third in hand, one third in three months, and one third in six months, with bond and security."

[12] Sara T. D. Robinson, *Kansas, Its Interior and Exterior Life* (Boston, 1856), p. 66.

eight hundred inhabitants. The same mushroom growth was in evidence in Saratoga, Nebraska. The secretary of the town company reported that when he arrived at the first of April there were only two houses on the town site. In the middle of August he recorded in his diary that fifty-six buildings had been completed and many more were going up. There were graded streets, vehicles of all kinds, two omnibus lines to Omaha, and a ship landing. A real city had grown up within one season. One could hardly believe the changes the enthusiastic secretary recorded. In the midst of this business activity the price of lots increased by leaps and bounds. One man bought two lots for $110. Less than a year later he sold them for $600. In the summer of 1856 men were refusing $3,000 for lots in Omaha.[13] Times were reported as lively, money plentiful, wages high, and the city improving rapidly. In this atmosphere towns began to appear almost spontaneously. The *Nebraska City News* of March 21, 1857, says: "New Towns. New towns are spring-ing into existence so fast that we can hardly chronicle their advents." A list of nine towns followed.

The boom prices of these frontier towns were unreasonable and not in line with the general development of the country. When the bubble was pricked by the panic of 1857, prices dropped like a plummet and did not recover for many years. In 1857 Peter Riden-our bought two lots on or near the corner of Sixth and Jackson

[13] The *Omaha City Times* gives the following sketch of the growth of Omaha:
"1853, June—Town claim made by the company and kept by them by paying tribute to the Indians whose title had not been extinguished.

1854, June—No settlements; but a single house, 'Old St. Nicholas,' of round logs, 16 feet square, built by the company as an improvement to hold the claim.

1855, June—Number of inhabitants from two hundred and fifty to three hundred. Best lots sold at $100.

. . . .

1856, October—Number of inhabitants sixteen hundred. Best lots sold at $2,500.

1857, April—Number of inhabitants two thousand. Best lots sold at $3,500.

1857, June—Number of inhabitants three thousand. Best lots sold at $4,000."
Governor Izard of Nebraska, in a territorial assembly, mentioned, as evidence of flush times and prosperity, that business lots upon streets where wild grass still flourished had advanced in price from $500 to $3,000 in a few months.

Streets at Topeka. He kept them for twenty years and sold them for less than he paid.

One of the strongest characteristics of the frontier was its optimism. In no section was it more manifest than in Nebraska. Every group which staked out a town site was certain that this spot was destined to be the scene of a great metropolis and trade emporium of the West. The town company and the few settlers beguiled to its environs lost no opportunity to boost their "city" with loud-tongued eulogies. These optimists felt certain their town was the gateway to the West, and without a doubt would become one of the leading points on the new Pacific railway which would surely come through in the near future. Nor was this boosting confined entirely to the cities. The newspapers gave much space to advertising the territories.

This same spirit of optimism led the early settlers to believe that the Kaw and Platte Rivers were navigable. It was thought that the Kaw could be navigated as far up as Fort Riley during the winter and to Lawrence throughout the whole year. In 1857 a small steamer drawing but fourteen inches of water was advertised to ply semi-weekly between Kansas City and Lawrence. Her first trip took ten days and her second five months. She spent the entire summer among the sand bars.[14]

Similarly those towns located on the Platte imagined themselves as river cities, and the legislature petitioned Congress to subsidize a man with 20,000 acres of land in the Platte Valley on the condition that he dredge out the river, put a steamboat on the stream, and run it between the mouth of the Platte and Fort Kearney.

It was to a company's great advantage if it could persuade a colony to locate on its site. The company which laid out a town near the junction of the Kaw and the Blue Rivers in Kansas, called the place Boston and offered a passing colony one-half the town site if they would stay and make that their home. The colonists decided

---

[14] In 1855 a boat made some successful trips to Fort Riley. A number of other boats from time to time made trips but in the end the navigation of the Kaw was given up as impractical.

to accept this offer provided the proprietors would agree to change the name from Boston to Manhattan as their constitution required their town to be named. This was easily arranged and Manhattan became a permanent city.

Hundreds of towns were laid out in Kansas and Nebraska in the days prior to the Civil War. Men came from the East and founded the river towns, and then in small groups these residents journeyed from place to place staking out town site claims in the interior.[15] Although there were many honest attempts to found permanent urban communities on beautiful spots, nevertheless, in scores of cases no such honest attempts were made. Crafty speculators founded "cities" for their own profit without any intention of actually giving value for the money invested by buyers. All that was necessary was to arrange a company under some tree or elsewhere. They staked out the site, made a plot of the "city," gave charming names to the streets, had hundreds of beautiful lithographs printed, filled out certificates of shares, and then went East to sell a fortune to friends. The lithograph showed pictures of broad shaded streets, churches, opera houses, elegant residences, and magnificent wharfs with puffing steamers. These brilliant fictitious documents, so attractively arranged, successfully parted many an unwary one from his money at a price which seemed dirt cheap. The town of Curlew, in Cedar County, Nebraska, was an example of the most glaring and successful fraud of all the fifty or more town sites in the river counties of northern Nebraska. Ten thousand lots were laid out and sold but no house ever was built there. The fascinating map and pictures, portraying the tremendous growth and importance of

---

[15] Of this period Mr. Albert Robinson Greene wrote: "It was a day of small things but great beginnings. . . . Everything was in a state of incipiency. Opportunity was knocking at every door. There were schemes of all sorts, rational and chimerical. The laws of the early legislative sessions furnish abundant examples. . . . It was a time of tremendous mental and business activity. Official sanction was given to operate ferries, toll bridges, and stage lines in every direction. Highways were projected to imaginary cities in the undisturbed prairie grass, where flaming lithographs exploited the sale of town lots at fabulous prices before there were any inhabitants except grasshoppers and prairie dogs." "In Remembrance," Kansas State Historical Society *Collections*, Vol. XI, p. 486.

A BOOM LITHOGRAPH OF SUMNER, KANSAS

This is the "engraved romance" that lured John J. Ingalls to the West in 1858. Courtesy of the Kansas State Historical Society.

Curlew, gave the lots a rapid sale in New York. Although house-less, the 10,000 lots brought the proprietors $150,000.[16]

John J. Ingalls, who was destined in maturity to become one of the nation's greatest orators and to represent Kansas for eighteen years in the Senate, was lured to the west bank of the Missouri by what he later called "a chromatic triumph of lithographed mendacity." The town which brought him from his New England home was Sumner, long since dead. It was heralded in Massachusetts as a commercial city of large proportions. There were none of the four churches represented to him, no respectable residences, no schools, no children, no society, no commercial exchange, no reshipment and forwarding, and only a few small grocery stores with the few common articles demanded by the impoverished citizenry. On the lithograph a college was imagined, but no one in the town had ever even heard the idea advanced. On the spot designated "machine shop" stood a rickety old blacksmith shop run by a decrepit Negro. Only one street, interspersed with stumps, had any pretentions of a grade. The others were footpaths leading up and down the wild ravines to shabby cabins and miserable huts. Of the two hundred houses some were without chimneys, some without windows and doors, some without shingles or clapboards, resting merely on heaps of stones or stumps of trees and scattered without any regard to order or regularity. Young Ingalls concluded his description: "I wish I could give you a photograph of the place, but a new western village is truly indescribable in language. It can only be compared to itself." [17] This was the typical western city which actually grew for a time.

Ordinarily large letters on all new town plots stated that they were located adjacent to the very finest groves of timber, surrounded by very rich agricultural country, abundantly supplied with building rock of the finest description, well watered, possessed fine indications of lead, iron, coal, and salt in great abundance. J. Sterling

[16] William Huse, *History of Dixon County* (Ponca, Nebraska, 1896), pp. 26–27.
[17] John J. Ingalls, letter to his father, October 5, 1858, Kansas State Historical Society *Collections*, Vol. XIV, p. 100.

Morton said: "In my opinion, we felt richer, better, more million-airish, than any poor deluded mortals ever did before, on the same amount of moonshine and pluck."

The only way to get a sound title to a town site was to get the town incorporated. The lack of inhabitants in no way interfered with this procedure. There were so many of these charters that the wording of acts was cut down to essentials. The following charter of a long lost town gives an example of brevity:

An Act to incorporate the town of Margaritta in the County of Lancaster.

Sec. 1. Be it enacted by the Council and House of Representatives and of the territory of Nebraska that the town site claimed by the Richland Company, upon which the town of Margaritta is situated and located, together with all additions that may be hereafter made according to law, is hereby declared to be a town by the name and style of the town of Margaritta.

Sec. 2. The said town is hereby made a body corporate and politic, and is hereby invested with the same power and corporate rights and privileges as are granted in an act entitled "An act to incorporate Nebraska City."

Sec. 3. This act shall take effect and be in force from and after its passage. Approved March 16th, 1855.[18]

Some town builders did not even take the time to have their companies recorded before rushing off to sell lots. A man in Burt County, Nebraska, is said to have secured a piece of land, mapped it out, and sold $20,000 worth of lots. During all this time he never had a claim on the land but was simply a squatter.[19]

Men out on a buffalo hunt, or on a trip through the country, or camping at night or noon, would admire the beauties of the country

---

[18] *Nebraska Council Journal*, First Session, pp. 142, 143, 144; *Session Laws of Nebraska* 1855–1865, p. 169.

[19] A. L. Child, *Centennial History of Plattsmouth and Cass County, Nebraska*, p. 78.

and decide to found a town to grace the beauty spot and line the pockets of the participants. Judge Wakely tells of a party crossing the Elkhorn River in Nebraska. One member of the party, observing the natural beauty of the nooning ground,[20] with the spirit of a seer, pronounced the spot an ideal site for a future commercial center and county seat and proposed that they found a town. In twenty minutes a company had been formed, the area stepped off, a name selected, a manager elected, and a few days later handsomely engraved certificates were distributed to the city fathers.

As a result of the many paper towns and the unbounded confidence of the pioneer in a time of prosperity, much traffic took place in town lots. Shares often doubled in price in two or three weeks. Even servant girls speculated in town lots. Men who never before owned fifty dollars' worth of property at one time, shortly after crossing the Missouri River had full pockets of town shares. The lots and the stock of many town shares were quoted on the market from day to day when there was not so much as a house in the alleged town. Ordinarily, however, lots or groups of lots were seldom sold. It was an almost universal plan to issue certificates or shares in the new city and to sell the certificates. The city would be divided into as many as four or five hundred shares according to its size and the optimism of its founders. Each share represented from two to twenty lots. The standard price was about $500 each.

It was not merely the newcomers or eastern residents who lost self-control in the rush of speculation; the older settlers were also carried along with the tide. Many who had really valuable properties in cities like Leavenworth, Atchison, Nebraska City, or Omaha, sold them and with the proceeds bought certificates of shares in new cities in the interior.

The Reverend Henry T. Davis in his early experience in Nebraska made an appointment for preaching services at a town on the map called Fairview. He rode on and on thinking it certainly

---

[20] Nooning—a term used to designate the time spent in eating dinner and allowing the horses to graze.

was about time he came into sight of the town. Finally he saw a shanty some distance off the road. Upon inquiry as to the location of Fairview he was told he had passed through the town two miles back. "How is that"? exclaimed the preacher. "I haven't seen a house for miles until I saw yours." "Oh, there are no houses in Fairview," returned the settler. "It was laid out only a few months ago." The squatter told the preacher to ride back two miles and look in the grass for the white stakes. Arrangement had been made to hold the service in a squatter's shanty some distance off the road. The minister found the stakes and when he arrived at the shanty found his congregation of about a dozen squatters waiting for him.

The *Boston Traveller* gave this story of the town boom of the fifties on the prairies:

A gentleman recently returned from the West relates that, in setting out early in the morning from the place where he had passed the night, he consulted his map of the country, and finding that a very considerable town, called Vienna, occupied a point of his road but some twelve or fifteen miles off, concluded to journey as far as that place before breakfast. Another equally extensive town, bearing as high sounding a name, was laid down as a convenient distance for his afternoon stage, and there he proposed halting for the night. He continued to travel at a good round pace until the sun had risen high in the heavens, and until he computed that he had accomplished more than twice or thrice the distance which he proposed to himself in the outset. Still he saw no town before him, even of the humblest kind, much less such a magnificent one as his map prepared him to look for. At length, meeting a solitary wood-chopper, emerging from the forest, he accosted him and inquired how far it was to Vienna.—"Vienna," exclaimed the man, "why you passed it five and twenty miles back. Did you notice a stick of timber and a blazed tree beside the road? that was Vienna"! The dismayed traveller then inquired how far it was to the other place, at which he designed passing the night. "Why you are right on that place now," returned the man; "it begins just on the other side of the ravine, and runs down to a clump of girdled trees which you will see about a mile farther on the road." "Are there no houses built?" faltered out the traveller. "Oh, no houses whatsomer," returned the woodman, "they hewed and hauled the logs for a blacksmith shop, but before they raised it, the town lots were disposed of in the Eastern States; and every thing has been left, just as you now see it, ever since." [21]

One enthusiastic town builder wrote *History of Kansas and Emigrants Guide*. In the preface he warned his readers:

Some writers, and the most we have observed on Kansas, write with such graphic and novel style that the reader going there would not suppose it to be the same country described. No man is considered a hero unless he can describe Kansas as a paradise. We profess to give its history as we saw it and understand it.

He then described a town which he laid out and in which he was interested:

Whitfield City is located upon the bank of the Conda river, in one of the most central and commanding situations in the territory. . . . No place in the territory can have more public access to roads. . . . One mile from the town is one of the finest free stone quarries in the country. Rocks one hundred feet long could be split off from the beautiful mass. . . . The roads designated . . . are the finest imaginable, rendering carriage traveling the most delightful in the world.

Whitfield City, a name of ancient remembrance among all Christian denominations, is laid out on a splendid and magnificent scale. . . . It is laid out at right angles, with a number of large public squares for schools, churches, etc. . . . On the east and west of the town plat and public square are clumps of shade trees overshadowing two large and limpid springs of water. . . . To the northwest you behold the smooth, serpentine windings of the Conda river (Soldier creek), studded with a black-looking forest, shooting off to the north through the Pottawatomie lands, like the great hydra for which it was named, retreating from view in the high rolling prairie.

Whitfield City is laid out with a view of encouraging scientific, literary and religious institutions. Liberal donations are made for schoolhouses and churches, and the fine springs insure comfort and convenience. . . . A railroad up the Kansas river will soon supersede every other thoroughfare. . . .

A manual-labor college is about being established at Whitfield City, under the patronage of donations from the town. The peculiar features of the college is its manual-labor department. . . .

[21] *Kansas Chief*, July 30, 1857.

J. M. Cole secured a copy of this *Emigrants Guide* on his journey to Kansas and decided to settle at Whitfield City but on his arrival was disgusted to find that it was a city of stakes only. There was not a single house nor even a tent to break the monotony of the bare hills and rolling prairie.[22] All of this bears out the words of Horace Greeley that "it takes three log houses to make a city in Kansas, but they begin calling it a city so soon as they have staked out lots."

Towns which had grown to a fair size sometimes declined and died. The town of Sumner, three miles south of Atchison, Kansas, once had a population of twenty-five hundred. Its streets were filled with busy traffic of the wagon trains as the thousands of oxen and mules transported hundreds of tons of goods from that river point across the plains. In a few years the overland traffic was superseded by the railroads running through other points, and the drivers' voices and the lowing of cattle were heard no more in the once busy town. Little by little the population drifted elsewhere until the community died out entirely.

Rome in Ellis County, Kansas, had a population of over two thousand and was the metropolis of western Kansas. Buffalo Bill was one of the chief supporters of the enterprise. Even the luster of its name and the prowess of Buffalo Bill did not keep it from oblivion.

Among the reasons for the death of thriving towns may be listed the following: The railway went through a rival town leaving the urban community high and dry; the trail changed; the county seat with its accompanying interests was removed to a rival town; the stage line shifted leaving a town isolated.[23]

[22] Fannie Cole, "Pioneer Life in Kansas," Kansas State Historical Society *Collections*, Vol. XII, pp. 354–355; George Martin, "Some of the Lost Towns of Kansas," *Ibid.*, pp. 426–490.

[23] Secretary Martin of the Kansas Historical Society has collected material concerning lost towns in Kansas covering in all only thirty-two counties. He gathered about 2,000 geographical names once familiar on maps, in documents and publications. These names are now unknown. *Ibid.*, p. 362; in 1931 Marshall County, Kansas, boasted of few more than a dozen towns. Forty-three other mushroom villages and towns had grown up and passed into oblivion. "Many Towns Have Vanished," *Marshall County News*, February 27, 1931.

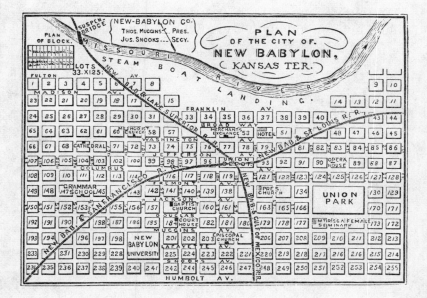

THE CITY OF NEW BABYLON ON PAPER AND IN FACT

Albert D. Richardson, *Beyond the Mississippi*, 1867.

CHAPTER IV

THE RIVER CITIES OF THE FIFTIES

THE ENGROSSING INK was hardly dry on the Kansas-Nebraska Bill when the voracious settlers in western Iowa, Missouri, and Minnesota crossed "Old Muddy"[1] or the Red River and, joining the trespassers there who had already taken claims at the sufferance of the red man,[2] laid out the first towns in the new territories. The Kansas-Nebraska Bill became a law in May, 1854, and on June 13 a company of Missourians formed the town company of Leavenworth at Weston, Missouri. Leavenworth thus became the first town in Kansas. On July 27 another group of Missourians, while still in their native state, formed the town company of Atchison, named after the senator from Missouri who is given credit for the repeal of the Missouri Compromise. Lawrence was founded in August and Topeka was born in the snows of December.[3]

Most of the important towns of the fifties were located on the Missouri River although several which have since become very important were to be found along its tributaries. These latter streams were at that time thought to be navigable.

There was little farming on the part of the first settlers. A few patches of sod corn were put out here and there. Some scattered gardens gave evidence of an attempt to produce vegetables, but

[1] The Missouri River.
[2] The treaty between the United States Government and the Indians in which the Indians relinquished their title to the lands bordering on the west bank of the Missouri River was concluded and ratified on April 17, 1854. President Pierce proclaimed this treaty and extinguishment of the Indian title June 24, 1854. A. L. Child, *Centennial History of Plattsmouth and Cass County, Nebraska*, p. 5.
[3] W. C. Simons, "Lawrence Newspapers in Territorial Days," Kansas State Historical Society *Collections*, Vol. XVII, p. 325.

there was little investment of means or muscle on this project. Mr. J. Sterling Morton quotes a speculator of the time as truthfully portraying the state of affairs when he said the inhabitants were only amateur farmers "merely aggravating the soil a little." [4]

These early inhabitants pinned their faith on the rapid development of the river towns and the trade that would soon flow into these "splendid emporiums of commerce." So great was the faith of the settlers that land rose to enormous prices in the vicinity of these promising "cities." In 1857 lots on the river landing 25' × 125' were valued at ten thousand dollars. Three or four blocks back they sold for two thousand, while those a half mile distant brought twelve hundred. One lot costing eight hundred dollars six months later sold for twenty-two hundred dollars. Eleven thousand dollars was offered for eleven lots which cost fifty-five dollars eighteen months earlier. Suburban lots three miles from the river sold for one to two hundred dollars each which had been bought during the previous winter for one hundred dollars an acre.[5]

The emigrant, having read in the Nebraska papers about the vast building program, the magnificent buildings, the splendid colleges, inviting parks, and the ever-rising real estate prices of the chosen abode, was often deeply disappointed at first sight of his future home. Instead of regular rows of well-built homes on well-graded streets, there was only a scene of the rudest character. Perhaps there was one graded street while the others were mere foot paths leading up and down natural ravines to the scattered dug-outs, log cabins, and other uncouth dwellings which composed the "city." These scattered habitations, surrounded on three sides with hazel brush, weeds, and briars, presented a gloomy aspect to the tenderfoot fresh from well-tilled fields and well-improved cities farther east. John J. Ingalls noted that his new home town had no fences and that the whole place was open to the incursions of dogs

---

[4] J. Sterling Morton, "Centennial History," *Daily Nebraska Press*, July 5, 1876.
[5] Albert D. Richardson, *Beyond the Mississippi*, p. 53.

and pigs [6] which existed in large numbers and seemed to constitute the greater part of the population of the town. Mr. Ingalls also complained most vigorously about the mud:

The worst feature is the mud. Kansas mud is incomparable; in the mud line it is a perfect triumph—slippery as lard, adhesive as tar, cumulative as a miser's gold, and treacherous as hope, it forms a compound unique and peculiar that defies description. There are three colors— black, red and clay, differing in no respect except chromatically. It sticketh closer than a brother, entering every crevice, and then accumulating in varied laminæ and strata, many shaped and many colored, that can neither be kicked off nor scraped off, nor in any way avoided. It dries as hard as a mortar wall. A brush glides over it as it would a lapstone or the Farnese Hercules, leaving a hammer and an old case-knife the only resource. The usual method of cleaning boots here is to take them by the straps and bang them against a brick wall. It is quite efficacious, the only objection being that the process would soon bury the house as effectually as Vesuvius did the city of Pompeii.

As late as 1866 Topeka did not have a foot of sidewalk or pavement. The dwelling places were of the rudest sort. At Omaha Mr. Estabrook, one of the leading men who later became a territorial attorney general, lived in a shack covered with hay. It was built of cottonwood boards nailed up and down to the frame work; it had one room with a hay roof but no floor. Dry hay was scattered over the ground and carpets laid over that, and when the rain leaked through the primitive roof and soaked both carpets and hay, the carpets were hung on the line to dry and fresh hay was placed on the floor.

At Lawrence, Kansas, many odd structures were to be seen. There were dugouts, sod houses, log cabins, shake structures, and other odd dwelling places. In the summer of 1854 it was a village of tents, but by the following year most of the houses were made of

[6] *The Peoples Press* of Nebraska City (June 28, 1860), stated that the city council, at a recent meeting, suspended the ordinance against hogs and "the porkers are therefore entitled to the freedom of the city."

sod. The sod house built at this time had not developed into the standard type which came into being on the plains in the next pioneer generation. Sod was used for the walls but not for the entire house as was done on the true sod-house frontier. A style which became fairly common and which was almost peculiar to Lawrence at this time was called "the hay tent." It was built by setting up two rows of poles and then bringing them together at the top and thatching the sides with prairie hay. The house was all roof and gable; the windows and doors were in the end. The gables were built up with sod walls. The "Pioneer Boarding House" was this sort of structure. It was fifty feet long and twenty feet wide. Here the first sermon was preached, and it served as a city auditorium, as well as furnishing board and room to a horde of speculators and home-seekers. This building burned down in the fall of 1854 and the St. Nicholas was built in the same way except that the walls of poles and hay were banked with sod to a height of three or four feet and lined with cotton cloth.[7]

The home of Governor Charles Robinson on Mount Oread where the University is now located, was made of sod and thatch. One of the best dwelling houses in Lawrence was made by setting four forked poles in the ground to support roof poles running crosswise. These, covered with hay, served as a roof. The sides were enclosed by a wagon cover and blankets. Mrs. Charles Robinson spoke of visiting one of her friends who lived in a little cabin with mud walls, cottonwood roof, and cloth covering the inside. It was tent-shaped and very small with an earthy smell which gave her a stifled feeling as she entered the low door.[8] In a year or two these sod and hay structures were replaced by shake houses. Shakes were made by sawing a log into thirty-two inch blocks and splitting off rude boards after the manner of making shingles in that period. The shakes were nailed directly onto the studding like

[7] Richard Cordley, *History of Lawrence* (Lawrence, Kansas, 1895), pp. 13–15.
[8] Many other New England ladies of culture and good breeding adapted themselves to these crude surroundings.

clapboards. John J. Ingalls described the buildings in western towns as shabby and rude in the extreme. The green cottonwood boards shrank and "crawled" in the sun leaving a superabundance of ventilation.

These frame buildings were so cold that the housewives froze their feet on the cold floor, and in Lawrence during the cold winter of 1855–1856, water froze only a short distance from the stove. Because of the leaky roof rain collected in puddles on the uneven dirt floor. The fireplace or cookstove was often the only heat all winter. The furniture consisted of the most meager equipment. Oftentimes a box was used for a table, a trunk or chest served for an improvised wardrobe, and rude benches for chairs. A bed was made of rough boards threaded with cords and covered with a mattress stuffed with prairie hay, proverbially called prairie feathers. Quilts and aprons answered the purpose of doors and windows. Seats were made of rough boards. Some of the early frame or shake cabins were papered with newspapers from the East.

Some companies in Pittsburgh, Cincinnati, and St. Louis built a type of ready-made houses. These were manufactured ready to be set up on their arrival by steamboat. In 1857 one of these Cincinnati houses fifteen feet square sold for two hundred dollars.

The inhabitants of the early towns, isolated as they were from the outside world, eagerly waited for the boats and stage coaches. The dull drone of the river steamer brought a large portion of the town rushing to the landing. They came on foot, on horseback, and in vehicles of every description, and waited patiently while the boat landed. Nor was it the boys and girls, the young men and young women only who went to the river; but the business men, the housewives, and even the aged and the infirm hastened to the wharf. The young men even forgot their training and left the church service when the first steamboat of the season whistled, and the deacons slipped out to see what had become of the younger members. Even the ladies and the more decorous became restless. The preacher, failing to hold the interest of his congregation, dismissed the service and all went to the river. The *Nebraska City News* of March 20, 1858, very vividly depicts the arrival of the first boat of the season:

THE FIRST BOAT

IMMENSE EXCITEMENT

THE PLATTE VALLEY TAKES THE HORNS

Our writings were disturbed last evening at 7 o'clock by the ringing of bells, the thrilling whistles of the engine, and the shouts of 'A Boat'! 'A Boat'!! The streets were at once filled with men and boys running to the wharf to meet the first boat of the season. It was the Platte Valley.

Naturally the first boat up in the spring was always considered the great event of the season as it brought fresh supplies of goods to replenish the stocks of merchandise which were very generally depleted during the long winter. Such an event was certainly worthy of celebration. Although these boats were not floating palaces, they did represent a degree of luxury and were a welcome connecting link with the outside world. Parties were quickly improvised and the provisions on board were levied by the people whose ordinary diet consisted of the rude fare of the prairies such as venison, wild turkey, prairie chicken, and other game. These were gladly exchanged for bacon, fruit, vegetables, and, not least, a good quantity of the elixir of the frontier—liquor. If there was not a band, a darkey was always on board with a banjo or a fiddle and so the festivities culminated in a dance.

In the year 1856 Peter A. Sarpy owned a trading post at the little town of Decatur, Nebraska; Clement Lambert was his chief clerk. Like most Indian traders he was fond of his quickest moving goods—whiskey. One evening a St. Louis steamer tied up at the wharf for the night. This was a signal for a general celebration. Lambert led the spree. Uproariously drunk, he stripped down to pants and Indian leggings; buckling a belt around his waist, he stuck in a pair of Colt's revolvers, sprang onto his pony, Billy, gave a few Indian war whoops, and raced to the river. At the wharf, with a gun in each hand, Lambert let out more savage whoops and threats which sufficed to open the gangway. Pony and rider ran into the boat, up the stairs into the saloon, and halted before the bar. Here the clerk ordered a big drink for the pony and commanded every person present to drink to the health of Billy and the President of the United States. It must not be supposed that all the frontier towns were as raw and uncivilized as those Indian trading posts, and yet it must be remembered that wherever civilization meets savagery, even civilized man is mastered temporarily by barbarism.

Erastus Beadle gives a classic description of the arrival of the steamer *White Cloud* at Omaha on the evening of April 15, 1857:

When the boat arrived it seemed onehalf of the inhabitants were at the landing. When the plank was put out they rushed on in such a body it was some minutes before the passengers could get off. Then such a peeping into each others faces to recognise some expected friend. The vicinity of the ladies cabin was one perfect jam of men eagerly peeping over the heads of more forward ones or crowding through to get a sight at some dozen ladies who were as eager to single out, their husband, brother, or friend. I mixed in but no one I knew was there. I was not however as disappointed as some hundred others must have been.

This interest in a boat arrival did not abate even when the boats became numerous. Every whistle brought an assemblage at the wharf to see the newcomers and any other new sight. It became a regular custom for boats on their first trip up in the spring to give a free dance to the citizens of the town. These were splendid affairs.

As time went on, the boats became numerous. J. W. Hacknew recalled having counted fifteen steamboats in the port of Brownville, Nebraska. In June, 1859, there were seventy-six calls at Nebraska City, and during the months from May to November of that same year there were two hundred and twelve landings.

Although the days before the Civil War are considered primarily as the epoch of the river city, further west some new cities were being founded. In an inland town the great event of the day or week was the arrival of the stage coach from the East. This vehicle was announced half a mile away by the prolonged blast of a horn and a cloud of dust. The lumbering coach, drawn by four horses, dashed up to the hotel with a final effort of the tired animals and amid the cracking of the whip. The town turned out to see the travel-worn passengers emerge from their cramped quarters. Bearded men in high hats and long tailed coats and ladies in deep, round bonnets, shawls, and mammoth hoopskirts, were indeed glad to disembark; running the gauntlet of the hotel loungers and inquisitive townsmen, they disappeared to enjoy the comforts of rest and refreshment in the hotel.[9] The residents of the straggling little western town were eager for any news from the East. The crowd anxiously awaited the coming of a wheeled messenger bringing intelligence from home. The driver and passengers were plied with questions and there was an air of expectancy as the group waited the distribution of the mail. A gloom of disappointment hung over all when it was found that the eastern mails had failed to come through or that the wires, the splendid new means of communication, had been broken.

There were many complaints about the mail and the poor service on the stage lines. The *Nebraska Advertiser,* of Brownville, Nebraska, reported that a man in Kansas, ninety-six miles away, wrote a letter to the editor inviting him to a Christmas ball. It was written December 21, 1856, and was received March 14, 1857, requiring eighty-four days to be delivered. If a man wanted his mail brought to his door he spoke to the postmaster about it and paid two cents for each letter delivered. If he went to the post office he paid only one cent per letter.

The river boats, particularly the earlier ones of the season, were welcomed because they brought a pleasant relief from the eternal corn-bread, sorghum, and other rude fare. Flour from which to make biscuits was ever welcome.

[9] *Nebraska City News,* March 20, 1858; Eliza Johnston Wiggin, *Impressions of Early Kansas* (Wichita, Kansas, 1915), p. 6.

These towns, soon after they were founded, supported eating houses with ultra-modern menus. As early as January 6, 1859, an advertisement in the *Nebraska Advertiser* announced that, although fresh oysters were quite a rarity in Nebraska, they could be had at the Brownville Eating Saloon, and that anything in the eating line could be secured at any hour. As early as May 27, 1858, the same paper announced that the druggist had lately received a supply of fresh goods among which the most important item was a soda fountain from which gushed forth an ice cold sparkling beverage. This luxury, although not in general use except in the larger towns, was not an isolated case by any means; for newspapers of the other more flourishing towns speak of ice cream on sale at the drug stores, bakeries, and candy kitchens.

At first almost the entire population of the new country was male. When Leavenworth was first laid out in September, 1854, the *Kansas Weekly Herald* said that "the population of this city is nearly as follows:—99 men, 1 woman, and 0 babies. Total 100." [10]

And yet in this land of opportunity for barbers there was not one barber shop until February 9, 1855. This is only one hint of the lack of conveniences and comforts in a new country. The *Kansas Weekly Herald* pled for skilled workers:

What we want now most, is mechanics. We have several kinds, but not enough of them. We have not got a Sadler, Shoemaker, Tailor, Cabinet Maker, Hatter, nor Milliner in the place, and every one of these trades would do the very best of business here. We are really afflicted for the want of a Shoemaker and Cabinet Maker; and if the eastern states will send us mechanics, *who are not abolitionists,* we may safely promise them fortunes out of their business.

The municipal service for fire and police protection was crude indeed. In July, 1857, a fire broke out in Lawrence, Kansas. Fortunately it was put out quickly by a hundred men supplied with buckets from the tinware store. By July, 1858, Nebraska City had a primitive system. There was a bucket and water company and also

[10] *Kansas Weekly Herald*, September 15, 1854.

an engine company. The inadequacy of these was proved two years later, however, when during a dry period the whole central section of the city was reduced to ruins.

The police department was little more efficient. The police were similar to the old night watchman. These majestic representatives of the law and preventers of deviltry carried lanterns for the alleged purpose of seeing the miscreant, but in reality this paraphernalia served most efficiently to indicate the whereabouts of these law enforcement officials.

A person who had read about the wonders of Kansas or Nebraska in the boom journals, would have thought that pauperism could not exist in this new land flowing with milk and honey. Nevertheless, before the Civil War pauperism did exist west of the Missouri River. In view of the lack of a poor house or county farm, the county commissioners received proposals from responsible parties giving the terms upon which they would undertake to keep paupers who had become charges of the county.

Another service, although semi-public in character, was in the hands of private individuals. This was the business of caring for the live stock of the town. For several years oxen and other cattle owned by the settlers were put into a common herd. At night they were confined in a substantial pen and during the day they were driven out onto the prairie where they grazed. A member of the community agreed to herd them and hired boys to do the actual tiresome work of watching the animals during the long weary days.

Today the business man of affairs seeks the control of air lines, radio companies, or automotive works. In the fifties the moneymaker sought control of the ferry. The man who owned a good ferry in that day had a venture equal to a United States air mail contract of the Hoover administration. These ferries were often awkward, crude contrivances. Frequently they were propelled by the force of the current flowing against a keel and were shuttled back and forth on a cable to which they were attached by a rope and pulley. As traffic increased, steam ferries displaced these earlier boats. In the coldest winter months the Missouri River was frozen allowing teams and sleds hauling hay and other necessities to cross the ice.

Despite the fact that these river towns were trying to assume city airs and to appear mature, they savored of the wild rugged West. They were surrounded on three sides by savagery, and this influenced the community. A few examples will illustrate the proximity of the people to the unconquered wilderness. In the year 1859 the first school-house in the inland town of Beatrice was burned by a prairie fire. On May 16, 1857, a large prairie wolf ventured into Omaha at nine o'clock in the morning and was about to kill a young colt a few hours old when he was discovered and chased out of town by two dogs. The Indians at this time were frequent visitors. In February, 1857, a frightened deer ran into Nebraska City and was captured in a ravine. In 1854 the sheriff pursued a black bear into the heart of the same city and there, assisted by men, boys, and dogs, killed the unfortunate beast.

The immigrant from the East was apt to feel that the people in the new country were dilatory and lacking in energy in their business pursuits. A resident of Omaha in 1857 complained: "We want more prompt energetic working business men here than we have. It is just the place for such men to make money."

In 1858 John J. Ingalls in a letter described the inhabitants of the frontier town of his choice as shabby, ill-dressed, unthrifty people like the inhabitants of the Irish quarter of a large city, wearing upon their countenances a look of discontent akin to despair. He felt that there was a good prospect ahead, for men of education and ability were scarce and in demand. He observed that offices were filled with dolts, and posts of honor and profit were held by irresponsible persons because there were more positions than worthy candidates. He was correct in his anticipation of a bright future, for within a few years he was one of the prominent young politicians in the territory.

The frontier towns were communities of broad contrasts. One

could find people of culture equal to those in the East. On the other hand one could find a turbulent class of people who cared little for the finer things of life. Many came West with no thought of making the new community their home. An idea persisted of making a fortune and returning home in three or four years. An early minister complained that this temporary citizenship created a feeling of instability and tended toward a low condition of morals. This, together with the spirit of worldliness and wild speculation, created a rough life. Sabbath breaking, profanity, and drinking were common. In many towns in the territories there was no Sabbath. Stores and shops were kept open and Sunday was the busiest day of the entire week.

Lawrence, Kansas, was an exception to the rule. On Sunday a hush came over the city and the sound of the church bell reverberated over the prairie. Hymns of praise swept through the Kaw Valley. On that day it was a little New England town set down in the rude environment of the frontier. Even the Puritan towns, however, were colored by the wild carefree spirit of the new country and in the rougher urban centers there were tumultuous times.

Elections were celebrated with plenty of liquor and not infrequently ended in excitement. On the occasion of the first Republican defeat in 1856 a general fight occurred in Nebraska City. A large proportion of the citizens participated with knives, pistols, brickbats, sticks, and fists. The mêlée lasted an hour or two. On the occasion of a trial friends of the litigants took sides and continued the battle in a free-for-all fight. The *Nebraska Advertiser* gives an account of one such uproar in 1859:

Several of our Nemaha City neighbors, who were in attendance as parties, witnesses, and lookers on in a suit before Judge Whitney, on Tuesday last, having imbibed rather freely, or 'were socially received' too often, ended the affair by a general free fight, in the Halls of Justice. Result—stove knocked over; several bloody noses, and a good deal of loud talk.

The cultural things were pitifully scanty. When the Kansas territorial legislature met at Pawnee in 1855, little was found at the so-called capital except a stone building which had been erected for a legislature. There were no accommodations for the board and lodging of the members; they were obliged to camp in tents. At another meeting of this august body the assembly was held at Shawnee at an Indian mission. At that time there were between two and three hundred Indians at the mission. The powwow of the white man was held in the environment of the past among Uncle Sam's red wards. One day as Governor Beebe, the boy governor of Kansas, was sitting in his executive mansion alone with his thoughts, a party of United States and territorial officials called to see him. He showed them about the mansion and entertained them with a recitation of the wonders of Kansas. They praised his hospitality and took a hearty interest in his furnishings. Finally one of the Washington visitors said, "You seem comfortably located here, but where is your library?" "Right this way," replied the youthful executive as he led the way through one room and into another; he softly closed the door and, to the surprise of the visitors, pointed to a farm almanac and said, "There is my library."

Nevertheless in spite of the crude beginnings, a few of the cultural things came in. A resident of Omaha in the summer of 1857 could proudly boast that his city had a dozen pianos. In the spring of the same year a Library Association had been organized and in May the secretary wrote to the *New York Weekly Globe* for a subscription.

The discovery of gold in the Rocky Mountain region in 1857 gave a big impetus to migration from the East and thus raised the river towns to the status of outfitting points. There was an intense rivalry among the Missouri River towns for the preëminence. The newspapers of the various towns vied with one another to induce the overland traveler. Shorter or safer routes to the gold field were advanced. Some of this campaign work to direct travel to different points was unscrupulous. The gold fever raged furiously in the straggling little river towns. Companies were formed for the purpose of making the overland pilgrimage. The Missouri River cities became the outfitting points for the Rocky Mountain mining industry. An Omaha man proclaimed in a newspaper: "Picks, Shovels, Rockers, Pans, Toms, Stoves, and all necessary mining articles, are already to be seen in the stores and shops of our merchants and mechanics."

The writer stated that ministers, lawyers, tradesmen, and gamblers were getting ready to leave for the mines where there would be abundant business for each.

The impatient miners could hardly wait until spring to start over the prairies for Pike's Peak. While the snow was still on the ground, wagon trains and pedestrians started for the Rockies. Men trudged across the weary distance pushing a hand cart or walking in search of the rainbow's end.[11] In a few instances lads from nine to sixteen ran off and, procuring hand carts or making their way however they could, journeyed to the gold field.

The gold rush made the Missouri River towns in reality mining towns.[12] They were crowded centers; the streets, lanes, and byways were filled with a multitude of prairie schooners. These monster wagons were pulled by ten yoke of oxen or from four to six span of mules driven by one line. The town presented a busy scene with its rumbling wagons, bellowing oxen, braying mules, cracking whips, and busy men. The shouting, yelling, and cursing of the teamsters rent the air. Men rushed up and down the streets in utter forgetfulness of everything except hurry and bustle. Almost everybody who could muster a vehicle went into the freighting business.

[11] Two men from St. Anthony on the Mississippi River passed through Omaha in March, 1857. Their conveyance was a hand rack which was so arranged that they could use it as a sled. They traveled across country without any reference to roads or settlements. A man on foot with his knapsack and a ham of meat on his back passed through one of the river towns on his way to the gold field. He planned to make the rest of his journey in the same manner.

[12] The chief outfitting towns were Leavenworth, St. Joseph, Atchison, Brownville, Nebraska City, Council Bluffs, and Omaha.

This as a rule returned a fine profit. The business ranged from a one mule cart or one team of oxen and a wagon carrying a few hundred pounds, to a train carrying over a half million pounds. Transportation was supplied in almost every conceivable style. Alexander Majors in 1860 dispatched a train of twenty-five wagons regularly every week. Each wagon was drawn by six yoke of oxen and carried three tons of freight, making in all seventy-five tons to the train.

Prices were high and on every hand was to be seen evidence of the booming prosperity of the frontier. Saloons, gambling houses, dance halls, and all manner of rough amusements flourished, taking the wages of the incoming and outgoing "bull whackers."

It was only natural that anyone inclined to riotous living took advantage of this last chance for a fling at pleasure before starting on the slow journey. Outlaws and other wild men frequented these cities. A minister who stayed overnight at Atchison, Kansas, in 1865, complained that sleep was out of the question until the early hours on account of the blasphemous language, groans of pain, and the ring of revolvers heard through the night. The wives and daughters of the respectable cultured class seldom walked on the streets and when they did, they wore veils or sunbonnets to hide their faces from the men. The War brought a large number of deserters, guerrillas, and bushwhackers who fled from the border to find refuge in the river cities. A Mr. Bentley wrote from Nebraska, in 1866, that for weeks it had been unsafe for an unarmed man to go on the streets alone after dark, for burglaries had been frequent and altercations had been a nightly occurrence. The whole thing had been spiced by two or three murders. On January 2, 1859, John J. Ingalls wrote that since Christmas there had been five murders in Leavenworth. Everybody carried two revolvers.

In spite of this martial atmosphere there was a calmer side to frontier urban society. Among the better class of people there was to be found a certain genteel element. A few carpets were to be found such as Brussells rugs with showy flowers. These were carefully rolled up each fall and striped rag rugs put down in their place. Ladies dressed in silks and tasty woolens, the skirts full and reaching to the ground. Shawls were worn summer and winter. Many men wore old army overcoats with bright brass buttons,[13] but some had plain dark coats. A few men even wore tall silk stove-pipe hats. These elegancies in dress were, however, confined to the few and more often both men and women dressed very plainly. Now and then a melodeon or piano was to be found.

Society conversation turned most often to the advantages of the old home, the elegancies and comforts of it in comparison to the rude surroundings and disadvantages of the new. But the universal optimism for the western home, its healthfulness, brilliant future, and opportunity, drowned despair.

Many had their own horses and saddles or carriages. Others hired the livery rig which was available in every town. The young people took moonlight rides over the prairies. In the earlier times the young men and their lady friends rode ponies since there were few rigs. These limitations were later remedied.

Young and old found amusement and social events. For the most part the long winter evenings were spent listening to lectures and debates, reading at reading rooms, arranging and looking at dramatic presentations, or dancing. Discussion clubs had various names such as Lyceum, Library, and Literary Society,[14] Debating Society, Debating school, Athenaeum, and Dramatic Association. These literary societies sprang up while the towns were in their infancy. At Lawrence, Kansas, during the first winter the Lawrence Athenaeum and Mechanics Institute was founded. When Leavenworth was only a few weeks old [15] the *Kansas Weekly Herald* announced an open air lyceum: "For lack of other amusement, our Citizens

---

[13] This was more particularly true immediately following the Civil War.

[14] On February 9, 1857, the Legislature of Nebraska incorporated the Brownville Lyceum, Library, and Literary Association. Its purpose was to promote a lyceum, library and reading room with a capital stock of $50,000 to be sold at $5 a share.

[15] The first house in Leavenworth was completed about September 20, 1854. The first sale of lots occurred October 10, 1854.

have organized a debating society which is held every night on the Levee in front of the *Herald* Office. They have no light on the subject except that of the stars and the various camps." [16]

At Brownville, Nebraska, there were two societies—a library and lyceum association and a debating society. Each was well patronized and grew. Many of the questions debated were live questions of state or economics. The following are representative of the subjects:

1. Resolved that the Nebraska legislature should pass a law releasing persons from debts contracted outside the territory after a residence of sixty days in the country.
2. Affirmed that all kinds of stock should be restrained from running at large.
3. Affirmed that the Missouri Compromise was right.
4. Resolved that men and women should be equal before the law in respect to legal right and liabilities.

The debates were not merely opportunities for the youth to practice theoretical academic polemics; they were open forums for the discussion of problems of the day. Lawyers, ministers, and the leading citizens of the town took part in the fiery art of Demosthenes.

Occasionally a dramatic association arranged a home talent play. These usually were of the Shakesperian variety.

Some lyceums made the practice of inviting lecturers to speak on technical or abstract subjects which could not draw a crowd today. At Brownville, Nebraska, doctors from the budding young medical college there lectured on such topics as "The Bones" or "Pathology." At other times ministers, lawyers, or other men of some education lectured on abstract philosophical, political, or classical subjects. During the winter of 1860 the Brownville Lyceum presented the following subjects: "Manifest Destiny," "Philosophy, Greek and Roman," "The Historian, Statesman and the Divine." The membership was one dollar for the season. In 1864 the society raised four hundred dollars to improve the building.

The river towns were blessed with a contact with the world de-

[16] *Kansas Weekly Herald*, September 22, 1854.

nied to the isolated prairie town. As a result of steamboat and stage
transportation occasional professional entertainers visited these
more fortunate communities. A magician, a troupe of saxhorn players, a blind flute player, a minstrel show, the New Orleans Serenaders, and a troupe of singers calling themselves "The New England Bards" followed the Missouri River giving concerts to crowded
houses during the years 1857 and 1858.[17]

An observer told of visiting a theater at Leavenworth in 1858.
The performance was offered in a barnlike building in the heart of
town. The crowd sat on wooden benches all at the same level and
listened to the three or four disreputable musicians who made up
the orchestra. The stage and auditorium were lighted with candles;
the floor of the stage creaked when the performers walked over it;
and the scenery threatened to topple over.[18] These performances,
although not as finished in technique as those in the East and although presented in rough surroundings, nevertheless formed a
pleasant feature of frontier life and were much enjoyed.

Hand organ grinders also followed the river. Some of these had
the proverbial monkey to collect the money. Others sang for small
change on the streets. These entertainers must have become somewhat of a trial to the population, judging from the comment of the
Omaha Times:

For the past few weeks, hand organs have been quite plenty in our
streets. First came a couple of foreign maidens with unwashed faces
and "unkempt hair discoursing on a hand organ at back doors for stray
half-dimes to the accompaniment of cracked voices and a ricketty tam-
bourine." Others followed. Most of these itinerant musicians claim to
be of noble birth from the old country.

Circuses kept pace with other immigration. The first one made its
appearance in 1857. Everybody in the whole country attended.
These circuses of the fifties were creditable for the period and the

---

[17] The New England Bards also visited Lawrence in July, 1857.
[18] Augustus Meyers, *Ten Years in the Ranks of the U. S. Army* (New York,
1914), p. 137.

country. Three daily performances were given at nine, at two, and at seven o'clock, with a change of program at each. There were wild animals, tight rope walking, equestrian feats, such as riders balancing on horses, stunts on horseback, such as two or three men doing acrobatics on as many horses while at full speed, the educated horse which did tricks, clowns, trapeze performers, and others.

Lodges such as the Masons, Odd Fellows, and Sons of Malta were organized west of the Missouri River in 1857 and 1858. Militia companies were popular. There was scarcely a county seat without its military company. Here and there a town had a band which was a prominent feature of local celebrations.

A wedding on the frontier was always followed by a charivari. This ceremony occurred on the evening after the wedding and consisted of ringing cowbells, beating on tin pans and all the other noise-making machinery that the genius of the younger citizenry could devise. In due time the groom and bride appeared before the assembled noise makers and invited them into the new home to partake of pumpkin pies, watermelon, cigars, or other desirable luxury provided by the groom.

The "infair" took place the day following the wedding. This was a visit of the closer friends of the wedding party to the bridegroom's parents or to the new home. In the latter case it was a sort of house warming affair. Not infrequently the young guests rode horseback, the young ladies riding behind their escorts or on separate horses.

In the speculative fifties, when every man envisioned himself a coming plutocrat, sports and professional amusements flourished. Lawrence and Leavenworth, Kansas, both had bowling alleys early in their history. Theaters and pool rooms also blossomed.

Lottery sales were occasions for congregation and intercourse. Outdoor sports such as hunting and riding were favorites. Wolf hunts were conducted in different ways. Sometimes a few friends mounted on horses, took a half dozen greyhounds, and enjoyed a spirited chase. With no fences, the open prairie was the sportsman's delight. At other times the hunt assumed the nature of a community affair, a veritable drive against the luckless prairie denizen. Acting on plans laid at a general mass meeting, the various parties closed in on the quarry at a place previously decided upon.

Horse racing was a favorite diversion. The natural prairie grass served as a track for both running and trotting races. These were announced in the newspapers and were the all-absorbing topic for days before the affair.

Ordinarily there were only two horses in the contest. The backers would put up fifty to a hundred dollars on each side and nearly as much was staked on side bets by outsiders. If the horses were from different towns or communities a strong spirit of community loyalty was shown by citizens and their money was arrayed on one side or the other. In addition to this more formal contests were held from time to time in which ladies displayed their horsemanship and side saddles were given as prizes for the best riders.

Horseshoes was enjoyed. Ball, although not as popular a sport for team contests as it became in the eighties, was nevertheless played in a simple form by children and young people.

The most elaborate occasion of the whole year came on the fourth of July. A typical frontier celebration in 1857 began with a huge dance on the evening of July third. The hall would be filled to capacity. After a midnight supper a recess was taken to sweep the dancing floor. The dance then continued gaily until broad daylight. Day was ushered in by the firing of salutes and the ringing of bells.

The whole country round about was invited to help celebrate. In the morning the settlers came thronging in on horseback, on foot, or seated in chairs in heavy ox-wagons, and in other conveyances.[19] These vehicles were covered with garlands of green, and flowers hid their rough exterior. About ten o'clock the crowd was escorted by the military company to a wooded place outside the city where a bower had been erected. At Lawrence, Kansas, in 1855, about two

[19] A. D. Richardson mentions having seen one family in Kansas ride triumphantly to the celebration on a stone drag.

thousand—a motley crowd of free-state men, Missourians, and Indians—attended the celebration. The easterners were dressed in eastern garb; the Missourians were distinctly marked by their dress; and the Indians in their bright-colored blankets added color to the whole scene. Arriving at the grove, they hoisted a flag and fired salutes for each of the states and "the great territory of Kansas." After this a formal program was rendered which inevitably included toasts beginning with the Fourth of July and running on down through a long list of subjects to the ladies who had provided the food for the occasion.[20]

The formal program was sure to include the reading of the Declaration of Independence, an oration, and volunteer speeches. There was a prayer by the chaplain and songs by a choir. A favorite song, which foreshadowed the homestead law, was "Uncle Sam is rich enough to give us all a farm." The program was followed by a tremendous public dinner. At Nemaha City, Nebraska, in 1857, a table over four hundred feet long groaned under the weight of eatables; over two thousand people were present. At Brownville, Nebraska, in 1856, a free barbecue was held. There was buffalo meat, venison, oxen, sheep, hogs, pigs, and other food; "enough," as the newspaper editor said, "to have fed the whole territory." Toward evening the streets were filled with men who had begun to feel the effects of liquor. It was fortunate if the day passed without some unpleasantness. The whole celebration ended with another huge ball which lasted until the morning of the fifth. This might be held on the green. At Lawrence, Kansas, on July 4, 1855, the good puritanical spirit was indicated by the fact that instead of a dance the settlers met in the largest hall in town and had ice cream and cake.

[20] At Bellevue in 1854 toasts were offered to the following: Fourth of July, George Washington, Army and Navy, President and Acting Vice-president, Spartan mothers of the American Revolution, The Union, Nebraska, Knowledge, Our friends crossing the plains, The Press, Bellevue, The ladies. Then followed nine volunteer toasts to various persons, including the Indian Agent and the ladies who prepared the food.

CHAPTER V

LOG-CABIN DAYS

AS HAS BEEN MENTIONED previously there was little farming during the first years. John J. Ingalls wrote to his father that the actual exports from the country—corn, pork, and hides—had not been enough before 1860 to pay for the whiskey that was drunk every month, and men lived on what they brought with them or on the charity of their friends. In due time, however, the agricultural frontier began to develop.

In the fifties the rural residence west of the Missouri was very much like the conventional dwelling which had existed on the frontier from the time the English first set foot on American soil. The home-makers settled along the streams where timber was available and naturally the log cabin was the type of structure built. The settler lived in his covered wagon or in a lean-to, tepee, or other improvised shelter until a house had been constructed.

It was necessary to find large straight trees from which to make logs for the cabin. In the eastern part of the territories near streams this was possible. The farther west settlement advanced, however, the more difficult it was to find trees sufficiently large and straight for building logs. These cabins ordinarily consisted of one room only and were about twelve by sixteen feet. The logs having been drawn up to the building site, the neighbors came in and helped the newcomer. If the logs were too crooked, small sticks were wedged into the cracks and the smaller crevices all chinked with mud. This had a way of drying and dropping out, leaving large openings in the walls through which the northern blizzards drifted and the dust storms blew. The huge fireplace at one end was made of sticks covered with clay mortar which was pounded in between the lath-like sticks until a fire-proof wall was formed between the fire and the log walls.

Nails were expensive and difficult to obtain. As a result not a dozen nails were used in a house; an auger and hardwood pins were substituted for them. There were no nails in the window or door. The more primitive cabin indeed had neither; the more comfortable ones ordinarily had one low door and a small window. The opening of the latter was covered with greased paper. The doorway, at first closed by a piece of old carpet or buffalo skin, was in time replaced by a door made of long clapboards hung on skin hinges and having a leather latch-string.

At first mother earth served for a floor but in time a puncheon floor was laid. This consisted of a kind of heavy plank split out of logs with axes and wedges and smoothed on one side with a broad axe. Even in this case a liberal floor space around the fireplace was left bare of wood to insure against fire. When holes wore in the earth, fresh clay was pounded into the hollows.

Heavy poles called ridge-poles were laid on top of the body of the house in such a way as to form the support for the home-made shingles. These were usually layers split from logs and were known as shakes. They were laid loosely on the poles. The same number of poles was then laid on the roof boards to hold them in place. These poles were called weights and were kept on the roof at the proper distance apart by braces from one to the other. This roof shed rain fairly well but the fine snow blew in the crevices, and it was not at all uncommon for one to awake in the morning to find snow drifted about the room. The Honorable J. Sterling Morton lived in such a cabin with an addition of a smaller bedroom. The inside was much better furnished than the ordinary cabin, having been lined with buffalo skins bought from the Indians for two dollars each. In such a cabin the first floor was frequently partitioned into kitchen, bedroom, and pantry by means of quilts and blankets. An attic might be divided off in the same way giving as many rooms as it would hold beds.

There were variations of this type of domicile. As sawmills were established and lumber became less expensive floors were laid. Even these were rough and unplaned and had to be worn smooth. Yet these kitchen floors of ash and hackberry, scrubbed with wood ashes to maintain their original whiteness, were the pride of many house-keepers. Cottonwood timber, although more plentiful, was not as enduring as harder woods. The boards shrank and warped leaving great cracks, and the shingles, steamed and cut from the logs, curled up until the roof leaked like a sieve. Sometimes the roof of such a cabin was made of bark and boards or even of poles, straw, and dirt.

As late as 1860 a frame house was enough to cause the neighbors to call the occupants "high-toned." These first frame buildings were constructed of the rough native lumber made at the primitive saw-mills. One kind was called the balloon frame house. The furniture, like the house, was of the rudest sort—homemade chairs, or stools, boxes for tables and cupboard, and trunks for wardrobes. When frame houses began to appear, stoves became numerous.

In 1861 when a few frame houses were being built the *Nebraska Farmer* gave the following estimate of the cost of making a farm on the prairies:

A House	$250.00
Breaking 40 A	120.00
500 Walnut posts @ 5¢	25.00
500 post holes dug	5.00
12,500 ft. lumber	125.00
1½ kegs 10 d nails	6.37
Total	$531.37

The first attempts at agriculture were crude indeed. Not infre-quently a settler without oxen or horse took a spade and mellowed the prairie sod sufficiently to plant potatoes. Breaking the tough sod of the virgin prairie was a difficult and trying task. In the first place it took more power than the average pioneer could command. The ordinary settler owned only one yoke of oxen; in order to

BREAKING THE PRAIRIE

From a drawing by Theodore R. Davis, *Harper's Weekly*, 1868.

break the sturdy turf it took a large plow with several yoke of oxen. It was necessary then either to hire the work done by an older settler or join forces with a neighbor and break a patch on each claim. The ordinary breaking plow turned a strip of sod from twenty to thirty-three inches wide and was drawn by six yoke of oxen or more. The man who guided the plow had a most difficult time holding it in the ground. Sometimes a second person sat on the beam to help keep the plow in the ground and to drive. It was often possible for a settler to give day labor to an older settler in exchange for breaking. Because of the violent struggle over slavery, in many instances men in Kansas broke prairie sod with their guns strapped to their sides.

Many crops and types of animal husbandry were tried. Tobacco, hemp, cotton, and sorghum were grown. One of the most interesting experiments was that of Valeton Boissiere, a French philanthropist who bought a tract of nearly 4,000 acres about twenty miles southwest of Ottawa, Kansas, in 1867, to found an educational and industrial coöperative institution for the development of certain industries. He enclosed 3,100 acres with fifteen miles of stone wall. He imported a large number of French workmen, planted mulberry trees, and began raising silk worms and manufacturing silk. The plan proved impractical in several ways. Producing raw silk was not a success and the Frenchmen could get higher wages in the country nearby than Boissiere could afford to pay during the period of development of a new industry. In time the workmen scattered and became a part of the new agricultural territory developing around them.[1]

The leading agriculturists experimented in many ways to find the best type of agriculture for the country. The usual procedure was to plant corn on the newly-broken sod. A man and a boy could do this nicely. Taking an axe the man drove it through the sod; the boy dropped in the grains of corn. Another lick with the axe

[1] George A. Huron, "Ernest Valeton Boissiere," *Transactions*, Kansas State Historical Society (Topeka, 1902), Vol. VII, pp. 552–564.

closed the cut. In many instances the wife dropped the corn and the husband covered it with the hoe.[2] Little cultivation was necessary the first year or two, but what little was needed was done by hand. Later a one-horse cultivator came into use. This had one shovel, making it necessary to take four trips to plow one row. Corn is an ideal crop for pioneer conditions. It is peculiarly fitted to growth with a minimum amount of preparation for planting and no machinery for harvesting. Although the price of this crop was low at first, the gold rush in the late fifties and the Civil War brought the price up to a high figure.[3]

When the first settlers arrived there was plenty of wood along the streams for fuel. It was not uncommon for settlers living away from the larger streams to move for the winter to these places where wood was plentiful.

Farm buildings were very primitive. A common type of barn was known as the hay shed. This was made by setting a row of forked posts in the ground about fourteen feet apart. These posts stood about seven feet high and rails were placed on them. From a center ridge pole rails extended to the ground. These were covered with prairie hay.[4] Primitive corn cribs made of poles were fashioned much as a log house.

A cow and calf were always kept together. The calf was penned up while the mother was turned out on the prairie to graze. The calf thus served as a decoy to bring the cow home at night without the services of a herder. The calf received a portion of the milk in

---

[2] An early Kansas settler saw thousands all over the eastern part of that state thus begin their farming in 1856.

[3] Price of corn January 1 over a series of years, 1848–1878:

1848—$.32	1854—$.40	1860—$ .54	1866—$.54	1872—$.48
1849— .27	1855— .60	1861— .35	1867— .61	1873— .41
1850— .31	1856— .40	1862— .28	1868— .90	1874— .60
1851— .40	1857— .52	1863— .50	1869— .67	1875— .67
1852— .28	1858— .31	1864— 1.10	1870— .77	1876— .41
1853— .42	1859— .75	1865— 1.10	1871— .52	1877— .44
				1878— .39

[4] See *Desoto Pilot*, Desoto, Nebraska, September 12, 1857, for description.

consideration of the services rendered. It was by no means milked and fed to him from a bucket, however. He had to secure it in fair competition with the milker. The milker on one side of the cow and the calf on the other each sought to get his share.

If there was any corn the hogs fared well enough. If not, they were allowed to run in the timber and fatten on nuts.

The comparative scarcity of timber made fencing a difficult problem. In the eastern states, whence many of the settlers had come, great forests had awaited clearing and it was not difficult to find material for enough rails to fence the farm. While wood was yet available the earlier settlers began splitting rails for the worm or stake-and-rider fences. One type of rail fence was called the Shanghai fence. If the farmer did not desire a fence clear to the ground, a stake was driven for the rails to set on, thus allowing a space below the bottom rail like the common barbed wire fence. Stake-and-rider corrals were made. It was plainly impossible to fence the prairies with the scanty timber found along the streams, and since the price of rails was beyond the reach of the farmer, necessity called for experimentation with hedges. The principal trees used for hedges were the white willow, the honey locust, and the Osage orange. The willow was soon displaced by Osage orange. The locust did not come into extensive use either although it was more successful than willow. Osage orange, or the Maclura plant as it is sometimes known, is the ideal hedge herb for fencing. It takes years for it to grow as large as forest trees, but in its early stages it grows very rapidly, quickly forming a wall if trained correctly. Nature has endowed the Osage orange with a long sharp thorn which procures for it the most wholesome respect of man and beast. As early as 1857 a firm in Bloomington, Illinois, advertised for sale one hundred and fifty bushels of Maclura seed which they estimated would produce fifteen million plants. In 1858 one man in Nemaha County, Nebraska, had set out a hedge enclosing one hundred and sixty acres.

There were several ways of starting a hedge. One way was to buy seed from the East and plant it. Another way was to plant the seeds in a bed and transplant them when they came up. Others preferred to buy the sprouts from the local nurseries which were established to meet the demand. Peddlers went through the country selling the plants. Later when the older trees began to bear fruit, the oranges were thrown into a pit and when the sprouts grew up in the spring they were transplanted; or the balls were soaked in water and the seed picked out by hand and planted. A furrow was run for a fence line and the plants put out in it. Great care was taken the first two or three years. Women and children cultivated the plants with a hoe. Water was hauled or carried long distances to give the tender plants a good start.[5] They cost but little, and the fences served their purpose admirably.[6]

The settlers quickly realized the value of all sorts of fruit and ornamental trees and shrubbery. In spite of the hard times in the spring of 1858, prior to April 22, there had been received in Nemaha County, 71,500 fruit trees.[7] The newspapers urged the prospective emigrants to bring fruit trees and shrubbery and to set them out and care for them. Friends sent shrubs and slips to the new country, but too often these were dead when the long journey was over. Trees were obtainable at nurseries just across the river in Iowa, Missouri, and Minnesota. Before long nurseries were established in the new country. Before 1864 little or no fruit had been gathered in the new region. The good crop of that year placed fruit culture in a respected position in the agricultural field. In 1869 the Kansas State Horticultural Society displayed in Horticultural Hall at Philadelphia a pyramid of one hundred and forty plates of beautiful apples and pears. Kansas was awarded the gold medal for the best display of fruits. This gave a great impetus to and enthusiasm for fruit growing. One man estimates that within five years over a

---

[5] The next generation, in the age of barbed wire, cursed the hardy perennial because it sapped the ground, shaded the crops and roads, and obscured the view. It was necessary to uproot the hedges in order to get rid of them.

[6] It was estimated in 1867 that a hedge fence could be made in Kansas at an expense of 50 cents a perch.

[7] One steamer, the *Asa Wilgus*, left 55,500 fruit trees, evergreens, and ornamental shrubs.

million fruit trees were planted, ninety-eight per cent of which proved to be entirely worthless. In spite of this, fruit trees continued to increase and the industry prospered.

In the fifties oxen were used almost exclusively for draft purposes. Indeed as late as 1859, horse teams were so scarce they attracted attention in Pottawatomie County, Kansas. There were numerous Indian ponies and riding horses at that time, but it was thought that oxen were superior to horses for heavy hauling and breaking. Even as late as 1882 a writer in the *Nebraska Farmer* urged the advantage of oxen over horses. He argued first of all that they were cheaper power, for a calf cost less than a colt, was cheaper to raise, and could be worked earlier. They were also cheaper to equip. Harness for a team cost thirty dollars while a yoke cost only five. The difference between the cost in equipment might be used to buy a team of cows which would be the beginning of a dairy. He pointed out that the depreciation was less also. When an oxen grew old he could be fattened for beef and sold at no great loss but an old horse was a dead loss. The only advantage of the horse, the writer argued, was that he was better to drive into town on Saturdays.

In the late fifties and early sixties farmers began to organize societies for the advancement of agricultural interests. Farm journals urged the formation of such societies, and in 1862 the Kansas legislature passed a bill encouraging their formation. It was argued that these societies would protect the farmers against the speculator, that they would enable farmers to buy and sell in lots from St. Louis, and finally that meetings for discussions would diffuse ideas and originate new methods of farming in a land so different from the old home in the East. Some of the early societies were those in Brown County, Kansas, Dodge County, Cass County, and Nemaha County, in Nebraska. The Nemaha Valley Farmers Club, organized in 1859 or 1860, declared that its purpose was helpful mutual contact. The members met once a month.

An important work of the early organizations was the promotion

of agricultural fairs. The fair moved west with civilization. At first
it was sponsored by the territorial government. Nebraska held its
first territorial fair in 1859. The orator of the day was J. Sterling
Morton, a youth of twenty-six. The speech was delivered from an
improvised rostrum made by placing a farm wagon in the shade of
a native oak tree. Towns vied with one another for the honor of
holding the fair in their limits. Ottawa, Kansas, offered the free use
of its park, no increase in hotel charges, free toll across the bridge,
and a guarantee of $2,000 in cash as an inducement to secure the
state fair in 1871.

The fair was much like fairs of today except that it was conducted
on a smaller scale. No permanent buildings were erected at first and
the whole project was conducted like a picnic. Prizes were offered
for cabbages, squashes, fruit, grain, and live stock. Jelly, cake, bread,
laces, and fancy work were entered by the women. Implements were
placed on display in an open field. Pulling matches and plowing
contests were often held. In the former, men entered their teams
in a contest to see which could pull the best. In the plowing contest the man who turned the straightest furrow and did the best
work was awarded the prize. Riding contests were also held. Prizes
were given for the best men and women riders. Sometimes there
was a display of men's clothing. There were always races. Since
there were no regular tracks these events were held out on the
prairie grass. One county advertised a purse of five dollars for a
three-hundred-yard race. Another allotted twenty dollars for the
races. As the country grew more opulent, regular grounds were
established and maintained. A balloon ascension was the attraction
of the day and the merry-go-round and side shows made the eager
country folk happy. Medicine shows, organ grinders, and stands attracted the passers-by.

The country boy looked forward for months to the time of the
county fair. Work was laid aside and the whole family, rising early
in the morning, loaded into the farm wagon and jolted over the
prairie. Arriving at the fair the horses were unhooked and given

provender while the family, after a look around the grounds, gathered at noon to consume a generous lunch taken from well filled baskets and spread on a cloth on the grass. After noon the rural folk strolled around the grounds eating candy, drinking red lemonade, and enjoying the unfamiliar sights. Perhaps the head of the family enjoyed the rare luxury of a cigar by way of celebrating the occasion. Neighbors and acquaintances, hungry for social intercourse, met in friendly association. Toward evening, when the last child had been hunted up, the wagon slowly moved over the prairie back to the lonely cabin. Aching heads and tired bodies bore witness to the strain of the unusual excitement.

Of all the manufacturing activities on the frontier, that which caused the greatest enthusiasm during the first three decades, was the production of sorghum and the attempts to make sugar. Sugar at that time was scarce and high priced. Consequently great quantities of syrup or molasses were consumed in lieu of the more concentrated sweetening. To meet the demand an effort was made to produce these staple articles at home. In the late fifties two kinds of cane were brought into the trans-Missouri region. These were sorghum or Chinese sugar cane and Imphee or African sugar cane. Sorghum yielded more and made a better quality of molasses. Soon almost every settler began to raise sugar cane and convert it into syrup at the molasses mill.

An ideal location for a molasses mill was on a gentle incline near a wooded stream. The mill itself was a machine turned by horse power to squeeze the juice from the long stalks of cane. One man fed the stalks between two rollers which mashed them and allowed the juice to drain out and run down the incline in a trough to the evaporator. In the more primitive mills the rollers were made of wood, but in time the more efficient ones had iron rollers.[8] The evaporator consisted of a large pan the sides of which were wood

[8] One correspondent wrote to the *Nebraska Farmer* that the best yield he had had with a wooden mill was sixty gallons an acre, but with the new iron mills a yield of two hundred gallons per acre was obtained.

and the bottom iron. It was used to boil the cane juice and was known everywhere as a molasses pan. It served very well as a boat in flood times or in case of an emergency to cross streams. There were hundreds of these pans in Nebraska, Kansas, and Dakota Territory.

A firm in Zanesville, Ohio, made and advertised nine models of molasses mills in 1861. They ranged in price from fifty dollars for the one horse capacity which ran twenty-five to thirty gallons per hour to one hundred and fifty dollars for the four horse capacity which produced seventy-eight to one hundred gallons per hour. Evaporators ranged in price from fifty to one hundred dollars.

The wooded stream furnished the two necessary items of wood for fuel and water with which to wash the pan and other utensils. According to the Kansas State Agricultural Report for 1864 sorghum molasses sold at fifty cents, and New Orleans molasses at seventy-five cents a gallon. The Kansas State Board of Agriculture reported the yield for that year as between eighty and one hundred and sixty gallons per acre. A Nebraska man reported an average yield of eighty gallons an acre for the years 1859 to 1862. This was certainly a profitable project for the poverty-stricken settler. A certain Mr. Mudge of Wyandotte, Kansas, made 1,300 gallons of syrup in fifty days. In the Rock Bluffs precinct of Cass County, Nebraska, twenty-three mills operated. In that precinct alone 6,685 gallons of syrup were made. This was ten gallons for every man, woman, and child. With the war time price of sugar, experiments were carried on everywhere for its production. Only a very few succeeded. Lime, chalk, alkali from hickory bark, and clay were used to refine the syrup by taking out the green substance squeezed out of the cane sheath. In using the clay process about a bushel of dry clay was thrown into a hundred gallons of juice and stirred. When the clay settled, juice as clear as water was drained off.

The demand continued so great that the College of Agriculture at the University of Nebraska, beginning in the autumn of 1882, offered a sixty day short course in sorghum making. The state farm had 250 acres of sorghum to be made up into molasses that year.

Vinegar was also made from molasses. A barrel of rain water was made into vinegar by adding three gallons of molasses and a little yeast.

CHAPTER VI

PIONEER FINANCE

THE FIRST SIGNS to be seen when a new town sprang up were "Bank" and "Saloon."

The Nebraska territorial legislature was more extravagant in chartering banks than the other territories. It was not difficult to secure the voting of a bank charter particularly if the would-be banker had some money to pass around to the legislators. When John M. Thayer expressed surprise that a certain man received a charter, the man opened a little book and called his attention to a list of members of the legislature with amounts opposite their names. That explained everything. The very first session of the Nebraska territorial legislature passed a number of bills chartering "wild cat" banks. Mr. A. D. Jones, then a representative of Douglas County, claimed to have been the only member to have voted against these banks. In a rhetorical speech he concluded that

when he should be gathered to his fathers, and an humble monument had been erected to his memory upon the site of his beautiful home in Park Wild, it would gratify his soul to look down from the high battlements of heaven—the region of the blessed—and read upon that monument the simple and truthful inscription: "Here lies an honest man— He voted against 'wild-cat' banks in Nebraska!" Allen H. Bradford, who was representing Otoe County in the council, was a large, fat man, with a squeaky voice. Concluding a short and sputtery speech in answer to Jones, he spoke as follows: "He [Mr. Jones] talks about the time when he shall be a-look-*ing* down from the high battlement of heav-*en*. I wish he was there *now*, a-singing forever more, among the blessed, instead of being down here a-makin' speeches which don't do any good away out here in Nebras-ky."

88

As has been noted previously, there was a great boom in 1856. So great was the rush and so vigorous the enterprise that in some cases houses were shingled by lamplight at night. Daylight did not furnish enough time for the consummation of the great schemes then afloat. One of these projects found expression in January, 1858, when the legislative assembly, thinking it necessary to have more money in circulation, created banks of issue under special charters. Six banks were created, one for every five hundred men in the territory. Each bank had power to issue as many dollars of indebtedness, in the form of paper money, as the individual stockholders might feel was desirable for their needs and ambitions. Often capital stock was raised by the simple method of taking the private note of the various stockholders. In that way $50,000 of stock could be readily created. The bank discounted these notes. After having been duly authorized these banks began to issue money. This territorial paper money was not fiat money but was in theory kept on a parity with specie by the promise of redemption in coin. Although it differed theoretically from the continental or confederate currency, in the long run the result was the same. Great quantities of this paper money were issued with only the word of the stockholders to protect the holders of the money. The newspapers in the states protested against this scheme, declaring that the banks started under this law had no legal existence. The *St. Joseph Gazette* of May 13, 1858, speaking of a Nebraska bank, said:

Bank of Tekamah

This is one of a brood of banks started and starting in Nebraska Territory, none of them having any legal existence. Large packages of it are being sent to this city for circulation, and ultimately it will fail and the people will be the losers. If there is any place of redemption in this city, go and get it changed at once, and then never take a dollar of it again. No banks can have a legal existence in Nebraska or Kansas until the act creating them is approved by act of Congress. This has not been, and will not be, given.

Some banks operated without charters; this was defended by some persons arguing that after all, the soundness of a bank depended upon the responsibility, honor, and integrity of the bankers. These characteristics, however, too frequently did not exist.

A banker in one of the states east of the Missouri, when asked how he got started in the banking business, confessed:

Well, I didn't have much else to do and so I rented an empty store building and painted 'bank' on the window. The first day I was open for business a man came in and deposited one hundred dollars. The second day another deposited two hundred-fifty dollars, and so along about the third day I got confidence enough in the bank to put in a hundred myself.

Some of these banks, chartered and unchartered, were started with almost no capital. DeSoto, Nebraska, had two banks. One had a visible office, safe, and cashier. The other had nothing to show for its existence but the name Waubeek engraved on its bills. This alleged bank, operated by non-residents who owned no property in DeSoto and held no charter, issued over $200,000 in notes. When the Bank of Nebraska at Omaha closed its doors a writ of execution by the county sheriff showed the following assets of that bank: "Thirteen sacks of flour, one large iron safe, one counter, one desk, one stove drum and pipe, three arm chairs, and one map of Douglas County."

The Platte Valley Bank was located at Nebraska City and the Nemaha Valley Bank was in Brownville. If a person called at the Platte Valley Bank to redeem one hundred dollars in its money, the cashier would throw out one hundred crisp new bills of the Nemaha Valley Bank. If the person seeking specie should take his paper to the Nemaha Valley Bank the cashier would hand out one hundred dollars of the Platte Valley issue. If then the particular person asked for money to be used in the East the cashier would hand out a roll of Omaha Bank bills. Although this money was not worth anything in the eastern states it was used extensively in the West.

WILDCAT CURRENCY

The bank that issued this five-dollar bill never even had a building but nevertheless printed and circulated its money. Courtesy of the Nebraska State Historical Society.

In accordance with the well-known Gresham's law, this cheap money circulated to the exclusion of other valuable paper money and specie. One conservative authority has estimated that the circulation per person in Nebraska in 1857 was $100.[1]

The use of cheap money to the exclusion of all else gave inflated values to claims, town lots, and other property. In the trade of the world the most plentiful substance is the cheapest. As a result land and other commodities were higher than money and kept sky-rocketing as the money depreciated. People rested in false security in this artificial prosperity. The governor was so far fooled by this pseudo prosperity that he mentioned in his message to the legislative assembly as evidence of the good times in Nebraska that town lots had advanced in price from $300 to $3,000 each.

Of all these banks, chartered and uncharted, which operated before 1857, only the Platte Valley Bank proved to be sound. This was in principle no more secure than the others. In 1857 a number of St. Louis firms, having taken in considerable amounts of paper money on Nebraska banks, sent an agent to secure the cash. All the banks closed except the Platte Valley at Nebraska City. When it was known there would be a run on this bank, men with quantities of silver and gold placed it at the disposal of the bank; it remained solvent. Every cent of the paper money was redeemed at face value because the chief stockholder, Mr. Nuckols, was reliable and his word was as good as gold.

With so many banks not only in the West but elsewhere issuing money, it was a difficult problem to know which paper was valuable. The newspapers sometimes warned their readers against worthless or counterfeit money. The *Omaha Times* of June 17, 1857, cautioned the public to beware of the Brownville, Nebraska, bank. The editor said:

[1] In 1894 the estimated circulation of the United States was put at $25, France at $40, and England $18; and yet England was reckoned as the wealthiest nation in the world. Henry W. Yates, "Early Nebraska Currency and Per Capita Circulation," *Proceedings and Collections*, Nebraska State Historical Society, Series II, Vol. I, p. 71.

We have received a letter from a party at a distance, enquiring if the Brownville Bank had a place of redemption here? The party making enquiry states that he has on hand some $800 of the bills, taken by him at par, in good faith, and the loss will fall heavily upon him in case it turns out to be worthless. Having mislaid the letter, we take this method of replying, that the Brownville Bank never had an office in this city—never redeemed a dollar of its issues here—and that the whole thing is a grand swindle—got up by foreign sharpers, who, by dating their wild-cat issues from our midst, have thrown upon our Territory and our people a stigma which we do not deserve.

It was very much as a senator from an eastern state had said when his state was passing through this experience. He remarked that the members of the legislature had to sort their money each morning after reading the paper and throw away what was worthless. Paper money was called by various names such as "stump-tail currency," rag money, and shin plasters.[2]

Along the Kansas shore, a steamboat captain pulled up to a wood yard and bellowed out, "Is your wood dry?" "Yep," was the reply. "What is your wood worth?" shouted the captain. "What kind of money der yer tote, cap?" asked the wood merchant. "The best money on earth, the new Platte Valley Bank." "If that's so, cap," was the rejoinder, "I'll trade cord for cord."

Apparently Kansas had only one bank of issue prior to 1864 and escaped some of the more severe effects of the unbridled financial chaos of Nebraska. Most of the paper money used in Kansas was issued by banks chartered and controlled by an eastern state or secured by pledges of state bonds. Unfortunately when the southern

[2] This worthless paper money was issued by various banks in the newer states just east of the frontier. In 1858 Major Joseph R. Hanson and a group of friends left Winona, Minnesota, for Dakota. They took enough provisions with them to last during their journey, expecting to revictual in Sioux City, Iowa. When they reached that city and asked a bank to change a fifty dollar bill, they were astounded to find it worthless. The bank of issue had collapsed during their journey. This was a calamity since it was about all the money the party had brought. "Reminiscences of Yankton's Early Days," *The Monthly South Dakotan*, May, 1898, p. 15.

states seceded, their bonds depreciated rapidly, in some instances becoming entirely worthless, and the money issued on such bonds naturally fell far below par.

When the panic of 1857 closed most of the banks, merchants issued money in the stress of hard times. Nebraska City merchants issued dollar bills and also twenty-five and fifty cent bills payable in merchandise. This passed as change. The merchant who had credit sufficient to do this conferred a favor on the community at a time when money was so scarce as to be almost an unknown quantity.

Various kinds of wild-cat paper money continued to exist as late as the seventies, confusing people, cheating them of their hard-earned cash, and creating confusion in commerce. Various currency handbooks were printed in the East and the wise man always had one of these at his command. If one man handed another a five dollar bill in payment for goods, the second stopped his work to look up the latest cash value of the money proffered. *Thompson's Bank Note Reporter* was issued weekly. *Peterson's Philadelphia Counterfeit Detector and Bank Note List* was a monthly which served the same purpose. Another currency guide was *White's Detector,* published at Louisville, Kentucky. These, besides detecting worthless money, gave information regarding defunct banks and quotations on money which was not current. They also offered a vast amount of choice editorial material upon the money question.

It was common for the home town paper to announce that certain worthless currency on a given bank was in circulation in the vicinity and that the readers should beware.

One very successful scheme was worked by two Indiana swindlers. At certain points in the West they circulated bank notes issued by the Orleans Bank of Connelton, Indiana. Along with these notes they issued a currency detector magazine which quoted the Orleans Bank notes at only a two per cent discount. These sharpers under the name, Orleans Bank, had issued notes to the amount of $13,346 and shut up shop with the following assets:

Whitewash	$2.00
Two pieces of boards	.50
One old plank	.18
One iron safe	75.00
Total	$77.68

The cashier sold the safe for enough to pay board and rent, and their transportation out of town, and the two rascals traveled through the West distributing their money to unsuspecting victims. The special detector they published and distributed was intended to validate their fake money and take people unawares.

In 1873 a so-called Professor J. D. Clark itinerated over the plains, making it a business of giving instruction to classes in the towns on the subject of detecting counterfeit treasury notes, bank notes, and drafts. He gave his instructions to the business men and chief citizens and presented it in such a charming way that it was entertaining as well as instructive, according to newspaper comment.

Frontiersmen totally disdained to be bothered with small change. J. J. Ingalls wrote from Kansas that one curious fact about the currency was that nothing smaller than a five cent piece was in circulation.

It was not hard to start a bank even as late as the seventies and people sometimes combined banking with their merchandise business. A vault and safe was installed in one corner of the store; pickles and cheese were sold, kerosene drawn, and money borrowed or deposited, all under the same roof. The securities of the seventies and eighties were largely chattels. There were few men whose name on a note was acceptable without security. Often the bank lost by the overnight departure of a client to parts unknown. It would never do to allow such a person to go unpunished for the effect on other borrowers would be disastrous. It was then necessary for the wide-awake banker to follow a trail through devious windings to the goal. Frequently this was unattainable. Mr. Theodore Ackerman of Russell, Kansas, followed the chase some two hundred miles into Colorado in search of a span of mortgaged mules. When he finally

located them he found the owner had endeavored to disguise his
property and had entirely changed the color of the docile beasts
from a grey to a brown by using a paint brush from head to heels. In
another instance Mr. Ackerman followed a trail two hundred miles
in the other direction to Kansas City where he located the team in
the basement of a livery stable and seized and sold the property,
fully recovering the value of the loan. The banker was not always
so fortunate with these runaway securities and frequently lost the
loan entirely. It is not strange then that a high rate of interest was
customary.

In October, 1857, the Reverend Reuben Gaylord, stationed at
Omaha, Nebraska, wrote that money was worth from four to six
per cent per month. In Douglas County, Kansas, in 1858, the county
board built a jail at a cost of eight hundred dollars. The board borrowed the money from a local merchant at the rate of five per cent
per month. It was not unusual for the money lenders to charge from
two to ten per cent per month on notes renewed every sixty or
ninety days. Additional charges for writing and recording the chattel mortgages or for a commission for securing the money frequently caused interest charge to range between twenty-four and one
hundred and twenty-four per cent per annum. Interest rates became
a bit cheaper in the seventies, but even then they were so burden-
some that many lost everything. It was impossible to mortgage a
claim until the homesteader "got his papers." As a result instances
were frequent when every horse, cow, hog, and chicken on the place
was mortgaged. At these exhorbitant rates the chances were greatly
against the borrower. When the homestead was patented, the owner
"plastered" a mortgage on it for $300 to $500 and tried to pay out.

The banker gave a favored few—well-to-do farmers or business
men—money at a lower figure. When the poor settler came for
money, the banker demanded a list of his property for security before a $25, $50, or $100 note would be made out with the settler's
horses, wagon, and other chattel property as security. The borrower
and his wife both signed the note. Interest above 12 per cent in the

seventies was classed as usury,[3] while bank interest was 24 per cent per annum on amounts below $100. To avoid prosecution the loan concern took the extra interest from the principal when loaning the money. For example, a borrower, giving a note for $100 for three months, received only $97 and then paid the other three dollars when the principal was paid. The three dollars subtracted from the principal at the time of the loan was called the "discount." Sometimes a penalty of 24 per cent was exacted if the principal was not paid promptly.[4]

Those unable to borrow from a banker depended upon the country loan broker. Young lawyers often took this means of adding to their slender income while building up a practice. Mr. G. E. Griffith of Lawrence, Kansas, quit store keeping and went into the mortgage and loan business in this fashion: A man in Connecticut from whom the firm bought goods wanted Mr. Griffith to invest some money for him in a mortgage. He received a commission and thus began a business almost unintentionally. Farmers and business men needed more money than the banks could supply so that the field was open for money lenders. Loan brokers became very objectionable to the farmers who were obliged to borrow from them at ruinous rates. In one case a young lawyer became a candidate for governor. He was branded as a loan shark and, as proof, one transaction was unearthed from the records in which a cow called Speck and a black boar pig were pledged as security for payment of a loan which carried a liberal rate of interest. This proof that he had engaged in this nefarious business placed a stigma upon him which lasted for many years. In spite of many cases of heartless extortion and ruinous rates of

[3] In Dakota Territory up until 1875 the legal rate of interest was 18 per cent. In that year it was reduced to 12 per cent.

[4] Cass G. Barns, *The Sod House* (Lincoln, Nebraska, 1930), pp. 235–236. In the eighties in North Dakota (Dakota Territory) it was called "12–10" borrowing. The borrower got $90 for each $100 on the face of the note and paid twelve per cent on the amount named on the note. For example, one approached the banker for a loan of $300. When the note was signed the borrower received not $300 but $270 although he paid interest on the $300. One had to borrow for five years to get that. John W. Scott, "The Pioneer Farmer," *Quarterly Journal,* University of North Dakota, Vol. XIII, p. 292.

interest, borrowers were plentiful who were anxious to secure loans even at these rates.

As time went on, merchants and farm implement dealers pressed the farmers to mortgage their land to buy horses, implements, and other improvements. This led to much unwise buying and mortgaging and in the end many were driven from their farms by foreclosures.[5] Many times a farmer bought a full line of farm implements and did not get them paid for before they had to be replaced.

The mortgage game was not entirely a one-sided affair, for some mortgaged their farms for all they could get, sometimes more than they were actually worth, and left the country, considering the place well sold. Hamlin Garland was glad to mortgage his claim for $200, which he judged a good price, before going East to more inviting work.

Certain mortgage companies composed of men in the eastern states with capital to invest employed agents throughout the West. Oftentimes these agents were unscrupulous lawyers, shifty land men, and others whose motives were inimical to both the homesteader and the loan company. The agents, eager to obtain their fees, frequently made loans which they knew would never be paid and that were certain to be a loss both to the company and to the homesteader. These agents made hundreds of loans between $250 and $500 on a farm of 160 acres. The records show that in a great majority of the cases the borrower lost his home. When borrowers failed to pay interest, the mortgage company was obliged to employ a loan inspector to travel over the prairies interviewing the homesteaders who desired loans and inspecting the property they proposed to give as collateral.

This move came too late, however, for practically every important farm mortgage company operating in the newly settled lands failed. Hundreds lost their homesteads willingly. Their one chance was to make as large a loan as possible, vanish, and let the mortgage

[5] Dr. Barns says it has been estimated that an average of two and a half settlers occupied Nebraska homesteads before one came who was able to stay.

company take the lands. Claims with frame houses costing as much as five hundred dollars were no better risks than one with a sod house, for the neighboring settlers moved the houses away.

One loan inspector told how he made a bad loan in Dakota Territory. He was called to the home of a Connecticut Yankee who had a good piece of land with a story and a half frame house on it. The New Englander seemed to be a conscientious man with astute business ability. He said the house was very good, too good in fact; it had cost him nearly five hundred dollars, all the money he had. He needed a little more to set him on his feet, and get his business in shape to make good financially. When asked if he did not want a larger loan than the amount he had named, he answered that he had figured out just how much he needed and there was no use to borrow more. The loan was made and thirty days later the whole family was on the way to California. A relative was holding open a job on a fruit ranch for him and the thing he had figured so exactly was the price of the tickets. A settler could go away for several months and leave his shack with his chattels lying about in perfect safety, but, once vacated, the buildings disappeared piecemeal or were skidded away in entirety. The loan company had no recourse because no official in the county would have helped the company against a local man.

In two instances the above-mentioned loan inspector caught men in the act of moving houses off mortgaged land. He took no action for he knew it was impossible to secure redress through the courts. One man made a specialty of collecting these houses from loan company land. Several served as lean-tos to his original house. Two or three thrown together served for a barn, others made a chicken house, a corn crib, and a hog house. At another time the inspector found a long frame shanty built across the line dividing two claims. Two men had built the structure and occupied it together, each sleeping on his own land. One mortgaged his claim and left the country; the other was moving the shack onto his land as the inspector came. When the inspector remonstrated, the house mover retorted that he was not moving the mortgaged shack. He was moving his own and could not help it if the other followed his. While the inspector was there, not a hand was laid on the mortgaged part of the shack.

Of forty-one pieces of land visited by this inspector in northwestern Nebraska and southwestern Dakota about 1889, three were occupied by the original mortgagors and three by squatters. Of the remaining thirty-five there was not a board to show they had been homesteaded.[6]

Sometimes financiers, taking advantage of the desire of homesteaders to sell out, played a game of high finance. In North Dakota a man named E. Ashley Mears organized a string of banks. He opened the National Bank of North Dakota at Fargo and a number of banks in smaller towns. Their purpose was to engage in the mortgage loan business. The homesteaders, who proved up as quickly as possible in order to secure the maximum loan and leave the country, were willing to sign a mortgage for a much larger sum than the amount of money they actually received. For example if a man thought his claim was worth five hundred dollars he would sign a mortgage for $1,000, but receive only five hundred. After accumulating a quantity of these mortgages, Mears went East, attended a church for a few months, got well acquainted, and won the confidence of the minister and the leading church members. Then it was easy to sell mortgages. The banks continued to pay the interest until the panic of 1893 when they failed. Shortly thereafter the investors began to realize that they had in reality bought western land at a high price.[7]

After the days of wild-cat banking ceased, money was extremely scarce on the agricultural frontier. Many times there was almost a dearth of that dear commodity. In Garden City, Kansas, a merchant sold a pair of boots and when the cowboy purchaser offered a ten

---

[6] Seth K. Humphrey, *Following the Prairie Frontier* (Minneapolis, 1931), pp. 103–175, *passim*.

[7] Samuel Torgerson, "Early Banking in North Dakota," *Quarterly Journal*, University of North Dakota, Vol. XIII, pp. 287–288.

dollar bill, the merchant hunted the entire community over in search of change. The hotel keeper and the liveryman were consulted, the whole settlement was combed, but no change could be found.

Even the states had difficulty in building up credit in frontier days. During the Civil War, Kansas state bonds were sold at prices ranging from sixty-five to ninety cents on the dollar.

One thing which alleviated the distress of the poverty-stricken settler was the fact that he did not need to pay taxes on his claim until it was patented. He could prove up on it in five years or he could wait seven and a half years. If a man wanted a loan he proved up in five years, otherwise he waited the maximum time before starting to pay taxes.

The experience of Mr. John Turner is representative of the terrific economic struggle through which the early settler fought his way. The little family, consisting of a husband, wife, and three small boys, having migrated to America from England in 1871, were lured from their city home in the East by the promise of a better livelihood on the prairie. Arriving in the territory described by the emigration agent in glowing terms, Mr. Turner and the eldest son worked in stores for a few months keeping books and running the many errands necessary to a general merchandise establishment. They received no money for this service. The custom in the West at that time was to pay the employees in goods or give them orders on some other store. In the late autumn, father and son selected a claim and, leaving the family in town, they began constructing a sod house. Having no horses, they were obliged to secure a team from a neighbor to haul the necessary timber and to plow the sod. Returning the horses, they carried the sod in their arms, laboring day after day for over three weeks. Having finished the house, the family was nicely moved in when a heavy rain came, caving in the roof with its tons of earth, mixing mud with bed clothes, clothing, utensils, keepsakes, and the meager furniture.

In order to meet the requirements for improvements on the

homestead, Mr. Turner and his son traded the labor of their hands with the neighbors for the use of horses or oxen. After one year a partnership agreement with a neighbor was arranged. Mr. Turner was to take care of the oxen and drive them when they were used on either claim, and for every day he used them on his own claim he was to give a day's work with the team on his neighbor's land. Thus far he had pursued a cash policy but now, tempted by the promise of greater prosperity, he forsook this policy and purchased an old undesirable pair of oxen together with a yoke and chain for $147 on seven months' time, with interest at the rate of twelve per cent per annum. It required a twelve and a half year struggle before the final payment was made. In eighteen months one of the oxen died, and after walking for miles in search of a single oxen and finding none, Mr. Turner was obliged to buy another team, although he was able to do little more than pay the interest on the principal for those bought the year and a half before. Once more he gave a note, this time for $130 at twelve per cent per annum. He did not tell how long it took to pay this second note, but no doubt it was years, for new machinery such as plows, mowing machines, binders, and pumps had to be purchased to enable him to work more efficiently toward the goal of economic independence.

CHAPTER VII

ROAD RANCHES

THE FIRST permanent settlers on the prairies were those adventurous ones who feared neither the dangers of Indian attacks nor the privations of life in a region remote from civilization. They formed a frail, thin line of settlement along the overland trails. These little frontier islands of settlements stretched out across the lonesome bleak ocean of savagery connecting two continents, so to speak, of settlement. This development was a new thing in the history of the frontier. It is true that settlement often followed rivers but never before had settlement pushed out across a barren area and formed a chain hundreds of miles long. There were several of these lines of settlement and each was occasioned by the same thing—a gold rush with its accompanying migration.[1] In 1849 the first great rush for California occurred from points along the Missouri River converging near Fort Kearney on the Platte and continuing westward. In 1858 the discovery of gold at Cherry Creek in Western Kansas (on the present site of Denver, Colorado) caused trails to be opened from the Missouri River towns to the Rocky Mountains of Colorado. In some instances these ran along the old route but in others new trails were formed. In the sixties the gold discoveries in western Dakota around Virginia City and in parts of that territory which were subsequently made into Montana and Idaho, caused the formation of new routes across the Indian country. The Black Hills gold rush of the seventies again caused routes to

[1] The Santa Fe Trail, Oregon Trail, and Mormon Trail must each be taken into consideration in making this general statement. Little or no settlement occurred along the Santa Fe Trail west of Council Grove. In considering the other trails it seems likely that very little settlement would have occurred along these routes had it not been for the greater traffic caused by gold rushes.

be made across unsettled country to the region of glittering promises. Naturally people began to settle along these routes.

Information in regard to these road ranches as they were called is indeed meager. Occasionally a traveler or freighter mentioned a place or gave a brief description. This mere mention together with a few reminiscences and the scant information in guide books forms our source of information.

Although universally called ranches these might well have been called eating houses or trading establishments. These isolated posts began to appear in the fifties and continued to become more numerous. In 1853 two men driving cattle to California along the north side of the Platte reported one such place, later known as Boyd's Ranch, about ten miles northeast of Kearney. In 1864, after a period of only ten years, Mr. J. Sterling Morton on his way from Omaha to Kearney on a buffalo hunt found the ranches twenty to thirty miles apart along the overland route. They were more numerous along the overland stage and pony express route.

It might be imagined that life at one of these road ranches along the overland stage line was lonesome but such was not the case. The later settler who located in a more isolated region, attracted by rich soil or other considerations, led a far more lonesome life. The trails were the main streets of the nation's east-to-west travel, and for years they were crowded with traffic in season. One witness said this line of vehicles was "one immense train. Wagons were never out of sight. Every house was a ranch, every floor was a sleeping place." In the last of April, 1853, six steamboats had come up the Missouri River to the vicinity of Omaha and the emigrant traffic was so heavy that the boats were used for ferrying purposes at the Bellevue Crossing. In addition to the thousands of emigrants bound for the gold field there were hundreds of freight trains carrying supplies and equipment to the mines. Mr. Albert D. Richardson, in 1865, reported passing much heavy quartz machinery including a boiler drawn by sixteen oxen. After 1860 there was a daily stage west and east bound. In the sixties in Lincoln County, Nebraska, it was no uncommon thing to see seven hundred to a thousand wagons pass through in a single day. On one occasion a lady of that county counted nineteen hundred wagons passing between "sun and sun." Great herds of cattle were driven from the states over this long journey to California. This highway, beaten annually with hundreds of thousands of hoofs and the wheels of countless vehicles, was indeed picturesque. Frequently the road was obstructed for hours by the immense herds of buffalo which almost daily crossed the path to drink at the Platte River. Indians rode up and down this historic highway, their wigwams pitched near some canyon or gulch or more often on the river bank conveniently near a trading post. The tired pilgrims and teamsters were happy to reach these road ranches and find a place of entertainment at night after their long tedious day's journey. Along the overland stage route between Atchison and Denver there were no towns or settlements of any kind except road ranches, once the traveler had left Marysville, Kansas, one hundred miles west of Atchison.

The typical road ranches were built only in groves of timber along the valleys since at that time no one considered taking up land any distance from living water.[2]

Road ranches varied in style of architecture and function. In general the buildings approximated trading posts more than mere hotels or residences. Some were made of sod with sod roof, dirt floor, and small windows somewhat like port holes. Others were made of stone with loopholes in the walls, and shining rifles, pistols, and ammunition at hand for instant defense. The western ranches were enclosed by palisades or walls and the ranch buildings strung out around the inside of the enclosure, leaving an open court or corral in the center large enough to contain all the animals belonging to the establishment. A long narrow horizontal opening about waist high formed a window in the outside of the storeroom which made up a part of the enclosing wall. Through this slit traffic was carried

    [2] F. A. Root and W. E. Connelley, *The Overland Stage to California* (Topeka, 1901), pp. 23, 235–265.

on with the Indians thus avoiding the necessity of allowing them admittance to the enclosure. In case of necessity a drop door closed the opening. A watch tower was frequently built on a prominent corner of the wall and in dangerous times a lookout was kept day and night.[3] Some of these sod enclosures had sod structures like bastions built on the corners for places of defense.

Farther east the buildings did not take on the aspect of a fort to the same extent as those in the west. Often they consisted merely of a sod house or adobe, as it was called, or a log house with dirt floor and roof and a corral. There was usually a herd of cattle, a band of Indian ponies, and some herders at these points. These institutions were hotels, bar rooms, and stores for general merchandise, and all the business was transacted in a single room. A stock of goods varying from a meager shelf to a "shebang" was kept. The latter was the name for a general merchandise establishment carrying a more or less complete line of goods.[4]

Horace Greeley, describing a road ranch west of Manhattan, Kansas, said:

It consisted of a crotched stake which, with the squatter's fence aforesaid, supported a ridge-pole, across which some old sail-cloth was drawn, hanging down on either side, and forming a cabin some six by eight feet, and perhaps from three to five and a half feet high—large enough to contain two whiskey barrels, two decanters, several glasses, three or four cans of pickled oysters and two or three boxes of sardines but nothing of the bread kind whatever. The hotel-keeper probably understood his business better than we did, and had declined to dissipate his evidently moderate capital by investing any part of it in articles not of prime necessity.[5]

In speaking of the fare at one of these wayside eating places Greeley commented: "—the dinner the hardest I ever yet paid half

[3] Robert Morris Peck, "Recollections of Early Times in Kansas Territory," *Transactions*, Kansas State Historical Society, Vol. VIII, p. 489.
[4] Sometimes used to indicate a dive or dance hall.
[5] Horace Greeley, *An Overland Journey from New York to San Francisco in the Summer of 1859* (New York, 1860), p. 74.

a dollar for. Doubtless, however, my eyes will be opened to an appreciation of cold hog and corn dodger as delicacies, long before they are blessed with a sight of Sacramento." [6]

The rancher actually made little attempt at farming but kept some live stock for trade, accommodated travelers at night, and sold articles which they needed. The goods were freighted from the wholesale houses in the Missouri River towns. The greatest business was in meals, whiskey, and trading oxen and horses.

Many of these ranches ran first-class eating establishments. Daniel Freeman, the man who took out the first homestead in the United States in 1862, started a road ranch at Plum Creek. He put up a sign "Bakery" and his wife used a hundred pounds of flour every day. She made yeast bread overnight and while it was baking in the forenoon, she set salt-rising bread to be baked in the afternoon. They used St. Louis flour which they purchased from the freighters en route to Denver. She sold her bread for fifty cents a loaf and made as much as thirty dollars a day. Mr. Freeman had seventy-five head of cows and milked twenty-five. They made cheese also. They allowed a young calf to fill its stomach with milk, then killed it and took the stomach, washed it and hung it up to dry. When dry, it was put away for rennet in cheese making. A small piece made new milk form into a solid curd. Mr. Freeman made a cheese press and mold. They got twenty-five cents a pound for the cheese and sold quantities of it. They charged two dollars for meals and people were glad to pay it. No doubt this ranch afforded much better meals than most places, for one stage hand said that west of the Little Blue there was no butter but plenty of beans, bacon, hominy, sorghum, and, on the western end, plenty of buffalo and antelope steaks.[7] Dried apple pie was the standing luxury on the prairie. One passenger who had made a score of trips over the overland stage line said it was "apple pie from Genesis to Revelation along the Platte." A good cabbage head sold for as high as fifty cents, a water-

[6] *Ibid.*, pp. 56–57.
[7] The only canned goods in the West in the sixties was sardines and oysters.

THE CHEESE CREEK RANCH

A road ranch on the Oregon Trail in 1864, so called because the proprietors made and sold large quantities of cheese. Courtesy of the Nebraska State Historical Society.

melon for a dollar, and corn for a dollar and a quarter to two dollars and a half a bushel. The ranchers charged two dollars for stabling and hay for a team, fifty cents for the privilege of sleeping on the hard dirt floor, fifty cents for boiling coffee and cooking a meal on a stove, ten cents a pound for green wood, and fifty cents for a drink of whiskey. One cattleman driving a herd to California paid twenty dollars a gallon for twenty gallons of whiskey which he felt was necesary for his men in case of sickness. This whiskey was made by mixing nineteen barrels of water with one barrel of alcohol which had been freighted out from the Missouri River. A Mormon, Joseph E. Johnson, ran Wood River Center Ranch in the vicinity of the present Shelton, Nebraska. He kept a bakery and eating saloon and in addition for three years published a paper, *The Huntsman's Echo,* the first effort at publishing a newspaper in that isolated region. He is rumored to have had a daguerreotype studio also. It was said "he did not have enough stock of goods in his store to make a wheel barrow load on a smooth road." Aside from running an eating house and selling liquor, Johnson's biggest business, like that of many of the other ranches, was in repairing wagons and doing the necessary blacksmithing which naturally came on the overland trip, and in trading stock. Many emigrants had broken-down or foot-sore oxen and horses that they were ready to trade to the ranchers at a bargain. These, when kept on grass for a few weeks, recuperated and in good flesh were ready to be traded for more lame, foot-sore stock at a nice gain for the rancher. Some travelers accused the ranchers of selling doctored cattle and horses which looked well for a few days and then gave out, thus cheating the purchasers. Some of the greatest ranching businesses in the West were built up from the trading business.

One of these road ranches of the Platte Valley was called the Turner Tavern. It was described as a one story log building resembling an old time country tavern. It had two apartments; the first was a combination dining room and kitchen, the second was a parlor and sitting room. The latter contained a large heating stove around which circled emigrants, traders, freighters, old miners, and mountaineers to relate their adventures.

The passengers of the overland stages always took their meals regularly twice or three times a day according to the reputation of the house and the hour the stage reached it. Some houses had the reputation of being very dirty, while others were known to be kept clean and to serve wholesome food. The latter houses became so famous that they were seldom passed by, provided they were reached at the right time. The ranchers raised live stock and butchered hogs and cattle to furnish fresh meat. Hay was furnished for the travelers' stock also.

Some of the stations along the overland stage line had very queer names; for example, forty-nine miles west of Atchison was "Log Chain," seventy-two miles out was "Frog Town," and one hundred and eight miles away was "Lone Tree."

Since all road ranches were not patronized by the stage travelers there was less business at some than at others. Life at some of these ranches was drab and monotonous most of the time; but a wagon train would stop and things were temporarily lively. One of these ranches was not as lonesome as one might imagine. Hundreds of new faces were seen almost every day going and coming along the great highway. Very often a grand dance was given at one of these stations. Although women were scarce on the plains some of these ranches were presided over by comely women who adapted themselves to their crude environment with heroic spirit and willing hearts; they turned their hands to the rude labors of cooking meals for the passengers and braving the ever-present danger of death or capture by the red man. When a dance was held the women went from one station to another within a radius of fifty miles to attend such a social gathering. Some of these road ranches were the scenes of the worst kind of depravity. Dances were accompanied by drunken revels which ran into the most degraded bedlam.

Towns originated and grew up around some of these road ranches due to their location on the trail. Beginning with a blacksmith shop, eating house, and trading post, the little town grew into a place of considerable importance. An example of this is Dobytown located two miles west of Fort Kearney. In 1859 this outpost had a population of three hundred. It was built just off the Fort Kearney reservation in deference to the United States rule that a town could not be built on a military reservation. The sod houses, or adobe as they were called, were one story high. It was a rendezvous for all sorts of outlaws, gamblers, and crooks who practiced their nefarious game on passing "pilgrims."

Grand Island, although born of more respectable parentage, was enabled to thrive because of the overland traffic. It was founded in 1857 and, inasmuch as it was the most westerly settlement, gave the settlers a chance to sell their products or goods to the trail travelers. The community had the usual outfitters post, or store, blacksmith shop, cobblers shop, and home bakery. Settlers were also given a market for their oats, hay, corn, and vegetables.

CHAPTER VIII

THE SOD HOUSE

NATURE cares for her own. When the pioneer in the eastern country moved west and built his home in the virgin forest, the timber which caused him so much work in order to clear his fields, provided him shelter and warmth. Likewise when the hardy settler began the conquest of the prairie, he found at hand material for shelter and fuel. The dugout and the sod house provided shelter, and buffalo chips and prairie grass served for fuel. Where timber was available it was natural for the people to make the conventional log house. Even in the eastern part of the trans-Missouri-Red River territories, however, dugouts and makeshift, hay-covered, sod structures were used at first for shelter.[1] As settlement crept westward and timber became more scarce, the homesteader came to depend more and more on soil and grass for homes. The typical prairie home was made of sod or was dug out of the side of a hill or ravine.

It was customary for the emigrant upon locating his homestead to arrange a temporary shelter until the permanent dwelling was ready for occupancy. When the wagon halted, the head of the family took out a spade and began to construct the dwelling. The dugout was more easily made than the sod house and hence many pioneers, anxious to get settled and to plant crops, made this type of dwelling their first home. In a few days excavation for the dugout was complete. The family meanwhile lived in the covered wagon box while the father used the running gears to haul the logs, poles, brush, and grass needed for the roof and front of the dugout. The mother of the family cooked the meals by a camp-fire and the group slept in

[1] These were made in both Omaha and Lawrence. See Chapter III.

the wagon or other temporary abode. Sometimes a hole dug in the ground and covered with canvas or sheets supplied the necessary shelter. Mr. and Mrs. M. E. Babcock of Fillmore County, Nebraska, made their first home by sewing four sheets together for a tent. Within a few days a windstorm blew down their shelter at night and wrecked their covering irreparably. The first residence in Antelope County, Nebraska, was a shack made of poles and grass.

The dugout was a room dug in the side of a hill or ravine. A few rails or posts were used to make a door frame and possibly a window. The door, of course, opened out into the ravine. The front wall was made of square cut turf, or logs if they were obtainable. A roof sloping back onto the hill was made of poles or logs covered over with brush, a layer of prairie grass thick enough to hold dirt, and finally a layer of dirt over the grass. It was by no means ideal, however, for after a rain the high water often drove the occupants from their home. It was necessary to dig a trench from the house to the drainage level to carry water off the floor. Then, too, a frog pond for a front yard meant mosquitoes in summer and a very unhealthful environment. Even in dry weather the place was dirty.

Governor Garber, of Nebraska, lived in such a house in 1870 and 1871 when, as a Civil War veteran he came West to seek his fortune. He was called to serve as governor from 1874–1876, a true instance of out of dugout and into the capitol.

Although it was bad enough for a man to live in a dugout, it was far more trying on the women. Mrs. John McCashland, of Fillmore County, Nebraska, did what a good many others of her sex no doubt did. When she first saw the dugout her husband had prepared for their home she was so discouraged she burst into tears. Her husband after due consideration arranged for a different type of home. Mrs. George Shafer of Delphos, Kansas, objected strenuously to living in that kind of hole in the ground like a prairie dog, as she said, but finally consented to do so. Like many other pioneer women she sacrificed her ideals for expediency. The Wright family, in Nuckolls County, Nebraska, had a dugout nine by twelve feet. There were six people in the family. In that little home there were a bed, stove, table, and several boxes. A boy and a girl slept on the table. It was not uncommon to place a bed-tick on the floor at night and carry it out in the daytime in order to have room enough to walk around in the house. When a family moved out of a little dugout into an eighteen by twenty-four foot house above the ground they felt that it was indeed a mansion.

It was no uncommon incident for a traveler driving across the prairie at night to drive over a dugout. Occasionally cattle wandered over the housetop shaking the dirt down onto the dining table.

Elder Oscar Babcock, a Seventh-day Baptist minister of North Loup, Nebraska, gave $2.78½ as the cost of a fourteen foot square dugout in 1872. He itemized the cost as follows:

One window (8 x 10 glass)	$1.25
18 feet of lumber for front door	.54
Latch and hanging (no lock)	.50
Length of pipe to go through roof	.30
3 lbs. nails to make door, etc.	.19½
Total	$2.78½

The dugout was a very common structure and was used for many purposes. Blacksmith shops, post offices, and even lodging places were located in them.

Not infrequently a combination sod house and dugout was made. The sod house, although a little harder to build, was much more satisfactory and lasted some years. It was widely used even in the eastern portion of the prairie states. The centennial historian of Butler County, Nebraska, in 1876, made the statement that more than nine-tenths of the citizens of the county had at one time or another since their arrival lived in homes constructed of earth.[2] Three types of sod houses were in vogue in McPherson County,

[2] Butler County is on the Platte River only three tiers of counties from the Missouri River and is much more accessible to timber than counties farther west.

A SOD DUGOUT WITH ADJOINING SHED

The most primitive type of sod dwelling. The wagonload of sod at the rear of the dugout is to repair the roof. Courtesy of the Nebraska State Historical Society.

Kansas, during the seventies. Some were laid up rough, others plastered, and still others hewed off smooth. These structures were of various sizes but a rather pretentious sod house followed a common building plan of sixteen feet wide and twenty feet long. The sod bricks were made by turning over furrows on about half an acre of ground where the sod was thickest and strongest.[3] Care was taken to make the furrows of even width and depth so that the walls of the cabin would rise with regularity and evenness.

A spade was used to cut the sod into bricks about three feet long. These bricks were then carried to the building site by wagon or by a float [4] made of planks or the forks of a tree. J. Clarence Norton of La Harpe, Kansas, related that in building the house on the homestead, the line for the wall was drawn after dark so that it could be located by the north star. For the first layer of the wall the three foot bricks were placed side by side around the foundation except where the door was to be made. The cracks were then filled with dirt and two more layers were placed on these. The joints were broken as in brick laying. Every third course was laid crosswise of the others to bind them together. This process was continued until the wall was high enough to put a roof on the structure. A door frame and two window frames were set in the wall and the sod built around them at the proper time. Sometimes the builder drove hickory withes down into the wall as a sort of reinforcement. The gables were built up of sod or frame according to the means of the settler. The poorer settler built a roof in the crudest manner. A forked post set in each end of the cabin furnished a support for the ridge pole. The rafters were made of poles and the sheeting of brush; a layer of prairie grass covered this, and over all sod was placed. The settler who could afford it put a frame roof on his sod house. In that event sheeting was nailed on the rafters and tar paper spread over the sheeting boards. This was then covered with sods thinner than those used to cover the side walls, and laid with

[3] Dr. Cass G. Barns, *op. cit.*, has given an admirable description of the construction of a sod house.

[4] A kind of sled.

grass side down; the cracks were filled with fine clay. From time to time this dirt filling had to be renewed as the rains carried it away. In a short time great growths of sunflowers and grass appeared on the roofs. If the house were to be plastered, a mixture of clay and ashes was used. If it were to be a smooth finish, the builder took a spade and hewed the wall to a smooth finish and symmetrical proportions. The whole thing, as one pioneer said, was "made without mortar, square, plumb, or greenbacks." All that was needed was a pair of willing hands, and many homeseekers came to the plains with no assets other than a wagon cover. The little sod cabin was frequently divided into two rooms by a piece of rag carpet or quilt. The windows and door were closed with buffalo robes or other blankets. The house was crudely furnished. A nail keg and a soap box did duty as chairs. A dry goods box made a table and a rude bed of boards was fashioned in the corner. When the migration immediately following the Civil War broke in its fury, the demand for doors, sashes, and blinds was so great that even small towns ordered in carload lots. The dealer at the little town of Milford, Nebraska, advertised in March, 1871, that he had three carloads of this type of merchandise on the way.

The ordinary sod house had grave faults. Its few windows permitted little light and air for ventilation. The immaculate housekeeper abominated them because they were so hard to keep clean. The dirt and straw kept dropping on everything in the house.[5] The most disagreeable feature of these houses was the leaky roof. Few of the sod-covered houses really turned water. A heavy rain came, soaked into the dirt roof, and soon little rivulets of muddy water were running through the sleepers' hair. The sod-house dweller had to learn to migrate when it rained. If the rain came from the north, the north side of the house leaked, and it was necessary to move everything to the south side; if from the south, a move had to be made again. When the roof was saturated it dripped for three

[5] Some housekeepers lined the roof with cheese cloth which caught the falling particles and thus insured a greater degree of cleanliness.

days after the sky was bright without. Dishes, pots, pans, and kettles were placed about the house to catch the continual dripping. One pioneer woman remembered frying pancakes with someone holding an umbrella over her and the stove.[6] A visitor at the home of a Dakota woman said that when great clouds rolled up in the afternoon the lady of the homestead began gathering up all the old dishes in the house and placing them here and there on the floor, on the stove, and on the bed. The visitor remarked that the prairie woman seemed to understand her business for when the rain came down in torrents a few minutes later every drop that came through the numerous holes in the roof of the shack went straight into those vessels. After a heavy rain it was necessary to hang all the bed clothing and wearing apparel on the line to dry. One old settler mentioned keeping the clothes in the covered wagon to keep them dry.

When the roof was well soaked its weight was immense. The heavy rafters sank deeper and deeper into the soggy walls until occasionally the roof caved in or the walls collapsed, burying people underneath the ruins. To prevent this kind of accident, heavy posts were placed in the house to support the roof; these were a great nuisance because they took up so much room. Frequently the cabin was covered with long coarse prairie grass. This type of roof also had the fault of dripping water after a heavy rain.

There were, however, some striking advantages of the sod house. It was cool in summer and warm in winter. There was no fear of the wind blowing it over and no danger of destruction by prairie fires. Neither was there danger of fire from a faulty fireplace. A fireplace was safely built of sod. The average life of a sod house was six or seven years.

One man related that upon moving into a frame house after five years in a sod structure, the change was so great from the dark cave-like dwelling to the well-lighted frame building that the family could not sleep on account of the light.

[6] In case of sickness someone had to hold an umbrella over the patient in bed. One old settler remembers that they often had to dispense with kneeling at family worship because the floor was in puddles.

Some careful housekeepers papered the walls of their houses with newspapers. Some in more recent times have been plastered and equipped with shingle roofs. About 1876 Mr. George Rowley built a seven room sod house at Wauneta, Nebraska.[7] They brought a piano with them, the only one in the whole country. The editor of the *Blue Valley Record*,[8] in speaking of a certain section remarked: "The neat sod houses, the beautiful flower gardens, and the well-cultivated farms all betoken a high order of things."

When the family moved out of the sod house or dugout, the live stock profited by the change. Sod shelters and dugouts frequently housed the live stock. Sod was used to make corrals, hen-houses, corn cribs, wind breaks, and even pig pens. A pig pen ordinarily was made by building a sod wall and digging a ditch with vertical sides around the inside of the wall. This kept the animal from rooting down the wall. Windbreaks were made by building a sod wall and perhaps putting up stacks of hay along one side of it. Sometimes a hay shed was built out over the wall.

Closely related to the sod house was the mud house whose walls were constructed from clay well tramped and mixed with straw like the brick made by ancient Israel while in slavery in Egypt. The walls, two or three feet thick, were sometimes whitewashed and were both comfortable and sightly.[9]

In the eighties a large proportion of the claim shacks was made of frame covered with tar paper. Lumber yards in the little boom towns did a thriving business.[10] The inside of one of these houses was papered with such periodicals as the family received through the mail.[11] In Union County, Dakota Territory, a frame house built of cottonwood boards was plastered with mud. Slough grass was

---

[7] This is noted for its very unusual character. The typical sod house had only one room and only one small window.

[8] Milford, Nebraska.

[9] John B. Reese, *Some Pioneers and Pilgrims on the Prairies of Dakota* (Mitchell, South Dakota, 1920), p. 36.

[10] See Chapter XXVII.

[11] N. J. Dunham, *History of Jerauld County South Dakota* (Wessington Springs, South Dakota, 1910), p. 24.

THE PRIMITIVE AND THE ADVANCED IN SOD CONSTRUCTION

The dugout in the foreground was probably the first home of the family. The sod dwelling at the rear was a later improvement. Courtesy of the Nebraska State Historical Society.

cut into one inch lengths for use as plasterers' "hair." A layer of dried prairie weeds was used to insulate the building against the cold. The weeds were placed next to the cottonwood boards and the clay was held in place over this insulation by means of strips of wood. When the mud had dried the walls were decorated with newspapers.[12]

At Jewell City, Kansas, at Ord, Nebraska, and at Sioux Falls, Dakota Territory, the settlers built sod forts for protection against the Indians. The Jewell City post was made in two days by united community effort in the face of danger. In two days' time the settlers had built a wall four feet thick and seven feet high around a fifty yard square. Thus the sod from the prairie served to shelter the settler from the weather, served as a shelter for his stock, protected him from the Indians, and crudely supplied his fencing needs.

[12] W. H. Fate, *Historical Glimpse of the Early Settlement of Union County (Dakota Territory)* (Sioux City, Iowa, 1924), p. 73.

CHAPTER IX

HOMESTEADING

FOR YEARS before the Civil War the frontiersmen had demanded easier terms on the sale of public lands to the actual settler. From the time of the land law of 1800, each succeeding piece of legislation made the public domain easier to acquire in small lots. The popular song of the fifties, "Uncle Sam is rich enough to give us all a farm," expressed the sentiment of the land-hungry agrarians and working-men of the country.

When the Northwest came into its own with the election of Abraham Lincoln in 1860, free land was assured. The Homestead Bill became a law May 20, 1862. It provided that "any person who is the head of a family, or who has arrived at the age of twenty-one years, and is a citizen of the United States, or who shall have filed his declaration of intention to become such," and who has "never borne arms against the United States Government or given aid and comfort to its enemies," was entitled to one hundred and sixty acres of land in certain areas or eighty acres if taken in more favorable locations. For example, only eighty acres could be taken within a railroad grant.

A fee of eighteen dollars was charged for each one hundred and sixty acres. Fourteen dollars was paid on making application and the balance when "final proof" was made. From the date of first application, usually called filing, six months was allowed to make improvements. On or before the expiration of that time the homesteader had to be on the land and begin improvements. He was further required to make it his permanent residence for five years from the date of the first papers. Any time after that date the settler could take out his final papers, provided, however, that he did it within seven and one-half years after filing. This final process consisted of giving evidence that the conditions had been fulfilled. If the evidence was satisfactory, a patent was granted on the testimony of two witnesses. This last formality was called "proving up." Later legislation made certain exceptions in the case of soldiers but only minor changes in the policy. One such change allowed war veterans to apply their service time in the army to the residence time required for proving up on a homestead. Another amendment allowed an ex-soldier of the Civil War who had served nine months to take one hundred and sixty acres of land within the limits of a railroad grant whereas all others could take only eighty acres. The first homestead in the United States under the Homestead Law was taken by Daniel Freeman on January 1, 1863, near Beatrice, Nebraska. Freeman, a Civil War soldier, was on a furlough and had to rejoin his regiment, consequently the other claimants allowed him to file first.

The greatest rush of settlement into the trans-Missouri region came in the seventies and eighties. After the Homestead Act passed, the thoughts of many of the soldiers turned to the West. As the boys in blue sat around the camp-fire they planned what they would do when the long bloody war ended. Many looked forward to the time when as comrades they would move to the new land and start out life together. In the course of time many of these plans were broken up; nevertheless, a large wave of migration flowed westward soon after the War. Other soldiers who had not previously planned seriously on migrating, upon arriving home were dissatisfied with the quiet life in the old surroundings. After a few years near the old home these men decided to cast their lot in with the West. Confederate soldiers after a few years of the carpet-bag rule in the South began to leave the chaotic environment forced on the people by military reconstruction. As a result of these combined factors, a mighty wave of migration poured out onto the prairies, rolling rapidly toward the Rocky Mountains until the grasshoppers stopped its flow in the middle of the decade of the seventies. Again the flow started westward only to sweep beyond the rain belt, but the droughts of the late eighties once more flung the home-seekers back toward the East. At a later time the tractor, combine, and dry farming have once more made this region habitable. During the peak years in the early seventies and eighties whole counties were settled in a fashion which rivaled the work of a magician who by means of the magic wand brought forth a prosperous city.

The first claim in Adams County, Nebraska, was made in March, 1870, by two typical plainsmen, the vanguard of civilization. By the fall of 1871 the county had a voting population of twenty-nine. Mr. T. J. Adams, writing on April 19, 1872, exclaimed:

One year ago this was a vast houseless, uninhabited prairie, with no trace of approaching civilization to frighten the timid antelope, or turn the buffalo from his course. . . . Today I can see more than thirty dwellings from my door yard aside from those in the village. . . .

According to the census of 1888 the county had a population of 10,235. The *Blue Valley Record* of Milford, Nebraska, on August 9, 1871, stated that in six months' time York County had increased in population from one thousand to nearly one thousand five hundred. The county seat, it remarked, was a thriving city with one business house, one school-house, two dwellings, and a number of lots sold. The *Republican Valley Empire* of Clyde, Kansas, stated that whereas in October, 1869, there were but four settlers on Buffalo Creek in Jewell County, on July 12, 1870, one hundred and fifty claims had been taken. On July 4, 1873, at a great celebration in Buffalo County, Nebraska, there were five hundred children singing Sunday school hymns where eighteen months before wild Indians and buffalo roamed at will.[1]

The methods of transportation to the West in post-War migrations were similar to those of the fifties except that the river traffic gave way gradually to the railroads until in the eighties few were

---

[1] The 1870 census of Nebraska showed a population of 123,000. The increase for the year 1871 was 40,000 or 38 per cent according to the State Superintendent of Immigration.

THE FIRST HOMESTEAD TAKEN IN THE UNITED STATES

Daniel Freeman, a soldier in the Union Army, while on a brief furlough, went to Nebraska to look over the highly advertised land there. Upon arriving at the land office at Nebraska City on December 31, 1862, he found the town thronged with settlers who had come to take claims. The Homestead Law went into effect on January 1, 1863, but New Year's Day was a holiday, and Freeman had to rejoin his regiment immediately. By common consent he was allowed first filing. In the midst of a New Year's dance at the hotel the land office was opened, and at five minutes after twelve the first homestead was taken, the land office was closed, and Freeman set out on his return journey. The homestead became a national monument in 1936. This early painting by Jack Tobias is reproduced by permission of Milan Evans, owner of the picture and copyright.

traveling by any other means. The covered wagon, which was used some in the fifties and the eighties reached its greatest use just following the War—in the seventies. During this period the type of vehicle which came to be used largely in the winter was a frame covered wagon. The *Beatrice Express* of February 27, 1873, noted that although it was cold, the usual grist of emigrants arrived on their way to western Kansas. The travelers were protected, it stated, by a frame wagon covering. A stove warmed the inside of the home on wheels. One such wagon, built like a box car, passed through Milford, Nebraska, in 1871, bearing the label "Monitor."

A typical representative of the soldier homesteader was E. D. Haney of Republican County, Kansas. He served in an Indiana regiment in the Civil War and was discharged in Texas. The next five or six years he spent in Minnesota and Iowa where he alternated attendance in high school and college with teaching. Haney subscribed to the *New York Tribune* and heeded the advice of Horace Greeley to go West and build up the country. During the winter of 1870–1871 he talked the matter over with two Iowan ex-soldiers and they all decided to go West. Mr. Haney bade his sweetheart good-bye with a promise to send for her in two years. On April 4, 1871, the group left Shueyville, Iowa. The three comrades found their military experience and their camp life helpful in this new venture. With a fine team of horses and a good covered wagon they made twenty-five miles a day. On arriving on the east bank of the Missouri River, opposite Nebraska City, a strong wind made it unsafe to run the ferry boat. While the comrades waited three days for the wind to abate, they met two other former soldiers on their way to take a homestead in Kansas; there was a natural affinity. The group crossed the river and traveled together into Kansas. They crossed the line just north of Belleville on April 28th. A day or two was spent in looking for claims before the companions drove to the land office some miles away. They homesteaded claims adjoining one another. Haney, having more education than the average homesteader, traveled a few miles east to an older settled region and taught school the first two winters. The money was used to buy farming equipment and household furniture. At the end of the two years he sent the money for his sweetheart to come to Kansas. Her father, having sold his farm, also came with his whole family to the new country.

Sometimes a family of grown children claimed homesteads adjoining one another. In one case a widowed mother and her three children homesteaded four quarters and built up a little village of sod houses and stables around the central surveyor's stake so they could live near each other and yet each live on his own homestead.

When a new settler came into a community already partially settled, he sought the services of someone on the ground to aid in selecting a claim. This task sometimes consumed a few days. The settlers were usually glad to aid strangers in this manner for every new inhabitant increased the value of the country and brought neighbors, and, with settlement, churches and schools were certain to be established. The settlers in a community were informed as to which land was vacant and were able to show the claimant the unoccupied tracts. In the eighties professional "locators" advertised in the papers and charged a regular fee for their services. Deception was practiced by some of the settlers. Certain homesteaders "reserved" select homesteads for their friends or for sons who would soon be eligible to take a claim.

A shrewd individual sometimes arranged his claims in such a way that large blocks of government land remained in his possession to be farmed for years without disturbance. A man in Potter County, Dakota Territory, filed upon 480 acres [2] within a square of 640 acres, leaving 80 unclaimed on the north side of the 640 (40 acres unclaimed on each side of the north 160's), and in the center of the 640 he left 80 acres unclaimed—20 in each of the four quarter sections. This 80-acre plot in the center of the section of 640 acres

---

[2] This could be done by taking a homestead, a preëmption, and a tree claim of 160 acres each.

was used for a long time before even the neighbors realized what he had done.

Again settlers told the emigrant that all the good claims were gone and that one would have to travel miles beyond to find good locations. Having established this untruth, the older settler offered to sell the newcomer a good claim. Frequently the strangers accepted the offer only to find later that good land could have been found near at hand by searching for it.

Shortly after the Civil War, an old soldier named Fred Hoppe settled in a fertile valley in Jefferson County, Nebraska. An old settler, Loyal Stevens, came over and asked him whether he intended to stay or was merely camping there for a few days. Hoppe asserted that he had bought the land from the government for $1.25 an acre and that he had every intention of staying. Mr. Stevens, angry at having his domain encroached upon, replied that the government had no land in that vicinity, that he owned the whole valley, and that he would drive out any settler. He tapped his gun in a significant manner. Mr. Hoppe replied that he had practically lived on lead during the past four years and that if his neighbor wanted to start anything there would be a funeral. The old settler took the bluff and soon the two were the best of friends.

The rush for claims was so great in the seventies and eighties that it was the part of wisdom on selecting one to plow a few furrows, lay four poles in the shape of a pen or dig a hole two or three feet deep indicative of the beginning of a well. These hints of the beginning of occupation sufficed to reserve the claim for a short time until one could go to the land office and file on the land. Some who thought there was no such hurry and delayed a few days lost their claims to others.

One thing, which no doubt added to the difficulties, was the fact that frequently the claims lay long distances from the land office. Mr. S. D. Butcher of Custer County, Nebraska, had to travel ninety miles to Grand Island to file and prove up on his land.

Claim-jumping took place during the homestead period in a manner similar to that of earlier times. Shooting over claim disputes was not extraordinary; many lives were lost as a result. When a jumper was killed, the case was dismissed, for the "unwritten law" condemned the claim-jumper. Sometimes the claim-jumper was right. Near Wichita, Kansas, in 1872, a man took a homestead and in connection with it was holding an eighty acre plot to which he had no title. A man tried to exercise his homestead right on the eighty. The illegal possessor raised a mob and compelled the party of the second part to relinquish the land and promise to let it alone.

Sometimes claim-jumpers merely hoped to secure a large sum as payment for moving off the claim of a settler who had been a bit lax in living up to the requirements of the law. If the settler happened to be careless with a gun, this frequently resulted in a dead jumper. Otherwise the settler, knowing he would be at a disadvantage at the land office in case of a lawsuit, either sold out to the jumper and relinquished his own filing, or "bought off" the jumper. A contest before the land commissioner involved considerable expense and it was rarely possible to secure impartial witnesses. Delays of a year or more were not uncommon and even then the decision was more often a matter of guess work than of justice. For this reason it was usually the part of wisdom for the settler either to relinquish to the other for a consideration [3] or to pay the jumper a sum to cancel his filing papers and thus give a clear title to the claim.

It was only natural that the settlers should stick together and protect each other in the possession of their right of homestead. All efforts of a newcomer to take possession of a claim were resented by the neighbors of the claimant. In order to protect themselves the settlers formed associations in some places. At Camden, Nebraska, the organization was styled the Homesteaders' League and its stated purpose was for the mutual protection and advancement of the farmers' interests. In Sherman County, Kansas, in the eighties,

[3] S. K. Humphrey, *Following the Frontier*, p. 83.

an association was formed for protection against the hated cattle-men.[4]

Owing to the poverty of the great majority of homesteaders and the lack of employment nearby many were obliged to leave their shanties for a few months out of the year. Legal provision had been made for such exigencies. It often happened that a tenderfoot came through the country and spying the inviting location proceeded to take possession of what he termed an "abandoned claim." In western Nebraska an interesting case of claim-jumping is recorded. A Civil War veteran, a son of the East, had taken a homestead on a beautiful stream. He built a sod house for his wife and three children and a sod stable for the two ponies and old Brindle. Having "wagered Uncle Sam sixteen dollars against a quarter section that he would make that his home for five years," he began his battle with the hot winds, droughts, insect pests, coyotes, and blizzards. In order to escape some of the hardships incident to the severe winters of the plains and possibly secure employment which would enable him to improve his claim, the horny-handed, sun-burnt son of toil took advantage of the legal provision, loaded up most of his possessions, and returned to "his wife's folks" beyond the Missouri River for the winter.

During the winter a prospector, a suspicious-looking individual, noticed the unoccupied claim and took possession. He was informed by the neighbors that the claim was not abandoned and was urged to vacate it. He contended that the land was forfeited and that he was going to stay. About the first of April the absent settler drove back to take possession of his home. The prospector refused to vacate. Legally he was clearly in the wrong but had the proverbial nine points of the law in his favor since he held possession of the settler's home. Here was clearly a serious case. A questionable character, intrenched and defiant, was confronted by a veteran soldier who had faced shot and shell unflinchingly. Strong language and bitter threats ensued. There was universal sympathy with the

[4] See Chapter XI.

settler, of course, and a score of the bronzed prairie homesteaders, only too glad to rid the neighborhood of this doubtful character, volunteered to help their fellow settler. To storm the intrenched man would no doubt have meant fatalities among the attackers. The sod house was not combustible and hence he could not be burned out. It was therefore resolved to smoke him out. A stove stood in the center of the building and the pipe extended straight up through the roof near the center of the comb. The claim-jumper sat near this stove with his rifle at hand scarcely daring to peek out lest a volley of lead meet his gaze.

On a dark, stormy night a dozen homesteaders, armed and with a good supply of sulphur and powder, surrounded the abode. They crept up to the gable of the sod shack out of danger of rifle fire from the windows. It was but the work of a minute to crawl along the roof and pour a pound of sulphur down the pipe onto the coals below. This produced a commotion in the house, a hurrying to and fro in a gasping effort to secure fresh air. This was merely an introduction to the scene that followed. A pound of powder was dropped down the same aperture. There followed a flash and terrific explosion with dirt and ironware flying about the house. A coatless, blackened individual was met at the door and the ultimatum delivered to him in vigorous frontier language. He was at first disposed to argue the case but seeing a lariat in the hands of one of the party he agreed to depart at once. He was escorted out beyond the limits of the neighborhood and advised to be gone as fast as he could travel.[5]

As a rule the homesteaders avoided the high broad tables and benches, preferring to settle along the valleys of the various streams and to build their homes under the protection of the hills in the vicinity of wood and water. The new arrivals one by one ventured a little farther up stream or a little farther out on the prairie away from the streams.

[5] Frank M. Vancil, "Jumping A Claim," *Frontier Days*, ed. Oliver G. Swan (Philadelphia, 1928), pp. 502–505.

LAND OFFICE BUSINESS

Front and rear of the United States land office at Garden City, Kansas, in 1885. Fifty thousand acres were taken daily, and when the crowds blockaded the halls and stairway, the land attorneys accommodated their clients through the back windows. Courtesy of the Kansas State Historical Society.

After a man located his future home, made some sign of occupancy, and traveled from forty to sixty miles to the land office, he found the office crowded. In 1871 when certain land in Gage County, Nebraska, was opened to settlement, ninety-four homesteads were taken on the first day. A deputy sheriff, a constable, and several citizen deputies were on hand to preserve order. The crowd gathered before daybreak shivering in the cold until the office opened. One of the land seekers was a woman. When the door opened, the room was jammed full in a moment. By common consent the woman was given first chance.

The *Beatrice Express* in commenting on the rush for land said:

The jam was terrible, and the poor woman was obliged to beg for more room from fear of fainting. The applications poured in as fast as they could be taken care of all day, the crowd inside and out never growing smaller, for as fast as one applicant, with papers properly fixed up, would worm his way through the crowd to the door, and be cast out, panting and dripping with perspiration, another would squeeze in, and become a part of the solid surging mass within.[6]

Men arriving at the land office early in the morning found a long line, two abreast, extending across the street in front of the land office at Concordia, Kansas. Some of these men had slept in front of the office all night in order to be the first in line the next morning. Observers at Marysville, Kansas, testified that a long line of men stood in line all night in front of the land office. An understanding was reached among the waiting men allowing each one to drop out occasionally to get some coffee and something to eat without losing his place in the line.

At one land office in Dakota Territory in July, 1874, the receipts of one day were over $1,800. At Garden City, Kansas, in the eighties the officials used a ladder to enter and leave the building in order to escape the constant crowd which was always in front of the land office long before opening in the morning and during the closing hours. This was lowered from a rear window.

[6] November 18, 1871.

In many instances application was made for tracts of land that were already taken; disappointed, the unlucky parties generally withdrew to try another application, or else they took the failure good-naturedly and quit. In cases of dispute between rival claimants the difficulty was settled at Washington.

As in other relations with the United States Government a certain amount of graft crept into the business of homesteading. Perhaps the majority who took up land never intended to live on the prairie. There developed a class of people who were chronic settlers; these men made "settling" a business. It made little difference to them that the laws of the United States allowed a man to exercise his homestead right only once. They filed claims under one name in Iowa, another in Kansas, and still another in Dakota. It was not even necessary to migrate to a different state to work this scheme. They might take five or six homesteads in the same state over a period of thirty years. A change of name was no inconvenience; in fact it was a boon, for the eastern prisons yawned in vain for many western pioneers.[7] Many, after living on a homestead for a year or two, sold their rights to others. The seller was said to have relinquished his right to the buyer who proved up in his own name. This was known as a relinquishment and the original settler was free to move on and take another homestead. Relinquishment, although frowned upon by the land office, became quite a business and land men frequently secured a fee for bringing these parties together. There was no set price for relinquishments. The consideration varied from several hundred dollars to a chattel of little worth. The price depended on how optimistic the buyer was and how desperate the need of the seller was. Sometimes a man with some money would offer good wages and very little work for a period of six months if the men would join his gang and use their preemption rights in concert, prove up, and after securing the titles in their own name, deed them to their employer. This gave the man of wealth a large tract of land in a single piece at a small cost.

[7] S. K. Humphrey, *op. cit.*, p. 80.

Government spotters, always on the alert, sometimes caught these employers at their game.

Frequently parents "saved" quarter sections for their sons who lacked a year or two of reaching their majority, which was necessary to exercise legally the homestead privilege.

A man living in another county filed on a homestead in Turner County, Dakota Territory, and hired someone to plow the required amount. Before time to "prove up" he secured two witnesses, and, taking three boxes about six feet long and two feet deep, in which apple trees had been shipped by a nursery, he and the two men placed them on end in a semi-circle with the covers off. This gave the three occupants standing room. Laying the boxes down, a man could sleep in each. The claimant and the two witnesses then appeared at the land office. The testimony ran as follows: The claimant is a single man. He works out for others but his claim has been his home the required time. He has dug a well. He was not asked how deep it was nor whether he found water or not. While they did not know the exact measurements of the house, the height was sufficient for a man to stand upright. It was made of lumber, had two outside doors and was big enough so the three had slept in it, each man having a separate bed. Soon after the final proof the boxes disappeared.[8]

Contrary to expectation, a noteworthy proportion of the first settlers were single or unattached women. These were especially noticeable in a land of hardship. They tried without training or physical strength to wrest a living where strong men had great difficulty in maintaining their hold. Many were sensitive, delicate, cultured women, unused to the harsh work involved in conquering the plains. They were plucky and staunch, taking things as they came, in an uncomplaining manner. These, if at all inclined toward matrimony were not left to bloom alone and unseen. A marriageable lady with a homestead certainly was not unattractive in a land of

[8] W. H. Stoddard, *Turner County Pioneer History* (Sioux Falls, South Dakota, 1931), p. 156.

unlimited bachelors who, batching in dugouts and very sorry figures at stag housekeeping, readily succumbed to the wiles of these prairie sirens.

Since many of the immigrants to the new country were bent on making a small roll of money with little effort and returning to their former homes, there was considerable loafing and little real effort was put forth to practice earnest, systematic agriculture. The main activity was that of holding the land for a raise in price. A few acres of land down on the creek or river bottom were scratched over in the slackest way. Some justified their idleness on the principle that probably little could be reaped anyway. One saying was: There's no use to "buck maw Nature." They hoped for enough "truck" to get through the season and let the next year look out for itself.[9]

The homestead law did not supersede the Preëmption Act and consequently it was still possible for a man to preëmpt an adjoining quarter section at the same time he was homesteading. Or the homesteader could at any time commute his original entry to a preemption and buy the land at the regular price of $1.25 per acre.

In the seventies Congress passed the Timber Culture Act. This provided that a man could file on a one hundred and sixty acre tree claim provided he planted forty acres of trees and cultivated and kept them in growing condition for eight years. The fee was the same as for a homestead. Natural conditions made the fulfilment of this law impossible.

Few who proved up under this law fulfilled its condition. The cottonwood tree was generally selected. This could be grown from cuttings. The cutting was laid down in the furrow with the top above the ground and covered by the next furrow from the plow. The claimant then skipped a few furrows and repeated the process. The weeds were kept from growing between the rows of trees with a corn cultivator. When they grew at all they made solid groves of

[9] Stuart Henry, *Conquering Our Great American Plains* (New York, 1930), pp. 182–183.

THE CHRISMAN SISTERS, HOMESTEADERS EXTRAORDINARY

These daughters of a ranchman near Goheen Settlement, Nebraska, took homesteads, timber claims, and preëmption claims, each holding three claims of 160 acres each. They arranged their living with one another to fulfil the residence requirements of the United States Land Office. Courtesy of the Nebraska State Historical Society.

young trees. Elm, ash, hackberry, and some walnut trees were planted in these groves. This created a great demand for forest trees during a short period.

The territory of Nebraska passed a law in 1869 encouraging land owners to plant trees. The law read:

That there shall be exempt from taxation of the property of each tax payer, who shall, within the State of Nebraska, plant and suitably cultivate one or more acres of forest trees for timber, the sum of one hundred dollars annually for five years, for each acre so planted and cultivated: *Provided*, That the trees on said land shall not exceed twelve feet apart, and shall be kept in a healthy and growing condition.

The same year a similar law exempted the land owner from "fifty dollars annually for five years, for each acre" of fruit trees planted. These laws were a stimulus to set out thousands of trees in Nebraska.

The great weakness in the Homestead Act lay in the fact that it made homesteading too easy. The government encouraged failure by not requiring more than the mere minimum of a shack for a home, only ten acres under cultivation, and a well. There was no mention of personal qualifications and equipment. Thousands were deceived into thinking that securing a piece of land was all that was necessary to make a competence for the owner. Following the great boom of the eighties when the tide of migration began to recede, central Dakota and western Nebraska and Kansas presented anything but a land of occupied farms. Everywhere was to be seen the scars of once-broken patches which were fast reverting to sod, a caved-in well, and the tumbled-down walls of sod shanties that had served their purpose in proving up for the settlers who had since left the country.

CHAPTER X

VIGILANTE DAYS

OWING TO THE VALUE of horses on the frontier and the ease with which horse thieves could escape on the borders of new settlements, public sentiment demanded the speedy extinction of this class of thieves. By and large the most heartily hated miscreants on the whole frontier down through the years were these culprits. Strange to say, horse stealing was regarded as a much more serious offense than ordinary murder. In accordance with the recognized code of the frontier, men were permitted under certain conditions to take one another's lives with impunity. If two men had a quarrel and decided to shoot it out, the public regarded it as a matter which concerned only the participants. It was expected, of course, that one would not take unfair advantage and shoot from ambush or shoot his enemy in the back. When, for example, a man announced that he would shoot on sight, it was expected that both would carry arms constantly and should one fail to arm himself it was his own fault because he had been duly warned. In such cases the antagonists began shooting at sight. This rule was so well established that after the courts were well organized few convictions could be secured although homicides were numerous. A horse thief was always presumed to be guilty until his innocence could be clearly established.[1] Many innocent men were hanged in the early years, but probably the majority of those executed were guilty.

In a new country jails were rare. It was, of necessity, quite common to take a prisoner fifty or a hundred miles to an adjoining state or older county. This afforded an excellent opportunity for escape. In one instance, for lack of a better place, two men were chained in

[1] T. A. McNeal, *When Kansas Was Young* (New York, 1922), pp. 76, 77.

a stall of a livery stable.[2] Again culprits were placed in the newspaper office. At Lincoln, Nebraska, the county treasurer's milk house
was used for a cooler of men instead of dairy products. In another
place when a man got so boisterous and drunk as to be dangerous to
the public peace, he was dropped into a dry well until he grew
peaceable enough to be released. At Warner, Kansas, a drunken
man was handcuffed around a telegraph pole until he sobered up
sufficiently to appear before the magistrate. At Wahpeton, Dakota
Territory, in 1874 a small building, sixteen by twenty-two feet, was
used by the county officials as their place of business until a court-
house could be constructed and since there was no jail, the attic was
used as a cooler and reformatory. The attic window, however, gave
hope to the evil-doer.[3] The civic improvement needed above all
others was the jail. Newspaper editors all over the West deplored
its absence and called upon the city fathers to arise and supply
this great need. An editorial in the *Frontier* published at O'Neill, a
town near the Nebraska-Dakota line, well expressed this general
cry: "The crying need of O'Neill is a safe place to put the many
drunken wretches that disgrace our streets day and night continually. Let us have a jail at any cost."

Even after the prisoner had been safely incarcerated in the newly-
built frontier jail either in his own county or in one only a little
farther east, he was in no special danger of his life or liberty.

It was usual for the prisoner to take "leg bail," as escape was
termed on the frontier. The newspapers were filled with stories of
escapes. Some dug under the sill and crawled through this excavation; others tore the shingles off and crawled through the roof.
Then, too, confederates had easy access to the flimsy buildings and
it was found necessary to patrol the place. This cost of guarding
made the jail one of the most expensive items of government in the
primitive communities. It was indeed, as an editor said, more ex-

---

[2] They escaped by turning the tap off the bolt which held the chain to the barn.
[3] Horace B. Crandall, "A Sketch of Richland County," *North Dakota Magazine*,
Vol. II, No. 4, p. 38.

pensive to hold prisoners than to catch them. Jailers and other officials were easily bribed. One sheriff made the following report to the clerk of the district court when a murderer escaped: "He effected his escape by slipping out of the back door and climbing over the wall while my deputy was in and had the door open for the purpose of emptying their slop pails."

The editor of the local paper flayed this sheriff unmercifully:

The allowing of Darling to escape ought to cost the sheriff and his deputy their official heads. It will be difficult to make some people believe that it was simply thoughtlessness on the part of "my deputy"—an accommodating "deputy," to leave jail doors open; he ought to be promoted and a wooden man put in his place. The sheriff, however, closes his letter with the consoling remark: "I will see that it don't happen again." Now, sheriff, stick to that. When Darling comes back and insists on being locked up, see that "my deputy" don't send him out after a drink, just before his trial comes off—he might forget to come back. We hope the sheriff will also stay at home and tell "my deputy" to come in when it rains.[4]

There is small wonder, then, that under these conditions the people should rise up in disgust and take the execution of criminals into their own hands. Anglo-Saxon society in semi-primitive surroundings, given a problem, finds some solution. The ability to solve its own problems was particularly characteristic of the American West. As the miners found a way to protect themselves in California and Montana in the fifties and sixties, so the agrarian settlers of the prairies solved their problem in a similar manner.

Before the beginning of the agrarian history of the prairies, when the never-ending lines of white-topped emigrant wagons slowly trailed toward the setting sun during the fifties, gangs of unscrupulous thieves had hide outs along the overland trails, from which they sallied forth and fell on luckless travelers journeying toward the land of gold. These gangs and other lawless groups continued to operate during the early period of settlement all along the

[4] *Republican Valley Empire*, August 16, 1870.

border. In response to this condition settlers' organizations arose. As early as 1858 an association was formed in Nemaha, Nebraska, to protect property against horse thieves. It had the customary president, vice-president, secretary, and treasurer. In addition there were ten riders. Initial membership dues were one dollar, and subsequently assessments were made to cover the expenses. When live stock was stolen, it was compulsory to report it immediately. Riders were then dispatched to recover it. The riders received one dollar a day and expenses. Meetings were held once a month.

During the War, lawless organizations appeared in Kansas and Nebraska which operated under the protection of sectionalism. The Red Legs was so called because the members wore red morocco leggings. It was a loose-jointed organization, its membership shifting between twenty-five and fifty men. Their original activity was horse stealing, but their depredations included rascalities of all kinds. Their headquarters were at Lawrence, Kansas, an abolitionist stronghold. At intervals they would dash into Missouri, despoil the citizens of that slave state of their property, and repair to Lawrence where the booty was defiantly sold at auction. Missourians who came in search of their property were in danger of their lives. Governor Robinson tried to break up the gang, but the Red Legs repaid his interference by an attempt to assassinate him, their plan barely miscarrying. In the heat of the slavery controversy, public opinion could not be rallied against this gang which was "spoiling the proslavery people." The activity of this organized band was one of the reasons for the destruction of Lawrence at the time of Quantrell's raid.

Other gangs operated under the protection of patriotism. These bands of thieves were called Jayhawkers and preyed on the people west of Missouri. If a man had a fine team of horses, he was at once marked by the thieves as a rebel sympathizer. Some of the victims actually were Southerners but little regard was paid to one's political feelings. One victim in southern Nebraska organized a posse, chased the thieves into Iowa, and, capturing thieves and horses, hanged the "loyal" culprits. This had a very definite tendency to promote safety for property and life.

Sometimes the prisoners condemned by "Judge Lynch" were given a trial in true vigilante style. At other times it was a matter of mob rule. An instance in which the former held sway was reported by a circuit rider. In a prairie settlement in 1865 a prisoner was accused of having killed a boy herding cattle and of bringing some of the stock to town and selling them. The citizens called a mass meeting at the public park. After addresses by several citizens an organization was effected for a jury trial. A president and a secretary were appointed, a jury impaneled, and a counsel was appointed for the prisoner. Seven witnesses were examined. The trial began at ten o'clock and at two o'clock the case was given to the jury. The verdict was guilty, and at six o'clock the culprit was hanged. It was all in a day's work. There was no long period of waiting for a trial with its inevitable escape of the prisoner or its expensive court proceedings. Justice was swift and certain.

In this early period wholesale executions were sometimes held. At Rising Sun, Kansas, six men were hanged from the same limb, four at one time and two a few days later. These culprits had been caught in the act of killing a man who had attempted to save his cattle from the thieves. Self-preservation dictated lynch law.

In other and probably the great majority of cases, if there were any suspicion, the prisoner was considered guilty and dispatched without a trial. In a little prairie town, which bloomed and then faded in the seventies and has long since passed away, a man and a half-grown boy drove along with a fine team of mules and a good buggy. The word was passed around that the mules had been stolen. A posse of citizens was rounded up and was soon in pursuit. The following day the couple was caught and both the man and the boy were hanged from the limb of an oak tree. Later it was learned that probably the boy was not actually guilty of stealing the mules and that likely an injustice had been done in his case. He had paid the penalty for being in bad company. The old oak tree remained for years a landmark to mob violence and a place to be avoided by playing children to this day!

It did not even pay to joke about stealing horses. In one instance, about 1860, a young man riding a horse, overtook a pedestrian and asked the man why he did not ride. The man on foot replied "I have no horse." Upon which the stranger smiled and remarked, "Why don't you pick one up"? The pedestrian invited the rider to eat dinner at his house close by and, while they ate, the host sent his boy to get some neighbors to help him hang the supposed horse thief. By the time they had finished eating, several of the neighbors had assembled. Some had lost horses at the hands of thieves. When the visitor went for his horse, they told him he was a thief and would be hanged and that if he had any prayers to say, it was time to begin. The young man declared his innocence explaining that he had only joked, and that if they would give him time he would prove that the horse he rode was one he had hired and for which he was paying; but his words were unheeded. They took him to the nearest tree, tied his hands, placed him on a horse, adjusted the noose around his neck, led the horse out from under him, and hanged him on the main road in broad daylight. He was left hanging there. When the news reached the county seat, the liveryman came and claimed the horse, saying the traveler was paying for the use of it. The stranger was an orphan boy who had come out to the new country and had no friends to take up his case. Hence there was no attempt to punish the guilty ones. Had some person interested in justice attempted to prosecute the lynchers, no doubt public sentiment as manifested by the jury, would have allowed the guilty parties to go free or would have let them off with a light sentence. Ordinarily, however, the men hanged were justly under suspicion, and although in many cases there would have been insufficient evidence for conviction in an organized legal court, they were guilty.

In the beginning apparently, vigilante justice developed as the result of some dastardly crime or of the organization of powerful gangs of criminals who made peoples' lives and property unsafe.

These gangs drew members from the best society and included officers and other individuals highly respected in the community. In response to this rule of thieves, the abler men of the community quietly began organizing a counter movement and carefully secured information concerning the membership of the horse thief gangs.

In the territory between Winfield and Wichita, Kansas, a powerful group was built up for the purpose of stealing horses. Among its members were numbered farmers, business men, city officers, sheriffs, and other officials. Their organization was so extensive and insidious that it was almost impossible to arrest a horse thief. In the spring of 1870 the gang drove two hundred and fifty stolen mules into Texas. A vigilance committee was organized by a group of Winfield men and worked so quietly that the gang, having become bold, suspected nothing. All members worked as detectives. Their work was so well done that they learned the names of members and officers, found out the times of the disbursement of funds, and located the headquarters of the gang. By autumn they were ready to strike. One of the stopping places of the gang was a country house. The committee, knowing when the agents of the thieves would make their trip, watched for them. Spies brought word that four of them had stopped at the house. In a few hours it was surrounded and the men were called out. They came to the door and were ordered to surrender; part of the group refused and were shot and part were taken to a tree and hanged. One man's body was laid on the bank of the creek and a placard carried the mute message, "Sold for stealing horses." The next day excitement rose high and hundreds of people gathered at the place. Among them were the vigilance committee who took five more men from the crowd so quietly that the move was not noted; a little later their dead bodies were found hanging from trees by the river. This greatly intensified the excitement, and in that atmosphere the vigilance committee made a statement in the newspaper giving the reasons for the organization of the committee and explaining the care with which it had acted. It then gave the names of the officers and members of the horse thief gang. This created a tremendous sensation for it included men in the country and towns who were not even suspected by their neighbors. Horse stealing ended abruptly, and many flush men, who had no honorable means of support, left the country immediately.[5] The newspaper, in giving a very meager account of the affair, closed with this mild-mannered remark: "It is regretted that the law seems to be inadequate to the occasion." In point of fact the press made little objection to this extra legal practice and even commended it. The editor of the *Huron* (South Dakota) *Tribune*, in speaking of a certain rascal, said: "He will undoubtedly stretch hemp in the course of a few months and we shall be glad to publish his obituary." [6]

Homicides resulting from disputes between neighbors or citizens were seldom punished by mob violence, but murder for the purpose of theft, was deemed worthy of death. At one of the Missouri River towns in 1857, a gang of twenty thieves made a business of luring people with money away from the pressing crowd of emigrants, murdering them, taking their money, and throwing their bodies into the river. Finally some boys discovered a body floating in the water. This led to the arrest of two of the gang who confessed. The people, aroused by the despicable crime, feeling that the judge was corrupt, hanged the criminals.

There was ample reason to fear that, unless the people took matters into their own hands, the criminals would go unpunished, for in very few cases was justice actually meted out by court procedure during frontier days. At Abilene, Kansas, when that was the cowboy capital, Tom Smith, city marshal, was murdered while attempting to arrest a homesteader. The murderer received a

---

[5] Reminiscences of Arnold Walden, *Kansas Reminiscences*, a scrapbook of clippings in the Kansas State Historical Society, Article undated, Vol. III, p. 114. This reminiscence does not agree in all details with the newspaper reports but seems more reliable than the papers; *Wichita Vidette*, November 10, 1870 and December 8, 1870.

[6] August 11, 1881.

sentence of only fourteen years. During the first six years of the territorial history of Nebraska, not one murderer met the punishment comparable to his crime. At times murder threatened to become an epidemic. In one county five men charged with murder were confined at one time in the county jail. There was room for only four and one was kept in the corridor. One frontier paper mentioned that six murders had been committed in the county in one year and only one arrest had been made. In a county in the short grass country a cold-blooded murder was committed. The detective trailed the murderer for nine months through the flint hills of Kansas into the Ozarks of southern Missouri, back into Kansas, and across the plains of Colorado, through New Mexico, and into the panhandle of Texas. He rode hundreds of miles alone risking hardships and dangers untold. He caught his man in a cow camp just ten months after the murder and took him back to the scene of the crime. A change of venue enabled him to get off with a sentence of only ten years and he was pardoned in three or four. Such miscarriage of justice was bound to create sentiment in favor of that quick, sure method employed by the vigilantes with their rope.

From the crimes of horse thievery and murder it was only a step to the execution of criminals for more petty crimes and misdemeanors. Men were hanged for robbing jewelry stores or committing other crimes. Drinking was the downfall of more than one who met death at the hands of a mob. In Pierre, Dakota Territory, during the winter of 1880 and 1881 a vigilance committee was formed to keep the peace, since the heavy snows had shut the town off from legal headquarters at Yankton. Some "bull whackers" [7] from Fort Pierre, across the river, visited Pierre occasionally. They considered it a "tenderfoot burg" and proceeded to shoot up the town and terrorize the inhabitants. A freighter named "Arkansaw" visited Pierre several times for the purpose of celebrating. He shot recklessly on the streets and then went out onto the roads leading into the town terrorizing all he met by shooting over their heads

[7] Freighters.

or at their feet. He was said to be a good man when sober and some of the vigilance committee tried to reason with him. He was told that he would be welcome if he would leave his gun at home. He mistook this kind warning for an admission of fear on the part of the committee and attempted to "hold up" and terrorize the occupants of a dance hall. The vigilantes were on hand and riddled his body with bullets. The citizens justified the committee and the incident had a very wholesome effect. The little town enjoyed unusual quiet during the remaining portion of the winter.[8]

In at least one instance the vigilantes took over a civil case and handed down a verdict. A man sold his farm but after the sale was made and the deed delivered, the railroad located the station at a point which greatly enhanced the value of the land. The seller regretted his bargain and asked if his buyer had recorded the deed. Upon receiving a negative reply, the former owner courteously offered his assistance to take it to the county seat and have it recorded since he was going there. This was not an unusual proceeding since neighbors always did errands for each other. Later the accommodating gentleman asked to buy back his farm since he still lived there. When this was refused, the purchaser was told to get out, since there was no proof that he held the title. (The accommodating neighbor had hidden the deed.) The wronged man went out and told his friends. A neighborhood crowd of about twenty-five was gathered together and filled with courage—they had fortified themselves with "old rye"—they elected a captain, called on the swindler, and demanded the deed. He said he had lost it. The mob demanded that he make out a new one, but he refused. He was then presented with a hemp collar which caused a prompt change of attitude. Someone went for a justice of the peace and a notary public. He and his wife signed the deed and the justice and witnesses made it legal. As one reported it, the "Regulators" went for more "old rye" and then returned home "to

[8] William Rhoads, *Recollections of Dakota Territory* (Fort Pierre, South Dakota, 1931), p. 29.

sleep the sleep of the just." [9] The man moved out of the country This no doubt gives us a hint as to why men were not given a fair hearing and why a mob often did brutal things. They "screwed up their courage to the sticking point" with whiskey.

The vigilante organizations, once brought into being by some unusual situation, continued to function in the case of less provocation and sometimes got out of hand. Men were hanged for things which did not merit the severe punishment of death. Then, too, the committees attempted to regulate the conduct of individuals at times. The organization took upon itself the job of cleaning up a city and ridding the place of undesirables. Having determined who these were, they notified them to leave, decorating their letter of warning with a rude drawing of a skull and cross bones or perhaps a rope formed into a noose. The persons to whom these missives were addressed usually left town at an early date. Many towns were cleared of gamblers and other undesirable citizens in this manner.

In a well-regulated civilized country a jail sentence is the principal punishment for crime. It was manifestly impossible for vigilantes to use this system since they had no jails and the jails used by the organized government were mere colanders. It meant, as a rule, either that a man was told to leave the country or that he was executed.

A verdict in a criminal case in a frontier Kansas court read: "Not guilty, but if the prisoner is sharp he will leave the town before night." The newspaper reported that when the prisoner was last heard from "his face was set like a flint toward Santa Fe, and he bore in his hand a banner with the strange device 'I'm off.' "

[9] Alfred T. Andreas, *History of the State of Nebraska* (Chicago, 1882), Vol. I, p. 589.

CHAPTER XI

THE HOMESTEADER-CATTLEMAN WAR

WHEN THE BUFFALO and Indian melted before white occupation, the ranching business developed. Following the Civil War, by reason of military use, cattle were scarce in the North and prices were very high in the East. On the other hand Texas, almost untouched by demands of the War, was teeming with long-horned cattle. In 1866 certain northern stockmen discovered that cattle could be bought in Texas for ten dollars a head and these men braved the many dangers involved to drive these cattle from Texas to the railroads which were pushing westward across the prairies. As early as 1867 Abilene, Kansas, near the end of the Kansas Pacific Railway, became a shipping center. A little later Newton, Wichita, and Dodge City, in Kansas, and Ogallala, in Nebraska, became large cattle centers fed from the "Long Drive." Hundreds of thousands of cattle were driven from Texas to these points each season. From the cow towns of the plains some of these cattle were shipped to eastern markets; but the larger portion was driven northward to be used by the United States Government for the soldiers or to be given to the Indian wards of the government and to stock the prairies with cattle as ranches began to spring up here and there.[1] The editor of the *Wichita Eagle* climbed to the top of the highest building in the little town one day in September, 1872, and was able to count twenty-one herds of cattle within two miles of the city. The editor of the Niobrara, Nebraska, *Pioneer* stated that thousands of cattle were driven across the river at that point bound for the Indians of northern Nebraska and Dakota. As many as

[1] Everett N. Dick, "The Long Drive," Kansas State Historical Society *Collections*, Vol. XVII, pp. 27–86.

5,000 of these Texas cattle were crossed over the Missouri River in one day, the editor observed.

Naturally when a score of herds were held in the vicinity of a cow town for days or weeks awaiting disposal, both the cowboys and cattle had a direct effect on the community. As the community became settled, the first homesteads taken were naturally those near town and soon friction arose between the herders and the settlers. The citizens and farmers at Abilene signed a circular inviting the Texans not to return. When the Santa Fe Railway extended further west, Newton and Wichita became convenient shipping points. The people of Wichita were wise enough in 1870 to attempt to hold the cattle trade. Through its newspaper the city invited the cattlemen to drive their cattle there guaranteeing them a passage. This guarantee would indicate that even at that early date the trail was closing up. Many, no doubt, felt that it was undesirable to have the cattle trail run near their farms. One settler mentioned the Texas cattle as among the worst pests with which the settler had to contend. They were vicious by nature, making it unsafe for a person to approach afoot, they stripped the settler of feed for his stock, and trampled and destroyed his garden. Worst of all, these rangy, long-horned, savage beasts brought with them the dreaded Texas fever. Wherever they traveled they left a trail of death among domestic cattle. If the latter even walked over the ground which Texas cattle had trod, they caught the Texas fever and whole herds were wiped out. The Texas herds seemed to be immune and simply acted as carriers of the disease which wrought havoc with native cattle. Many theories as to the cause of the disease appeared, but the mystery went unsolved until a later day.[2]

The tick fever, although annoying and destructive at times, was not the cause of the war between the homesteaders and cattlemen. Farming and ranching did not flourish together. The rancher was no more favored by agrarianism than were the trapper, the Indian,

---

[2] It has since been discovered that the disease was carried by ticks which dropped off the Texas cattle and infected the susceptible native cattle.

or the buffalo. These inhabitants of the wilds naturally melted away before the homestead frontier.

At first the few scattered homesteaders who lived near the cattle trail were glad to have the cowboys "bed down" for the night on their claims. There were two or three reasons for this. In the first place a herd of twenty-five hundred cattle would leave the poverty-stricken settler several hundred pounds of fuel at a time when cow chips were in demand. Furthermore in a mixed herd one or more calves were born each night. These were given to the homesteader because it was impossible for them to keep up with the herd. Often among the "drags" [3] there were lame or crippled cattle which the drover traded to the settlers at a bargain or gave away. After a few days' rest and grazing these became strong. Many homesteaders began herds of their own in this way. Some secured a yoke of good oxen by breaking a couple of these lame old Texas steers which became sound when they had recuperated from a period of hard driving.

Nevertheless when the country became populous and settlers began to fence off their holdings and plow up the cattle trails, there was trouble. When the settler remonstrated at the damage done by the cattle, the cowboys drew their guns and cowed him into a resentful submission. Such incidents soon led to organized opposition by the homesteaders. As early as 1871 the settlers on the Little Blue River [4] began to harass the herds. In one instance sixteen armed men met a drover and tried without shooting to frighten him away, stampede the herd, and steal as many as possible. In Butler County, Nebraska, the homesteaders put an end to the trail in 1872. A fearful night storm had stampeded several thousand "steers" and dispersed them over the plains and hills in every direction. The following day a dismal blinding fog had settled down on the country. Word was passed from mouth to mouth. Horses

[3] Cattle which walked in the rear of the mammoth herd each day as it stretched out on the line of march toward the North.
[4] Kansas and Nebraska.

were mounted by armed settlers and a dreadful carnage ensued. Hundreds of the longhorned cattle were killed, butchered, and packed away in various receptacles. The flesh was eaten and the hides were later cut up for lariat ropes. Prosecutions, arrests, and threats followed this daring episode, but, of course, no convictions were secured since the jury and county officials were fully in sympathy with the agrarians; the trail in that community came to an abrupt end.[5]

The line between stealing and honorable warfare is very indistinct in the war between the cattleman and the homesteader. As one looks back over the scores of years, some of the acts of the settlers seem little less than thinly veiled thievery. The cattlemen considered the settlers as mere rustlers stealing their cattle purely for economic gain.

In all history there was perhaps no more favorable opportunity for the development of the ranching industry than that which presented itself on the prairies of the United States just following the Civil War. Within a decade the ranching area of the United States became larger than the total cultivated area. Capital from Europe migrated to the plains for investment in this profitable undertaking. English earls, French counts, and German lords established ranches in this fairest of grazing regions. Some of these remained in America to manage their ranches and add to their wealth. Others, leaving a manager in charge, returned to their native land to come back occasionally to look after their interests. Eastern financiers invested their money in ranches and some Eastern men of wealth even came to live on the plains.[6]

The ranching industry paid enormous dividends especially in the earlier years. The money used to purchase cattle was almost the only outlay. The rancher had first to find a spring or other permanent water supply; he secured this either by squatter rights,

[5] George L. Brown, *Centennial History of Butler County, Nebraska* (Lincoln, Nebraska, 1876), pp. 21, 22.

[6] Of these, one of the most noted was Theodore Roosevelt who lived on his ranch near Medora, North Dakota.

preëmption claim, or homesteading. The man who thus controlled a permanent watering place was able to monopolize the pasture within a radius of five miles. A crude structure of logs or sod was built for the rancher's dwelling, and a few buildings were erected to house the employees and horses. A corral made of poles completed the building equipment of the ranch. Often the buildings were roofed with dirt and seldom represented any large outlay of capital. The cattle belonging to such a ranch naturally would not wander far from their watering place. Sometimes a rancher owned a number of such ranches; the general manager or ranch owner made his headquarters at the home ranch; the others were supervised by managers or foremen. If different ranchers occupied territory along the same stream, the cattle frequently intermingled necessitating branding them for identification. With an abundance of grazing land free even of taxation, cattle raising proved a bonanza. In later years when the ranges became overstocked and the pasture was short, it ceased to pay such large profits.

When the homesteaders began to push westward and file on the land which had been freely used as personal pasture land by the cattle barons, the latter naturally did not surrender their privileges without a struggle. They held back the relentless waves of farmers as much as possible but in the end inevitably went down to defeat before the pitiless attacks of the "nesters." [7]

The ranchers conducted their struggle along several different lines. Many times they or their employees conjured up Indian scares, causing the temporary depopulation of whole regions and even scaring many away permanently. A second means of preventing settlement was to discourage the homesteader. The emigrant was told that it never rained, that the land was unproductive, and that the homesteader's family would starve. In western Kansas the settlers were told that Dodge City was as far west as civilization would ever go and that the place was hardly fit for a civilized man with a family. When these means failed to stay the inflow of the

---

[7] A name which cowboys and ranchers gave to the despised farmers.

grangers, as the farmers were called, threats were used. A lonely settler attempting to homestead a fertile spot within a rancher's range would receive a call from a number of cowboys who threatened death. Anyone but the most resolute would turn back to a less-favored spot nearer other grangers. Threats could not dam the westward flow of settlement long, however, and the ranchers had to concoct other means of saving as much as possible of the public domain for grazing purposes. Some ranchers had each of their cowboys homestead, preëmpt, and take timber claims. Sometimes they preëmpted a number of sections on the outside of a square of grazing land; a barbed wire fence around the land enclosed many sections of government land within the hollow square.

Frame shacks were constructed for the use of the cowboys in proving up. Many of these were upon wheels or runners and were moved from claim to claim for this purpose. In the long run none of this availed for the homesteaders made entries in the pastures, contested and canceled the entries of the cowboys, and destroyed the fences. Bloodshed resulted; but there was little chance of final victory for the ranchmen in the courts when the jury was composed of homesteaders.

In Custer County, Nebraska, in the fall of 1884, a few settlers located homesteads in the pasture of the Brighton Ranch Company. This pasture was about fifteen miles square and was enclosed by a barbed wire fence. These settlers served notice on the company to remove the wire fence within thirty days. When the company paid no attention to the request at the expiration of the time, the homesteaders made a raid on the fence and took the posts for rafters for the roofs of their sod houses. The ranch foreman had the settlers arrested and taken to the county seat for trial. While the settlers were in custody, the foreman with a number of cowboys drove from home to home tearing down the houses to recover the posts. They hitched their team to the end of a ridge log and in a few seconds the neat little home was a shapeless mass of earth, hay, brush, and sod intermingled with the furniture, utensils, and other property. The

THE MARSH TYPE OF HARVESTER

The first grain harvester on the prairies, widely used between 1875 and 1883. Courtesy of the International Harvester Company.

cowboys then extricated their posts and took them along in their wagon. While the merry-making, rollicking cowboys went about their work of destruction, a boy on a fast horse was sent to the county seat for help. A posse of men from the town started in pursuit of the celebrating cowboys but they, having been warned by a cowboy from the town, fled to the hills escaping the wrath of the posse. The ranch company failed to win their case against the settlers since the homesteads were illegally fenced in. The foreman was arrested and fined for tearing down the settlers' houses.[8] The settlers were not always so fortunate, for many times the ranchmen and their employees had control of the county government and the decision went against the grangers.

Upon one occasion, when two men went near a ranch to do some breaking on a tree claim, a dozen cowboys saddled their horses, filled the magazines of their Winchesters, and rode off in the darkness on an "errand of mercy." The next morning nothing was seen of the breaking party. Afterward it was discovered that several gentlemen had called on the tree claim farmers, helped them hitch up their horses, and actually accompanied them a long way to prevent the savage men and beasts of the plains from hurting them.

In Rice County, Kansas, the war between the granger and the cattleman took this turn: Many cattle died in the winter of 1871 and 1872. Others, faring a little better, huddled together along the streams trying to keep warm. Many of the living were on the verge of death. The homesteaders skinned the dead animals for the hides. The cattlemen were widely separated and did not know what was happening over the range. After a time the cowboys came to the conclusion that the settlers were killing some cattle which might have survived. The cattlemen sent an ultimatum that the first settler found skinning an animal would be killed on the spot. The settlers answered the threat by stating that if any settlers met death at the hands of the cattlemen the prairie would be fired. Each group

[8] S. D. Butcher, *Pioneer History of Custer County* (Broken Bow, Nebraska, 1910), pp. 185, 186.

had the other at a disadvantage and the matter was allowed to subside.

From skinning dead cattle and shooting dying cattle or killing cattle which became a nuisance, it was only a step to stealing cattle. Probably a considerable number practiced "rustling" under cover of the excuse that the cattlemen were holding the range illegally. In a war one of the chief means of inflicting punishment on the enemy is by despoiling him of his property. Hence butchering the rancher's cattle was a fairly common occurrence. Probably the whole truth concerning the range wars will never be known, but many homesteaders probably stole cattle under the pretext that the cattlemen were abusing them. On the other hand, no doubt, the stockmen used the pretext of rustling to drive out the small rancher.

The homesteaders of Sherman County, Kansas, in 1886 organized to protect themselves against the ranchers' charges of butchering range cattle. Since there were no herders with the cattle to prevent them from roaming the country tramping and destroying the homesteaders' crops, not a few settlers killed the ranchers' stock. The cattlemen, sensing their losses, sent out cowboys to protect the cattle and punish the culprits. Of course no one was caught for it was said it took only five minutes to kill and dress a beef on a foggy night. The brand was cut out of the hide and the proof of ownership was destroyed.

The cattlemen offered a reward of $500 for evidence leading to the conviction of a man for killing range cattle. This came close home, for the man who bought or ate range beef was just as guilty as the man who killed it, and very few settlers were not guilty of eating range beef. It was customary for a man to kill only one yearling but to sell twenty quarters to his neighbors. With the cattlemen offering such an attractive reward someone was almost sure to be tempted to betray his guilty neighbor. One man in the community was of doubtful loyalty to the range butchers and some of the guilty parties organized the Homesteaders' Protective Association to protect themselves. They then invited a number of the neighbors to join the organization. Among them was the man who was suspected of betrayal. The applicants gave many oaths regarding claim jumping and other items of general interest to which any honest man would subscribe; the last and most solemn oath of all was: "I do solemnly swear not to tell anything that may in any way lead owners of cattle which are running at large contrary to law and destroying settlers' crops to discover who had killed or crippled or in any way injured these same cattle, . . . If I do, then I shall expect this society to use me thus." At this point a straw man with a rope around his neck was suspended before the astonished candidate who promptly said "I do"! Other members were taken in until the whole county was organized. There were thirteen lodges bound together by secret pass words and secret grips and signs. Later, when the cattle were all rounded up and the range controversy had disappeared, the lodges were united into a central organization called the "Homesteaders' Union Association" which tackled the problem of settling a county seat struggle. This was done effectually and decisively within three months' time. It is estimated that the organization saved the county $100,000 in litigation and other costs incident to a long drawn out county-seat quarrel. The organization died out almost immediately following this effectual settlement of the controversy.[9]

In 1882 a vigilance committee of about fifty members was formed by the cattlemen in eastern Montana and western North Dakota with the avowed purpose of catching or driving out cattle and horse thieves. The active members were mainly irresponsible shifters hired on a salary of thirty-five to fifty dollars a month. As a matter of fact the expedition moved about the country burning the homes of the small permanent settlers. Much property was destroyed and miles of prairie were burned but no thieves were caught.[10]

[9] E. E. Blackman, "Sherman County and the H. U. A.," *Transactions*, Kansas State Historical Society, Vol. VIII, pp. 50–60. Mr. Blackman was the secretary of the H. U. A.

[10] Zena Irma Trinka, *Out Where the West Begins* (St. Paul, Minnesota, 1930), pp. 349–350.

In Custer County, Nebraska, a homesteader by the name of Ketchum was accused of rustling. He and a man called Mitchell lived together. Robert Olive, a rancher, determined to arrest or drive the alleged thief out of the county. The sheriff deputized Olive who together with a group of cowboys attempted to arrest Mitchell and Ketchum. The homesteaders resisted and in the encounter Olive was killed. The homesteaders later gave themselves up to be tried. A brother of Olive secured possession of the prisoners from his friend the sheriff while they were being taken to the county seat for trial. He and his cowboys hanged the two homesteaders. The perpetrators of this crime were tried in a different county, found guilty, and sentenced to life imprisonment. A year later the Supreme Court handed down a decision that the prisoners were entitled to a trial in the county where the crime was committed. When the case came up, strangely enough no one appeared to testify against them; the case was dismissed.

It must not be thought that all homesteaders and cattlemen were at swords' points. One kind-hearted ranchman in Custer County, Nebraska, gave water to the settlers. Cisterns were dug near his deep wells and the water was pumped into the cisterns for his needy neighbors.

The cowboys naturally caused some trouble in the drowsy little towns and in their vicinity. On the train cowboys monopolized the seats without a protest from the passengers. On the streets they shot at random and took special delight in testing the courage of strangers against the whiz of bullets about their ears. A favorite trick was to shoot near the toes of a tenderfoot and compel him to dance. Frequently the unsteady hand of the drunken cowboy allowed the gun to shoot holes through the feet of victims. When the cattlemen returned from having sold their stock at the markets in the East, they usually put on a spree and determined that everyone in the vicinity should celebrate. Those who did not want to drink were obliged to hide. Sometimes a cowboy crazed with drink went wild and shot up the town. Two men in this condition terrorized Anselmo, Nebraska, for hours. Tin cans were placed on the hitching posts along the street and shot full of holes regardless of the danger to passers-by. Tiring of this, they went into a store and shot a hole through the stove pipe, the bullet almost grazing the storekeeper. They shot holes in the floor and ceiling of the saloon, accidentally shooting a man in the foot. They rode into the stores, helped themselves to cigars and other articles. After visiting all the stores in town they rode into the saloon again and played pool on horseback shooting off their guns to emphasize the game. The sheriff's posse killed both of them in attempting their arrest.

The friction between settlers and cowboys developed into a pitched battle in Kearney, Nebraska. The cowboys shot up the town, making a target of the guests on the veranda of the hotel, sending them scurrying indoors amid a hail of bullets. Finally the citizens armed themselves and a pitched battle ensued. The citizens drove the cowboys out of the town; but, while awaiting a return attack, drilled daily and appointed sentinels at night.

Settlement gradually pushed the rancher farther and farther west. The winter of 1880 and 1881 greatly weakened the stock interests. Early in the winter the rain began falling and saturated the grass. A cold spell then froze every spear of grass covering it with ice. A heavy snow was followed by rain and another cold spell which turned this to ice, covering the snow with a thick crust. This crust remained until spring. Temperatures ran as low as ten to twenty below zero for weeks. It was almost impossible for the cattle to get to the grass which was plentiful beneath the snow and ice. Cattle died by the thousands. It is estimated that from seventy-five to ninety per cent of the cows and calves on the range died that winter and sixty per cent of the steers lay in piles behind the hills where they had sought shelter. This marked the beginning of the end of the range cattle industry and the beginning of the final triumph of the homesteader. This, however, was only a step in the final defeat of the ranchmen by the agrarian settlers through sheer weight of numbers.

CHAPTER XII

HUNTING AND TRAPPING

FOR A HALF CENTURY before the coming of the permanent settler, hunters, trappers, fur traders, and others had roamed the prairies. With this group of migratory men this volume is not concerned. Even when the settlers came, intent on building cities and carving out homes, there was in connection with their activities considerable hunting and trapping.

The earliest settler of the fifties, like his predecessor the Indian, took to trapping. Except at a few places along the trails or the river cities, there was no market for agricultural products above his own needs, but furs and hides were always in demand. These were easily transported and commanded ready money. Then, too, observers testify, these squatters were none too fond of work, but loved the wild free life of the hunter and trapper and held their claims only long enough to realize a sum of money on them before moving on into a new region to repeat the process. These people, the trapper-hunter settlers, became the precursor of city building and home construction. They traveled here and there spying out the land and locating on the best sites. One such individual, as proof of his good judgment, recounted how five towns had grown up on or near his locations.[1] These advance guards of civilization searched out the land and many settlers learned of good locations from them. Frequently these trappers made their headquarters at a road ranch and, operating from there, penetrated the unexplored country on each side of the trail, staying out for weeks and months.

Then, too, among the early agrarian settlers there were adven-

---

[1] J. R. Mead to George W. Martin, August 2, 1908, *Transactions,* Kansas State Historical Society, Vol. X, p. 624.

turous young men usually without families who loved the wild solitude and liked to spend the winter trapping. When the first frost came and the autumn leaves began to fall, these young men itched for the solitude of the wild. Two or more would get together and make final plans for an expedition. The steel traps were gathered, rifles put in shape, and laying in a winter's supply of ammunition, provisions, and feed, they started for some favorite trapping ground. Along the streams were to be found the haunts of beaver, otter, mink, raccoon, and wild cats or lynx, while on the hills and prairies roamed the big buffalo, wolves, and the slinking coyotes. All of these animals were valued for their pelts and the more expert the trapper the greater the winter's dividends.

The trappers camped for the winter in the protection of some little grove along the stream. Sometimes a log shanty was built or a tent pitched, but more likely a dugout was made by digging a hole about ten feet square back into the bank of the creek and building a front of logs or covering the opening with brush and grass.[2] Next they would string out their traps for several miles along the stream to catch the forest denizens and would scatter poisonous bait on the prairie for the unwary dwellers of the highlands.

Busy days and exciting times followed. In the forenoon came a long tramp through the heavy snow, baiting, setting traps, and searching for poisoned victims. Sometimes the tired trapper returned almost empty-handed; again he was heavily laden with game. The afternoon was spent skinning animals and caring for the furs and pelts, with an occasional hunting expedition to supply the larder. An expedition on the prairie sometimes netted a buffalo skin and enough meat to last for weeks.

Their meals were not always regular but they ate well. The cooking was largely done over the camp-fire and consisted principally of game. Beaver tail soup was a trapper's dish par excellence. Roast

[2] When the Kansas Pacific Railroad was built west from Kansas City to Denver, dugouts were made all along the line by grading gangs. These were used in after years for headquarters by trappers. Adolph Roenigk, *Pioneer History of Kansas* (Lincoln, Kansas, 1933), pp. 191–192.

wild turkey or duck, roasted, fried, or boiled venison, buffalo, or antelope meat, and other dishes were delicacies. A big chunk of buffalo or deer meat was often spitted before the bright embers of the fire and roasted to a savory brown, juicy and sweet, ready to serve at a moment's notice when the hungry trapper returned. A spit was made by fastening the meat to a straight pole in a balanced position and placing the pole in a horizontal position over the embers with each end resting on a forked stick. The cook sat by the fire turning it occasionally with an improvised crank.

The history of these trappers is somewhat barren inasmuch as their very independence, and for the most part illiteracy, combined to sentence them to obscurity. It seems probable that few if any books were read at night. Their semi-savage life was unbroken by social activity. They no doubt played cards by the light of the cheery evening camp-fire. Talking, story telling, and wondering what was going on in the outside world were their main occupations. Now and then an evening was spent in molding bullets, repairing clothes, or making moccasins and leggings. Each evening that trusty friend, the rifle, had to be cleaned and oiled. While they did this pleasant task, memory drifted back to hunting exploits or narrow escapes from wild animals or Indians; over and over during the winter these exploits would be recounted. The short evening soon passed and the companions lay down to a night of unbroken sleep begotten of vigorous physical exercise in the pure fresh air.

Their wants were few. Simple beds made of prairie hay covered with buffalo skins, a few simple cooking utensils, some stools for chairs, a crude table, a box for a cupboard, and a rustic washstand completed their simple house furnishings. By the door stood the trusty axe used to secure the fuel supply.

The trapper was compelled to be ever on the alert for the prowling Indian visitor who would rob him of his catch as well as supplies. To guard against the loss of a large catch, the partners frequently dug a hole and, lining it and protecting it against dampness, stored their furs in it. This was well hidden and the surroundings camouflaged to prevent detection. It was better to lose part of the catch than all, and this guaranteed saving a part.

Barring accidents, the winter passed quickly and happily. If successful, with the coming of the first warm days of spring when the grass began to carpet the valleys, the trappers slowly wended their way homeward with several hundred dollars' worth of furs and turned to their agricultural pursuits in a half-hearted manner, always longing for autumn and the trapper's life among the haunts of wild animals.[3] In the seventies by the time the homesteader came, the country had been pretty well stripped of the larger, more valuable game.

Although certain settlers made a business of leaving the settlements and establishing a trapping camp during the winter months, many who stayed on their claims also did some trapping. Even professional men did not disdain to trap. Dr. George B. Lambert of Moran, Kansas, caught enough mink one winter to make himself a fur overcoat. Homesteaders found plenty of room to run a line of traps on their own land and on that belonging to the railroad, on school sections, or on unclaimed land. In the eighties muskrat and mink were commonly trapped. Skunks were also in grave danger of their lives from the numerous school-boy trappers who plagued the teacher by coming to school bearing the scent of that odoriferous animal on their clothes and persons. Along the streams near the Missouri River raccoons were trapped. The sides of many smoke houses and barns were covered with drying hides.

The wolf was especially sought after in Dakota in the eighties because in some sections a bounty was offered in addition to the price which the fur brought.[4] Probably more wolves and foxes were taken by poison than with traps. The settler hitched a horse to the front quarter of a buffalo or the carcass of a farm animal, and dragged it in a great circle of several miles dropping pieces of poi-

[3] William D. Street, "Victory of the Plow," *Transactions*, Kansas State Historical Society, Vol. IX, p. 41.

[4] Dillman, *A Human Life* (Excelsior, Minnesota, 1934), pp. 17, 18.

soned meat along the way. The wolf or coyote that happened to cross the trail, followed it and picked up the poisoned meat. The greatest drawback to this system was the fact that the dead wolves were often difficult to find. They would slink away in search of water and die in out-of-the-way places where they would not be found until the pelt was spoiled. When a fresh snow was on the ground, the trapper could track the victim and find the fur. Sometimes a great many wolves were secured in one night. It was not unusual to get seven or eight at one time.[5]

In preëmption days game was abundant. Turkeys were plentiful among the timber along the streams; the prairies were alive with prairie chickens; antelope, deer, elk, and buffalo roamed a short distance inland; wild ducks and geese were plentiful along the streams and lakes. Even bears were to be found in the woods along the larger rivers. Most of these animals melted before civilization like snow before a chinook wind, but prairie chickens, strange to say, actually increased following the occupation of the country by the homesteader. An abundance of waste grain made it possible for the country to support more birds than formerly. When the country became more thickly populated, they decreased again before the withering fire of many hunters and more efficient firearms. One Dakota woman recalled that when the country was only partially settled a drive across the prairie resulted frequently in ruining the nests of these birds; the wagon wheel rolled around dripping with the yolks of the broken eggs.

The preëmptors quickly slaughtered the larger game in the eastern part of the prairie states. One man recalled having killed thirty-three deer and eight elk in 1856. In the same winter another man and his three sons reported having killed over seventy deer, elk, and antelope. A deep snow had driven the animals to seek protection in the wooded valleys along the streams. The snow then crusted over with sleet firm enough to bear a man's weight, but the animals broke through. The settlers went about killing them with axes. While no

[5] Adolph Roenigk, *op. cit.*, pp. 191–192.

doubt this happened very infrequently and cannot be taken as a regular occurrence, yet it does give some idea of the enormous quantity of game that existed and was slain at that period. As settlement crept west the larger game moved before it.

In the autumn some of the settlers would organize hunting expeditions. One early resident remembered a hunt organized in 1860 at Garnett, Kansas. In the early part of October sixteen men with four wagons, a good supply of arms, ammunition, saddle horses, and other equipment, left for the buffalo country. Samuel Crawford, who a few years later became governor of the state, was elected captain of the expedition. On their return from the hunt a month later they brought four wagonloads of game of all kinds—buffalo, turkey, geese, ducks, deer, and a train-load of romantic experiences. The game was distributed to the people of the county and the girls in calico gave the heroes a buffalo dance.[6]

Sometimes these expeditions were for the express purpose of laying in a winter's supply of meat for a few families. Others were community expeditions which took the form of a more local hunt of a day or two, a kind of game drive, and ended in a big community feast or barbecue. Game formed a larger proportion of the diet than now. When short of supplies people sometimes lived for weeks on game alone.

Hunters were very wasteful. Many buffaloes were killed merely for the tongue which sold for fifty cents. At other times only the hump, a tasty morsel, was taken. J. Sterling Morton estimated that the average number of pounds of meat saved from each buffalo killed between the years 1860 and 1870 would not have exceeded twenty.[7] In the early seventies there was a limited demand for the meat in the East. The hind quarters only were taken for this purpose and were not skinned but shipped with the hides on. The front quarters were left on the prairie for the wolves to gnaw. Thousands

[6] Samuel J. Crawford, *Kansas In The Sixties* (Chicago, 1911), pp. 13, 14.
[7] J. Sterling Morton, "My Last Buffalo Hunt," *Nebraska Pioneer Reminiscences* (Cedar Rapids, Iowa, 1916), p. 224.

of bones cluttered up the prairie as a witness to the great destruction. The settlers camped near some stream or pool of water where the buffalo often came to drink. The hunter concealed himself behind some bank or in some low place where the unsuspecting beast was compelled to come for water. In this way the hunter often got four or five animals before they could get out of range of his rifle. There were millions of buffalo, and consequently few hunting parties returned without a good supply of hides and meat.

Buffalo hides were in good demand when properly tanned. Everyone on the prairies in the fifties slept over and under "buffaloes" as these robes were called. In most hotels or rooming houses the guest was obliged to find his own bedding and all travelers carried these furry skin blankets.

In order to keep the meat it was "jerked" or dried. There were two methods of "jerking" the meat. If the weather was the least bit damp, a scaffold was built by driving four forked sticks into the ground and laying other sticks on these until a complete scaffold was formed large enough to dry the flesh from a large buffalo. The flesh was cut from the bones and sliced into thin pieces, then dipped into boiling specially prepared brine; it was then hung over the rack. A slow fire of hot embers was used to cure it sufficiently to prevent spoiling. This could be done in less than a day's time. If flies were bad the smudge also kept them away from the meat. The second method was used when the weather was warm and dry as it usually was on the high plains in the buffalo country. The meat was prepared in the same manner except that no fire was placed under it; the wind and sun dried it in seven or eight hours so it would keep all summer in a dry place.[8]

The settlers often secured the services of Indian squaws to tan the hides for robes. Only those killed in the late fall or early winter were suitable for robes. These robe hides commanded as much as

[8] Charles Wesley Wells, *A Frontier Life* (Cincinnati, 1902), p. 27; "Donahoo Reminiscences," *Superior Express*, June 22, 1933; E. D. Haney, "The Experiences of a Homesteader in Kansas," Kansas State Historical Society *Collections*, Vol. XVII, p. 311.

SHOOTING BUFFALO ON THE LINE OF THE KANSAS PACIFIC

Frank Leslie's Illustrated Newspaper, 1871.

five dollars each. The ordinary hide probably averaged about two dollars and seventy-five cents in the seventies. The buffalo also furnished the tether with which his kin, the tame cow, was lariated. The hide of the buffalo made good raw-hide for all uses. The homesteaders cut the green hides into strips and dragged them behind their wagons. When cured, the hides were used in the dozen and one ways that hay wire served in later days—to repair things, to braid into lariats, and even to tether the pig or the old hen with her brood of chicks.[9]

Deer and elk were hunted in much the same manner as buffalo. They came into the wood along the streams for protection in the winter and were frequently easy prey for the settlers. The antelope was hunted by strategy. Old hunters, concealed among the grass or sandhills, placed a cap or handkerchief on the end of a ramrod, stuck it into the ground, and awaited developments. The antelope was a curious animal; lured on by this weakness, it circled the bait, drawing nearer at each circle until it fell by the hunter's bullet. The plains were heavily populated with antelope and the flesh was superior to mutton. The hide was also used in a variety of ways. When well tanned it was used for making trousers. The finest and best was used for shirting and was long a favorite shirt for hunters.[10]

Turkeys were plentiful and furnished a most savory dish. In the spring and summer the hens kept away from the damp tall grass and marshes of the lowlands and reared their flocks. The old birds kept their flocks where insects, weeds, and wild fruit sufficed for food until fall, when they brought their brood into the timber and corn fields. Settlers sometimes rode them down on the prairie. They could not fly far and were easily caught when tired, but usually they were hunted in the timber. They were wary birds and it was hard to slip up on a flock. Dogs were used to tree them. When scared, the bird sometimes forgot to hide and sat on a limb where

[9] Ibid., p. 309.
[10] A. D. Richardson, Beyond the Mississippi, p. 165; Charles Wesley Wells, op. cit., pp. 27–28.

the hunter killed it easily. They were frequently hunted by moon-light, also. Turkeys had a habit of roosting in flocks in the trees along the streams. The pioneer boys, having ascertained the roost by a daylight reconnoitering trip, arranged a hunting party at night by moonlight. Rifles were used and sometimes one person killed two or three birds but ordinarily one volley disturbed them too much for further success.[11]

Coon hunts were great sport for early settlers. Boys and young men particularly enjoyed getting together and sharing such a social evening. The raccoon lived along the wooded streams and was hunted with hounds. The dogs took up the trail of the animal which fled up a tree when closely pursued. In the earlier days it was cus-tomary for the husky young men to cut down the tree and watch the dogs fight the coon. Sometimes the coon would get away and climb another tree. Thus the great giant trees of the creek valleys were felled for sport. At a later time the coons were shot out of the tree. Men often stayed out all night at this sport.[12] Catamounts were sometimes killed in the same manner. In a limited way grey-hounds were used to hunt jack rabbits. No fences interfered with the sport, and, mounted on horses, the hunters followed the chase with the zeal of the fox hunters of old. Although timid by nature, the trained greyhounds also learned to kill coyotes.

The prairie chicken presented the easiest prey of all to the home-steader. They were very difficult to shoot and for that reason were not hunted much with a gun by the poverty-stricken homesteader. They were easily trapped, however. Some hunters set a figure four trap; this, when sprung, allowed an inverted box or chicken coop to drop to the ground imprisoning all under it. Others placed a covered box in the field with corn fastened on a swinging trap door. Sometimes as many as a dozen or fifteen chickens were caught in one night. In the seventies great quantities were shipped east each week

[11] G. Webb Bertram, "Reminiscences of Northwest Kansas," *Transactions*, Kan-sas State Historical Society, Vol. VII, p. 201.

[12] Noah Ard, personal interview, January 2, 1934.

from the little towns. One woman said that one year they ate about one hundred prairie chickens. They used only the smaller pieces; the breasts were dried and suspended on strings in the dugout for use in cold weather. Townsmen with fowling pieces and money to buy ammunition did more prairie chicken hunting than the rural dweller. Without the help of a dog these men were known to kill thirty or forty grown chickens during an hour in the field. By the middle seventies it was necessary to prohibit the killing of deer and to allow only a limited open season for prairie chickens.

Various kinds of fishing were engaged in. In some places shooting fish was a favorite sport. When the ice was on, two different methods of fishing were used. The first was by stunning. When the ice was crystal, the fish could be seen swimming along just underneath. The hunter struck the ice violently with the back of his axe just above the fish; this stunned the fish. The axeman then chopped a hole and brought out the fish with an improvised net. In an hour's time a fisherman could take as many fish as he could carry home. Snaring was also good sport and the means of capturing hundreds of pounds of fish. A hole was cut in the ice and a heavy brass wire loop, attached to a stick, inserted. When schools of fish sought the vent for air the choice fish were hooped out on the ice.

CHAPTER XIII

WHITES AND INDIANS

IN THE LAST FEW YEARS of the first quarter of the nineteenth century the United States made its first really serious effort to formulate a policy for handling the Indians. John C. Calhoun, Secretary of War in the administration of James Monroe, who was in charge of Indian affairs by virtue of his office, studied the question, and rendered his report to President Monroe on January 27, 1825. He advised that the Indians be moved to the territory beyond the Missouri River. The best scientific opinion reported that white men could not live there and yet this "Great American Desert" abounded with game which the Indians were accustomed to use for food.

Congress accepted Calhoun's scheme when Monroe presented it, and it remained a cardinal policy during the next fifteen years. The Plains Indians were induced to surrender a portion of their land to be used for homes for the eastern tribes which were moved beyond the Missouri River. In 1834 the Indian Intercourse Act forbade any person without license from the Indian commissioner to set foot on this Indian reserve. Furthermore a large part of this area was reserved permanently to the various tribes by clauses which guaranteed the territory to them forever.

As late as the end of President Jackson's second term, George Catlin, a man who knew Indians and the West, pronounced this region "almost one entire plain of grass, which is and ever must be, useless to cultivating man." [1]

The Sante Fe trade, the travel to Oregon, and later to California

---

[1] Frederic Logan Paxson, *History of the American Frontier* (Cambridge, Massachusetts, 1924), pp. 276–278.

upon the discovery of gold there, served to threaten the safety of the Indians in their new home. At first the emigrants merely traveled *through* the Indian country, but as the travelers saw fertile spots in the "desert" and began to start "road ranches" with a certain amount of primitive agriculture, ranching, and merchandising, the Indians' permanent home was doomed. Bit by bit the red man was pushed westward by various treaties. He was always near white settlement on the plains and was continually feared by the often panicky settler. For the most part, the relations between the two races were peaceable; indeed, the normal condition was one of peace. Occasional raids and massacres on both sides were exceptional. Hardly a battle of any consequence between armies of whites and Indians took place within the borders of Kansas, Nebraska, or the Dakotas.

In the fifties and sixties the Indians' tepee was no uncommon sight as the tribes migrated here and there. The red blankets of a group of Indians often made the Fourth of July celebrations picturesque and colorful.

When the first settlers crossed the eastern border of the Indian reserve, the aborigines, knowing their rights, demanded payment of each settler for the right to make improvements on land or town lots within the reservation and to which the Indians had neither relinquished their rights nor received payment. The settlers were anxious to locate on choice sites and paid the sums without complaint. At Omaha, Nebraska, the sum demanded was ten dollars from each man who built on the Indian holdings.

Indian manners and customs were different from those of the whites and often, when the Indian meant no harm but was following the best tribal etiquette, he alarmed the suspicious white people. Indians, like other primitive peoples, were very sociable and hospitable. They made frequent friendly calls and followed tepee etiquette. All the white man's houses which they had frequented were trading posts open to everyone. Their wigwams accommodated eight to ten families and property was held more or less in common.

Habit and usage, therefore, taught them to walk right into any dwelling without knocking, squat on the floor, smoke, or make themselves generally at home. The ways and habits of white men were strange and interesting, and they would pick up every cooking utensil and examine the women's clothes. The housewife, living under the constant dread of Indian attack, was naturally frightened nearly to death when she became conscious of a visitor and looked up from her work at the fireplace to see a burly bronzed warrior in her house. These children of the forest moved stealthily, and oftentimes the first warning the woman had of her unwelcome company was when she became aware of the presence of someone else in the room. In McPherson County, Kansas, Mrs. Finan Roy was absent-mindedly wiping dishes one day when without warning an Indian slapped her on the shoulder and yelled in her ear. She learned that he wanted some dead chickens which had died from cholera. She advised him not to eat them as he might get sick also, but he took them away. He also begged her for the family dog because it was fatter than the Indian dogs and consequently would make better eating.

In a settlement they entered every house they could and ate all they could get. Thus they went from house to house stripping the entire neighborhood of victuals. Their password was "Eat! Eat"! or if they could speak a little more English it was "Me heap hungry!" If the residents saw the redskins approach and fastened the door, the would-be-visitors sought a window, flattened their noses against the glass, and with the patience of the race watched the family program until the frantic house mother was glad to feed them to get rid of them. Groups of Indians often visited homes begging for food and picking up loose articles. They were the most persistent beggars imaginable, and it was a favorite saying among the settlers that they would steal the tires from a man's wagon wheels while he was driving at a trot. Sometimes settlers would take with them the cow, the coop of chickens, the stove, and practically everything they owned when going away to visit or to attend a social function some miles away, for fear the Indians would take the property while the family was gone.[2]

Albert D. Richardson, while traveling the overland trail in 1859, met numbers of the Indians begging and stealing from the travelers, asking particularly for whiskey and tobacco. Nearly all of these highway beggars bore certificates of good character from some white man. One solemn old brave proudly presented Richardson with this testimonial written by some wag: "This Indian is a drunkard, a liar, and a notorious old thief; look out for him."

When settlers became more numerous and less fearful of Indian attacks, they sometimes set the dog on the red men or applied a blacksnake whip to their bare legs.

In the territorial period, John Peterson, a shoemaker, and his bride, Mathilda, landed in eastern Nebraska. Mr. Peterson began to erect a frame building for a hotel. Since there were no lumber yards, he took his axe and adze and daily wrought lumber from the trees of the nearby forest. Among the inhabitants of the community was an Indian named No-Flesh who bore the reputation of being "no good." One day while Mr. Peterson was in the woods, his wife was busy frying doughnuts; No-Flesh and his companions sauntered around the log cabin, entered the room, and squatted on the floor. Although terrified, the young wife maintained her self-possession and continued with her doughnuts. The young woman accidently dropped one of the boiling hot morsels of baked dough; it rolled to the feet of No-Flesh and stopped. The wily son of the forest needed no invitation to reach out and pick up the sizzling circle but immediately he dropped it with a howl of dismay. To alleviate the pain, the Indian thrust his fingers into his mouth. The flavor caused him to forget the pain, and, picking up the cooling doughnut, he devoured it and called for more. For more than an hour the young matron stood over the fire baking the tasty morsels for the hollow redskins. Mr. Peterson arrived home just in time to see the last of

[2] Clara M. Fengel Shields, "The Lyon Creek Settlement," Kansas State Historical Society *Collections*, Vol. XIV, p. 150.

the supply disappearing down their throats. The young husband drove the unwelcome visitors away and the young bride collapsed from the strain. No-Flesh did not forget the doughnuts and later visited Mr. Peterson and proposed that they trade wives. The shoemaker, thinking it a joke, consented. No-Flesh was to bring three Indian women in return for the young wife who could fry doughnuts. One day while Mr. Peterson was called away on an errand, the young wife, busy at her work, looked out of the window and noticed No-Flesh accompanied by three squaws. Unadvised of the joke and frightened beyond measure, the young woman darted from the house and sped to the home of a neighbor a quarter of a mile away. No-Flesh, seeing the cherished prize dash away, gave pursuit. She reached the cabin a few steps ahead of the Indian and cried, "Save me!" No-Flesh was stopped at the muzzle of a rifle and explanations were demanded. It took a council of war and a bushel of doughnuts to heal the breach.

Often the relations between the two races was cordial. Humboldt, Kansas, was very prosperous in the fifties owing to a large traffic with the Indians to the southwest.[3] Sometimes the Indians did considerable trading with the settlers in the rural sections also. They secured calico, beads, bead pocket-books, and other merchandise from the trader and exchanged them with the settlers for something to eat. Raw-hide lariats were bartered for pork, watermelons, and other food. In the hunting season Indians, returning from a hunt, often stopped at the settlers' homes offering to trade buffalo for "hoggie" meat, as they called it, or for corn meal. Ordinarily the settler was glad to make the exchange, for pork became monotonous and fresh meat was welcome. In one vicinity a colony of Germans became very intimate with the Indians. The Indians furnished the Germans with fresh meat in return for wine and baked foods which were much appreciated. The congenial relationship grew to such an extent that some of the Indians learned to speak German.

[3] Charles F. Scott, *History of Allen and Woodson Counties* (Iola, Kansas, 1901), p. 93.

Contrary to the ordinary conception that the Indian is stolid and lacking in humor, the red man appreciated a joke and laughed as heartily at the discomfiture of a comrade as did a white man. The story is told that when Chief Red Cloud and his group of twenty warriors were on the way to Washington to see the Great White Father, they stopped at Fort Kearney and Major John Talbot invited them to his house for dinner. One took a big bite of mustard but kept a straight face. The others all around the circle did likewise until all had a mouthful and then all broke out in laughter together.[4]

The red man also had a sense of fair play and could relish a joke on one of his own race at the hands of a white man. Ben Vanthusen was boiling salt not far from where the city of Lincoln, Nebraska, now stands. A young Indian brave wanted to play a trick on him and approached him with the usual salutation, "How," and at the same time offered him a ramrod. When the white man reached out for it the Indian struck him across the knuckles. Ben returned the blow with his fist just under the Indian's ear. The latter fell backwards into the pan of boiling salt water. The accompanying braves made fun of their companion, calling him a squaw, and lionized the white man.

Sometimes the gratification of their sense of humor led to the so-called Indian scares. Lusty young men, like their white brothers, were ready for a romp and a frolic. A few drinks of the white man's fire water, procured from some unscrupulous member of the white race, added to the vigor of the frolic. In 1855 a straggling band of Omaha braves passed through the vicinity of Plattsmouth, Nebraska, and, having nothing else to do, began to yell and race their horses around the settlers' huts. This demonstration was interpreted as an attack and a tremendous "scare" followed. Men hooked up their cattle and horses, put their families and household goods into their wagons, and took flight to the nearest settlement for safety.

[4] Told by a granddaughter of Major Talbot, *Minden Courier*, Minden, Nebraska, March 27, 1931.

The Indians seeing the flight, in mere devilment, pursued. Faster the wagons flew, harder the men plied their whips, and louder the women screamed and the men cursed. In the panic, bedding, bureaus, tools, and effects were thrown overboard to lighten the loads. At last the Indians, tiring of the sport, halted, rode back, gathered up the discarded property, and putting it safely in a pile, rode away to brag over the exploit.

Sometimes an Indian scare was perpetrated by a small group of white men who were imbued with a spirit of deviltry or a desire to play a practical joke. Such a scare was often enough to throw a whole region into a panic.

A dance was held at Pierpont, Day County, South Dakota, on Thanksgiving in 1890. There was some talk that evening about Indian troubles nearby. Some reported that a number of settlers had been massacred in other places. Some of the young men had been drinking a little and were ready for some fun. They threw red blankets over their shoulders and chased one young man, firing a few shots to give the attack color. When the young man reached home and told his parents that people were being killed and that he had been pursued, the parents, who had been in an Indian raid in the sixties and remembered their earlier experience, drove to Bristol and gave the alarm. It spread quickly and, since there was no telephone to Pierpont to verify the matter, the panic spread widely. Newspapers came out the next day with stories of how the Indians had swooped down upon Day County and killed most of the people. Train crews were prepared to carry away the women and children. The train was crowded with the sheriff standing guard on the rear platform to club off the Indians. When the people learned of the joke, they were almost ready to lynch the jokers, who were arrested but were released on payment of their fines.[5]

In 1882 a report was spread in Aberdeen, South Dakota, that settlers had been massacred in Spink County. The scare came about

[5] L. G. Ochsenreiter, *History of Day County* (Mitchell, South Dakota, 1908), pp. 48–49.

in this manner: A party of men had set out to establish LaFoon and sought to liven up things a little by making some fun. Some of the men dressed in ragamuffin style and arranged for a confederate to take a German lad out for a trip; this wild-looking crowd bore down upon the youth and felled the confederate with a blow. The boy fled to Redfield telling that he had been attacked by savages and his companion slain. The authorities sent word to Fort Sisseton and United States regulars were ordered into the field. The president of the North Western Railway went from Huron on an engine at high speed and offered to transport help at once. Citizens got out firearms of every description and an "army" of thirty or forty men on horses was dispatched to the camp of the town founders. A short distance from town they met men from the camp who had started out to look for the frightened German boy and who explained it was all a joke.[6]

Sometimes the settlers were victims of their own imaginations. In one instance the alarm was spread and the people all rushed to town. A reconnoitering party was sent out to investigate. They found the "Indian camp" and the objects of their scare, about one hundred and fifty shocks of cane.

White families were always more or less in danger from marauding parties of Indians who stopped to beg or steal and commit minor depredations. Ocassionally a settler was killed in the defense of his property or by a drunken celebrator.

At other times, however, the Indians, goaded on by the relentless westward pressure of white settlement which pushed them farther and farther into the more arid and unfruitful portion of the plains, and seeing the game, their living, melt away before this invasion of their domains, rose up in organized rebellion. Sometimes these outbreaks were caused by the white man's violation of treaties. Again they were caused by the failure of the Indian agent to deliver their annuities or provisions. Unscrupulous Indian agents were to blame for many breaches of the peace. Sheer hunger at times forced the

---

[6] *Aberdeen Argus News*, June 1 and 2, 1931, p. 2.

Indians to leave their reservations in search of food. Indians were often given whiskey until they became drunk and traded their furs off for a song. Sobering up and becoming conscious of the deception, they went out to wreak vengeance on the innocent settler or prairie traveler.

Sometimes certain members of a tribe signed a treaty giving away the tribal lands. Many, not in agreement, declared themselves not bound by a treaty which they had no part in making. One such occurrence happened in the eastern Dakota Territory. A group of Yanktonais Indians claimed they owned an interest in all Sioux lands and they resented the presence of the white settler in the valley. They threatened to kill the chiefs who had signed away their lands, and vowed they would drive the white men from the Sioux Valley. Chief Lean Dog with 1,500 warriors advanced on the settlers at Medary. The settlers tried to buy off the chief by offering the band provisions for a feast. Lean Dog, however, refused the offer saying he did not care about a feast; he could have all the food in town since there were only sixteen men holding the townsite. He ordered the whites to leave before sundown. They allowed the settlers food enough to last four days and plundered the settlement. Behind the refugees arose the smoke of the burning buildings of the new town. It was not uncommon for so-called friendly or treaty Indians to rob trains and frontier settlers, hoping the deviltry would be charged against the hostile tribes.[7]

One of the most notable general attacks of the Indians was that of 1864. On August 7, the Indians attacked every ranch and station between Big Sandy and Denver. It was a beautiful morning and the attack was made at nearly the same hour, near mid-day, all along the stage line. A certain number of warriors were allotted certain points along the trail. This simultaneous attack of the Cheyenne-Sioux led by Black Kettle and others, was the consummation of plans laid a month before. In nearly every instance it was successful.

[7] Albe B. Whiting, "Some Western Border Conditions in the 50's and 60's," Kansas State Historical Society *Collections*, Vol. XII, p. 8.

The Indians appeared at the stations as they were in the habit of doing and were received kindly. Without a moment's warning, they began to shoot down their victims, mutilate bodies, burn houses, and carry away captives and plunder. Captain H. E. Palmer, on his way to Fort Kearney near Big Sandy, met ranchmen, freighters, and stage coach passengers on horseback fleeing from the Little Blue Valley. They told a terrible story of how the Indians just to the west had massacred none-knew-how-many people. He passed a ranch and there found little children from three to seven years old who had been taken by the heels and swung around against the log house until their heads were beaten into a jelly. The hired girl was found not far from the ranch, staked out on the prairie, tied by her hands and feet, her nude body full of arrows and terribly mangled. The owner of the ranch was not far away, horribly mutilated, and the buildings were burned. The next day Captain Palmer passed seventy wagons which had been loaded with merchandise en route to Denver. The teamsters had mounted their mules and made their escape. The Indians had opened boxes containing dry goods, taken great bolts of calico and other goods, carried off all they wanted, and scattered much more over the prairie.[8]

This attack naturally caused great fear among the settlers all over the plains. In Buffalo County, Nebraska, the settlers placed their movable property in wagons and driving their cattle before them, took the trail for the Missouri River. Practically the whole country as far as the Missouri River was deserted. When the fleeing settlers reached Omaha, one hundred and fifty miles to the east, they found the stores closed and every able-bodied man pressed into service; armed mounted men patrolled the country for miles outside the village of Omaha. This was known as "the stampede."

The speculative settlers were disturbed most of all by the fact that these Indian scares stopped immigration. As soon as the first sharp

[8] Captain H. E. Palmer, Company A, 11th Kansas Volunteer Corps, "History of the Powder River Expedition," *Transactions and Reports*, Nebraska State Historical Society, Vol. II, p. 197.

pangs of the attack were over attention was directed to minimizing the scare and keeping the news from traveling beyond the borders of the territory involved. In the very midst of an Indian scare in South Dakota, James M. Allen in a letter to his father said:

> The news of this Indian difficulty will travel all over the country and we cannot expect any more immigration this way before next spring; and from all accounts there were large numbers enroute to settle in the Big Sioux valley who will now turn back. I fear immigration will be retarded for several years.

The German settlers of Grand Island, in characteristic German fashion, took steps to defend their town. They built a fort of logs twenty-four by twenty-four feet with twenty-five loopholes. They had ample ammunition, a good supply of provisions, and were well organized. In one corner of the fort a well was dug. They built an underground stable eighty-eight feet long and a cattle yard within range of the guns of the fort. Another fortification consisting of a sod wall was built around the business houses. At each corner was a tower of green cottonwood logs projecting out far enough to permit the defenders to shoot anyone who might crawl under cover of the breastworks from the outside. The government gave them a cannon, and squads of men were sent out daily to reconnoitre. At different points piles of straw and brush were placed to be set on fire to alarm those absent of the approach of hostile Indians. This thorough preparation enabled the citizens to remain in the settlement during the great stampede. At Tekamah, Nebraska, as the result of an Indian raid, the settlers appealed to the governor of the territory who responded by organizing the settlers into a company, and enlisting and mustering them into the United States Army. Regular army equipment was supplied and each man drew rations of flour, sugar, bacon, coffee, and so forth, which was transported from the capital. A government blockhouse, forty feet square and two stories high, was made of logs. After the Indian scare had subsided the company was discharged. This organization performed a double service to the settlers. It provided protection, paying the settlers for protecting themselves, and furnished welcome provisions free.

In some instances individuals built protections against the savages for themselves. In 1866 two Union soldiers, fresh from the front, went to a spot near Junction City, Kansas, took up land, built a log cabin of split logs and covered it with dirt so that the savages could not burn it. To further protect themselves they built an underground passage-way leading from a trap-door inside the cabin to a square fort built up like a pyramid outside the cabin. It was made of solid logs and dirt; it had four loopholes but no entrance above ground.

When on the war path, the redskins often pillaged and plundered for the sheer joy of breaking things. In one instance the flour was mixed with the molasses. In another, the feathers were picked from the chickens and those fowls which had not died, were found running around in a nude condition when the settlers returned. This was presumably the work of squaws who seemed to have a cruel desire to mutilate and destroy. The primitive red man also valued certain things which were not held in the same esteem by the settlers, and he often destroyed valuable property in order to secure what he fancied. Canvas and bed-ticking were valued highly by the Indians and they quite frequently emptied the feather beds and pillows to secure the ticks. One Kansas woman remarked that after an Indian raid the prairies looked as if a June snowstorm had visited the country. Mr. I. N. Hunter of Nebraska said that his mother had picked up enough feathers from two feather beds to make two pillows after a raid on her home.[9] When a Kansas emigrant train was robbed in 1857, the Indians took the covers off the wagons, looted them of all clothing and bedding, emptied flour, meal, and dried fruit on the ground, and carried off the sacks.

In the trail attack of August 7, 1864, in Hall County, Nebraska, two boys, Nathaniel, fourteen, and Robert, eleven, the sons of

---

[9] I. N. Hunter, "Recollections of Weeping Water, Nebraska," *Nebraska Pioneer Reminiscences* (Cedar Rapids, Iowa, 1916), p. 36.

George Martin, had a narrow escape which was noteworthy indeed. The boys had come to Nebraska with their parents in 1862, homesteading twelve miles north of Juniata. The two boys and their father had been out making hay all day. When they were almost ready to drive their loads home, nine Indians rode up. They attacked the father first, who was a quarter of a mile ahead of the boys. They shot at him, but he flattened himself out on the top of the load in the depression made by the boom or binding pole. Grabbing his repeating rifle with its six shells, he wounded one Indian and shot a pony in the neck just as its rider drew back his bow to shoot from under the pony's neck. The wounded pony was unable to hold up his head, and the Indian abandoned him and started toward the boys. The boys, seeing him coming, unhitched, and the older boy placed his brother on the horse and climbed on behind. They rode to a little knoll and hid there.

In the meantime George Martin continued his fight with the Indians. Letting the horses go, he devoted his attention solely to repelling the attack. When the Indians heard him shoot the third time, they dropped back in surprise. They were not used to a gun shooting more than twice, and thought they had him after the second shot. One followed cautiously, however, and succeeded in shooting from behind the load. The arrow struck the father in the neck, slicing the jugular vein and lodging in the collar bone. The team, unguided, passed close by the house and as they went by the door the man dropped off. The Indian followed him around the load and would have killed him had it not been for his daughter, Hepzibah, who rushed out of the cabin with the old shot gun and scared the Indian away. The wife dragged her husband into the house. She fastened up the gash in the jugular vein with a pin and, racing to the barn, secured a horse hair which she twisted around and around the pin closing the wound and stopping the flow of blood.

The savages, finding the family at the house well armed and fortified, turned back and found the boys in their hiding place behind the ridge. The old mare which the boys were riding had a colt in the barn and made a dash toward her offspring. The Indians apparently did not care to hurt the boys but wanted the horse and attempted to head her off from the house. When cornered, the mare became belligerent, grabbed one Indian's pony by the nape of the neck and shook it, almost throwing the rider. When another got too close, the mare grabbed his blanket and jerked. The boys tried to grab his bow, but failed. The Indians then began shooting. The first arrow lodged in Nathaniel's elbow. Nearly distracted with pain, he broke it off before he thought. The second also struck the older boy, entering his back just under the shoulder blade near the backbone. It went through the right lung and came out below the right breast sticking into Robert's backbone tight enough to hold. A third grazed Nat's hip, making a flesh wound, and stuck into Bob's hip. The horse rushed on toward the house at break-neck speed, while the arrow shaft with its feathers working back and forth in the lung with each bound of the horse, caused intense pain. Finally when not far from the house, the boys fell off the horse together, the fall tearing the shaft of the arrow out of the younger boy's body. The blood began spurting from Nat's wound. The Indians finally captured the mare after she became entangled in the lines. Three Indians went back to see the boys. They paid no attention to the older boy, no doubt thinking a person with an arrow entirely through his body could not possibly live. They hit the younger boy on the head a number of times to be sure he was dead. One said, "Shall we scalp them?" Another answered, "Papoose scalp no good," and they left the brothers. The boys finally crawled to the barn and lay down there. Weak from loss of blood and the shock of the experience, they lost consciousness.

The family, thinking the boys were dead and afraid to remain on the ranch, started for Fort Kearney. The next day on the insistence of the family, a party of freighters went back with them and found Nathaniel and Robert twenty hours after they had received their supposedly mortal wounds. The mother was overjoyed at finding her sons alive. The father found the string attached to the arrow-head of the shaft which had broken off in the older boy's elbow and pulled the arrow-head out with a pair of shoeing pincers. The arrow-head measured four inches in length. The arrow which had pinned the boys together was pushed and drawn through Nat's body. The family then loaded the boys into a wagon and started for the nearest doctor at Nebraska City, one hundred and sixty miles away. Nat felt he could never stand the terrible jolting and the family stopped en route. After hanging between life and death for days, the boys both recovered and the unbroken family returned to their home. Nat lived to tell of the experience three score years afterward.

During the years 1865 to 1868 there were numerous attacks on the frontier. In Jefferson County, Nebraska, two men, Bennett and Abernathy, who had a ranch between Meridian and Hebron, were attacked and retreated to a cave in the bluffs. The Indians carried combustibles, filled the entrance, and set fire to them. The two white men were smothered.

These raids of the sixties were numerous and general all along the frontier. Men and boys were shot, and women and horses were taken captive. Devastation, death, and fear reigned on the prairies. At Dwight, Nebraska, a seventeen-year-old girl and her twin brothers were captured by the Sioux while the rest of the family was away from home. Another sister escaped from the house and spread the alarm. The children had nothing to eat for days on end and at one time in order to keep from starving, the girl scraped a deer hide that had lain in the sun for several days. One week she had nothing to eat but a handful of corn.

On July 23, 1867, a party of Indians attacked a small settlement on the Blue River in Jefferson County, Nebraska. Approaching the home of Peter Ulbrick they found the father, mother, and two children, Peter Junior, aged twelve, and Veronica, aged fifteen, in the field hoeing corn. The children were on the opposite side of the field from the parents who did not notice the Indians until the screams of the children startled them. The parents were powerless to assist and hastened to the house where two other children were busy with household duties. Loading them into a farm wagon with a few household goods and other cherished possessions, they fled to a ranch some miles away. There they met other neighbors who gathered to tell tales of depredation and slaughter. It was a sad meeting, for hardly a family had escaped unscathed. After a few days a searching party took the trail of the Indians. Proceeding about two miles they found the boy's body, his head crushed by a tomahawk blow and his scalp torn off. There was no trace of the girl and the searchers gave up the chase. A petition signed by the heads of sixty-seven families asked the governor to aid in securing military assistance from the Federal Government.[10] Veronica Ulbrick was kept a prisoner for eighteen months, subjected to nameless abuse and mistreatment, and was finally returned through an exchange of prisoners with the Indians at North Platte. Her mind was never normal again and in 1933 she was living the life of a recluse, cared for by friends.

During the middle sixties many settlements were attacked, men scalped, and women taken prisoners. At North Platte at the time Veronica Ulbrick was returned, sixteen other women and girls were released by the Indians. The Indians began to feel that the more women they captured and held the better ransom and terms they would secure. To the mind of the Indian it became more profitable to steal women than horses, prized though these anmials were.

Above and beyond the actual losses suffered from savage attacks was the terrible strain on the pioneers who lived in daily dread of an Indian. Women, having heard of recent savage attacks with kidnappings, rape, and murder, lived in awful fear of what might come to them any day. With husband gone for a three-day trip to the mill or to town, the strongest heart quailed. Ted Oliver of Buffalo County, Nebraska, recalled vividly having spent long hours on the roof of his log house looking for Indians. Sarah Finch of Custer

[10] In 1931 upon the construction of the new Nebraska state house and razing of the old state house, a large accumulation of papers was consigned to the bonfire. When a workman threw a quantity of these into the incinerator, a document fell to the floor. The workman picked it up and found this petition which had been sent to the governor sixty-four years before. His attention was arrested when he saw the name Ulbrick on the petition. His sister had married Alfred W. Ulbrick who was caring for Veronica Ulbrick.

County, Nebraska, was left much alone and her husband prepared a box of sugar mixed with strychnine which she carried with her for three years. She knew Indians liked sugar and whenever one obtained any, he would never taste it until the whole band was present. Then seated in a ring he would pass the delicacy around, dropping a small portion in each hand. At a given signal when all had been served, they ate it. It is easy to see what would have happened had the Indians captured her and eaten her sugar.[11]

One of the last and most striking battles between the Indian and the white man on the central plains, was the battle of Arickaree fought near the boundary line separating Cheyenne County, Kansas, and Colorado. This battle was an event culminating the numerous Indian raids. A body of Indians, called renegades, composed of parts of several tribes, raided the settlers in the Saline and Solomon Valleys, killed a number of people, drove away horses, and took two young women captive. Many of the settlers were soldiers, discharged from the Union armies only three years before, and were ready to grapple with the foe. Consequently, when General Philip Sheridan announced that he would raise a company to attack hostile Indians in the western part of Kansas, in a few days a large number of these ex-soldiers, buffalo hunters, and other frontiersmen appeared at Fort Harker. It was not difficult to secure fifty select men with Colonel George A. Forsythe of Sheridan's staff in command and Lieutenant Fred Beecher, a nephew of Henry Ward Beecher, second in command.

Hastening up the Smoky Hill River two hundred miles to Fort Wallace, they were supplied with ammunition, sustenance, pack mules, and horses. About the tenth of September this little company of fifty left Fort Wallace in pursuit of approximately two hundred and fifty Indians. After following the trail for a few days, the old scouts became convinced that they were following a much larger number of Indians than had at first been estimated. Nevertheless the command was anxious to push onward. One evening the com-

---

[11] S. D. Butcher, *Pioneer History of Custer County*, p. 42.

pany camped on the bank of the Arickaree, a branch of the Republican River. Fearing an assault, the scouts selected a sandy island, in the middle of the dry river bed as a place to make a stand in case of attack.

Just at daybreak, September seventeenth, the sentinels gave warning and rode into camp followed by the mounted savages who were shouting and waving blankets. With exultant shouts and battle songs Cheyenne, Arapahoe, and Sioux warriors, stripped naked and painted, bore down upon the little company like a mighty cloudburst. The white men rushed to the island and, sheltering themselves as best they could, resisted the charge of the relentless red men. The oncoming warriors, riding at high speed, were determined to obliterate that little handful of resolute defenders. The repeating rifles in the hands of unerring marksmen wrought havoc with the swift riders. Volley after volley was poured into the charging braves. The painted warriors reeled and fell from their saddles. Soon the remnants of that majestic charge, riderless horses and unharmed warriors, swept over the defenders' position, mingling friend and foe in one mass of disorganized confusion. The Indians rode back to the hills skirting the river, picking up some of their dead and wounded as they went.

As opportunity offered, the soldiers lying on the ground dug into the sand with knives and scooped it up with their hands, improvising sand pits which afforded protection from the enemy. Indians, in the meantime, began crawling toward the trenches through the tall grass. Whenever a scout raised his head it became a mark for the Indians, and whenever the grass moved, a bullet sped on its message of death toward the redskin creeping there. During the first hour every horse was killed. A little after ten o'clock the scouts noticed Roman Nose, a gallant Cheyenne chief who claimed he bore a charmed life, preparing to lead an attack. The riflemen felt that their last hour had come. Dead men's rifles were loaded and placed in readiness for fast firing and every man resolved to sell his life as dearly as possible. Several scouts centered their fire on the chief. His spear fell from his hand. He was about to fall from his horse when, grasping the mane of his steed, he steadied himself; his warriors gathered around him and bore him from the field mortally wounded. Thus the second magnificent charge was turned back.

Several more futile attempts were made to reach this island. Suddenly at about two-thirty in the afternoon, the defenders discerned by aid of their field glasses that Dull Knife, an old celebrated warrior of the Sioux tribe, was preparing to lead a charge. He was a favorite chief and was considered a sage and a prophet. He now appeared in full dress wearing a gorgeous war-bonnet reaching from the crown of his head to the ground and which distinguished him among his people as a warrior of renown. He addressed the braves, formed his mounted fighters in line, took his place in the lead, swung his gun over his head, and encouraged his speeding warriors to battle. Colonel Forsythe, lying wounded in a pit, ordered his men not to fire until the enemy was in close range. Before this new charge was near the island those grim plainsmen picked off the gallant old chief. His horse turned and fled to the hills, followed by the warriors. Here they were met by the squaws with poles, clubs, and sticks, threatening them and urging them to return for the chief. They responded to this by marching on foot in a body and bearing away the great leader amid a hail of bullets. At the foot of the hills they were met by the acclamations of the squaws. The battle had ended. Hundreds of warriors lay on the bloody sand of the Arickaree.

Half the little frontier company was wounded. Colonel Forsythe lay with a broken leg caused by a bullet through his thigh. Lieutenant Beecher, for whom this island was later named, died from wounds that evening. The doctor was disabled and died during the day, depriving the wounded of medical care. No food nor water was available that long day. When the friendly shades of night finally fell, the survivors dug a hole six feet deep and secured enough muddy water to fill the canteens. Before midnight a council decided to send a request for aid. Jack Stillwell and Pete Trudell volunteered to attempt to pass through the Indian lines to go to Fort Wallace, eighty-five miles away on a straight line. The Indians would be watchful for communications with the fort and it would be necessary to take a circuitous route, increasing the distance to one hundred and twenty-five miles. Capture by the Indians meant certain death, yet these brave men risked their lives for the good of the group. Starting at midnight, they were only three miles from Beecher's Island by daybreak. They sheltered themselves in a hollow bank overhung with grass and sunflowers. The second day they hid in a swamp which was unfortunately close to an Indian village. The morning of the third day they concluded they were far enough from the scene of battle to travel by daylight. To their dismay they sighted a group of Cheyennes. Fortune favored them again, however. They found the carcass of a buffalo which had been killed some time before. Enough hide hung to the bleaching bones to form a shelter; and the scouts gratefully crawled into this acceptable though inelegant hiding place. The scouts met two colored messengers en route to the camp of Company H, Tenth United States Cavalry, only seventy miles from Beecher's Island. These messengers hastened on to their company. Colonel Carpenter in command of that unit, started at once to look for Beecher's Island. Meanwhile the two scouts had reached the fort. At midnight of September twenty a command left the fort with ample ammunition, wagons, and supplies.

While this was taking place the Indians continued to besiege the island. The wounded suffered greatly. The carcasses of the horses supplied food. The boiled horse meat was sprinkled with plenty of powder to cover the taste of the badly tainted flesh.

On the night of the third day no help having arrived, it was concluded that the two messengers had perished. Two more men started for relief. They fortunately intercepted Colonel Carpenter whose only knowledge of the location of Beecher's Island was what his messengers had obtained from the first two scouts. One of the men mounted a mule and guided Colonel Carpenter to the scene of the battle. On the morning of the ninth day after the battle, the guard aroused the worn and weary men with cries of "Indians! Indians"! With ammunition low and spirits still lower, every man felt that the end had come. Grasping their rifles, the resolute plainsmen stood ready to sell their lives as dearly as possible in this final attack. On the distant hill could be seen a dark line of mounted men riding at great speed. Suddenly the sabers and carbines gleaming in the sun, showed the grim veterans that help had arrived. Cheer upon cheer was given by those powder-stained scouts for the dusky-skinned members of Colonel Carpenter's colored rescuers. Men embraced one another, and tears rolled down cheeks that had withstood the shock of battle. Tenderly the survivors of this clash were taken to Fort Wallace. The battle of Arickaree became traditional among the Indians as one of the most disastrous events in the long roll of clashes between the red man and white. In recent years it has been ascertained through Indians who were engaged in the battle that they lost between seven and eight hundred braves.[12]

[12] Winfield Freeman, "The Battle of Arickaree," *Transactions*, Kansas State Historical Society, Vol. VI, pp. 346–357.

CHAPTER XIV

COLONIES AND COLONIZING AGENCIES

THERE WERE three distinct boom periods in the settlement of the trans-Missouri prairie. The pre-Civil War period brought in a rush of settlers which engulfed the eastern portion of the tier of prairie states and which was ended abruptly by the panic of 1857. During the War only a very small migration continued. With the close of the War and the release of a large number of men onto the labor market by reason of mustering out a million men to take their places in civil life, a second migration began. This was stopped as abruptly as the first by the panic of 1873. For a time there was little movement of population, but by 1879 the last and greatest boom period of our whole history as a nation had begun. This period lasted from 1878 to 1886. In 1880 the population of Kansas was 996,096. In 1887 it was 1,518,552, an increase of 552,456 in seven years. The population of Nebraska likewise increased more than 600,000 between 1880 and 1890.[1] In Dakota a great expanse of hitherto almost uninhabited territory became, in a decade, a sufficiently populous region to be admitted to the Union in 1889 as two states. During the eighteen year period ending June 30, 1880, the whole number of homestead and preëmption claims filed was only 44,122. The land office records show that in the following year and a half 16,718 claims were entered.[2]

Of the various factors which caused the great rush of settlement

---

[1] Hallie Farmer, "The Economic Background of Frontier Populism," *Mississippi Valley Historical Review*, Vol. X, p. 410.

[2] Harold E. Briggs, "The Great Dakota Boom, 1879 to 1886," *North Dakota Historical Quarterly*, Vol. IV, p. 78. The total number of acres filed on in Dakota prior to the census of 1880 was 7,381,880. In the nineteen months succeeding it was 1,029,280.

in the eighties the first in importance was probably the natural land hunger of the people in the eastern states who began to long to exploit the new western domain. Hamlin Garland who left Iowa to take a claim in the Jim (James) River Valley in Dakota gives us something of the popular psychology in the eighties.[3] Settlers were stampeding toward Dakota. Nothing else was talked about when the neighbors met. In vain the papers and Farmer's Institute lecturers advised cattle raising and diversified farming, predicting wealth for those who stayed in Iowa, but the exodus continued toward the prairies west of the Missouri River. "We are wheat farmers and we intend to keep in the wheat belt," they answered. Some who were well fixed in Iowa, said, "It seems a pity to waste all my rights." They referred to the fact that by staying in Iowa they would miss a chance to take advantage of their rights as citizens to file on government land.[4]

Others emphasized the usual allurements of a new country—the deep black soil, the coarse wheat stubble, the heavy growth of prairie grass; and in addition it was being populated with genial people. To the Iowa farmer's protest that North Dakota was too cold, the "boomer" replied that it was a good thing for the ground to freeze, that the soil froze down five or six feet and kept in the water. The spring thaw was gradual, it was argued, and the grass roots went down with the thaw and were well supplied with water. Stock lived right out on the prairie grass all winter.[5]

A second factor, and one of the greatest agencies, was the railroad. The railroad companies endowed with land by a benevolent national government, were anxious to convert the land into cash before it became a tax liability. Then, too, every settler in the territory served by the road became a potential customer, raising crops to be shipped and requiring manufactured goods on the transportation of which the railroad reaped a profit. In short, the railroad cared little

[3] Hamlin Garland, *A Son of the Middle Border* (New York, 1917), p. 234.
[4] J. H. Shepherd, "Tales of the Early Settlers," *Quarterly Journal*, University of North Dakota, Vol. XIII, p. 269.
[5] *Ibid.*, p. 270.

whether an emigrant bought railroad land or took free land from the government. Settling up the country enhanced the value of the railroad's alternate sections and created future business for the company.

A third factor was the immigration activities of the local governments. Each state had its immigration board. Many counties had immigration commissioners, and cities and towns through chambers of commerce, real estate boards, and other organizations, presented claims that their particular localities were better than others for settlement.[6] In some cases a hundred dollars was collected by public subscription for printing pamphlets to inform prospective settlers of the virtues of the country.

As a result of the work of the railroads in advertising the land, numerous colonies were organized and immigrants came in bodies to the new country. In the early seventies the competition between the various railroads for settlers waxed warm. The Santa Fe, Union Pacific, and Burlington Railways, were keen competitors. Each sent agents to Europe to agitate for migration to the New World. These agents vied with one another in their glowing accounts of the territory through which their particular roads ran. The railroads printed lithographed pictures, maps, flowery descriptions of the productivity of the country, and glowing accounts of those who had succeeded on the prairies. Free land was the big drawing card. Probably an attempt was made to give a fairly accurate picture, yet no pains were spared to depict the favorable side, although no mention was made of the hardships and more unfortunate aspects of the country.

The railroads made luring offers, among which were greatly reduced transportation rates for passengers and their baggage and freight. Seed was sometimes given to the emigrants, feed for stock was hauled free, and other accommodations were rendered. Emigrant houses were built in central locations where land hunters might stay without payment for lodging while they hunted for land.

The states also entered into keen competition for foreign emi-

---

[6] Hallie Farmer, *op. cit.*, p. 409.

grants. The following letter from Mr. C. B. Neilson, Nebraska's immigrant agent for Denmark, Sweden, and Norway, gives a view of the situation:

Dear Sir: Victory! The battle is won for our state, but it was a hard fought battle; a great deal harder than I imagined. The fall emigration to Nebraska of people with sufficient capital to commence work on our prairies will be very large. On Monday I go to Sweden and Norway, and will have easy work there. I shall try my best to beat the agent for Minnesota, Col. Mathison, formerly secretary of state, but now in Sweden. The truth shall and must be known all over this country.

All the papers here will now come out in favor of our state; but I had to face them by threatening to lecture publicly about Nebraska—a step now unnecessary.[7]

Group after group of foreigners was sent across the ocean accompanied by agents or representatives of the state or railroad. In some instances in which there was no official representative on board ship of the company which started them from Europe, a rival company's agent persuaded them by smooth talk or better offers to settle in a territory far from the original destination.

The terms for railroad land were easy. The Union Pacific offered eleven years' credit. Only one-tenth of the purchase price was to be paid at the time of sale. Deferred payments bore interest at the rate of six or seven per cent but for the first three years the purchaser was required to pay interest only. If an emigrant chose to buy on six years' credit a ten per cent reduction was made in the price and one-fifth of the purchase price was due at the time of sale. For cash a twenty-five per cent discount was made from the original price of the land. At Gibbon, Nebraska, in 1871 the price was three dollars per acre. Another way in which those with money secured land at a discount was by buying railroad bonds and trading them for land. The land grant bonds of the Atchison, Topeka, and Santa Fe Railway were selling at sixty-five per cent of their face value in the seventies. These bonds, however, were accepted at face value on payment for land. A Mennonite bishop at Berdiansk, Russia, entrusted the Santa Fe representative with $56,000 in the form of a draft on Hamburg to invest in land grant bonds of the Santa Fe. The bonds were then offered in payment of land at face value. When the Union Pacific was selling land at four dollars an acre, one man reported that he had secured his land for $2.70 an acre by means of this financial maneuver.

The Santa Fe sent Mr. C. B. Schmidt to agitate for removal among the German Mennonites in Russia. The Russian authorities objected to his agitation and he was obliged to leave secretly. The Santa Fe and the state of Kansas joined in making the Sunflower State an attractive field of migration. In 1874 the state law was amended to free from military service those who belonged to non-resistance groups. The Santa Fe printed this law in German and distributed it in Russia. The company carried seventeen cars of goods free of charge from Pennsylvania to Kansas and carried Mennonite passengers free for three months.

Since most of the Mennonite emigrants were ignorant as to methods of withstanding the wiles of land agents and of buying tickets, making transfers, and other matters of travel procedure, a Mennonite Board of Guardians was created. The Board had Mennonites who had resided for some time in America, meet newcomers and assist them in every possible way. The Mennonites left various parts of Russia in July, 1874, and, arriving in New York, scattered to different sections of the United States. A large group, if not the largest, about 1,900 persons, settled in Kansas. Arriving in Topeka at one time, they attracted much attention. Their peculiar dress and manners were very apparent. They brought a quarter of a million dollars in gold. The railroad housed them in large empty brick buildings which had been built for car shops but in which the machinery had not been installed. These buildings, encompassing several acres, sheltered the aliens for four weeks. The Topeka merchants did a thriving business during their stay. Daily processions of these people were seen traveling between their improvised dormitory and the mercantile establishments. They also purchased 60,000 acres of land.[8]

Like most other people, large numbers of Mennonites arrived in America very poor. The Guardianship helped them to the amount of $100,000.[9] The well-to-do among them built frame houses while the poorer classes lived in dugouts. Since these people had been in the habit of living in villages in Russia they tried to carry out the old plan in their new home in certain places. One such interesting experiment occurred at Peabody, Kansas. Twenty-four families from the Crimea founded "Guadenau" or Grace Valley. This plan was followed: Five sections were purchased and the village was located in the center of this block of territory. The other sections were arranged in such a manner as to edge with the center section. Every other section was government land. The five sections purchased were railroad land. A street was laid out through the middle of the center section. The variety of types of houses indicated the financial ability of the owner. Some were sod, some frame, and some were sod with a wooden roof. The village scheme would not work in the new country. In 1925 there were seven sects of Mennonites in Kansas numbering 10,250 adults over fifteen years of age. In smaller numbers they were scattered through the other states. A group on its way to Kansas in 1873 was intercepted by the Dakota commissioner of immigration. He stopped the group and took three representatives to see the Dakota land which was all free. They returned with a satisfactory report; and that is the origin of the Mennonite settlements on the James River. This valley houses practically all the Mennonites in the Dakotas.[10]

In numerous places the railroads built immigrant houses for the

---

[8] The following Kansas counties received the most of this first tide of immigration: Marion, Harvey, Reno, McPherson, and Barton. Abraham Albrecht, *Mennonite Settlement in Kansas*, MS. Master's Thesis, University of Kansas, 1925, p. 36.

[9] *Ibid.*, Chapter I.

[10] Gertrude S. Young, "The Mennonites in South Dakota," South Dakota Historical *Collections*, Vol. X, pp. 485–486; Herbert S. Schell, "Official Immigration Activities of Dakota Territory," *North Dakota Historical Quarterly*, Vol. VII, p. 15.

settlers to live in while building their houses. One of these, built by the Burlington Railway Company, was described as a long frame building of one room with a cookstove in each end. The Sante Fe made each settlement a present of four sections in the middle of the settlement valued at $3,200 and built two large emigration barracks, eighteen by two hundred feet each, where they could live near to their future homes until the dwellings were completed. Later these buildings were used for churches until suitable buildings could be constructed. At length these gift sections were divided into eighty acre tracts which the poor people could buy at a low figure. The money went into the poor fund. In some places barracks housing eight poor families were built. As a rule friends of the poor people living in the barracks would bring them vegetables and sour milk in abundance. Soup made of flour and water constituted a principal item on their menu. Railroads often ran box cars and even passenger cars on a siding and allowed the emigrants to occupy them until they could prepare habitations. In 1876 a colony of one hundred and eight families of Russian Catholics, said to be the largest single expedition to leave Russia for America, settled at Hayes, Kansas.[11]

In a few instances English colonies were established on the prairies. In Harper County, Kansas, a town called Runnymede was established reminiscent of a high point in wresting rights and privileges from the king in Merrie England.[12] Ned Turnley, an Englishman who settled in Kansas, evolved a scheme in high finance. He went to England and talked up his scheme. Many of the English lords were anxious to get their wild sons away from an environment of evil companions and liquor and to shelter them while they were growing to be country gentlemen.[13] Turnley painted a glowing pic-

---

[11] *Golden Jubilee of Russian Settlement in Rush County and Ellis County, Kansas,* (pamphlet in Kansas State Historical Society Library), p. 15.

[12] King John signed the Magna Charta at Runnymede in 1215.

[13] There can be no doubt but that this motive caused many parents of noble blood to send their sons to the West. A considerable number of young men were sent to Russell County, Kansas, for the same reason.

ture to the fathers. To the sons he presented a different story, but equally attractive. He emphasized the vast spaces of the West with its adventure—the paradise of the hunter and his hounds. This naturally appealed to the young bloods. For five hundred pounds each, Turnley offered to take the young men to Kansas and train them for man's estate, to be country gentlemen. He secured one hundred of these young men. A locality fifty miles southwest of Wichita was selected and the town of Runnymede founded. For months the young Englishmen found the sport fully up to expectations. They followed the hounds joyfully in the chase.

A large hotel was built for their accommodation and the whole experience became a holiday. They drank immoderately and wasted their fathers' substance. The funds soon ran out and a steady drain on the paternal resources began. Finally the fathers back home grew weary of the continual call for money and, no doubt, hearing something of what was actually occurring, sent for their sons to come home; the colony died out.[14]

Other English colonies were peopled largely by middle class farmers or experienced laborers seeking economic independence. Unlike American settlers, they had no accurate idea of pioneer life. For generations the Americans had been battling against the inhospitable savagery always just to the west. Usually the settlers in a new region were not more than a few years removed from pioneering. Ordinarily their fathers or grandfathers had conquered the wilderness. The English farmers had to unlearn one type of farming and learn another. As a result, in a few years' time, many of them returned to England abandoning their homes. There were Scotch and English colonies in the Dakotas also.

In addition to the colonies mentioned above a considerable number of French, French-Swiss, and Belgians settled in the northeastern part of Kansas in colonies. There were also some colonies of Canadians on the prairies. Most of the foreign emigrants who

[14] T. A. McNeal, *When Kansas Was Young*, pp. 57, 58.

came to the Dakotas, however, were Scandinavians.[15] Carlton Qualey states that:

> If the American born Norwegians were included probably fully thirty percent of the total population of North Dakota in 1890 was of Norwegian stock.
>
> At the time North Dakota became a state the census figures show that the Norwegian foreign-born formed 14.1 percent of the total population.[16]

This large Norwegian population does not include the other Scandinavian people, the Danes and Swedes. In addition to these a large portion of the land of Pembina County, North Dakota, was taken by Icelanders.[17]

The Saxon colony in Buffalo County, Nebraska, was formed among the laboring classes of Martin Luther's home country. Many in that land looked with longing eyes toward the New World. Living there was poor, wages low, and the people in the over-populated factory districts were anxious to migrate. Many did not have the means to pay their passage across the ocean. They, therefore, organized themselves into classes and agreed to pay a stipulated amount, in some cases fifty cents and in others one dollar per month, into a common fund and, when the amount contributed sufficed to pay the transportation charges of a few of their number across the ocean, the members drew lots for the opportunity to go. When they arrived at the place of the settlement, they had no oxen to draw the poles for the rafters for their sod houses and had to *carry* this heavy timber five miles from the Loup River.

Although the larger colonies migrated from alien shores, there were many colonies of strange peoples from the East. One of the earliest of these was the vegetarian colony located six miles below

<hr>

[15] Harold E. Briggs, "The Settlement and Development of The Territory of Dakota, 1860–1870," *North Dakota Historical Quarterly*, Vol. VII; p. 142.

[16] Carlton Qualey, "Pioneer Norwegian Settlement in North Dakota," *Ibid.*, Vol. V, p. 37.

[17] Sveinbjorn Johnson, "The Icelandic Settlement of Pembina County," *Collections*, State Historical Society of North Dakota, Vol. I, pp. 112–114.

Humboldt, Kansas, on the left bank of the Neosho, by a group of reformers whose central aim was a vegetarian diet as a boon to mankind. This was one of a number of projects put forth by a national vegetarian society. The organization was based on the idea that its members would abstain from the use of meat, tea, coffee, tobacco, and other stimulants. The society also promoted the idea of hydrotherapy as against the conventional types of medical treatment. The purpose of this group was to form an ideal community on the fertile prairies in the West. The plan perfected embraced the idea of a large tract of land to be held in common by the colonists and small tracts to be held individually.

The colony was organized in the fall of 1855 and in the spring of 1856 the secretary arrived with a number of colonists. Others came later during April, May, and June, until more than a hundred reached the new town called Neosho City. According to plan, a large house in the center of the prospective settlement was to be constructed and ready to receive the colonists when they came. This was to serve as a lodging place, and a community dining room in this building was to furnish food for them while they were building their own dwellings. Quantities of grains and vegetables were to be stored in a common depot for use until crops were raised. A sawmill and a grist-mill were each to be ready to serve the colonists when they arrived. Had these plans been effected the rigors of pioneer life would have been ameliorated, the colony would probably have been a success, and the majestic scheme might have been partly realized. Among the other items called for in the plan when the colony became well established, were a hydropathic establishment, an agricultural college, a scientific institute, a museum of curiosities and mechanic arts, and an efficient common school system.

When the groups of settlers came in the spring it rained and rained. Everything was gloomy and forbidding. The settlers had to move to high ground to get out of the wet lowlands where the city had been planned. In addition to the untoward reception which nature gave the peculiar colony, there appears to have been gross mismanagement, if not out-and-out dishonesty, on the part of the officers of the concern. One lady, who later wrote about the adventure from the vantage point of the East, said that when their party arrived, expecting to find a place to stay while they erected their individual dwellings, they found no sawmill, no grist-mill, only one house—a log cabin sixteen by sixteen with neither door nor window. There were only two stoves in the entire company. Some families were living in tents of cloth, and some in homes of cloth and green bark peeled from the trees. On top of this, the food supply was not copious. The weather got hot, drying up the shallow springs which had been described in the glowing prospectus as "inexhaustible"; and the settlers were compelled to use water from the stagnant pools of the creek which ran through the settlement. Soon nearly the whole settlement was afflicted with ague, bringing suffering and death.

Then, too, the speculative fever, more deadly than the ague, gripped the members of the company and did as much to wreak havoc with the colony as did that disease. The earlier colonists, seeing the good government lands all about them, instead of working in harmony with the original plan, spread over the country beyond the colony's domains, taking up the choicest claims with the expectation of holding the land for a raise in price to sell to a later comer. Had the colony succeeded in establishing a town the land beyond would have become very valuable in a short time and the original settlers could then have sold out at a profit.

There was only one plow in the colony and the little patches of melons, pumpkins, squashes, corn, and other food stuffs, were raided by the Indians. Under these discouraging circumstances the lady wrote: "Disappointment has darkened every brow, however hard they may have striven to rise above it. We are 100 miles from a grist mill, and 50 from a post office."

Family after family left for their old homes. By spring there was not a trace of the colony. Its members had either gone back East or spread over the country and succeeded without the aid of a paternal company. Today the only permanent reminder of the vegetarian colony is the name Vegetarian given to the little creek which flowed past their town into the Neosho River.[18]

In the late seventies and early eighties Kansas was the scene of another interesting migration which was important. This was a movement of colored people from the South to the frontier and was known as "the exodus." The migration was so large that it attracted not only national but world-wide attention for a half decade. Benjamin Singleton, of Morris County, Kansas, headed an "invitation committee in sunny Kansas" and stirred the ex-slaves of the South. In all he moved about 8,000 colored people out of Tennessee. One man reported his favorite argument as:

Hyar you is, a-pottering around in politics, and trying to get into offices that you aint fit for, and you can't see that these white tramps from the North is simply usin' you for to line their pockets, and when they get through they will drop you, and the rebels will come into power, and then where will you be? [19]

There was a tremendous appeal in the thought of coming to the land of Old John Brown.

Governor John P. St. John in June 17, 1879, wrote:

It seems as if the North is slow to wake up to the importance and magnitude of this movement of the colored people. No longer ago than last Saturday I had a call from a delegation of 100 leading colored men from the states of Mississippi and Alabama, who are here canvassing Kansas and other Northern states with a view of migrating this coming fall and spring. I had a talk with them for nearly an hour in the Senate chamber, in which I gave them a full and fair understanding of the condition of things in Kansas, and what they may and may not expect by coming here. They answered me that they had borne troubles until

[18] Miriam Davis Colt, *I Went to Kansas* (Watertown, N. Y., 1862), pp. 1–100 *passim*. Mrs. Colt was one of the settlers who journeyed to the banks of the Neosho. Through sickness and death she lost those near and dear to her and returned bereft and disillusioned to the East.

[19] Singleton began his agitation in 1869–1870 during the carpet-bag and scalawag period. I. O. Pickering, "The Administration of John P. St. John," *Transactions*, Kansas State Historical Society, Vol. IX, pp. 385, 386, footnote.

they had become so oppressive on them that they could bear them no longer; that they had rather die in the attempt to reach the land where they can be free than to live in the South any longer.[20]

A contemporary, writing April 1, 1880, stated that from 15,000 to 20,000 colored people in Kansas had settled there during the previous twelve months. Of these, thirty per cent had come from Mississippi, twenty from Texas, fifteen from Tennessee, and smaller numbers from other states. He stated that about one-third was supplied with teams and farming equipment and gave promise of becoming self-sustaining. Another third was employed as house servants and laborers in the older settled regions, and the last third lived from hand to mouth, working and farming where they could.

So many Negroes left that it caused great alarm among the planters in certain sections of the South. One section, twenty-four miles long by four or five miles wide, was nearly depopulated by the exodus. The complaint of the Negro was that he had no political rights, no representation in government, and no vote. The emigrants came in crowds, from babes in arms to aged cripples. Nearly all were poor and brought all their belongings in innumerable baskets, boxes, trunks, and other baggage. Homeless and without food, at the mercy of their hosts, in a strange land, they were cheerful and little worried about the future. They were well received; temporary quarters were provided in a number of places and large sums were raised by the citizens to relieve their needs.

Those who desired to continue rural pursuits settled in Graham County at a town which they named Nicodemus after a noted slave who was said to have come to America in the second slave ship, bought his freedom, and become an outstanding figure. During the first years their farming operations were very crude. There were only three horses in the whole settlement and most of the work was done with hoes and mattocks. *Many acres were put in with the aid of only a spade and a grubbing hoe.* In some families with the help of the women two or three acres were planted by this process. After

[20] *Ibid.*

they became economically independent, so far as aid from the people was concerned, they broke up the colony organization and thanked the people for what they had done. This was one of the few colonies planted on the prairies which did not go to pieces through internal dissension.[21] This community had its own Masonic lodge, one of the best bands in northwest Kansas, an academy, and it furnished the state with a state auditor some years later.

Certain church colonies, held together by peculiar religious beliefs, migrated from different places and settled in a given area. An example of this was the Seventh-day Baptist colony at North Loup, Nebraska. Through the medium of the church paper, people from Wisconsin, Iowa, Missouri, Ohio, Kansas, and eastern Nebraska united their fortunes to found this community. The Ebenezers, a peculiar communistic religious group located near Buffalo, New York, sent their trustees to Kansas to select a plot of 9,000 acres. They had originated on the Rhine.

An example of later day pioneering is furnished in the Dunker colony which left Walkertown, Indiana, on a special immigrant train of thirty cars in March, 1894. The coaches each had two cookstoves, one at each end. At St. Paul the Great Northern Railway furnished the immigrants with a free lunch of coffee and buns. The sleeping accommodations were limited; the women and children had beds, but the men had to sit up. The immigration agent accompanied the colony on the entire trip and, in order to arouse the Dakota fever, had the train travel through Indiana, Illinois, and Wisconsin in the day time. Large banners were placed on the coaches conspicuously setting forth the opportunities of North Dakota. One banner read "From Indiana to the Rich Free Government Lands in North Dakota, via the famous Red River Valley, the Bread Basket of America." The group settled at Cando, North Dakota.

As has been suggested, colonies often broke up on the way to the new home or shortly after arriving. Frequently the break came over

[21] O. C. Gibbs, *Lawrence Daily Journal*, April 30, 1879.

a disagreement as to where to locate, over a division of the land, or over the choice of locations. In the spring of 1864 the New York Colony, organized at Syracuse, started for Dakota. Their object was to locate on government land in a suitable place, start a town, and build up the country around it. The plans were well laid and executed. One hundred families left by a special train of twenty cars. When they arrived at Marshalltown, some, dreading the three hundred mile journey across the uninhabited prairies through miry sloughs, became discouraged after listening to the woeful tales of terrible Iowa roads told by the Iowa people who wanted them to settle among them; they remained in Iowa. The main part of them, however, settled along the Missouri Valley between the Bix Sioux River and Yankton.

Many times people in a given community formed a mutual aid arrangement for the purpose of moving into the unknown country. The Nebraska Mutual Aid Colony, organized at Bradford, Pennsylvania, in 1882, is a good example of such an enterprise. Oil had fallen in price from $1.30 to $1.10 a barrel and the market fluctuated from day to day giving everyone a sense of economic insecurity. At first only ten men responded to the call of the organizer, but the number grew daily until fifty men had enrolled. The members elected officers and in good old American fashion adopted a constitution and by-laws with the following points:

1. Every name had to be accompanied by $2 for an initiation fee.

2. On payment of an assessment of $5 one became a charter member. This money was to be used to purchase 640 acres to be plotted in a townsite with streets and lots, reserving the necessary lots for churches, schools, and other public places.

3. Each charter member was to have two lots—one for a residence and another for a place of business; in addition to this each member was to have a pro rata share of, and interest in, the remaining lots.

4. Every member taking or buying land was to do so within ten miles of the townsite.

When the membership reached seventy-five, a committee of three was sent out to look up a location. At last the time came to leave the Keystone State. Farewell parties were given, presents exchanged, homes broken up, and large hampers of food made ready for several days' journey. Many wakeful heads were pillowed late on Tuesday to rise early on Wednesday. Accompanied by loved ones, those departing gathered at the station on that cold, gray day to say a last good-bye. They were leaving behind those whom they could scarcely hope to see again, the aged father and mother, brothers, and sisters. The good-byes and God-bless-you's were repeated again and again. The train rolled into the station. There was a last clasping of hands and hurried farewells. As the train puffed out there was a flurry of tear-stained handkerchiefs. Swiftly the iron horse drew the home-seekers farther and farther away from familiar scenes. The passengers busied themselves stowing away luggage and dinner baskets and arranging everything for a comfortable journey. This task finished, everyone began getting acquainted, for all were bound together to share the same toil and hardships as well as the pleasures and prosperity of the new home in the land of opportunity. After a long tiresome journey the travelers arrived at the lonely station on the prairie. The first meeting was held on a pile of boards near the depot. Since the coming of the colony from Pennsylvania had been heralded abroad in the newspapers, and people were coming from every direction to secure a home near them, the best of the land was fast being claimed by strangers. Arriving at the chosen location, they found the townsite claimed by others and the land so far taken that the colonists had to go farther northwest. In a panic to secure good land, they became so scattered that few were neighbors. This was a disappointment, since they had expected to be so located that the same school and church would serve all.[22]

When a colony arrived on the prairie it was customary to plot off the land and draw claims by means of numbered slips taken from a hat by a blindfolded member of the colony.

[22] Francis I. Sims Fulton, *To and Through Nebraska* (Lincoln, 1884), pp. 1–38 *passim*.

The Soldiers' Free Homestead Colony at Gibbon, Nebraska, was an interesting project and is representative of many soldier colonies.[23] Colonel John Thorp originated the colony. He was to receive for his share in the project the increase in value of a considerable tract of land which he owned adjacent to the colony. A man was sent to spy out the land but was told by a rancher that the soil was so dry nothing would grow. The cattleman hoped to scare the settlers away because the ranch had an ideal location and he did not wish to be disturbed by nesters. The homesteaders' spy found a corn-stalk butt one and a half inches in diameter in a field on the ranch and took it back East as evidence. The immigrants came in box cars and the railroad company built a siding and left the cars there for the settlers to live in until their homes were completed.

[23] The Ohio Soldiers' Colony located in Allen County, Kansas, and founded a town which has since been named Colony after this enterprise.

CHAPTER XV

NATURE FROWNS ON MANKIND

TO the poverty stricken homesteader, struggling to wrest a competence from the face of the virgin plains, all nature seemed hostile. In the spring, floods menaced the cabin or dugout built too close to the stream; in summer, drought and hot winds withered the promising crop, and insects everywhere took a terrible toll of the scanty cultivated areas; in the autumn, the prairie fires swept furiously across the plains, jumping creeks and sweeping everything before them, destroying crops, fuel, food for man and beast, homes, and even whole towns; in the winter came the dreaded blizzards and unbearable sub-zero temperature. These manifestations inflicted damage all the greater because the pioneers in a new and strange country were unprepared to meet such difficulties.

When the first small areas were broken and planted, the cultivated crops were much more succulent than the native plants and prairie grasses. Hence insects flocked to the patches of the homesteaders and greatly damaged or completely destroyed the crop. Again and again they visited the frontier region, wreaking havoc with the cultivated vegetation. As early as 1857 the grasshoppers, or Rocky Mountain locusts as they were called, made incursions into the little cultivated area along the Missouri River.[1] At Ponca, Nebraska, on August 3 of that year a party of men going home from an election, saw a dark cloud approaching rapidly from the North. As it drew near they saw it was neither a rain nor a dust cloud. Someone suggested that it might be a collection of cottonwood seeds

---

[1] As early as 1818 a swarm of grasshoppers descended upon the Red River Valley, Pembina County, North Dakota, and devoured all trace of vegetation at the Hudson's Bay settlement. Linda W. Slaughter, "Leaves from Northwestern History," *Collections*, State Historical Society of North Dakota, Vol. I, p. 209.

floating together high in the air. When near, part of the cloud came to the earth and the hungry grasshoppers devoured everything. Again in 1866 Richardson observed them. They darkened the air like great flakes of snow and in a column one hundred and fifty miles wide and one hundred miles deep they appeared near Fort Kearney, Nebraska, and passed southwest. In the same year they appeared in such vast quantities as to stop the horse races at Fort Scott, Kansas. They covered the track from one to three inches deep. In 1867 they made a raid on the harvest in Dakota and nearly destroyed it in a single day.

The great calamity of the year 1874, however, surpassed anything before or since and caused such great damage that on the plains it is generally called the grasshopper year. The grasshoppers came suddenly. They traveled with a strong wind, coming with it and leaving with it. Rising high in the air with their wings spread, they were carried along with very little effort; they appeared from the North. Their ravages reached from the Dakotas to northern Texas and penetrated as far east as Sedalia, Missouri.

The spring and early summer of the grasshopper year had been very favorable for growing crops. Small grain such as wheat and oats were mostly in the shock. Late in July, according to S. C. Bassett, a keen observer in Buffalo County, Nebraska, the family had sat down to dinner on a bright sunny day. Gradually the sun was slightly darkened by a cloud in the northwest which looked like smoke or dust, and it was remarked that it looked as though an April squall might be in the offing. Presently one of the family who had gone to the well for a pitcher of fresh water cried, "Grasshoppers!" The meal so happily begun was never finished. At first there was no thought of the destruction of the crops. All looked upon the insects with astonishment. They came like a driving snow in winter, filling the air, covering the earth, the buildings, the shocks of grain, and everything. According to one observer their alighting on the roofs and sides of the houses sounded like a continuous hail storm. They alighted on trees in such great numbers that their weight broke off large limbs. The chickens and turkeys at first were frightened and ran to hide from them. On recovering from their fright, they tried to eat all the insects. At first when a hopper alighted, a hen rushed forward and gobbled it up and then without moving she ate another and another until her crop was distended to an unusual size and she could hold no more. Then when a hopper flew near her, she would instinctively make a dash for it, then pause and cock her head as if to say, "Can I possibly hold another"? [2] The turkeys and chickens ate themselves sick. One pioneer reported that a herd of forty hogs and a flock of fifty turkeys fattened themselves by eating nothing but grasshoppers and a little prairie hay. The pork and turkey both had a peculiar taste of grasshoppers.

At times the insects were four to six inches deep on the ground and continued to alight for hours. Men were obliged to tie strings around their pants legs to keep the pests from crawling up their legs. In the cool of the evening the hoppers gathered so thick on the warm rails of the railroad that the Union Pacific trains were stopped.[3] Section men were called out to shovel the grasshoppers off the track near the spot where Kearney, Nebraska, now stands, so that the trains could get through. The track was so oily and greasy that the wheels spun and would not pull a train.[4]

When people began to see the danger of the destruction of their crops, they brought out bed-clothes and blankets to cover the most valuable garden crops. Yet the insects ate holes in the bedclothes or crawled under the edge and destroyed everything; even hay piled on the plants seldom availed much. Smudges of dry hay and litter were tried. In Dakota old straw was piled around a field and set on fire. Some put a salt solution on the grain, all to no avail. A heavy

[2] A. J. Leach, *History of Antelope County* (Chicago, 1909), p. 58; S. C. Bassett, *Ravenna News*, July 1, 1910.

[3] This seems like a piece of fiction, but so many witnesses testify to the occurrence that it must be so.

[4] Apparently in this particular case the reason for the great drifts of grasshoppers was because the insects met a storm and heavy wind. The trains were stopped in North Dakota in 1873 by the same cause and could be moved only after the tracks had been sanded. Clement A. Lounsberry, "Popular History of North Dakota," *North Dakota Magazine*, Vol. II, No. 4, p. 54.

GRASSHOPPERS STOPPING A TRAIN ON THE UNION PACIFIC

From a drawing by A. P. Smith, *Harper's New Monthly Magazine.*

rain was best; it drowned millions of them. Men with clubs walked down the corn rows knocking the hoppers off, but on looking behind them they saw that the insects were as numerous as ever. The grasshoppers alighted in such large numbers on the corn that the stalks bent toward the ground. The potato vines were mashed flat. The sound of their feeding was like a herd of cattle eating in a corn field.

Every green thing except castor beans, cane, and native grass, and the leaves of certain native trees, was eaten. Onions seemed to have been a favorite food for the hoppers. They ate the tops and the onions right down into the ground to the end of the roots leaving little hollow holes where the succulent bulbs had been. One observer claimed in all seriousness that when a large number of these insects flew past his cabin door, their breath was rank with the odor of onions. Turnips were likewise eaten out of the ground. They seemed to have been very fond of tobacco, red peppers, and tansy. Trees, denuded of their leaves and having the bark stripped from their smaller trunks, died.[5]

The water in the creeks, stained with the excrement of the insects, assumed the color of strong coffee. The cattle refused to drink until compelled by extreme thirst. One writer reported that it was his daily task to climb down into the well and clear the hoppers out to keep them from polluting the water. Even the fish in the streams tasted like grasshoppers.

The grasshoppers cut the bands of the sheaves and let the grain shell out on the ground. A piece of harness or a garment left on the ground was quickly ruined. Fork handles, scythe snaths, and such things were so roughened as to become uncomfortable to the hands. The weather-beaten boards on the houses and fences were so eaten that within a few hours they looked as though the structure had been built of new lumber. If any of the creatures were tramped underfoot, their companions quickly devoured them. They ate the

[5] One observer said the willow hedges were peeled so clean of their bark that one would think a basket maker had done it.

mosquito bar off the windows and even invaded the house and ate the window curtains in at least one place in Kansas. A lady with her small children was caught out in the deluge of grasshoppers. The insects crawled inside the children's clothing, frightening them until they were almost distracted. When the insects left a few hours later, the whole country was a scene of vast ruin and desolation. The jaunty waving fields of corn in twelve hours' time were reduced to bent-over stalks entirely denuded of their leaves. Even the large weeds were destroyed. The grasshoppers usually stayed from two days to a week and then on a fair day left with the wind. They came in 1875, 1876, and 1877, but never again did they become the scourge they were in 1874.

The results of the grasshopper plague were marked. In the first place those who had the money to get out of the country did so. This caused a considerable exodus. A spirit of humor prevailed as the people left the country. It was a common sight to see the sides of covered wagons ornamented with humorous or catchy phrases or comic poetry. The following are fair samples: "From Sodom, where it rains grasshoppers, fire, and destruction." "Going East to visit my wife's relations."

Akin to this was another bad result; the news of the plague printed in the papers, together with the woeful story told by those who left, gave the country a bad name and greatly deterred immigration. A country which was so destitute as to call for aid certainly did not appeal to the home-seeker.

To the mind of the clergy this great calamity proved to be a blessing in disguise. It made the individualistic frontiersman see how weak and helpless man was in the face of God's providence. He was humbled. The result was wonderful revivals. One minister said, "Quarterly meetings were seasons of revivals and God overruled this great scourge for the people's welfare."

Farmers were compelled to butcher or ship East a large proportion of their live stock. In the long run, however, this proved to be an advantage, for they naturally shipped the poorest animals; in time these were replaced by better animals. This left a better grade of stock for breeding purposes.[6]

The scourge temporarily resulted in dire distress and groveling poverty for the settler just starting life anew in a strange country with no capital. Those who did not have to ask for aid lived in the most straitened circumstances. One lady in speaking of this time said:

We always had plenty of such as it was to keep from starving, but it was cornbread seven days in the week.

Father traded a neckyoke to neighbor for a bushel of potatoes. Mother would boil one or two for the younger children, and the older ones would eat the pealings, this would make mother cry. . . .

Another in reminiscing of this period called it the sorghum and hominy winter. There would not even have been hominy if the corn had not been shipped in.

Settlers in the stricken region called meetings to devise means of relief. It was agreed to appeal to friends, relatives, other people in the eastern states, and also to the state and Federal Governments. Committees were chosen to go East to appeal for and receive contributions for the stricken and hungry settlers. Committees from the East visited the plains and reported the situation as they saw it. Letters were sent to friends and organizations in the more favored region. It was not long until contributions began to flow generously in response to the appeals. They did not consist of delicacies but for the most part were low grades of flour, corn meal, bacon, cast-off or second-hand clothes, old blankets, and the cheapest kind of groceries and dry goods. Several different agencies distributed the aid to the people. Relief societies distributed large quantities of food and clothing. Churches and individuals sent boxes to acquaintances or fellow church members. Governor Osborn of Kansas called a special session of the legislature and a state bond issue was voted. Over $70,000 in cash was distributed among the sufferers. In Ne-

---

[6] One man went eastward driving his hogs and peddling them for corn or anything he could get. He traded one to a hardware man for a dish pan.

braska, likewise, a bond issue was voted. The bonds usually referred to as the "grasshopper bonds" ran for ten years at an interest rate of ten per cent. This money was used primarily for seed for the spring planting.

In Dakota Territory the legislature passed an act to issue $25,000 in bonds. Public sentiment was against it, however, and nothing was done. The settlers were proud and no doubt feared emigration would stop if people in the East ever heard that the frontiersmen were on relief. Mr. W. H. Pelton, of South Dakota, went to Chicago and eastern points to secure aid for the destitute. Great censure was heaped on him by the public, and emigration authorities hailed him as an impostor; yet there is no doubt that he did much to relieve destitution. Finally the settlers were obliged to swallow their pride and a territorial committee was appointed by the governor to receive and disperse money for relief purposes.[7]

The United States Government also passed a law appropriating $150,000 for the relief of the sufferers.[8] This consisted primarily of supplies of food and army clothing and shoes. The next spring quantities of seeds were furnished by Washington also. General Ord, of the United States Army, had charge of the distribution of these relief goods. In some instances counties and precincts voted bond issues for relief. The amounts received from these were small because of the expense of negotiating the bonds. The needs were great. At one time in 1875 over five hundred teams were waiting at Plum Creek, Nebraska, for aid.

The administration of such relief work was difficult indeed. At such times the worst in humanity comes to the surface. Selfishness, envy, jealousy, and covetousness were manifested. There were many accusations of partiality and preferences. In some instances these were well founded. In Fillmore County, Nebraska, it was complained that when the needy one went to the distributing officer

[7] Harold E. Briggs, "Early History of Clay County," *South Dakota Historical Collections*, Vol. XIII, pp. 130, 131.
[8] *Ibid.*, p. 131.

for assistance he was compelled to sign a receipt for quite a large quantity of goods before leaving the office. Upon arriving at the cars or storehouse he could get but a small portion of the goods he had signed for; if he demanded satisfaction or the return of the receipt, the distributing officer refused the request, explaining that someone had stolen the goods and that the receipts must be held so that the accounts with the superior officers would balance. This course was condemned by the settlers, but it is not known who stole the goods. In any case an underhanded graft was worked on the suffering settlers.[9]

Some abused the aid and displayed a mean, grasping disposition. One woman sold her own quilts and accepted blankets from the aid society while another used all the food provided for her by the society and saved her own to buy a sewing machine. On the other hand there was many a deed of mutual kindness, and the noblest attributes of humanity were also revealed. In Nebraska two men had charge of the distribution in each county and a deputy was appointed in each school district. Although there were few residents in a given county, much information had to be gathered and sent in.

Printed forms were supplied which furnished full information as to the crop raised and property owned by the settler. A census was carefully taken. There was no remuneration for the men in charge of the work of distribution. Clothing and other relief supplies were brought in over railroads free of charge for the most part. Relatives and friends were granted reduced rates to send supplies to the stricken areas. Much of the clothing was hardly worth the cost of the freight. It probably never entered the heads of the contributors that the recipients could hardly raise enough money to buy a spool of thread to sew up the rents in the badly used clothing. The rumor was current that the clothing was "pretty well culled" before it reached those for whom it was intended.[10]

The boxes or barrels sent by relatives, friends, or benevolent aid

[9] A. T. Andreas, *History of the State of Nebraska*, Vol. II, p. 851.
[10] John Turner, *Pioneers of The West* (Cincinnati, 1903), pp. 209–210.

societies, were a source of joy to the lonely harassed family on the plains. The father traveled miles across the prairie for the precious burden, and on his return the fun of unpacking began. The whole family gathered around the barrel and began to pull out prizes. "Here's something for mother," cried one of the children, or, "Here's something for little Jane," and so on until the box was empty and the precious gifts were distributed to all. The donors in some eastern state never realized what joy their benevolence brought.

There were many acts of generosity and good faith during the year of 1875. Although the country was not swept clean by grasshoppers, that was a lean year. That winter Charles Clark of Furnas County, Nebraska, was the recipient of kindness from some of his more favored neighbors. The fare at his home was indeed poor. One night the family sat down to a meager supper and was looking forward to the same kind of breakfast, but that night the neighbors got together just after dark and brought in bushel baskets of potatoes, cabbage, and other good things. They had a feast and a glorious good time.

One man described the home of one of the South Dakota grasshopper sufferers: The bed was set next to the dirt wall and consisted of a frame covered with straw. Upon it lay the wife, too ill to rise. The father wore cheap coarse clothes; his shoes were of plaited straw. By the stove, the fuel for which was hay or straw, stood two little children scantily clad, hungrily watching their father prepare from a little milk and flour a dish for his wife that she might have some nourishment.

The winter of 1874 and 1875 dragged out its dreary length. The skimpy little driblets of relief coal were supplemented by hay, weeds, and cornstalks. The people hailed with joy the first approach of spring. The green grass springing from the prairie brought joy to the lean horses and cattle, and the first vegetables brought happiness to the "relief-fed" population.

For several summers the settlers lived in constant dread of a recurrence of the terrible plague of the grasshopper year. As a result of this fear numerous inventions were brought forward. Even state legislation was enacted to eradicate this pest. One such invention put out by a Nebraska City man, was called the grasshopper exterminator, a machine which sold for fifteen dollars and which could be run by a man and two boys. He expected to save his nursery with it.

Another machine used in the spring of 1875 in Kansas, was known as the grasshopper dozier because the minute an insect got into it he went to sleep. It was a long tin and sheet iron pan, having a front side only a few inches high and the rear side two feet tall. It was pushed through the fields by horses. The little hoppers could not fly nor hop very high and dropped into the pan which was partially filled with kerosene. When the pan was filled, the insects were dumped in piles sometimes five or six feet high on the fields. For several years thousands of these little hillocks dotted the highways, meadows, and fence corners—mute monuments to one of the greatest plagues in the history of the state.[11]

In Minnesota thousands of dollars were spent in an attempt to exterminate the pests. A bounty of fifty cents a bushel was offered for dead grasshoppers. They were piled high and on still nights the citizens made bonfires of them.[12]

Many and varied were the remedies proposed to combat this great plague. One man advocated the destruction of the insects and eggs by concussion. He argued that a charge of one hundred pounds of powder buried in the ground and ignited after a heavy rain would kill all the insects for miles. He was optimistic enough to venture a guess that it would kill the hoppers in an area twenty-five miles square.

The Nebraska legislature, fully alive to the problem, passed the Grasshopper Act in 1877, which placed the grasshopper in the category of a public enemy and required all able-bodied citizens to rally

---

[11] Reminiscences of Charles C. Hollebough, *Kansas Reminiscences*, Vol. III, p. 50.
[12] Alma Tweto, "History of Abercrombie Township, Richland County," *Collections*, State Historical Society of North Dakota, Vol. III, p. 163, footnote.

to fight the pest. This act provided that the supervisors of each road district should, when the grasshoppers hatched out, notify every able-bodied male resident of the district between the ages of sixteen and twenty to perform two days' work eradicating the insects. If it took more than that to kill the hoppers, the supervisor could require up to ten days in the work. The supervisor was required to give a receipt to the person performing his duty. A fine of ten dollars was the penalty for refusal to work.

Lack of rainfall over long periods was another serious obstacle to the settling of the prairies, and constituted a menace to populating the plains. The first great calamity of this kind was the drought of 1859–1860. From June 19, 1859, until November, 1860, not one good rain fell and there were but two slight snows in winter. The roads never became muddy, and the earth broke open in great cracks. Day after day the burning rays of the sun beat mercilessly down on a dry and parched land. During the summer of 1860 hot winds from the southwest swept the prairies as if the very breath of hell itself had been released. For sixteen days and nights during that memorable summer, these scorching, blighting winds prevailed.[13] Fall wheat did not come up until spring and then withered and died. The bottoms, however, gave evidence of the great fertility and strength of the soil by producing some wheat. Even the prairie grass withered and presented a seared brown appearance. Streams, springs, and wells dried up. Day after day the harassed and discouraged settlers looked for rain. It seemed that it would never rain again. Not until it was too late to help the crops did a good rain come to water the parched surface of the earth.

Prior to this time there had been a heavy migration and the settlers had spent most of their resources in improving their claims, and endeavoring to wrest a meager living from the newly broken sod. As a result, thousands faced the winter of 1860–1861 without sustenance enough to stave off suffering during the frigid season

---

[13] W. W. Cox, "Reminiscences of Early Days in Nebraska," *Transactions and Reports*, Nebraska State Historical Society, Vol. V, p. 69.

just before them. Marcus J. Parrott, the Kansas representative in Congress, described the needs of his constituents in extravagant words stating that "many people were then living on acorns and were clothed in bark." [14] As winter drew near everyone who could do so fled from the Territory. Nebraska was only a little less destitute than Kansas. Claims were abandoned; farms sold for a song. The slavery struggle died out and a struggle for existence took its place. Bleeding Kansas became starving Kansas. It was computed that thirty thousand people left the territory of Kansas temporarily to secure food. Forty thousand stayed, however. [15]

Thaddeus Hyatt, an eastern visitor, made a tour of observation through the country and sent back stirring appeals for help. The presiding elders of the Methodist church in Kansas sent solicitors to the eastern churches and appointed agents at Atchison to take charge of the distribution of goods. The missionary board appropriated one thousand dollars for the benefit of the ministers of that faith. At a public meeting of the settlers at Lawrence in November, 1860, a territorial relief committee was chosen. S. C. Pomeroy was made chairman. Mr. Hyatt prepared a sixty-eight page pamphlet entitled "The Prayer of Thaddeus Hyatt to James Buchanan, president of the United State, in behalf of Kansas." President Buchanan gave him a check for one hundred dollars, a copy of which appeared in the *New York Tribune*. Relief then started moving toward Kansas. Judge W. F. M. Arny, having been appointed receiving and disbursing agent, camped by a railway depot in Illinois and kept the relief goods moving toward Kansas where Pomeroy carried on the work night and day distributing it to the needy. Atchison became the great distribution center since it was the only railroad town west of the Missouri River. The East generously donated over one hundred thousand dollars for the relief of the stricken people.

[14] George W. Glick, "The Drought of 1860," *Transactions*, Kansas State Historical Society, Vol. IX, p. 482-483.

[15] *Ibid.*; E. C. Manning, "In at the Birth and —," *ibid.*, Vol. VII, pp. 203-204; William H. Coffin, "Settlement of the Friends in Kansas," *ibid.*, p. 354.

E. C. Manning, a shrewd observer from Kansas, described this relief program as follows:

Opportunely, the thrify and sympathetic people in the regions eastward were aroused, and money, clothing, grain and food were sent from legislatures, societies, and individuals, by mail and rail, in response to the wail. All supplies from the East were delivered at Atchison. Thither from the stricken frontier men wrapped in comforts fastened with strings, and often with feet clad in raw buffalo hide, drove their teams to receive the timely aid. As the emaciated horses or oxen propelling the wagons dragged their weary hoofs along a sinuous tremor shook their frames at each colaboring step. . . . Boxes of clothing, sacks of meal, flour, beans, corn, rice, sugar, coffee, bacon, and everything that could sustain life, were delivered at Atchison by train loads, marked in large letters, "W.F.M. Arny, Agent." This was distributed by local committees throughout the famishing districts, and starvation was averted.

In January, 1861, empty, fine-woven manila sacks could be found in every community, all marked "W.F.M. Arny, Agent." Later on, men and boys could be seen wearing pants and coats made from these sacks, with "W.F." or "Arny" or "Agent" in sight; and if perchance a Kansas zephyr lifted a faded calico dress, the impertinent eye would see "W.F.M. Arny" staring at the landscape from a sheltering petticoat. Those petticoats did not rustle like the silk petticoats of today, but they were the drapery of a pioneer womanhood which has bred a hustling generation of citizens who have given Kansas fame.[16]

George W. Glick, later governor of Kansas, gave Mr. Pomeroy and his associates the highest praise for their diligent and faithful work. It was an onerous and trying task. Provisions arrived at irregular intervals and in irregular lots; small quantities arrived almost daily. This condition was a source of great annoyance and subjected Pomeroy to abuse and censure. Often fifty persons were there asking for aid when there were only five sacks of flour and five hundred pounds of corn meal on hand. Mr. Glick said he had seen as many as a hundred persons insisting on a distribution when there

[16] E. C. Manning, *loc. cit.*, p. 203.

was not flour enough to make bread to feed those in attendance for one day. The supervisor tried to learn the condition of each applicant, the number of needy people represented by each one, and the distance traveled en route. He and his corps of workers then made an effort to divide the goods on hand equitably. The employees often worked all night waiting on applicants for aid.

The winter of 1860 was cold and disagreeable, with considerable snow. The roads were bad, and feed for teams was scarce. Teams suffered for hours while their owners waited to be served. The animals were fed and two large rooms were fitted up for sleeping quarters for the men. Goods coming in had to be hauled or ferried over the Missouri River. Teams had to be hired, bills paid, goods opened, sorted, and arranged in a warehouse which was built west of the river. In the spring field and garden seeds were distributed.[17]

This relief was fortunate indeed, for starvation faced many. Hardly a family was able to live comfortably, and the great majority had barely enough to support life. Many saw no flour throughout the winter, subsisting on corn meal and the game they occasionally killed. Volumes could be filled with the accounts of the early settlers. One Kansas woman in telling of her experiences said:

We found one day that our scanty supply of provisions was growing alarmingly small. My husband said the next morning he would start out to replenish the wasting stores. When morning came it brought a severe snow-storm and blizzard. To go out with no neighbors within a mile or two would have been to risk his life. At noon that day we cooked the last morsel of provisions in the house. When the shades of evening gathered around that prairie home no preparation for the evening meal was made. The little ones could not understand it, and soon commenced their importunities—'Mamma, why don't you get supper?' 'Mamma, I am hungry!' 'Mamma, can't you give us some bread?' No explanation could satisfy them, and during that long winter evening that poor woman suffered untold agony because she was not able to gratify the hunger of her little ones. At last, worn out with their im-

[17] George W. Glick, *op. cit.*, p. 483.

portunities, they dropped to sleep, and she put them supperless to bed. The next morning the husband succeeded in getting a little food from a neighbor.

The hardships drew the settlers together and a kindly feeling existed among them. All were on a common level and felt their dependence.

One of the greatest terrors of the settler was the prairie fire. A prairie fire was a grand and startling spectacle. It was described by the great correspondent Richardson as

never dangerous to men or animals, [?] as depicted in our school-geographies, they are always startling and grand. The sky is pierced with tall pyramids of flame, or covered with writhing, leaping, lurid serpents, or transformed into a broad ocean lit up by a blazing sunset. Now a whole avalanche of fire slides off into the prairie, and then opening its great, devouring jaws closes in upon the deadened grass.[18]

The greatest danger from these fires occurred in the autumn when the grass was dry and seared. The camp-fire of a careless traveler, the burning wads from the discharge of a gun, a streak of lightning, or sparks from a steam boiler were enough to start a blazing, leaping, consuming force which moved across the prairie with the speed of the wind, destroying settlers, homes, barns, feed, winter range, stacks of hay, stock, and even devastating entire settlements. Although ordinarily, as Mr. Richardson says, not many human lives were lost, occasionally fatalities did occur. In 1860 there were four deaths in Cuming County, Nebraska, from this cause.

Very little could be accomplished by fighting a head fire but the side fires could be put out by dragging a skin over them. This method was considered so effective that cases were known where some of the fighters stopped to slaughter an animal, strip the hide from the carcass, tie a rope to each side of the green skin, and drag

[18] Albert D. Richardson, *Beyond the Mississippi*, pp. 143–144.

it over the side fires, putting them out as fast as the men could ride.[19] Sometimes iron rings were fastened to a skin and the skin dragged by this means in order to extinguish the blaze. A prudent person traveling alone on the prairie, always carried a few matches with which to save himself from a prairie fire. It was only necessary for him to burn a little spot, thus making an island on which to stand while the roaring blaze passed on each side.

In Dakota in 1859 one woman, caught alone at home in a terrible fire which swept the prairie and set the woods ablaze, and finding herself in imminent danger of certain death, took her child and crawled down into the well. Hardly had she gotten down into the well when everything about her was enveloped in flame. She was nearly suffocated from the heat and smoke, but held out until the danger was past and by her sheer nerve and resourcefulness, saved herself and her child.

Dugouts often protected refugees from prairie fires. There was much perspiring and coughing on the part of those protecting themselves but they came through the fiery ordeal none the worse for the experience.

So intense was the heat from a prairie fire in Dakota in 1871, that even the James and Vermilion Rivers were crossed at various places by the withering flames which appeared to leap across large streams as if attracted by a powerful magnet.

Settlers of Wells County, North Dakota, in the eighties observed that fires starting far to the North would burn six weeks or more. Each day the smoke grew more dense until at last the sun would be entirely obscured for days. At night the reflection of the fire on the clouds could be seen gradually drawing nearer and

---

[19] Theodore Roosevelt and the men on his North Dakota ranch near Medora, used the following method: They killed a steer, split it in half length-wise and then two riders dragged each half steer bloody side downward along the line of flame. The rope fastened to the saddle horn of one rider, was attached to the hind foot of the slaughtered beef, and the rope of the second rider was attached to the front leg. The two horsemen, one on each side of the line of fire rode as fast as their horses could run, smothering out the blaze. Men following on foot with slickers, wet horse blankets, or sacks, beat out any flickering flame left.

nearer, illuminating the sky more each night. Finally after about ten days of this, it would pass through, sweeping everything before it unless every precaution had been taken. On a calm night it was a splendid and awe-inspiring sight to see the fire pass through, lighting the heavens as bright as day.[20]

Some of the worst disasters, however, came after the country was comparatively well settled and the people had somewhat relaxed their vigilance. In 1889 in Turner County, Dakota Territory, in less than a half hour after attention was attracted to a fire, one family saw seven neighbors' homes in flames. Jack rabbits, birds, and here and there a loose team, went rushing by. The closest neighbor was terribly burned while his horses were roasted with the harness on. One woman was out pouring milk on her house to save it. Many saved their lives by sitting on the plowed ground.[21] On numerous occasions prairie fires destroyed towns. Leola, South Dakota,[22] and Sykeston, North Dakota, were almost entirely destroyed after the country was settled.

In November, 1873, Vermilion, South Dakota, was seriously threatened by fire. The whole town was alarmed, rallied under the direction of the town marshal, and broke fire guards around the threatened city. The Dakota Southern Railroad coupled up all their available cars with an engine attached ready to pull out with the people and their goods if it became necessary. The superintendent placed the entire rolling stock of the company at the disposal of the panic-stricken people. The Vermilion River lay between the fire and the town and it was only with the greatest exertion that the alert citizens were able to keep the flames from gaining east of the river although it did leap the barrier and make a beginning.[23]

---

[20] Walter E. Spokesfield, *History of Wells County, North Dakota* (Jamestown, 1929), p. 59.

[21] In one instance in Turner County (Dakota Territory) a team of oxen escaped with the plow and was found several miles away. The plow handles were burned off and the oxen severely burned.

[22] *McPherson County Herald*, June 14, 1934, p. 4.

[23] *Yankton Press and Dakotaian*, November 27, 1873.

The settlers attempted to protect their range and their homes by plowing around them. Two sets of furrows were plowed two or more rods apart and on a calm day the grass between was burned. This was called a fire-break. Occasionally fires were started in this way by some careless person letting the fire get beyond control. These fire-guards caused no end of trouble among the settlers. Often they were used for boundary lines. Some of the more contentious forbade persons to cross their fire-guards, and the more timid were forced to go miles out of their way in traveling across country.

The alternate sections of land belonged to the railroads and were for years unoccupied and covered with prairie grass. This was a fine place for fires to start and proceed across the prairie, destroying as they went. In the small towns the church bells pealed out the alarm of a prairie fire. In the country the conflagration could be seen for miles. It was the unwritten law that upon the outbreak of a fire every able-bodied man should come with fire-fighting equipment to help extinguish the blaze. The man who slept while the neighbors fought fire all night was considered a traitor or slacker. One writer who went through the experience of fighting prairie fires in Kansas while a girl, said:

The darkness that follows the going out of a prairie fire is something portentous. From being the center of a lurid glare you are suddenly plunged into the bottom of a bucket of pitch. Nothing reflects any light, and there is nothing to steer by. You don't know where you are nor where the house is; everything is black. Your throat is full of ashes and you can hardly breathe for the choking of the fluff in the air. If you call to your nearest pal on the back firing line the chances are that he or she has moved away, and may be half a mile distant. You may feel as if you were the last survivor in a horrible world of cinders and blackness. At length a welcome shout is heard—in our case it was my father hailing us and bidding us gather in. And so once more the fire danger is over, and we may rest.[24]

[24] Adela Elizabeth Richards Orpen, *Memories of the Old Emigrant Days in Kansas, 1862–1865* (London, 1926), pp. 72–73.

For hours after a prairie fire the black ashes blew, filling the air until day was almost turned into night. The black dust blew through the cracks into the house until the paper, the carpet, and even the peoples' faces were smudged.[25] A man traveling over the prairie was soon as black as a Negro.

It was easy enough for a person to get lost on the prairie at night under any circumstances, but it was doubly easy on a burned-over prairie or during a storm. Some of the most amusing and inexplainable incidents occurred along this line. One pioneer testified that when out on the prairie on a dark night a person lost all sense of direction and hardly knew "straight up." He could scarcely believe his own eyes when he came to a familiar scene. A certain kind of panic seemed to seize individuals which so completely bewildered them that they did not know their own residences or friends. In Fillmore County, Nebraska, a man upon coming to his own home, was so mystified that he not only failed to recognize his own house and barn but with difficulty was persuaded to unhitch his horses. In the same community a man by the name of Job Hathaway called on a neighbor one evening and visited until after dark. It was a very dark night and a little while after he had left, a man knocked at the door and asked if they could tell where Job Hathaway lived. "Why what's the matter with you, Mr. Hathaway? It is only fifteen minutes since you left here." The lost man replied, "You are mistaken; I never was here in my life." The neighbor went home with his guest and it was some time before the latter recognized his own home.[26]

It was not uncommon for a man, endeavoring to walk in a straight line, when lost on the prairie to travel in circles unbeknown to himself. Mr. Stephen C. Beck started across the prairie to a neighbor's home, one and one-half miles away. He had been on his way only a few minutes when he saw a bright light to the left. He kept on

[25] Edna Nyquist, *Pioneer Life and Lore* (McPherson, Kansas, 1932), p. 106.
[26] G. R. McKeith, *Pioneer Stories of Fillmore County, Nebraska* (Exeter, 1915), p. 22.

FIGHTING A PRAIRIE FIRE

From a drawing by Frenzeny and Tavernier, *Harper's Weekly*, 1874.

and on, when again a bright light came to view. He thought himself lost, went to inquire, and found his own family. He had seen his own light several times and thought he had seen a number of lights. To find one's bearing when traveling over the prairie, one had to look for some stove-pipe sticking out of the ground, the sure sign of a dwelling, and ask the township and section numbers of the occupants and the lay of the land.

Many strange stories are told of people lost in blizzards. One man who had been visiting his brother on a winter night, set out for his farm-home four miles distant. He was overtaken by a blizzard and, losing his way, sat down and waited until morning. Daybreak revealed that he had been sitting right next to his house.

Storms of various kinds added to the discomforts of frontier life. Electric storms which completely filled the air with the smell of sulphur and lurid flashes of lightning, brought fear to the hearts of the uninitiated. Those caught in these storms never forgot the electrified air which caused balls of fire to jump off the horns of the oxen or roll along the prairie. These storms were frequently accompanied by hail which beat down on the traveler so mercilessly that he was obliged to crawl under his wagon or take the saddle off and cover his head to escape injury from the infuriated elements. In the seventies Mr. Zedekiah Blake was driving to Fort Riley, Kansas, with a lot of garden truck when a storm came up and hail stones, some of them the size of eggs, rattled down so furiously that he was obliged to empty out his wooden tub of vegetables and get under the receptacle himself.

Of all these indications of displeasure on the part of nature, perhaps the most trying were the blizzards. Too often man and beast were poorly prepared to parry winter's icy thrusts. Certain winters stand out in the minds of frontiersmen as particularly "hard winters." Certain storms in these winters, and others, are remembered as particularly severe.

One old-timer in a reminiscent mood, averred that the average horse or ox was minus one or more ears as a testimony to the hard winters. Many were the men who had different parts of their anatomy frozen at one time or another as they pursued the tasks which obliged them to take long journeys to the mill, to town, or after fuel. Not infrequently settlers were frozen when caught out in these terrible frigid outbursts of Mother Nature. When caught in blizzards men have been known, in their efforts to preserve their lives, to kill their horses, rip them open and crawl into their vitals so as to have the warmth of the animal's intestines to preserve them from death in this peculiar fashion. One man, attempting to save himself in this manner, was found frozen to death in this strange death-bed. The storm had been so long in passing that the temporary warmth had subsided and the carcass of his mount had become the man's tomb.

The settlers had hardly stepped foot on the fair soil of Kansas and Nebraska until they were greeted by the awful inhospitality of one of the most severe winters in the history of the states. The winter of 1855–1856 lashed the settlers at a time when they felt it particularly keenly because of their unpreparedness. The frigid attack broke on the recent arrivals in all its fury in December. The thermometer hung between twenty and thirty degrees below zero at Lawrence, Kansas, for some days. Water froze in tumblers at breakfast and everything intended to be edible was frozen hard. The bread could be cut only after thawing the loaf out by the fire and cutting one slice at a time. Potatoes, squashes, pumpkins, apples, and other products were frozen as hard as rocks, and the glass jars of pickles and ketchup split open from top to bottom. Those who tried to write could do so only by keeping the ink bottle on the stove and the pen and writing material near-by, for the ink froze on the pen.

One pioneer testified that at Council Grove, Kansas, it was no uncommon thing to get up in the morning and find from two to four inches of snow on the floor, beds, and everything in the house. It blew and snowed three days out of the week, and even the comparatively mild climate of Kansas gave way to the frigid blasts of an

Arctic winter, which held the country in its grip for weeks. When the wind blew, no one could see to travel. A woman at Lawrence, Kansas, who lived in a good log house cemented inside, with a carpeted floor and a good sized cellar under it, froze her feet while about her home duties.

The road between Sioux City and Seargeant Bluff, Iowa,[27] was five feet above the level of the fields. When two teams met there was grave difficulty. One man said the snow over eastern Nebraska during the winter of 1855, averaged three feet on the level. In 1856 at Fremont, Nebraska, it was necessary for one man to hang blankets around the stove and put his wife and children inside the inclosure to keep from freezing. He spent the two days of the storm cutting wood and firing.

The blizzard was a storm peculiar only to the open plains. It was less of a snow storm than an ice-dust wind storm which drove a smother of pulverized ice into the air from the ground and carried it along in a veritable cloud of icy particles which beat with such stinging cold that neither man nor beast could stand to face it. The whole landscape was obscured by this sweeping frigid storm.

Unfortunate indeed was the man or beast caught in a blizzard. A person's face was covered with ice instantly, the eyes frozen shut, and his breath taken away, while the fine particles were driven into his clothing until he was encased in icy armor in a moment. The cattle which were saved were stranger sights than Whittier's clothes line posts in old New England. Their bodies were completely encased in ice. Their heads assumed the size of bushel baskets as they became covered with masses of ice formed from congealed breath, and the animals, unable to support the great weight, rested their heads on the ground. It was necessary to knock the ice off with a club.

Blizzards were attended by electrical phenomena. When the poker was touched to the stove, a shower of sparks leaped out to meet it. There was a crackle and snap of electrical energy when the hand was passed over someone's head. When the cook took the

[27] A road running North and South just East of the Missouri River.

baked potatoes out of the oven each tine of the fork emitted a flash upon touching the potato. Shocks were sustained when a person touched the stovepipe or the grate to "shake down" the stove.

Two outstanding blizzards occurred in the seventies, one in 1871 and one in 1873. On November 15, of 1871, it was so warm men went barefoot all day and had to stop frequently to allow their teams to rest while doing the fall plowing. The next morning people awoke thinking it was time to rise, but darkness still reigned. They found that they were snowed in. The blizzard raged for three days and two nights. The weather bureau at Lincoln, Nebraska, reported a temperature of seventeen below zero and a seventy-mile an hour gale. The storm came so suddenly that many were taken completely by surprise and were absolutely unprepared for it. Many were without food and froze trying to secure supplies. Many had to live on bread made from flour, salt, and snow water. One homesteader went to the next door neighbor's dugout which was nine by ten feet, and found in it the man, his wife, their two small children, bed, cookstove, two or three trunks, some other household furniture, and a team of large horses. He stayed, adding another to the strange assortment. For two or three days they all remained, packed like sardines in a can. The woman, a recent arrival in the West, wept bitterly at this cold reception.

It was not at all uncommon during a blizzard for the family to bring the calf, colt, pigs, chickens, or other farm animals into the house to keep them from freezing. At times fuel became so scarce that it was necessary to chop up the bed and other furniture and even to empty the straw-tick from the bed for fuel.

Animals suffered acutely. Cows were sometimes kept in tepees or half-faced sheds. A. G. Welch, a Nebraska man, got up and wrapped his blankets around his mules which were in an exposed place, and bound the blankets on with the lines. One man, while walking over a drift three feet deep ten days or two weeks after a snow storm and blizzard, came on some of his hogs. They had been there ever since the storm. They had found a warm place but no feed; they survived in good condition.

The snow particles in these storms were as fine as flour and penetrated every crevice. Stables ordinarily considered good shelters were filled more compactly and solidly than would have been possible with a shovel. Hundreds of heads of stock died of suffocation and exposure. Horses tied to the manger kept climbing on top of the snow as it sifted in until, when found, they were standing high on the snow with their backs lifting the flimsy roof and their heads down as far as they could reach, firmly held there by the halter ropes. Some animals in dugouts which were completely covered by snow, died of suffocation. Farmers in many cases were unable to get to their stables ten or twelve rods away. During the blizzard it was necessary to run the clothes-line or a rope from the house to the barn and follow it so as not to lose one's way between the two structures. In the spring after the great blizzard of 1871, the whole country was literally strewn with the carcasses of animals whose lives were lost in that terrible blizzard.

The Easter storm of 1873 was one long remembered on the plains. The morning of April 13, 1873, dawned bright and clear and was welcomed as the first day of spring. Toward noon the sky became overcast, the wind changed to sleet, and hail was reported in some places. It soon became almost impossible for pedestrians to make their way about town. In Hastings, Nebraska, a rope was tied from a store to the well and people guided themselves in that way. Business ceased. Only the most daring and foolhardy ventured out. Homesteaders in town had to stay until the storm was over, causing a world of anxiety on the part of the women who waited at home. A boy left a hotel in Central City, Nebraska, to go to a print shop one block away, but got lost and was found three days later frozen. Drifts were as high as houses.

Live stock, much of it bought with borrowed money, perished by the thousands. Some animals died endeavoring to cross streams, some in stables and corrals while their owners were unable to give relief, and some in cars on the railroad sidings, for railway traffic was abandoned. Some sought shelter in depressions and perished beneath the snow drifts many feet deep. It was not the intense cold which filled man and beast with terror, but the fine particles of snow, driven by the furious wind, which wet to the skin and chilled living things to the bone.

In Antelope County, Nebraska, a man named Al Wolfe lived alone in his dugout on the south side of a big hill. The hill furnished some shelter but made the snow drift badly. After the storm one of his neighbors went to hunt him up and see how he was faring, but could find no trace of his dugout. The location of the dwelling was marked by a smooth snowdrift. The friend got a number of neighbors together and started digging. They found the man insensible; in a very short time he would have died. His door opened outward, preventing him from working his way out alone, and the snow packed almost as solid as ice, encased him like a tomb.

During this same Easter storm of 1873 a man of Clay County, Nebraska, housed in the same room his family of eight persons, one hog, one dog, all his chickens, and four head of cattle. It was a frequent occurrence for the barns to be so completely covered with snow and for the snow to drift in such a fashion, that it was impossible to open the barn door. In this event a hole was made through the flimsy hay roof, and hay and grain were thrown down into the stable. Occasionally snow was thrown down for the animals to eat instead of water. This was seldom necessary, for the fine snow penetrated every nook and crevice of the ordinary frontier barn. One man fed his cattle in this way for two weeks, traveling between the house and barn guided by a lariat rope. In one county alone in Kansas eight people perished in this storm.

In Turner County, Dakota Territory, a party was in progress at the pastor's home and the group was snowed in for three days. The days were jolly but the nights were uncomfortable. The men spread their buffalo robes and blankets on the floor and slept there. The women and girls placed chairs along the side of the bed and a half dozen crawled into it, sleeping crossways with their pillows arranged on the chairs. In this manner, crowded to suffocation, they managed to get through the nights.

The winter of 1880–1881 was often called the hard winter. A severe blizzard occurred in October; most of the snow disappeared, only to be followed by a coat of sleet which covered everything. A foot of snow covered that and on top of the snow there fell a drizzle which froze to about the thickness of an inch. It is remarkable that any range cattle survived when it is remembered that at this time range cattle had to subsist on what they could pick up from the prairie. Mr. Doane Robinson, for years the Secretary of the South Dakota State Historical Society, says that in Dakota in the hard winter of 1880–1881, more than eleven feet of snow fell. Since there was no thawing weather throughout winter it all accumulated on the ground.[28] In the spring of 1881 no trains entered Nation City between January 30 and April 19, a space of seventy-nine days. For six weeks they were without mail. What was brought in was brought on snow shoes. Two small stores in the town were completely sold out. For two months they had no tea, coffee, sugar, vegetables, nor fruit. Many families lived on cracked wheat and antelope for weeks.

Thus it was all over the Dakotas. Although hundreds of snow shovelers were employed by the railways leading into Dakota, it was impossible to keep the roads open. During the day they shoveled through the drifts in a cut and during the night the heavy winds would fill the cut to the brim. Even in open places the telegraph wires were buried under these great mountains of snow.

On February second when it seemed the storms would have to cease, a great storm set in and continued without stopping for nine days. In the towns the streets were filled solidly to the tops of the buildings; and tunneling was used to secure a passageway about town. Farmers dug well-like holes down through the mountains of snow covering their barns and fed and cared for their stock through

[28] Doane Robinson, *History of South Dakota*, Vol. I, pp. 306, 307.

these openings. Fuel was scarce and the farmers burned hay. In town the lumber from the lumber yards, small buildings, fences, snow fences, and other available wood was burned. After the train service stopped, the kerosene supplies in the stores lasted but a few days and the whole country was obliged to sit in darkness for months. In the urban communities the business men formed themselves into relief committees to apportion out in an equitable fashion such supplies as were obtainable. Several families would colonize in one home to save fuel. Most of the settlers were young, however, and accepted this hardship as a lark. Very little real suffering resulted from the lack of food and fuel.[29]

In a blizzard in 1885 near Fargo, Dakota Territory, a man was doing his chores in the barn when the storm came on suddenly. He became lost in trying to reach the house, and his wife, hearing his cry of distress, went out quickly and answered it. He heard it, and following in the direction of her voice, reached the house in safety.

The great blizzard of 1888 is sometimes called the "school children's storm." The morning of January twelfth dawned clear, warm, and bright. The children started cheerfully off to school. Before long a fifty-six mile wind was blowing and the temperature dropped to thirty-six degrees below zero in Nebraska. Children coming home from school were caught. Parents coming after their children lost their way and were frozen. Many heroic deeds of schoolteachers are recorded. Many, knowing the children could not reach their homes, stayed in the school-house for one or two nights. There they encouraged their little flock and cared for them through the long weary hours until relief came. Others had the members of their groups hold hands and, forming a living chain, guided the little ones to a neighboring home.

The Knieriem school-house in Jerauld County, Dakota Territory, was about one hundred and forty yards from a settler's home. Thirty yards beyond the house was a stack of flax straw. All day the

[29] *Ibid.*

storm raged and by four o'clock the fuel supply in the little school-house was exhausted. Fred Weeks, the oldest boy, was sent out to see whether the road was clear and the journey to the nearest house possible. When he returned, the group joined hands and with Fred in the lead, started toward the haven of refuge. They lost the path, missed a foot bridge, and plunged into a little ravine. One child's wraps that were tied about her shoes were lost. When just at the point of exhaustion, the group struck the straw pile. Fortunately they found a fork and a lath at the stack, and clearing away the snow, they dug a hole in the side of the pile and teacher and pupils crowded in out of the death-dealing blasts of the frigid wind. They had missed the house by only about six feet. They tore the little girls' aprons in strips and made a long string. Fred took one end and went out into the storm in the hope of finding the house. This was impossible. The storm raged furiously, blinding, suffocating, bewildering. He returned to the straw pile. Fruitlessly they called, shouted, and screamed singly and in unison. They made prepara-tions for the night. They dug back farther into the stack and Fred took his place at the entrance. They kept all awake, made them sing, talk, move about, and laugh between the periods of tears. They told stories, sang, and called the roll every few minutes, any-thing to keep the little ones from falling into the grip of that sleep which never wakes. About four o'clock in the morning the storm abated sufficiently for them to see the house through the flying snow. Teacher and pupils were taken there. All were more or less frost-bitten; one girl's feet were frozen so badly that they had to be amputated. Fred Week's feet were so badly frozen the flesh dropped off, but he finally recovered.

In Buffalo County, Dakota Territory, one man and his wife perished in their own dooryard searching for one another. Another man and his wife tried to reach the school-house in an attempt to take food and clothing to their children. They lost their way and, having a shovel with them, the man buried his wife in a large snow-drift and he tramped in a circle about the spot all day and all night.

They called to each other occasionally, greatly encouraging one another. Many parents were frozen while seeking their children.

Etta Shattuck, a school-teacher, near O'Neill, Nebraska, got lost in going home and remained seventy-four hours in a haystack before she was found with both feet frozen. The whole plains region was under a tremendous nervous strain. After three days the tension was broken by the reappearance of the sun. Parents separated from children and husbands from wives, were reunited in happy family circles. But not all circles were unbroken. Over two hundred persons, many of them little children, had lost their lives.[30]

Dust storms were also experienced on the plains in the eighties. In April, 1889, the dust arising from a gale and the smoke from numerous prairie fires, caused a cloud to hang over the whole country obscuring the sun. The dust was so fine it entered the tightest houses. Wheat that had been sown, was carried and deposited in the prairie grass at the field's edge or in the road at the end of fields. In places this grain lay so deep in the road that it could be shoveled up and hauled away.[31]

Floods also took a heavy toll in frontier times. The settlers, not knowing how large the docile looking plains' streams became, fell an easy prey to the raging torrent of spring floods. A stream which was nearly dry in summer, became a swirling, boiling menace to life and property in the spring. Indians, watching the builders of new communities lay out their towns said: "White man heap big fool build lodge by river. Water wash away." The settler, however, wiser than the child of nature, paid little attention to the advice of the red man. Following the blizzards with the unprecedented snowfall of the winter of 1880–1881, in March, as the result of Chinook winds in the Yellowstone country, the Missouri River ran like a wild sea down the entire valley from Pierre to Sioux City. Below Yankton settlers were driven out of the valley to Sioux City. Ice

[30] The authentic death list carried the names of one hundred and nine known Dakotans; over one hundred perished in Nebraska, besides a large number in Kansas.
[31] William Rhoads, *Recollections of Dakota Territory*, pp. 44, 45.

gorges in the river at Vermilion caused the water to rise rapidly, destroying three quarters of Vermilion and sweeping the valley between Vermilion and Gayville clear of everything. The farmers of Clay County were left with nothing but the clothes upon their backs. Their houses, barns, fences, farming implements, and all their stock were swept away. One hundred and thirty-two buildings in Vermilion alone were totally destroyed.

CHAPTER XVI

WOMEN AND CHILDREN ON THE FRONTIER

SAID one trained observer who traveled on the prairie frontier in the fifties: "There is profound truth in the remark that 'plains travel and frontier life are peculiarly severe upon women and oxen.' "

A new country is made up of young people. Generally there were from three to thirty times as many unmarried men as unmarried women. The demand for marriageable women was so great that a young woman sometimes had more beaux than fingers and was at a loss to decide which one of a number of well-qualified suitors to accept. Indeed, a young girl was a rare creature on the plains and was quickly given an opportunity to accept the love and protection of a vigorous young man who could offer her a primitive cabin on a quarter-section for a home.

The great disparity of numbers between the two sexes decreased rapidly, however, for young men returned for sweethearts in the East. Some had arrangements made to return for their fiancées. Others returned to the East to stay during the winter with the intention of becoming acquainted with a suitable person and after a whirlwind courtship, bring her back to the frontier. It was not at all unusual to find a notice tacked up on a settler's door with the simple notice warning away claim-jumpers: "Gone to get a wife."

These young emigrant couples, having joined their life interests, came west with high hopes and optimistic plans for the future. With little more than their health and hands as initial capital, they were ready to brave any hardship in the hope of securing a home on the prairie. In fewer instances older couples with children came to improve their circumstances and face the unfavorable conditions of nature.

Four factors in the life of the plains' settler made life difficult: the perpetual winds, the absence of water, the terrific heat, and the absence of trees. A fifth, the deadening cold, was particularly severe in the Dakotas. There can be no doubt that the real burden of these adverse conditions fell upon the wife and mother. Courageously the frail girl broke old ties in the East hardly daring to hope ever to see her old home and friends again. Resolutely and tearfully she turned her back on the comforts of the East, the excellent furniture, flowers and garden, to face life on the bleak prairie in a dugout with but meager furniture and the monotonous solitude of the prairies.

Often, no doubt at the time of leaving the old home, the romantic spirit and the air of adventure obscured the unpleasant features and it was only when the plucky woman got her first view of a dugout and realized that such a hole in the ground was to be her home that she sensed the utter loneliness and drab realities of her future life. Many women were reduced to tears when they first caught sight of their future dwelling. One witness tells of a refined woman born in New York near the Susquehanna River amid the pines and maples near the brooks and rocks. She settled on the Kansas plains about 1860. She was found crying—crying because there was nothing beautiful at which to look; everything was hopelessly ugly. The inside of the house was crude and inartistic. There was nothing graceful indoors or out, only the vast measureless prairie with nothing but unending grass, green in the spring, seared and brown in the early autumn, and burnt and black in winter. There were no trees, no rocks, not even a sky line, only the shimmering waves of blistering heat rising from the tropical prairie.[1]

Tender, clinging vines were torn from the conveniences of an eastern home and transplanted amid the rude surroundings of the

[1] Adela Elizabeth Richards Orpen, *Memories of the Old Emigrant Days in Kansas, 1862–1865*, pp. 51, 52.

frontier. Cultured New England women were taken from the comforts of living rooms carpeted with rugs and furnished with pianos, and placed in dugouts with only one window and the bare dirt for a floor.

These solitary women, longing to catch a glimpse of one of their own sex, swept their eyes over the boundless prairie and thought of the old home in the East. They stared and stared across space with nothing to halt their gaze over the monotonous expanse. Sometimes the burning prairie got to staring back and they lost their courage. They saw their complexions fade as the skin became dry and leathery in the continual wind. Their hair grew lifeless and dry, their shoulders early bent, and they became stooped as they tramped round and round the hot cookstove preparing the three regular though skimpy meals each day. There was little incentive to primp and care for one's person. Few bothered much about brushes and combs. Hollow-eyed, tired, and discouraged in the face of summer heat, drought, and poverty, they came to care little about how they looked. Some begged their husbands to hitch up the team, turn the wagon tongue eastward, and leave the accursed plains which were never meant for human habitation. They were willing to sell out for a song—anything to get out of the country. Letters from home during droughts and grasshopper years, telling of the good crops in the old home, accentuated this feeling.[2]

How much of the retreat from the frontier from time to time was due to the women, is not known, but it is certain that many stayed until the prairie broke them in spirit or body while others fled from the monotonous terror of it.[3]

There was nothing to do or see and nowhere to go. The conversation each day was a repetition of that of the day before and was primarily concerning the terrible place where they had to live. Even the children felt the monotony of the life. One day in the eighties in southwestern Kansas a little boy came into the house

[2] Stuart Henry, *Conquering Our Great American Plains*, pp. 256, 257, 323–325.
[3] S. K. Humphrey, *Following the Frontier*, pp. 131–132.

to his mother and, throwing himself on the floor in hopeless grief, exclaimed, "Mamma, will we always have to live here?" When she hopelessly replied in the affirmative, he cried out in desperation, "And will we have to die here, too?" [4]

By no means were all the women crushed and defeated by the rude frontier. Many a member of the fairer sex bore her loneliness, disappointment, and heart aches without complaint. Brushing away the unbidden tears, she pushed ahead, maintaining her position by the side of her hardy husband, a fit companion of the resolute conqueror of the plains. Together the two unflinchingly waged a winning struggle against the odds of poverty and loneliness.

One woman in recalling early homestead days exclaimed: "It did seem so good to see the women coming in!" Although toil, fear, and dangers, were disagreeable, the dreariness and loneliness were the most oppressive. As the days and weeks passed, the prairie woman hungered for an opportunity to exchange thought and speech with one of her own sex. Mrs. James McClure was at one time deprived of the sight of a white woman for over a year. Hearing that at last one had come to live on a claim some miles away, she determined to see her; setting out early one morning accompanied by her two little children, she walked several miles. At length she reached the other's cabin door and—joy inexpressible! —there stood one like herself. They were utter strangers, neither knowing the other's name, but they threw their arms about each other and wept, then laughed, and wept again.

The Victorian age esteemed woman lightly in many ways. Her status universally was held to be secondary to man. Women, the necessary half of humanity for the propagation of the race and the comfort of man, received scant consideration from the male population. Legally they were subject to their husbands and all but lost their identity at marriage. Husbands sold their homes or their business without consulting their wives and it was held to be the

---

[4] Leola Howard Blanchard, *Conquest of Southwest Kansas* (Wichita, Kansas, 1931), p. 68.

latter's duty to follow the head of the household silently. It was especially distasteful to have women speak in public.

Although the life of woman on the plains was rude and hard, her position was legally, educationally, and socially, higher than in the more conservative East. Nevertheless in man's story of the conquest of the prairies, woman is given scant credit for her part. In prairie grass cemeteries in unmarked, forgotten graves sunken with the passing of time, lie the heroines of the far-flung vanguard of permanent civilization, the Marys, Hannahs, Margarets, and Sarahs. These martyrs who paid the price of the prairie, however, live in the grateful hearts of posterity.

The poverty of the frontier bore especially hard on the woman. Usually the family was poor and striving to climb the economic ladder. Many had to borrow money to make the journey west and pay the filing fee. Others found themselves without money after paying the fee and beginning life on the claim.

A woman in Cloud County, Kansas, said their total cash expenditure during the first year of married life, was sixteen dollars. Looking back in a reminiscent mood on the early hardship, she felt that life under those circumstances was peaceful and serene as compared with the more modern times when money was freer and wants harder to satisfy. Very little actual cash was ever seen. When neighbors exchanged work, the balance was paid in barter. The creditor received turkeys, lumber, wood, ox-bows, or seed grains.

The life of the women was much more tedious than that of the men. The latter seemed to have a jolly time as their exchange of work took them from farm to farm or on trips to the distant town; but women were tied down to their homes by the tiny children and the lack of adequate means of travel. Much of their time was spent alone in surroundings that compared very unfavorably with the old home. The invariable wind blowing day after day, tended to make them nervous. Moreover, the good housekeeper who had been used to an immaculate house never felt at home in a hole in the ground or in a home made of dirt above the surface of the earth.

Even those who had the good fortune to live in frame houses in the prairie town, had their trials. The gritty dust filtered into the house filling men's beards and women's hair. A newly washed window was almost as dirty within a day's time as before it had been washed. The hard water succumbed to no devices for softening it. This water hardened and roughened the skin and left the clothes in bad condition. The woman set about to supply herself with wash water by strewing tubs, dishpans, and other available vessels, under the eaves. The wind scattered these hither and yon; a little later the rain barrel, a well-known institution, appeared at the corner of the house to catch the raindrops which dripped from the eaves and were carried to the barrel by means of a trough. This receptacle became the reservoir to draw on for any soft water needs. In time cisterns were dug.

Swarms of hungry flies buzzed through the house. There were no screens, and the insects possessed the house from kitchen to bedroom. They drowned in the food, annoyed the diner, and woke the children up at such an early hour that they remained irritable throughout the day. In many places a smudge was built regularly in the evening to scare the insects away and make sleep possible. As the torrid sun beat mercilessly down on the little shack and the hot winds breathed their infernal breath upon the once smooth cheek of the tanned mother, she often wondered whether the country would ever become worth while and whether her children would ever have an opportunity in life.

Occasionally children became lost on the prairie. In 1868 in Lancaster County, Nebraska, two children, seven and eight and a half years old, wandered out to where their brother was herding cattle. They became lost in the high grass. The parents sought for them for four days and, thinking that the wolves had eaten them, mourned them as dead. A neighbor brought word they had been at his house and he had given them some food but, not knowing they were lost, had let them go. Finally after they had been absent eleven days, the father found them purely by accident. They were sleeping in the high grass. Their clothing was torn and they were so weak from lack of food that they could not walk. The father carried the little girl on his back some distance, then set her down and went back for the little boy; thus alternately carrying his precious burdens, he finally brought them back home safely.

The work of Mrs. LeRoy Otis of Tecumseh, Nebraska, is typical of the help which the pioneer woman rendered her husband. She planted ten acres of pumpkins, squashes, watermelons, muskmelons, and other garden truck. In the fall she put up a forty gallon barrel of cucumber pickles. She traded a load of pumpkins for a runty pig one day while her husband was away, cut saplings, and built a pen for her newly obtained property. She washed for a woman in exchange for a loaf of wheat bread, and at another time made a pleated-bosomed shirt for the husband of the same woman for another loaf. She likewise earned the first peck of seed potatoes by washing for a neighbor. Once more by washing she secured some turkeys and chickens and went into the poultry-raising business.

Wash day brought its problems for the frontier woman. As one woman remarked, wash day meant Monday and Tuesday and the term should have been "wash days." In the earliest times there was no bar soap. Soft soap and hot water were put into a keg and then the clothes were dumped into this mixture. The clothes were first vigorously prodded with a stick, then taken out and laid on a block and pounded with a mallet. When the clothes were sufficiently clean they were hung on bushes or fences to dry. Wash boards, boilers, and machines were unheard of. Great care was taken not to break any of the buttons with the mallet for buttons were too scarce and costly. They were made of pearl or bone, mostly bone. The clothes were seldom blued; if they were, commercial bluing was not used. Sometimes a piece of old blue calico was rinsed in the water and the clothes were run through the bluish solution. Frequently the women folk of the family migrated to a little creek or branch on wash day. The large ten gallon iron kettle and the clothes were taken to the bank of the stream and there, where wood and water were plentiful, the washing was done and the clothes hung on the brush and high grass along the bank to dry. When the washing was over, the big kettle was turned upside down and left there and the dry clothes were taken to the house.

Soap-making was another interesting home process. The ashes were saved and thrown into a V-shaped hopper called a leach. Wood ashes were best, with the exception of black walnut. Corn-stalk ashes were used largely on the treeless plains. While the ashes were accumulated during the winter, the meat scraps were collected in another receptacle—all kinds of fat, bacon rinds, scraps from lard fryings, the drippings of tallow and lard, and bones, for marrow makes excellent soap grease. When the time arrived to make soap, water was poured over the ashes in the leach and the liquid which soaked through the ashes, was caught in a pail. For good soap this brown liquid had to be strong enough to hold up an egg. The meat scraps were put into the large iron kettle and the potash added. After several hours' boiling, this combination formed a slippery mass called soft soap. It was usually kept in this form, but in later years by adding salt and continuing the boiling process, hard soap was made. When at the right stage, this liquid intended for hard soap, was poured into a bread pan or other shallow receptacle lined with cheese cloth. When hardened, it was cut and when fairly dry was pulled out of the mold by the cloth.

One of the greatest trials of the pioneer woman was remaining alone in the isolated cabin for days and even weeks while the husband went to the mill, to town, or worked away from home to secure sustenance for the little family. The danger of Indian attacks was ever present and every object seen approaching the cabin, was looked upon with apprehension. At such a time a visit from a stranger was unwelcome. A woman in Lincoln County, Kansas, was alone with her two babies while her husband was to be away several days. The larder was running low and one day as the young housewife looked out she saw an ox team approaching. The driver, a powerful man, got out and carried a quarter of fresh buffalo meat to the house. In answer to his inquiry as to whether she would like some meat the lady replied that they needed it but her husband was away and had left no money. He replied, "Oh, that's all right, he can just pay me any time," and left the meat. It was some years before they learned the identity of the hunter.

Of all the hardships, privations, and sacrifices, sickness weighed most heavily on the discouraged plains dweller. On one of the coldest nights of the winter of 1870, a man burst into a restaurant in Wichita, Kansas, saying: "Say, Landlady, there is a woman dead out east. Don't you want to go with me and see what can be done"? At the end of a long cold ride across the unfriendly arctic prairie, they entered a dugout. The place was dimly lighted but the good Samaritans were able to make out through the shadows the figure of a gaunt-looking man and near him several half-clothed children. Just opposite the door under the remnants of a dirty wagon cover lay concealed the object of the journey. Drawing aside the dirty rags, they found a comparatively young woman. An old faded calico wrapper was the only garment covering her. A wedding ring encircled a finger of the hand extended toward two small objects shivering in the corner. The woman had died giving birth to twins. The next day the first aid society was formed in the community. Forty dollars was raised to bury the woman and buy clothing for the older children. The twins lived to have homes of their own.[5]

Childbirth, a severe trial under the most comfortable circumstances, became a terrible dread on the lonely frontier. Miles stretched between the patient and the nearest doctor. Blizzards or floods often made it impossible to secure the help of a doctor. Many times the child was born without medical aid. At Lakin, Kansas, in the eighties the conductor of a passenger train telegraphed Mrs. William Loucks, a midwife, to be at the depot ready for service when the train pulled in; but the child was born on a freight truck

[5] "Pioneer Womèn of Peerless Princess," *Wichita Eagle*, March 8, 1908. In the early days Wichita was called the "Peerless Princess" of the plains.

on the depot platform before the patient could be moved to a private place.

Hard indeed was the lot of the woman who was called upon to give up a loved one in death. Perhaps the family was traveling through the country in search of a location when sickness seized a little one. Deprived of the comforts of life, the devoted parents struggled to provide for the most pressing wants. Their hearts nearly broke when they were unable to give the loved one the little luxuries for which it so earnestly pleaded. More bitter still was the hour when they were called upon to part with the little one. Kind friends among the strangers dug a small grave and, as the little group stood about the grave of the sunshine of the lives of the broken-hearted father and mother, they took a last look and laid the precious one away. There frequently was no minister to speak words of comfort to the bereaved parents. The mother found it almost impossible to tear herself away from the scene and leave her precious treasure alone on the bleak prairie. Scenes similar to this one occurred again and again making the woman's lot hard to bear.

In Sioux County, Nebraska, a young school-teacher married and went to live on a claim. Their shack was made of lumber with cracks large enough to stick the fingers through. When a little daughter was born the mother suffered much with bealed breasts. There was no doctor for miles around, no milk could be secured, and the baby died of starvation.

There is a longing in the heart of every woman for beautiful things. One observer who visited a sand hill homestead, found the husband away earning money for his family. The wife, a refined intelligent woman with honest unassumed yearning, confided to the stranger that she had always wanted a floor in her home. They had lived there six years always hoping to have enough money to buy lumber for a floor but never did. Now she hoped that since her husband had work she might have a floor before winter closed in.

Illumination was usually a problem which involved the woman

in a special way. As a rule the family regulated its program by the sun as closely as possible so that they might get along with a minimum of artificial light. This was possible during the summer, but the winter with its long evenings made lights necessary. In the homes of the more prosperous, candles were used. These were made at home; the manufacturing work fell to the lot of the housewife. There were two common methods of making candles. If there was no candle mold available, the dipping process was used. The wicks, consisting of twisted string, were dipped into a kettle of hot tallow. When withdrawn a certain amount of tallow stuck to the wick and hardened quickly in the cool air. After it had solidified it was dipped again. This process was continued until the wick had accumulated layer after layer of tallow and formed a regular-sized candle. In the second method, a candle mold consisting of a dozen tubes, was filled with tallow. Wicks were drawn in the center of the tubes and hot tallow was poured into them. When the tallow had hardened the mold was dipped into hot water for a moment and the candles slipped out readily. This was a great improvement over dipping and the candle molds were lent often. The tallow for candles was secured from buffalo and deer in the earlier times and from beeves in later years. In the late sixties after the discovery of petroleum in Pennsylvania, the kerosene lamp made its appearance. Although a great improvement over former rural lighting, it brought an endless round of cleaning sooty lamp chimneys and filling smelly kerosene lamps.

During the early years of settlement the woman spun the wool into yarn and knit the mittens and stockings. She frequently helped milk, cared for the milk, made butter and cheese, and raised a large flock of chickens, turkeys, ducks, and geese. She had charge of a large garden and did most of the work in it. In the absence of most of the modern conveniences she was obliged to do the best she could with the help of crude makeshifts. Having no refrigerator, she had to cool her milk and butter by lowering them into the well in a pail or tub.

In the earlier days there were no bedsteads, and one pioneer of 1856 wrote:

Sleeping on the ground is not confined to camping out but is extensively practiced in all our cabins. Floors are a luxury rarely seen here. In our own dwelling part of the inmates rest on the earth, while others sleep on sacking over our heads. . . . I noticed yesterday a member of our family making up his bed with a hoe!

Crowding was customary and a large number sleeping in a little cabin meant to take part of the meager furnishings out-of-doors before there was room enough to set the table. Crockery was used frequently on the table for dishes.

CHAPTER XVII

HOMESTEADER DAYS AND WAYS

ONE of the greatest hardships of frontier life was the great distance to town, to the mill, the blacksmith shop, or the railroad. There were no roads at first and the settlers stalked across the prairie along the line of least resistance like the buffalo had done for centuries. The trail usually followed the ridges carefully avoiding patches of cultivated land. Where timber was procurable, the people sometimes erected poles here and there across the prairie in a line to mark the road to town. Near Hay Springs, in western Nebraska, early settlers indicated the way across the plains with pieces of rag tied to an occasional weed, thus marking the trail between the lonely homesteader and civilization. The homesteader invariably gave the location of his dwelling by the section and township numbers.[1] Distance was measured by tying a handkerchief to the wheel of a wagon and counting the revolutions.

The traveler was obliged to ford the rivers since there were no bridges, and ferries were few. This presented difficulties. A heavy rain necessitated a wait of one or more days until the flood subsided. In certain parts of the plains quicksand proved very dangerous, engulfing man and beast. In other places muddy stream bottoms caused the wagon to stick fast so that the horses were unable to pull the load up the steep, slippery bank. This necessitated unloading the wagon and carrying the freight bit by bit to the bank, pulling the unloaded wagon out, and reloading, before continuing the journey once more.

In Furnas County, Nebraska, in 1874 a settler went to town for a load of seed grain. When he forded the Republican River on the

[1] J. Clarence Norton, personal interview, December 28, 1933.

return trip, he got stalled when about two-thirds of the way across. He had to unhitch and carry every sack on his back to the shore. When this stupendous task was completed, the team could not even move the empty wagon out of the mud. In order to proceed he had to float the box to shore, take the wagon apart, carry it out piece by piece, put it together again, and reload. The weather at this time was so cold icicles formed on his clothes while he worked.

Oftentimes three or four settlers would start out together on one of these trips to be gone for a week or two. When they reached a stream, they took all teams across but one and then ran the wagons down the bank into the stream with the aid of the remaining team. Then with a chain long enough to reach across the stream, the teams which had solid footing on the other side, easily pulled the wagons across. This process was repeated until all the wagons in the company were over the stream.

The gun and the grub box were two of the essentials of any trip. The grub box, generally an empty cracker box about twelve by sixteen inches, with a hinged lid, usually contained the following: Coffee pot, coffee knife (usually a hunting knife with a buckhorn handle), frying pan, tin cup, tin plate, fork, teaspoon, salt, watertight box containing matches, pepper, butter in a closed can, grease in a closed can, pancake flour, baking powder, a piece of bacon, and whatever food the particular person could afford. On these one-to-seven-day trips one never knew what might happen. On the way home the larder was sometimes enriched and the diet varied by the addition of crackers and cheese to the menu.[2] A dime's worth of cheese stretched out over several meals for one of these thrifty, poverty-stricken settlers. Many times meals were omitted and sometimes only one meal a day was taken.

The travelers carried their own bedding. In the summer it was an easy matter to spread a blanket on the ground and make a simple but hard bed there. On colder nights they often stopped near some

[2] George Gale, *History of Old Clay County*, MS. County Scrapbook, Nebraska State Historical Society Library, Chapter IV.

settler's haystack and let the oxen eat hay while they made a mattress of "prairie feathers." This famous bed was made by spreading a thick layer of hay on the ground, placing two blankets over it and covering the blankets with another thick layer of hay. The traveler then took off his overcoat, for use as a pillow, and, fully clothed, wiggled down between the two blankets.

When the homesteader arrived at the mill or town he sat around the store, or office of the livery barn, ate his lunch, and soaked up the heat until closing time; then he took his blankets and went to the hayloft to sleep. The custom of settlers' sleeping in the hayloft or an empty stall in the livery barn, was so universal and respectable that the district judge might crawl out of the hay and proceed to the bench without loss of prestige. Of course, when the lodger came from the hay in the morning it was only natural that a few straws or seeds adhered to his clothing or hair. This gave rise to the well-known nickname, "hayseed."

There were two more nicknames which were applied to the rural folk. Great quantities of sorghum were made each year and consumed by the country people. With many, corn-bread and molasses was the principal diet. This was so extensive that it gave rise to a term which was applied to the settlers, "sorghum lappers." Still another nickname apparently originated from the fact that the farmer had to follow the walking plow and avoid the clods as best he could; he became known as a "clod hopper." [3]

Many times trips to town were made in the winter in order to save the good weather of the year to improve the claim, work for a neighbor, or attend to farming operations. If the journey was made in the spring or autumn, it many times was quite pleasurable, and the women folks sometimes went along, for they liked to go to town then as now. Ordinarily camping was pleasant, but, should inclement weather prevail, the travelers were welcome to spread their beds on the floor of the cabin of a neighborly settler. There were certain

[3] F. Turner, *Pioneers of the West*, pp. 248–260, *passim;* A. Roenigk, *Pioneer History of Kansas*, p. 312.

places along the route very popular as lodging places. Some settlers were especially hospitable and entertaining. In the cabin of such a road-side dweller the group sat in front of a fireplace, radiant with blazing logs, and swapped yarns. The town-goer always started on one of these trips with the expectation of reaching certain well-known places at which to camp at night. In summer it was planned to camp near town one night and the next day go into the city, attend to the business, and return to the camping place the next night.

While the men and possibly some of the women from a given community, were gone on the long trip, those left behind in the settlement looked after their families and stock. When it was time for those absent to return, the ones at home would walk to the crest of the nearest ridge and peer across the prairie in a strained effort to catch the first sight of the home-coming group. Sometimes the families gathered at the first house on the road to meet their loved ones, get the first news, receive the letters from friends in the East, and, if there were children in the family, receive their presents, for in spite of poverty the parents managed in some way to bring something for the children among the packages from town. Under the conditions which maintained in the sixties and seventies, children frequently were sixteen years old before they ever saw a town.

Anyone going to town informed his neighbors and did errands and transacted business for the entire vicinity. This accommodation was appreciated and reciprocated. Among other things, the man who went to town brought the mail for the community. Frequently the neighborhood met and made definite arrangements for carrying the mail. It was left at the home of a respected citizen of the community who acted as postmaster by common consent.

Sometimes the settler hauled products to town. Some who lived near streams or wooded land, hauled logs or posts. Occasionally game such as venison, wild turkey, or buffalo, was salable although it brought a meager return for the hard work and exposure of bringing it to market. Hauling wood and game was usually done in mid-winter and, without overshoes, the settler trudged along beside the sled for miles, his feet freezing in cowhide boots wrapped in sacking. There were many hardships incident to these trips. Now and again a tire came off or some other misfortune happened to the wagon. Again a raging torrent, unwisely risked, took away a valuable load of tools, grain, or other possessions.

In the earlier times frequently the settler was seventy to a hundred miles from the mill. As population spread westward more mills were established, bringing a mill within thirty or fifty miles of each community. In the meantime, however, the fringe of settlement spread westward and the new settlers were again seventy or eighty miles away from the mill. Although the number of mills increased and pushed westward, population always kept in advance.

Mills were frequently unable to grind all the grain. They often worked night and day, Sunday and holidays. It was no uncommon thing to find twenty or thirty teams at the mill. There was plenty of company and the waiting crowd visited, engaged in athletic contests such as foot racing, wrestling, and playing simple games like horseshoe, or in fishing in the mill stream. The length of the wait depended upon the traffic and the capacity of the mill. One man spoke of having arrived at the mill at nine o'clock at night and finding thirty teams waiting. By morning the mill was grinding his grist. On the other hand in 1855 at the United States Government-built mill on the Otoe Reservation in eastern Nebraska, the grinding was so slow and the rush so great that people were compelled to camp and wait for weeks for their grist. One old settler found that others who came after him were getting their grain ground first. This angered him. Upon investigating he found that a bottle of whiskey did the trick.[4] If any part of the machinery of a mill gave way, it was necessary to send it to St. Louis for repairs.

Hospitality was one of the cardinal virtues of the West. Even utter strangers were welcome to the settler's table and bed. Though it might be supplied at a sacrifice, the settler's hospitality was always

---

[4] J. H. Graham, Speech at old settlers' program at Northbend, Nebraska, July 4, 1889.

extended. Rarely was any payment expected or given in return. "The pioneer was hotel-keeper and distributor of alms to all the world that came his way."

Neighborly helpfulness was manifested on every hand. If a prairie fire burnt a man's hay, a neighbor sent a load over to him. If he lost his crop by some accident, the neighbors each donated a few bushels to tide him over the winter. When sickness prevented the head of the house from putting in his crop, the whole neighborhood turned out with tools and in a day or two put the more unfortunate neighbor on the way toward economic stability and opportunity.

Settlers were inveterate borrowers. Before the settler got his wheat threshed he borrowed from his neighbors. When a settler returned from the mill the neighbors often came in such numbers to borrow that almost all the flour would disappear. It came back a little at a time after the borrowers had been to the mill. Neighbors borrowed sausage grinders, horse collars, scoop shovels, hay-racks, and a host of implements and tools. There was the proverbial borrower who never returned what he borrowed. Since there was no telephone it was necessary to visit the neighbor to bring back the property.

Furniture and house equipment were fully as crude as the clothing and food. Stoves and bedding were ordinarily brought with the settler. The furniture was either of a makeshift variety or crudely made at home. The first furniture was likely to consist of a nail keg and trunk for chairs, and a box for a table. The little dugout was so small that in many cases the table had to be set outside in order to make room in the house for the family to get around to do the work. Often the beds were "knocked down" during the day for the same reason.

A bed was made in the corner by sticking two poles into adjacent dirt walls. A short post set in the floor at the point where the two poles joined formed the only leg of the bed. A third pole was thrust into the wall at the corner of the house. This pole and the one at the foot formed a support for other poles laid lengthwise of the bed.

The tick of prairie hay and a feather bed, if they had brought one from the East, were spread on this. In the morning it was the work of but a moment to take the bed down, carry it out-of-doors, and bring in the table and chairs. The bed was doubtless stationary in most cases. Sometimes the grass was knee-high under the bed where it was not tramped down.

The cupboard was an open box in the corner by the stove or fireplace. The clothes were often kept in the covered wagon to shelter them from the water which continually dripped through the roof of the sod-covered house after rains. When chairs were made they were stools of the three-legged variety. A little later splint bottom chairs were afforded by the more fortunate. The table, made of cottonwood and soon cracked and warped, was covered with an oilcloth or floursack table-cloth. Tin plates, case knives, and earthen bowls graced its top. Cardboard mottoes, worked in bright colored yarns, were found in many of the better furnished homes. The town house that could afford a floor covering, had a rag carpet laid over a mat of prairie hay. Sometimes sacks were used for rugs. In one home in Buffalo County, Dakota Territory, for four years a hay carpet was used. Every Saturday the lady of the house took up the old hay, swept the ground clean, and put down fresh hay in order to have things "spick and span" for Sunday. In some cabins there was no clock and no looking-glass. The lady had to use the water bucket for a mirror.

In the absence of a fireplace and cookstove, a trench was dug two feet long and just wide enough to set a skillet on. A Dutch oven was used on this improvised stove. This was a skillet set on three short legs. The lid was first heated in the fire. When the blaze had died down to coals, corn-bread was baked slowly in the oven which had been covered with the hot lid and buried in the live embers. Corn-bread, thus cooked in the coals, was delicious.

Many utensils were scooped out of solid blocks of wood with a tool called a gouge. Pails and small tubs called "piggins" and "noggens" were made of staves at home.

Starch for use in laundering was made of the dross which forms at the bottom of the vessel when potato water is allowed to stand for several hours. Another method was used after wheat growing had been introduced. Wheat or bran was soaked in tubs for several days; the mixture of water and softened grain was then strained through clean straw and poured back into the tub to settle. As soon as the water was clear, it was drained off and the white pap placed in the sun to dry and bleach.

Rough brooms were made of buckbrush. Scrubbing brooms were made of straight poles of green hickory with the lower ends cut into slivers. Bunches of broom-corn were tied together to form a rude broom for house use.

Corn meal was often produced by grinding corn in coffee mills or rubbing the ear of corn on a large grater or a tin pan with the bottom perforated by driving nails through it.

Fish hooks were costly and many times the pioneer merely bent a large pin. Not every house had a pair of scissors in it. Knives took their place. Little work was required to make a sack garment to clothe a child. Three holes were cut in the bottom end of the sack through which to poke the child's head and arms.[5]

An axe, a wagon, a team of oxen, and an ox yoke, were the principal needs of the head of the household. Some pioneers did not even own a team of oxen or a wagon for some time after reaching the West. They worked for their neighbors and borrowed or hired oxen for their own use. Men have actually come West on the railroad, selected a claim, built a house, made a garden, and occupied their new domain for months without a team. As many as three families were the joint owners of a team of oxen. For several years, of course, life on the frontier was a fierce combat against poverty. Some became discouraged and left; others, not having the means to leave, stayed and grew rich.

Mrs. LeRoy Otis says that for a long time after they came to Ne-

---

[5] Mrs. Nancy Chouteau and Mrs. N. M. Harris, "The Makeshifts of the Pioneers," *Kansas City Star*, November 11, 1911.

braska they had no light at night. They retired early and rose as soon as it was dawn, thus using nature's light. They managed if possible to get the work done before dark. Sometimes they would open the stove door and, sitting around it, allow the blaze to light up the family circle. One time her husband killed a fat skunk which gave two quarts of oil. This made an excellent odorless light when used in a crude wick lamp. Such a lamp popularly known as an "old hussy" was made by filling a bowl or cup half full of sand and placing a stick upright in the center. A wick was then wound around the stick and enough animal oil poured over the sand to fill the cup. Often lard was scarce and oppossums, badgers, coons, and other animals fell a prey to homemade lamps. The wick was lighted at the top and made a fairly good blaze.

Sickness and death, always pathetic, was well-nigh tragic on the frontier. Said a writer at Lawrence, Kansas, during the slavery troubles in 1855:

The graveyard is one of first apportionments, and the soonest to be thickly inhabited. Quite late in the autumn, one of our merchants returned east to bring his wife out here. She died of cholera on the Missouri river, and was buried where many other immigrants have found a last resting-place, upon its wild uninhabited banks. The forlorn husband, Mr. Wilder, continued his journey, and reached this place in safety. He inherited consumptive tendencies, and this sad misfortune aggravated and increased them. He died this week. He had made every preparation to return to his former home in Vermont, and waited only for better weather and better traveling. They both came too late.[6]

When sickness came it was often impossible to have a doctor because the nearest practitioner was frequently fifty to a hundred miles away. Home remedies, the remedial suggestions of kind neighbors or Indians, were often the only medical help for the stricken one. During a protracted illness the neighbors offered their help and two or three "sat up" with the patient every night. When death came, kind neighbors closed the eyes of the deceased. Riders

[6] Mrs. H. A. Ropes, *Six Months in Kansas*, p. 185.

were dispatched to carry the word throughout the little community. There was no undertaker except in the larger cities at a comparatively late day. The neighbors came and "laid out" the body, washing and clothing it and making it look as presentable as possible. The arms were folded and held in position until the body grew rigid.

On the ruder frontier where no lumber was available, bodies were often buried wrapped in a blanket or sheet. Men took their wagon boxes to make coffins for their wives. Floors, clothes closets, and cupboards were torn up and sacrificed to furnish caskets for a loved one or a neighbor's loved one. On the occasion of the first death in Garden City, Kansas, a coffin was made of rough pine boards and blacked with shoe polish.[7] When sawmills came, coffins were made to order from black walnut or other native wood by the coffin-maker according to measurement. They were somewhat triangular in shape, wide at the shoulders and narrowed down to a peak at the feet. Newt Ard of Elsmore, Kansas, remembered that as a boy in the sixties, he rode on horseback to the coffin-maker carrying a stick with marks on it indicating the length and shoulder breadth of the corpse. In town the casket for an older person was nicely covered with black alpaca, and those for children were covered with white cloth.[8]

While the coffin was being fashioned other neighbors met, and, if a graveyard had not been provided, set apart a new cemetery; strong arms supported by willing and sympathetic hearts, dug the grave. If the death occurred in the night the burial was held the next day, for with no embalming the body disintegrated quickly. If death were too late in the day for burial, friends "sat up" with the body, keeping on the face of the corpse a cloth wet with vinegar in order to deter mortification as much as possible. Ministering neighbors placed the muslin shroud on the body and laid it in the casket.

If opportunity permitted carrying out the formalism of eastern

[7] Soot or lampblack was often used to black the new boards and make a coffin look presentable.

[8] *Buffalo County History* (Dakota Territory), (Gann Valley, South Dakota, 1934), p. 16.

burials, there was an awful blackness surrounding the burial and all the death trappings. This, however, was usually not permitted on account of the lack of equipment. If a minister was near at hand a funeral was conducted in a formal way at the home or school-house. The neighbor having the best wagon or ox cart, volunteered to use his vehicle for the hearse. A service was also held at the grave. A funeral was the minister's great opportunity to make an impression on the rough frontiersmen. They would listen on an occasion like this which placed them in a receptive mood.

More often, however, a minister could not be called and the body was buried with a prayer or a few words from some member of the community. Possibly the Sunday-school superintendent or some religious woman spoke a few words of comfort in the trying hour, and the next time the circuit rider came around, weeks or months later, he held a funeral service at the lonely little grave on the prairie.

There was very little evidence of mourning in the dress of those in attendance at a funeral. Ordinary clothing was worn. If there were flowers on the prairie or near the homestead residences at the time of the burial, the women brought them to garland the coffin. Bereavement is hard to bear in a home of comfort and ease where friends and kinfolk surround the mourners. It must have been far harder for the bereaved ones to return to a bare shack to face the hardships of frontier life without the helpmate, the parent, or the little child, the light of the home.

In the year 1867 at the funeral of a victim of the Indian massacre of that year, the armed funeral procession wended its way over the level Kansas plains and lowered the body into the grave. The ceremony was barely over when a buffalo was seen coming toward the mourners. Because of the restlessness of the Indians, the settlers had kept close to their homes and were short of provisions. Here was meat walking into their hands. With no thought of disrespect the scene quickly shifted from a funeral to a buffalo hunt. The buffalo was killed and the meat divided among the needy people of the community.

CHAPTER XVIII

FUEL AND WATER

TWO VITAL NECESSITIES for the people in any region are fuel and water. The prairie pioneer was called upon to face the difficult task of providing himself with these essentials under circumstances to which he was unaccustomed. The pioneer of Daniel Boone's day had a different set of problems to face than did the prairie settler. There was an abundance of timber for fuel and building. In fact there was too much timber. Clearing the land was the bane of the farmer's life. Years passed before the land was under cultivation, whereas on the prairies, with no clearing to do, the land was producing almost immediately. Water likewise was readily procurable in the timber country from the numerous streams, springs, and easily dug shallow wells. On the other hand as settlement crept westward toward the mountains it became increasingly difficult to secure a good supply of water.

The first settlers naturally located along the streams and secured their fuel from the timber which grew there in abundance. As settlement pushed out of the valleys onto the high lands, the upland settlers went to the streams for wood. The railroad grant and any land owned by people in the East, was cut over. It was argued that it was fair to cut over the railroad grants because the railroad, a great corporation, was securing an enormous profit. There was a general feeling that stealing from a railroad was not unrighteous. Then, too, it was thought to be all right to steal from the speculators for they remained in comfort in the East while the "actual settlers" lived on their land, improved it, and thereby increased the value of the speculators' land. One witness at one time saw as many as two hundred teams in the sparse timber in Union County, Dakota Territory. Finally the owners sent an agent threatening to prosecute the trespassers.

In some places land kept in trust for the Indians, was robbed of its timber. In Barber and Comanche Counties, Kansas, for several years after settlement a large number of people made a living by cutting and hauling cedar posts off the Osage lands to Wichita and Hutchinson. Various other kinds of timber grew there also and was likewise hauled into the towns and sold for fuel. There was considerable rivalry between the residents of Barber County and residents of adjacent counties over the wood rights. While it was considered legitimate to take the wood from the Indians, the filchers drew the line on allowing non-residents to share in the profits. This was done by threatening to report them to the United States authorities. It was not uncommon for citizens of the county to make a new resident give up his load of wood and even his money on threat of prosecution.[1] In Turner County, Dakota Territory, in the seventies two men each took a load of wood from government land, and, while passing through a community, hostile because of a county seat struggle, were reported to the Federal authorities. They were arrested late in the summer and taken to Yankton where their trial was appointed for the next April. The judge freed them on each other's bond and they returned home. They went to Yankton at the appointed time and refused to go on each other's bond any longer. This forced the government to pay their board and keep while they were there. They were tried before a judge who had been reared on the frontier himself and knew something of its hardships. He decided it was simply a case of moving timber from one piece of government land to another and discharged them. After the court adjourned he went to the men and shook hands

<hr>

[1] Contributions of members of the Old Settlers' Association, "Historical Sketch of Union County, South Dakota," South Dakota Historical *Collections*, Vol. XI, p. 571; T. A. McNeal, *When Kansas Was Young*, pp. 11, 12.

with them, saying: "Boys, I am sorry you have got to walk home. I wish you had your team with you so you could go home by way of the gulches and get another good load." [2]

People went twenty, thirty, and even forty miles, to haul firewood of even the poorest quality. Later arrivals even grubbed up the stumps of trees which had been cut by earlier wood hunters.

Many pioneers kept the oven full of green cottonwood to cure it sufficiently to burn well. The fitful fire of green wood burned with a continual hissing and sputtering as the sap and steam oozed from the ends of every stick in the fire-box and oven while the stove seemed barely warm to the impatient cook.

The first settlers on the table-land gathered buffalo and cow chips for fuel. They hauled them in and stacked them in ricks like haystacks to keep them dry for winter use. The settler was glad to have the cowboys bed their trail herd on his land for it meant several hundred pounds of cow chips. As this fuel became scarce it was customary for those traveling across the prairie to take along a sack and play a sort of "I spy" game wherein every stray cow chip as big as one's fist was picked up and taken to the house.

When the ranching area was curtailed by the homesteader and the great herds of cattle were pushed westward, people had to find other material for fuel. The poverty was too great to permit the purchase of coal, and the settlers in their dire extremity were forced to grasp at every possible opportunity for the substitution of light material for wood. Woody weeds such as sunflowers were advocated. Mr. G. C. Clark of Canton, Dakota Territory, advertised sunflower seed for sale in 1871, claiming that one acre would produce twelve cords and would furnish enough fuel for a winter.

The fuel that was almost universally used, however, was hay twisted into convenient form. Ingenious men tried to invent devices to twist hay. These were used with varying degrees of success. One Dakota man's invention consisted of two upright pieces of wood

[2] W. H. Stoddard, *Turner County Pioneer History*, p. 295.

carrying a crank and roller. Hooks caught the long prairie hay and wound it until it was a solid stick of the proper size. These sticks were then cut into lengths like stove wood. Many other devices were contrived to make hay fit to burn. The greater part of the twisted hay, however, was made by hand. These twists were known as "cats." [3] The tiny shacks were so filled with it in winter that there was hardly room for inmates or visitors. The wise husbandman always had a large pile of hay near the house to last over the period of a possible storm.

Hay-burning stoves were invented and put on the market. One unique style used magazines. It was built somewhat like an ordinary cookstove with a fire-box in the front part. Two pipes about thirty inches in length, filled with weeds, hay, or straw, were fitted in below the oven with an end opening into the fire-box. The hay was set on fire in the box and as it burned a spring at the other end of the pipe pressed on the hay pushing it into the fire-box as fast as it was consumed. A supply of eight or ten pipes was kept filled and on hand; when one pair of magazines was burned out, a ratchet was turned, winding up the spring, and the fireman inserted a loaded pair of pipes. [4]

Another type of hay-burning stove was known as a drum from the fact that drums of sheet iron held the hay. The stove, constructed similarly to the "Round Oak" stove so familiar a generation ago, stood about four and one-half feet high and consisted of a base which rested on legs and a top which lifted up to allow removal of the drum. The drum, which sat on the base and on which the top part of the stove rested, was about two feet in diameter. There were two or more drums, and while one was being packed tight with straw or hay at the nearby straw pile or hay stack, the other was in place on the stove. When the fuel burned out, the empty drum was

[3] Doane Robinson, "The Education of Redcloud," South Dakota Historical Collections, Vol. XIII, p. 162; W. L. Smith, "Early Life in McCook County," Monthly South Dakotan, October, 1901, p. 186; John B. Perkins, History of Hyde County, South Dakota (1908), pp. 26–27.
[4] Ord Quizz, Ord, Nebraska, June 21, 1923, p. 17.

THE MAGAZINE TYPE OF
HAY-BURNING STOVE

Courtesy of the Nebraska State
Historical Society.

replaced by the full one. One of these drums packed tight with heavy slough grass would keep a good fire an hour or two.[5]

Another hay-burner consisted of a wash-boiler-shaped contraption which when filled with hay or straw was set upside down over the stove with its lids off. Sometimes the smoke went out through the stovepipe and sometimes through the room.[6]

The Mennonite immigrants brought with them the idea of a hay-burning stove which they used in their old homes in Russia. It was built of brick and was six feet high, five feet long, and two feet wide. It was built in the wall between two rooms so that the sides would heat both rooms. The walls were kept warm by the circulation of heat and smoke. Hay, buffalo chips, corn-stalks, and weeds were burned in it. It had such a big fire-box and the circulation was so arranged, that firing was necessary only twice a day—evening and morning.[7] For some reason, perhaps the cost, it never gained wide usage.

Hay, although used for several years, was unsatisfactory as a fuel. It made a hot fire but it required constant attention. There was a saying that it took two men and a boy to keep the hay fire going. Furthermore, quantities of gas were released in the house during the process of continually replenishing the fuel. The fireman frequently was afflicted with a severe headache from inhaling these gases.

The fire hazard was greatly enhanced by the use of this fuel. Large quantities of hay in the house made a conflagration easy and probable. Changing drums or opening the stove to insert new "cats" gave an opportunity for embers to get out and start a blaze. The *Huronite*[8] of Huron, Dakota Territory, gave an account of one such mishap which destroyed the home of William Bishop of that

[5] Personal interview with Professor W. E. Nelson, former president of Pacific Union College. Mr. Nelson remembers that when he was a boy in Dakota he took the drum out to the straw pile and filled it. *History of Buffalo County*, p. 73.

[6] *Ibid.*, pp. 39–40.

[7] Edna Nyquist, *Pioneer Life and Lore*, p. 80.

[8] *Dakota Huronite*, February 23, 1882.

city in 1882. When the stove door was opened a large charred bundle rolled out on the floor. A strong wind blowing through the open door of the house caught this and scattered fire in all directions. The occupants were immediately driven from the house and everything was consumed.

Astonishing as it may seem a brickyard was established at Ord, Nebraska, in 1881 and bricks were burned with hay. A house built of bricks burned in the kiln in 1881, has stood in that city for over fifty years. It took great quantities of hay and weeds to burn a "batch." One month was spent in preparing for the burning. About two-thirds of the kiln was very good. The other third was rather poor.[9]

After the production of corn became established it brought new fuel. The cobs were burned in the kitchen stove and the stalks were burned in the fireplace or heater. A company at Omaha, Nebraska, manufactured a "fuel press." It was a hand power device which pressed corn-stalks and other similar stalky materials into compact bundles so that they could be bound with patent steel bands. A knife on the machine cut the bundle instantaneously into a convenient size for burning. According to the advertisement a bundle burned from twenty to forty minutes. A man or boy could make three bundles at once in sixty to ninety seconds, so the manufacturers claimed. The bands could be recovered from the ashes and used from seventy-five to a hundred times. The machine sold for twenty dollars.[10]

One man found himself without fuel when a snow-storm came. The only available fuel was corn-stalks and these had to be taken

---

[9] *Ord Quizz*, June 21, 1923, p. 17.

[10] *Nebraska Farmer*, October, 1877, February, 1880. In discussing the vitally important subject of fuel the *Nebraska Farmer* gave the following table, rating the effectiveness of various fuels in an attempt to show the value of corn-stalks:

Shell bark hickory	100	Pine	42
Oak	81	Corn stalks	35
Beech	65	Soft coal	85
Maple	60	Hard coal	103
Elm	58		

With greater pressure and better management of fire corn-stalks could be made more effective.

from snow knee-deep. He took a spade and, pushing it down near the stalk, cut it off close to the ground and pulled it up. When he had secured as much as he could carry, he slung it in a rope and took it home. This fuel made a good fire but required a man's entire time to get it and feed it to the stove.[11] When corn was cheap, it was burned on the cob in quantities. It made an excellent hot fire for it is an oily and concentrated bulk.

The first settlers who located in the valleys got their water from springs, or from the running streams. Often the women folk had to carry the water long distances from springs or neighbors' wells. One lady mentioned sinking some salt barrels in the ground near the river. The barrels soon filled with water and if they were dipped dry, they filled up again overnight. Shallow wells, twenty to thirty feet deep, usually provided an abundance of water. It was different on the ridges and high table-lands, however. Water was not to be had closer than a hundred feet and frequently it was two hundred. The buffalo wallows held the water from rains. This water, although it was warm and distasteful, was used to drink. Ponds were made but the water they held was no more palatable than that in the buffalo wallows, however, for it was filled with snakes, bugs, frogs, and larvae of various sorts. Cisterns were dug in draws or bordering lagoons. Many people hauled water from some distance and the old water barrel was a well-known institution. It stood in front of the house and supplied the household. In the summer its water became warm and insipid. In the winter it was taken in the house to keep it from freezing solid.

Hauling water in barrels occupied much of the early settler's time. If water was near at hand, a barrel was placed on a "lizard" or sled. If it was farther away, two or three barrels were placed in a wagon. The barrels were the ordinary wooden kerosene variety. To keep the water from slopping out, the top hoop was taken off, a cloth placed over the barrel, and the hoop driven back on again.

[11] B. E. Bengston, *Pen Pictures of the Pioneers* (Holdrege, Nebraska, 1931), Vol. II, p. 22.

According to the custom of the time when a man wanted to dig a well he secured the services of a water witch to locate a vein of water. Usually in every vicinity there dwelt an individual who claimed to be able to "locate" water. This individual was sought far and wide to render this important service. The water witch secured a forked stick of willow or peach, and grasping its ends firmly, he held his hands against his knees, stooped low, and proceeded to walk back and forth over a given locality in which the settler hoped to sink a well. Usually in a certain area the divining rod showed activity and at a particular spot the main stem of the rod inclined unmistakably to the ground. This marked the spot where a good vein of water would be struck.

To put down a well two neighbors often helped one another. The equipment needed was a rope, log windlass, and two iron-bound buckets. In some parts of the country strata of rocks made blasting necessary. One of the great dangers of well digging was from damp. There were two kinds of damp: black damp and fire damp. Damp was simply a heavier than air gas which gathered in the bottom of the well and overcame the digger.

In one instance a man and his wife in Dakota Territory were digging a well. The man was lowered into the well in the morning; after some little time his wife noticed that all was not well and that he had been overcome. Help was summoned and she went to her husband's aid. Soon it was noticed that the woman had been stooping motionless over the prostrate form of her husband for some time. Another person was sent down. This time the precaution was taken to fasten the rope to the waist of the rescuer. He fastened ropes to the others and they were brought to the top. Every effort was made to resuscitate the suffocated ones but all in vain. Another tragedy was added to the long list of casualties in the conquest of the prairies.

In August, 1870, a certain Mr. McKinley was digging a well one and one-half miles west of Belleville, Kansas. The well was forty feet deep. At noon when he did not return home for lunch Mrs. McKinley went to look for him. Seeing him prostrate in the bottom of the well and thinking he had fallen, she called a neighbor and went down into the well. When help arrived, she was found motionless stooping over him. She died before she reached the top, making another double tragedy in the warfare man waged against nature.

Scores of heroic deeds were wrought in digging wells on the high table-lands. Sheet water was to be found at a depth of two to three hundred feet and since the settlers had no money to pay for drilled wells, many were dug to that great depth. In 1918 the Nebraska State Historical Society received a pick and shovel used for more than thirty years by Nels Christensen in digging wells on the high table-lands between Niobrara and Lodge Pole. He had dug more than two miles of wells, perpendicular measure, with these tools. Digging wells at this depth carries with it a heroism equal to service on the battle-field. Once Mr. Christensen was at the bottom of a well two hundred and eighty feet down when the rope broke with a bucket of dirt near the top. Noticing what had happened he straightened up as flat as possible against the side of the well; the falling bucket shaved the skin from his nose, tore the clothing and skin from his chest, and landed with a terrific thud at his feet. The man on top, certain that his partner was dead, left the windlass and ran to get a neighbor to help get the corpse out. When he returned, he was astounded to hear Christensen calling from the depths of the earth.[12] Not a few of these heroes of the deep well-digging business were smothered by cave-ins.

These deep-dug wells not only proved dangerous for diggers and repair men, but occasionally those on deserted claims became death traps for the passer-by who happened to stray into them at night. The homesteader, having been driven from his claim by hard

[12] *Nebraska History and Record of Pioneer Days* (Lincoln, Nebraska, n.d.), Vol. II, No. 3, p. 7.

times, often took no particular pains about protecting the passer-by, and the luckless man or beast who on a dark night fell into the depths of one of these wells, was unfortunate indeed.

In Custer County, Nebraska, F. W. Carlin, while driving through the country about fifteen miles north of Broken Bow, found he had taken the wrong road and driven up to some old sod buildings; he turned the team around and started on what looked like a good road. Suddenly one of his horses seemed to step down into a low spot. Sensing that something was wrong he got out of the wagon and walked along the side of the team to be sure the road was all right. Suddenly without a moment's notice he became aware that he had stepped into an old deserted well and was dropping through space into the bowels of the earth. With a prayer on his lips he placed his feet together and prepared for the end. When he struck the bottom, the mud and water completely covered him. He was stunned but able to raise his head above the water, and, extricating his feet from the mud, stood on his feet arm-deep in the cold water. The well was curbed with wood and he managed to break off a piece at the bottom large enough to place in a crack of the curb; perching himself on it, he sat there until morning. While there one hundred and forty-three feet below the surface, he heard his team running away. In the horses lay his only hope of escape for no one knew he was there and the nearest house was a mile and a half away. In the morning by the light of day he noticed that the slimy wooden curb did not extend to the top. There was a place from six to sixteen feet curbed and then a place without any curb. The curbing was plastered with mud and there was not a crack where he could get his fingers in. He searched for his knife and began cutting foot-holes in the side of the curbing. When he got to the top of the curbing he took the board broken loose and made a seat. By this method he crept up fifty feet the first day. In the afternoon he came to a curbing which he thought he could not get through. It was solid one by six inch material and was fitted together so closely that he could not get a hand-hold. He stayed there all night and all of the next forenoon calling for help. One foot injured in the fall was paining terribly and he had to do most of his climbing on the other foot. Resolving to gain the top he finally decided he must make a desperate effort or die. Taking some sand, he placed it on a board, sharpened his knife, and, by alternately cutting and climbing, reached the top of the difficult curb. When within sixteen feet of the top he encountered his greatest difficulty. It was a round curb perfectly smooth and four feet high. Water had washed the dirt away from behind it until it was held in place only by a peg on one side. His only chance was to crawl up between the curb and the wall. In a half hour he had dug a hole large enough to let himself through and shortly afterward reached the top where he lay exhausted. The team had been found the day after he fell into the well and the finder took them to the justice of the peace, filed an estray notice, and turned them loose in his pasture, thus complying with the law and destroying the last chance of rescue for the unfortunate man in the well. By good fortune and great determination the apparently doomed man, with a sprained ankle and a broken rib, had climbed to the top and painfully made his way to safety. Few men have survived such a harrowing experience.[13]

In some parts of the country it was possible to drive a well. A company patented such a scheme and charged the settler a royalty for using it. The price was ten dollars for each well.[14] The principle was that of driving a sharp-pointed pipe into the ground and adding lengths as it was driven. When the point struck sand which was filled with water a pump was placed on the top of the pipe.

Another type was the bored well. These were put down in two different ways. The most common way was to drill the well with an expensive machine. The cost of the process varied with the difficulty of the job but it was quoted at one dollar a foot in some places in the seventies. Another method was that of using a common

[13] S. D. Butcher, *History of Custer County*, p. 314.
[14] *Nebraska Farmer*, January, 1880, p. 3.

post auger. By lengthening the handle of the auger as necessary it was possible to dig a "post hole" perhaps fifty feet deep and secure a supply of water. The hole was then "cased" to keep it from caving in.

CHAPTER XIX

FOOD AND CLOTHES

THE FIRST YEAR or two the settlers had to get along with
the clothes they had brought with them from the East. Said
one pioneer, "After we had been here a short time we carried our
whole wardrobe on our backs and our feet stuck out." Poverty was
a badge of honor which decorated all. The old blue army overcoat
from the Civil War was a prominent and comfortable article of
wear for some years following the War. Boots, when obtainable,
were purchased a size or two too big in order to allow for shrinkage
when they were wet.[1] Since many people did not have the money
to buy boots, they wore moccasins which could be bought for fifty
cents or which they themselves might fashion out of elk skins, cloth,
or sheep skins. Shoes were sometimes made by tacking leather
"uppers" to wooden soles. Children, clad with these shoes, clacked
across the bare cottonwood floors of houses and school like a troop
of cavalry.

In the summer nearly all the men and children went barefoot
habitually. On dress-up occasions they usually tried to wear foot-
gear, but even then it was not uncommon to see a barefoot man
dancing, or acting as superintendent of the Sunday-school, master
of a lodge, or chairman of a grange meeting. One lady remembers
seeing a whole family (man, woman, and five children), all barefoot, drive up to the photograph gallery and make preparations for
a picture of the family group. Even the women frequently went
barefoot around home. In order to save shoe leather they sometimes

[1] Hamlin Garland paints a picture of the difficulty farm boys had with shrunken
boots. As the boys attempted to put them on in the early morning light, they kicked
the mop-board in their annoyance, exclaiming "Plague these old boots; I wish they
were burnt."

walked and carried their shoes and stockings until near the place of public meeting, then sat down and put on the footwear. Older boys and girls went barefoot winter and summer. A doctor declared he had seen settlers' children running around out-of-doors barefoot in February apparently without ill effect.

In the absence of socks in winter men wore rags wrapped around their feet. When out on a trip in cold weather, they wound gunny sacks over their boots to keep their feet from freezing. Boots were blacked with soot off the inside of the stove-lids. Men wore their trousers inside their boots as they waded about the muddy unpaved streets.

The trousers were made of duck, jeans, or denim. Heavy grain sacks purchased for fifty cents each, often were used to make dress trousers. The shirts were hickory, blue or checkered. A garment something like a shirt worn outside the trousers was called a jumper or "wamus." Those who kept a few sheep made homespun jeans for the men and linsey for the women. This homespun cloth was usually dyed brown with walnut or other natural dye. A suit of homespun would last a year. In one instance, when a Kansas lad enlisted in 1861, his mother provided him with a pair of blue overalls and a blue hickory shirt tied up in a pillow-slip.

Women wore calico sunbonnets and long "sweepers" made of linsey-woolsey to church services. Nobody thought anything of a man's attending church in blue overalls and jacket. Often the color of the garment had washed out or faded in the sun, and a striking contrast was given the whole garment by a dark blue patch of new material above the knees or on the seat. Brown overalls were patched with flour sacking on which the brand and description of the flour still shone in bright blue letters. This made a novel and startling piece of raiment, not to say anything of the advertising value to the milling company. Men had to lie in bed while their wives mended their only pair of trousers.

The dress of men in official position was hardly less humble. A member of the first Kansas state legislature in 1861 said:

A SOD-HOUSE FAMILY

Custer County, Nebraska, 1886. Bare feet were the custom even for grown girls. Courtesy of the Nebraska State Historical Society.

So I roused myself out of dreamland, dumped into my saddle-bags a pair of blue woolen shirts, saddled the cayuse, and hiked to Topeka, across the boundless prairie, dressed in my only suit of clothes, which served for week-days and Sundays alike.

. . . There were few "away out here in Kansas" in the spring of 1861 who had better clothes than blue jeans, unless the Aid Society had contributed them out of the cast-off garments of the opulent East. But in blue jeans I felt equal to the occasion, . . .

Doctor M. H. Clark, a member of the Nebraska legislature in 1855, wore the buckskin attire of the hunter and frontiersman. Almost everyone carried a revolver or two.

After the War when clothing of all kinds was so extremely expensive, the settlers were fortunate in being able to secure condemned army blankets which were first made into shirts and later made over into undershirts. Occasionally the blankets were made into trousers.

Hats were fashioned from wildcat, coon, or badger skins, or some other garment was ripped up and made over into headgear. Horse blankets were tailored into coats. Mittens were rudely fashioned from the skins of animals—elk, coon, or whatever came to hand. Some were made of old pants, meal sacks, or other cloth. Everyone wore long mufflers of wool which were wound around their heads and over their ears. The girls often "worked" scarfs for their sweethearts. Strips of bed ticking were used for suspenders. Occasionally a man wore tanned and dressed buckskin shirt and breeches, the dress of the trapper and plainsman.

The man who wanted to dress up wore a fancy "boiled," pronounced "biled," shirt made of calico or other dress goods with two or three rows of white frills down the front. Since men did not wear vests, this showed off to good advantage.

Some of the women from cultured homes in the East, brought a good wardrobe with them. In a few years, however, these dresses gave way to the customary frontier garb of calico. Calico was worth from five to eight and a third cents a yard. It was the year-round fabric. Women took eggs and butter to the general store to exchange for this useful material. Pains were taken to beruffle the long, full skirts and trim them to look beautiful. The waists were high-necked and long-sleeved. Two of these calico dresses composed a woman's wardrobe for a year. Sometimes old chests, brought out from the East, were rummaged and old bed spreads, woven by some ancestor, were unearthed as a last resort and made into skirts.

Sunbonnets were the popular headgear although faded blanket shawls of other years were also worn. Hats were not numerous and caused little social competition. Mrs. Butler, wife of the first governor of Nebraska, wore one hat for five years. It served well until a man returning from the East brought his wife a new one; then Mrs. Butler had to have another one.

In the towns those who wanted to keep fully abreast of the styles wore hoop skirts and bustles. In the limited urban circles *Godey's Lady's Book* was reflected in clothes with flounces, tucks, pleats, a profusion of rosettes, jets, beads, and other ornaments. This kind of clothing was unknown to the prairie home where the garb that held sway was plain cotton clothing; the only ornaments were the patches of new material which all too soon made their appearance on the drab faded garments. The belle of the evening at the dance at the Fourth of July celebration at Blue Springs, Nebraska, in 1859, was fortunate enough to have a silk dress, although it did not match well with her sunbonnet and brown cowhide shoes.

If frontier food was unhealthful it was not because of its richness and high seasoning, but rather on account of the sameness which made the menu monotonous and unappetizing. Corn was the staple article of diet. In the *Nebraska Farmer* of January, 1862, thirty-three different ways were given for cooking corn. According to this article one dollar's worth of corn would furnish the same amount of nutriment as two dollars and fifty cents' worth of wheat or four dollars' worth of potatoes. Among the thirty-three recipes were:

1. Corn-meal mush or hasty pudding.
2. Dry corn and milk (parched corn, ground and eaten with milk).

3. Samp (yellow corn crushed, but not ground, and boiled the same as for hasty pudding).

4. Corn on the cob (green corn or roasting ears).

5. Dried corn.

6. Hominy (a dish made by taking the hulls off corn with lye and boiling the kernels).

7. Corn cake.

8. Apple corn-bread (corn meal and other ingredients mixed with raw apples and baked).

9. Corn dodgers.

10. Pumpkin Indian loaf (a kind of corn cake made of corn meal, pumpkin, and molasses together with other ingredients).

11. Corn-bread.

12. White pot (milk, eggs, corn meal, and sugar or molasses).

13. Indian dumpling.

14. Corn muffins.

15. Griddle cakes.

16. Baked Indian pudding.

17. Maize gruel (for invalids).[2]

For weeks and even months at a time pioneer families never saw any other kind of bread except corn-bread. When flour was needed, the whole family gathered around a wash-tub and in an evening shelled it full of corn. This was taken to the mill and ground into unbolted meal. When the housewife made bread, she sifted out the hulls with a wooden-rimmed shaker sieve.

Children tired so of corn-meal that in later life they could not be persuaded to eat so much as a bite of corn-bread. The children carried corn-bread and molasses to school for sandwiches.

Mush and milk was not infrequently served at parties as a dessert. A news item in the *Beatrice* (Nebraska) *Express* of January 9, 1873, advertised a "mush and milk festival." [3] Many times the cows were dry in winter and the pioneers had to eat their corn-meal mush with salt alone or perhaps with meat scraps. The Masonic

[2] The recipes in the *Nebraska Farmer* during the years 1859 to 1862 reflect the poverty of the frontier and the pinch of war conditions during the early years of the Civil War.

[3] This was given for the benefit of the band.

lodges served at their suppers, mush, corn-bread, molasses, and other corn products along with their more sophisticated foods such as pumpkin and mince pies, and meats.

Coffee was another staple article of diet. During the War and for some years after, money was so scarce on the frontier and coffee so high-priced that various substitutes were brought forward. Among these were parched barley, rye, or wheat, okra seeds, dried carrots, and "coffee essence." The latter was a mixture of ingredients more or less burnt. In one of these mixtures pumpkin or squash was baked very dark brown, and a piece one-half the size of the hand was put into the pot and boiled fifteen minutes. Another mixture consisted of two parts peas and one part coffee. This was declared to be better and stronger than coffee. Still another substitute consisted of corn-meal and molasses fried together until they were powdered. This semi-burned mixture, when boiled, produced a makeshift coffee.[4]

In the earlier times game was plentiful and every year two or three settlers would go out on the prairies for a big hunt when the weather became cool enough to preserve the meat. Buffalo, deer, and antelope, were the principal kinds of game brought home from these hunts. In addition to these, rabbit, wild turkeys, prairie chicken, and wild ducks and geese, were numerous near home. By the middle of the seventies this hunter's paradise was beginning to fade. Buffalo hunters practically exterminated the prairie monarch in the first half of the decade. When the settlers began taking homesteads around Dodge City and other places in the western third of Kansas and Nebraska, they found the whole country covered with the decayed bodies of buffalo slain by the hide hunters. Even as late as that there was an abundance of small game, however. The number of prairie chickens actually increased when the land was broken and they could forage on the grain which the settlers grew.

[4] *Nebraska Farmer*, May, 1862, p. 71; Henry T. Davis, *Solitary Places Made Glad* (Cincinnati, 1890), p. 195; "Donahoo Reminiscences," *Superior Express*, June 22, 1933.

When settlement became too dense, however, bringing with it countless hunters, the number decreased again.

After a period of settlement, a few hogs were available to butcher. This supplied the larder with a much-appreciated addition, and hog-killing time was looked forward to with keen anticipation. For the adults it meant hard work, but for the children it meant fresh meat, a welcome change from the summer diet of corn-bread, molasses, and greens. Ordinarily neighbors exchanged help in this task, for there was much heavy lifting. They used a small crane, or derrick, and block and tackle. The big kettle once more came into good use for the purpose of scalding the hog. When the day's work was done, the neighbors took home portions of meat in exchange for like portions when butchering time rolled around at their homes. Some of the pork was salted down for later use and formed a large part of the meat diet during the summer.

In the eastern portion of the prairies along the streams, a considerable quantity of wild fruit and nuts was to be found. Walnuts, pecans, hickory nuts, and hazel nuts were especially plentiful. Families went into the woods and gathered a supply of these in the fall. Among the wild fruit to be found along the streams, were strawberries, gooseberries, currants, plums, blackberries, raspberries, grapes, and elderberries. These fruits were welcomed for use as fresh sauce and as a palatable raw item of diet. They were also preserved for winter. One year in a certain Nebraska county there were thirty-seven varieties of plum jelly exhibited at the county fair. A Kansan gave the following method of preserving these wild plums: They were to be gathered fully ripe, placed in barrels, tubs, or jars, and covered with pure spring water. A scum formed over the top of the water and all was well. When ready to be made into pies, the plums were mashed and sweetened and a little of the water they were preserved in was added.

One who ate this kind of preserved fruit testified that although it was edible, it was sour and unpalatable. In spite of this the dwellers of the plains, accustomed to corn-bread, molasses, salt pork, and hominy, welcomed even this poor quality of preserve. If store fruit were to be had at all, the staple was dried peaches or apples. In fact, everything was dried that possibly could be. Green beans, corn, rhubarb, berries, and even pumpkin were dried. Rhubarb was cut in slices one inch thick, strung on a thread, and hung in the sun. Pumpkin was sliced thin or cut up into little dice and strung for drying. The meat became dark and leathery, but when soaked at Thanksgiving or Christmas time, it made a fair pumpkin pie.

The process of canning was not in use on a large scale during the frontier period, and, hence, the only other methods of preserving food was by means of salt brine and boiling sweets. Tomatoes were placed in a barrel of strong brine, and kept submerged by weighted boards. When the housewife desired tomatoes for a meal, she took a few from the barrel and soaked them in cold water, changing the water frequently. When the brine was finally soaked out, the tomatoes were cooked.

There was very little sugar in the homes of the early homesteader. The housewife looked long at that precious little package of refined sweetness before she would use it. In the eastern section of the country and along wooded streams a few maple trees grew. These were tapped and the sap was boiled down until it formed sugar. Likewise in this region there were many bee trees from which wild honey was gathered by the barrel. As population moved westward over the prairie, the trees were less numerous and sorghum molasses formed almost the sole source of sweetening.[5] Everything from coffee to preserves, was sweetened with molasses. Pudding, custard, pies, pickled cabbage, and even preserves were made with molasses. Recipes calling for molasses instead of sugar were published regularly in prairie papers.

The prairie produced some wild plant foods. In the summer, wild greens formed a large part of the diet. Buffalo peas were pickled. Sheep sorrel, sweetened with molasses, made a tart pie

---

[5] Some sweetening was made of watermelon juice boiled down to the consistency of syrup.

which was keenly relished by the corn-bread and salt-pork fed population.

Flapjacks, or pancakes, was a universal dish on the plains. The flour for this dish could easily be carried, could quickly be mixed with water, and the finished product made a substantial meal served with the ever-present sorghum. Another dish of recurring frequency was gravy made by browning lard and flour together in an iron frying pan, adding water, and bringing the mixture to a boil. Fried potatoes or game, when procurable, helped out materially. For the few pastries used, a little white flour was available, but for weeks and even months a morsel of anything made with white flour was never seen in many prairie homes. Sometimes wheat middlings or shorts, a stock food, was made to serve the purpose of white flour. White flour biscuits were considered the rarest treat and were eaten like cake, a food fit for the immortals. One dish which came with wheat culture, was boiled wheat eaten with molasses. Lard was often substituted for butter. Turnips were eaten instead of potatoes. One Nebraska woman, whose husband was working in town to buy supplies for his family, lived on watermelons after her supplies ran out. Although nursing a baby, she sustained life during the whole melon season but was so weak she could scarcely stand.

Children often became so tired of the monotonous diet of cornbread, sorghum, and salt pork that they cried and begged their mothers for something to eat. Some children had scurvy through lack of vitamin-content foods; sometimes their bodies were covered with scrofulous sores.

Campers, as well as early settlers, covered their fire at night so as to have some coals alive to start a fire the next morning. The settlers were usually too poor to buy matches. If anyone was so unfortunate as to let his fire go out at night he had to carry a pot or pan to the neighbors to "borrow fire."

The poverty of the early settler is well illustrated by an incident in the life of a Kansas man. He and his wife owned two hens which laid eggs occasionally. The couple agreed to save these eggs until their needs became greater. The wife often wished for some saleratus, provided they had eggs enough to make the trade. He and his wife took invoice and found they had only eleven eggs. He then made a thorough search to see if an egg might not have been laid that day, making a full dozen. Unfortunately he could not find a single one. On the next morning he yoked up the oxen, and with his eleven eggs drove to Council Grove arriving there a little before night. He intended after camping to do his trading so that the eggs would not freeze, and so that he might be ready to start home early the next morning. Before going to the store he met a neighbor who lived a few miles from him. He told the neighbor of his embarrassment at being one egg short. The kind-hearted neighbor said he had one over a dozen and the storekeeper gave it back to him. He gave it to his friend who went on his way rejoicing with the full dozen eggs, made the exchange, slept in the wagon, and early the next morning started home. He had spent two full days and a night on a trip in order to buy a package of soda so that his wife could bake biscuits.

CHAPTER XX

SPORTS

SPORTS on the frontier were in many ways similar to those in the East, but were adapted to conditions in the West. Some sports in their very nature fitted into the rude Western surroundings better than others and were perpetually popular. Regardless of the nature of the event, the element of gambling was ever present. No sporting affair could be run off without sizable bets first being laid. Everything, even the wearing apparel of the participants, was wagered, for cash was scarce.[1]

In the main the most common and popular sports were those requiring little or no equipment. Racing was among the outstanding, all-time, popular sports of this type. A race was always in place and always enjoyed. The equipment was at hand, namely, two pair of legs or two horses. On the way to the new home in the West, when the boat ran aground or when a flood or high wind prevented crossing a river, damming up the natural stream of traffic, the waiting home-seekers turned to racing and competitive sports. When the new home was reached and people from different places met for the first time, it was natural to match skill. In the railroadless small towns, especially when business was dull and time hung heavy on the hands of the citizens, racing was the favorite form of diversion. No member of the male population ever missed such an event unless he was compelled to do so by illness.

Probably the most popular was the horse race. A good horse was a precious possession, appreciated, and admired by all. It was quite the thing to possess a fast horse that could pass all the other citizens on the road. The editor of the *Wichita Eagle* in 1873, uttered his

---

[1] *Aberdeen-American News*, June 1, 2, 1931, p. 6.

gratification at riding with the owner of a fast horse and passing everyone on the road. Naturally other fast horses came into the country and in the endeavor to pass one another impromptu racing resulted. This eternal racing must have become as monotonous to the townspeople as sport-racer speeding in the modern college town, for the editor of the *Neosho Valley Register* of Iola, Kansas, in May, 1874, suggested: "An excellent way to fix a street is to plow a deep ditch across it. It prevents horse racing."

Frequently someone with a bit of sporting blood got up a race between two horses which were thought to be fast. Each horse had its backers. Often the horses were from different neighborhoods and appealed to local patriotism or loyalty. Many times such a race resulted from the braggart remarks of a member of one neighborhood. Sometimes such a race would be arranged on the spot and the whole town would close shop and go out to a smooth spot on the prairie to watch the race. The three judges lined up with tree or post or even the end of a wagon or other available fixed object. The starting was by the "ask and answer"—"Ready?" "Yes!" "Go!" or by the "lap and tap," wherein the horses were walked about fifty feet back of the starting line and were trained to whirl and break quickly. Often an assistant led the horse by the bit to keep the spirited animal from whirling too soon in spite of the rider. The riders, having turned, rode toward the line, attempting to keep even as they crossed the starting line. If this was the case (that is, if they were in lap) the judge tapped them off. The distance was short, usually from a quarter of a mile to a mile.[2] Often a race was arranged a few days in advance and was announced in the newspapers. A race of this kind for a half mile was announced at Clyde, Kansas, in 1870 with the statement that stock to the amount of five hundred dollars was wagered. The news report gave the crowd as four or five hundred and estimated that a thousand dollars changed hands.[3]

[2] Zoe A. Tilghman, "Quarter Horses and Racing in the Southwest," Kansas State Historical Society *Collections*, Vol. XVII, p. 348.

[3] *Republican Valley Empire*, August 23, 1870.

In Stromsburg, Nebraska, a drayman had a big horse which the citizens thought was a winner. Often this horse was unhitched from the wagon to uphold the town's honor in a matched race. Once a traveler came through town with an old sway-backed horse which apparently had difficulty in walking, let alone running. After some conversation a race was arranged and the old sway-back took the sporting boys' money.

As the country became settled and fields were plowed, work horses were not suited to racing, and the contests took on a different aspect. Tracks were laid out and the sport became more professionalized. The *Wichita Eagle* of July 12, 1872, gave a description of this sport as it later developed:

The event every Saturday afternoon in Wichita is a horse race. The track is just north of, and in plain view of the town. Last Saturday the race was between a Texas horse and a Wichita mare. The mare won the race, and it is said over a thousand dollars changed hands. It was estimated that over one thousand men were present, besides some five carriage loads of soiled doves. So great was the rush that Main Street for an hour or so seemed almost deserted.

Foot racing was second in popularity only to horse racing. Races were run at various distances. Boys and men were at it continually. Often men who thought they could run would go out on the prairie, take off their boots and socks, and run barefoot. Foot racers would come to town and challenge the local talent; and the home town boys felt called upon to defend their reputation. For days before a race the contestants would carry a load of shot on each ankle as weights. The sporting group of town would back their champion financially to the last ditch. One time at Salem, Kansas, a stranger appeared and shortly afterward built up a substantial bet with the sports that he could outrun any man in town. A local "whirlwind" was selected to compete with him. When the stakes were set on the prairie, the stranger stripped down to running trunks, and the home town boys knew they had been tripped up. As luck would have it, however, the local boy happened to be a real runner, and the down-hearted betters were gratified when the home talent sprinter won. The challenger had to beg his way out of town.

Broad jumps, running and standing, were in high favor. High jumping was also common. Poles were driven in the ground and notches made to indicate the various heights. Men then held a string at the height indicated by the notches.

The *Wichita Eagle* in commenting on the sports of March, 1873, said: "Baseball, croquet, mumble peg, and keno are the most popular games at present." Ball was not new in frontier days. Man had been playing with spherical objects since time immemorial. The game developed into its present general form, however, in the last half of the nineteenth century. Youngsters or their parents made the baseballs by unraveling the yarn of an old woolen sock or collecting wrapping thread from packages, winding it tightly into a ball of the proper size, and covering it with leather from the top of an old boot. In the earlier days the chief variations of ball were ante-over, two-old-cat, three-old-cat, and four-old-cat. Four-old-cat was most similar to present day league ball in that there were four bases. The Civil War greatly stimulated the game, for it brought together large groups of men who sought amusement and who gave attention to playing ball.

By the early seventies it was the rule for the prairie towns to have baseball teams. Each team adopted uniforms and catchy names. The Oakdale, Nebraska, team called themselves the "Striped Stockings." [4] The team of the neighboring town was called the "Antelopes." [5] Members of a team got considerably more exercise on the prairies of that day than in the ball park of the present time. On August 18, 1871, for example, the Milford, Nebraska, Blue Belts played the neighboring town of Seward. The game began at two o'clock and lasted four hours. The winning team made six home

---

[4] *Pen and Plow*, Oakdale, Nebraska, March, 1878.
[5] *Oakdale Journal*, September, 1874.

runs. The score was twenty-five to ninety-seven in favor of the Blue Belts. One need not be surprised at the large score and the long playing time when one considers that those doughty players gathered on the prairie and played without backstop, masks, protectors, gloves, or equipment of any kind except a bat and ball.[6]

In 1885 Wano and Bird City, Kansas, played a series of three games, the winning team to receive a new ball and bat. The first matched game of ball between Elk Point and Vermilion, South Dakota, occurred in 1872. The Vermilion boys had to drive over and the one available lumber wagon would not hold them all. Apparently they took turns, half riding and half running, and were well limbered up by the time they reached Elk Point.

Junior ball clubs consisting of the youngsters of a town, were organized. These teams, sponsored by an older ball fan, journeyed to neighboring towns to play other bantam teams. As early as 1873 Wichita, Kansas, had organized a young ladies' club.[7] Baseball was played after tea on week days in the town and on Sunday in a rendezvous outside the city.

Croquet came into vogue about the close of the Civil War and by the late sixties and the seventies assumed first place in the sport world in the West. The equipment was simple, inexpensive, and easily set up. As a courting game it has had no equal. When a family in a neighborhood bought a set, the people came for miles to play. They were so enthusiastic that they played on moonlight nights or with the aid of a few lanterns. The manufacturers came to the rescue in 1875 and produced a set with candle sockets in the top of each wicket and post just where the light was needed. Another valuable improvement in equipment was the invention of indexical balls. In this system the two teams were designated by stripes and the individual players, by the general colors of the several balls. This enabled players to avoid vexatious mistakes of confusing an

[6] *Blue Valley Record*, August 24, 1871.
[7] *Wichita Eagle*, February 13, 1873.

enemy for a friend.[8] Croquet parties were formed and the champion teams of the town journeyed to the neighboring towns to match skill with champions there.

In the sixties a type of velocipede which had pedals on the front wheel and a seat between the front and rear wheels came into favor. At first apparently this machine was taken about the country to be demonstrated and the people taught to ride. Probably an agent taught people how to ride and at the same time sold the velocipedes to those interested. An item from the *Neosho Valley Register* of Iola, Kansas, of July 7, 1869, gave an idea of this sport:

Quite an excitement has prevailed within a circle of young men for a few days last past because of the opening of a velocipede school in Iola. For several evenings and during the entire day of Saturday last, Odd Fellows' Hall was crowded with young bloods who were bound to "ride her or die." A great deal of sport was manufactured and many sore shins, lame ankles, swelled knees, varicose veins, sprained wrists, and painful backs were contracted by those who were the most determined. . . .

In the eighties when the bicycle craze swept the East, this sport became popular on the dusty streets of the prairie towns.[9] Roller skating took the country by storm during the same decade. Pierre, South Dakota, had three roller skating rinks in 1884 and one ice rink.[10] As early as the seventies large crowds went out to skate especially on moonlight evenings on the streams near the towns. In the rural districts nearly all the boys and girls in the neighborhood met and went skating on the sloughs or ponds. At these "skating parties" games were the order of the evening. Dare goal, pom-pom pullaway, cross tag, and other games were enjoyed. Sometimes the boys played hockey, or shinny as it was called, batting a stick of drift wood around with clubs. When it was cold they built bonfires on the edge of the ice in the districts where timber

---

[8] Introduced in 1869; *Neosho Valley Register*, June 16, 1869.
[9] *Pierre Free Press*, Pierre, South Dakota, January 31, 1884.
[10] *Ibid.*, January 10, 1884.

could be procured. This gave warmth and good cheer and lent a certain mystery, splendor, and enchantment to the night. Around the fire the older boys and girls coquetted.

At school when the new-fallen snow was fresh on the ground, dog and deer, or fox and geese could be played. In the former a series of loops were laid out on the snow by the whole group of players moving in a single file and scuffling out paths. The dogs were forced to run through these loops and the deer were allowed to leap across the narrow necks where the loops approached one another. Two of the players were selected to act as "dogs" and the rest became "deer." Fox and geese was similar. Two circles were made, one inside the other; paths from the circles ran to a haven of refuge in the center. The fox tried to catch the geese when they ventured out of their roost in the center. Other games were hide and seek, ball, blackman, and crack the whip. In bad weather the rowdy group passed away the time playing "I spy" or some other indoor games.

At home in the evening, checkers, dominoes, or cards, formed the diversion. In strict religious homes authors were substituted for cards. Among the older people seven-up, euchre, poker, and Sancho Pedro, were nightly enjoyed.

The frontier was a hunter's paradise. To the west within a few days' journey, was big game. Near at hand ducks, quails, turkey, prairie chicken, and other small game, abounded. Large groups of men sought companionship as well as sport in rabbit and wolf drives. Spearing fish was also a pleasant amusement. Torches were made of corn-cobs soaked in kerosene and placed on long sticks. Spears were often made of broken pitchforks. After dark the spearmen entered the shallows of the river, and, while the torches were held high to light up the stream, they were able to gig some fish.

In a Dakota county a gopher club was organized by the boys of one township. The county offered one cent each for gopher tails. The boys were divided into two groups, one representing the eastern half of the township and the other the western half. Two neighborhood boys were chosen captains. The side which secured the most points by the end of the season was to be proclaimed the winner.[11] The losers were to give a dinner in honor of the victors. The rivalry was keen. The record of each side was kept secret until the date of counting, but many guesses were made especially when news of an unusual capture filtered through. On the evening of the count the schoolmaster held the honored position of master of ceremonies in the dimly-lighted little sod school-house. He chose the judges and asked the leaders to sit on the platform with the judges. Each boy handed in his package marked with his name and "East" or "West." As the tally was recorded, the counters called out the numbers which were chalked up on the rude blackboard on the sod wall. The count went merrily on with first one side ahead and then the other, the girls clapping their hands and dancing around as their favored side drew ahead. The East side apparently had won the contest judging from the way their totals mounted up higher and higher. When nearly all had turned in their reports, the West put forward some of their heaviest scores which they had saved to the last. Then like a flash of lightning one boy turned in ten wolf scalps—1,000 tallies; another, five coyotes and five wolves—875 tallies. A third turned in one wild cat and ten wolves—600 tallies. Finally the West was declared the victor with 4,210 tallies as against 3,456 for the East. After the count a number of the boys regaled the crowd with stories of how they had captured their trophies in the hunt.

In the fifties and sixties all men went armed, and shooting matches were frequent. In Pottawatomie, Kansas, they took place three or four days a week when no farm work could be done to advantage. Each community had its local champion. Men from other communities would drift in looking for a match. The visitors

---

[11] The following points were allowed: wild cat, 500; wolf, 100; rattle snake, 100; coyote, 75; fox, 50; badger, 25; hawk, 25; gopher, 1. Clarence Wilbur Taber, *Breaking Sod on the Prairies* (Yonkers-on-Hudson, 1924), p. 134.

usually had something to "put up"; the local men bet on their champion. As a rule the shooters would each contribute a certain amount toward a prize. The man who shot best in three tries, won the prize. Sometimes it was merely a purse made up by the participants. Turkey shoots were numerous, and one man mentioned shooting for a beef. In some places the gunners actually shot at the turkeys which were placed on a box some distance away. The rules provided that the man had to fire standing upright "off hand" and must at least draw blood to get the bird. This barred the Indians for they were not used to firing from a standing position but when kneeling to fire, they could outshoot the white men. More often, however, the group of shooters each threw a sum of money into the treasury, bought some birds, and shot at a mark, the best shot securing a turkey. At a later date different towns had rifle teams which traveled here and there matching their prowess with the riflemen of other communities. At Huron, South Dakota, in 1881 one of the attractions at the Fourth of July celebration was a contest among the boys, each of whom shot at fifteen glass balls. The shooting was done from a rotary mole trap. One boy shot fourteen.

Raffles of various sorts were held occasionally and were a sporting event. The boys in town played marbles and the traveling men, waiting at the hotel for the local train, watched them "play for keeps." Guests and townspeople also played penny ante at the hotel during the winter months and, in warm weather, horseshoe near the hotel, livery barn, or blacksmith shop.

Wrestling matches like dog fights, took place on the street corners and were enjoyed without gate receipts. Football, no doubt considerably different from our modern game, was played by the boys.

As soon as a town was laid off and houses sprang up, one of the first places of business was the bowling alley. Leavenworth, Kansas, had such a ten pin establishment a year after its founding. Law--ence, in the midst of all its woe and misery and within a few months after its sack by Missourians, built a bowling alley. In 1862 a man in Nebraska City erected a double ten pin establishment with two well-laid alleys each seventy feet long.

Billiards were equally popular. The *People's Press* of Nebraska City remarked in 1860, "No matter how hard the times are people will have their amusement and the fever now is for billiards." In that year four billiard tables were brought by one steamer for three establishments in that city. When a public official brought a table to Niobrara, Nebraska, it had but two and a half hours' rest during the four days and nights following its arrival.

Newcomers in the plains country were susceptible to much jesting and trickery. These people were called "tenderfeet." One such trick was to get the tenderfeet to catch a gopher. They were told that all one needed to do was to pour water in the hole, hold a sack over it, and catch the little animal when he jumped out. The greenhorns stood there for hours waiting for the half-drowned rat to jump into the sack.

The snipe hunt was even more fun when a gullible victim could be secured. The old settlers would talk a great deal about the pleasure and sport in snipe hunting. After they had boosted the sport for a while the newcomer was eager to accept an invitation to participate in the good time. The guest, of course, was invited to take the place of honor, namely, that of holding the bag while the other hunters did the disagreeable work of beating the brush or tall grass to drive the snipes toward the sack. The victim had a lantern to draw the snipes to the bag, and it was his duty to sit patiently there for an indefinite length of time until long lines of snipes would follow each other into the bag. If the weather was warm, he was instructed to wear very heavy clothing to keep the man scent in. If it was cold, he was told to discard his hat and coat in order to rid himself of the scent. The drivers would then leave, uttering occasional snipe calls from different points of the compass, and, assembling at the means of conveyance, ride back to town enjoying the thought of the tenderfoot sitting there holding the sack. After some hours the victim came back wearily and for days was the laughing stock of the entire town. If he took it as a good sport he was heartily welcomed into the community. If not, life was made miserable for him.[12]

Men and boys went swimming in the summer. Boys went to the buffalo wallows, ponds, or creek holes. Conditions, especially in the buffalo wallows and ponds, were far from sanitary, but oblivious of their germ-laden surroundings, the youngsters splashed about in these mucky, stagnant pools; the secluded nature of the places offered complete privacy to the nude bathers. A period in midsummer was commonly called "dog-days" and was ruled out for swimming purposes by public opinion. Sometimes groups of men from the town went to near-by swimming pools for an evening plunge after a sweltering day in the sun-parched little prairie towns.

On the whole, although commercialized sport had a small place in the lives of the people, the settlers had many sports and enjoyed them fully as much as do later generations.

[12] Will E. Stokes, *Episodes of Early Days in Central and Western Kansas* (Great Bend, Kansas, 1926), Vol. I, p. 18.

CHAPTER XXI

BEGINNING OF MACHINE FARMING

AMONG the first inventions to ease the load of the toiling farmer were those perfecting mechanical devices for lightening the work of harvesting and threshing grain. As early as 1831 in the Shenandoah Valley, Cyrus McCormick had brought forth a mechanical harvester. The machine was unwieldy amid stumps and hills, however, and did not come into wide use until the great prairie wheat lands with their broad level fields, unhampered by stump or stone, were opened to settlement. The great impetus to the increased use of machinery resulted from the Civil War. The imperative need for breadstuffs sent prices soaring. A surplus of money during the War boom, and a shortage of man-power, caused the displacement of men in the harvest field. In the days before the War the trans-Missouri farmer had harvested his little patch of grain with a cradle and bound it in the same fashion as it had been done since the dawn of history.

The Kirby Patent Harvester which reached the prairie frontier during the early part of the Civil War, was a crude machine constructed somewhat on the order of the present day binder [1] with a platform and reel. The reel knocked the grain onto the platform. Two men operated the machine. The driver sat immediately over the bull wheel; the second man, directly behind him with a rake, pulled the grain off onto the ground where it lay in gavels and was bound up by five to eight men; depending on the heaviness of the grain, each binding station covered a fifth to an eighth of the

---

[1] The binder of today has the bull wheel on the opposite end of the machine and the machines travel around the field in the opposite direction from the Kirby, which worked like a mowing machine.

field. The man on each station bound up his portion of the swath while the reaper was making the next circuit of the field. In the evening cutting was stopped and all hands shocked the grain.[2] The small acreage grown then made it possible for the owner of one of these machines to cut all the grain in the community. He secured labor largely in exchange for this service. Before the War was over the self-raking reaper appeared. It was operated by one man, the driver only. The machine, as its name indicates, raked the bunches off automatically

Binding on station was grueling work of a competitive nature. The man on station kicked the gavel together with his feet while he jerked a handful of wheat from the sheaf. With a quick twirl of the wrist he spliced a straw band, stooped to gather the grain in his arms, and rose with the bundle on his knee. With a fast pull and a twirl over his thumb, finally tucking in the end, he dropped the bundle into the stubble and rushed to the next gavel. To allow the machine to make a round before the man had all his station bound was a disgrace. A hand who allowed that was said to be "doubled." Binders vied with one another in contests of endurance and speed. Individual binders would urge the driver to go faster in order to disgrace the worker on some other station. The whip cracked, and faster and faster the horses went around the field until one or more binders were "doubled."

The self-rake was the last word in the harvest field for a decade. In the early seventies the Marsh harvester came out and immediately it became the popular machine from the Red River Valley in the north to Kansas. This was the first machine used extensively in the trans-Missouri and Red River regions. This implement may be said to be the first prairie harvesting machine. The harvester elevated the grain over the bull wheel by means of slatted endless canvas aprons and delivered it in a stream upon a table. There two men, standing in a box-like compartment, alternately seized arm-

[2] Doane Robinson, "The Pioneers," *South Dakota Historical Collections*, Vol. XII, p. 146.

fuls from the stream and bound them with straw as on station. It was severe work, in some ways more taxing than binding at station. Hour after hour the men bound until their hands became raw and bleeding from the briars and smarting from the rust spores on the grain. A harvester averaged ten acres a day. After a twelve-hour day the tired binder, having taken care of his five acres of grain, was ready to rest his weary muscles. Three men and a boy could run this outfit. The boy drove the machine, two men bound, and a third shocked. In spite of the severity of the work the harvester was a marked improvement over the reaper, for two men could bind as much as four on the ground. Then, too, the labor of walking and gathering the grain from the hot ground was at an end because a sunshade protected the operators while the motion of the machine kept a breeze stirring.

Harvest started while the wheat was still unripe because in most communities many acres were cut by a single machine. The crew, therefore, worked at break-neck speed to get the grain harvested before it became too dry and brittle to bind well. This condition came altogether too soon. The machine was then operated in the morning and evening hours. At times the harvesting became a night task lighted by the feeble yellow glow of the lantern.[3]

In the late seventies the self-binder came into use. It was similar to the harvester except that a mass of machinery replaced the two binders. When sufficient grain for a sheaf had accumulated, a wire was drawn around the bundle, a knife cut it, and a mechanical foot kicked it to the ground. It was a heavy machine but with it two men could cut, bind, and stack more grain than a crew of six or eight could in the days of the self-rake reaper. In a short time every farmer had a self-binder.

About 1880 the Wood Company brought out a twine binder. About the same time McCormick and Deering put on the market the Appleby binder which became standard within five years. Dur-

[3] Dillman, *A Human Life*, p. 39.

ing the seventies another machine, the header, was manufactured which came into general use in some sections, especially in the western part of the prairie region. It was a large machine which cut a swath nearly twice as wide as the binder. As its name indicates, it merely clipped the heads off the wheat and elevated them into a tight hayrack which was driven alongside this machine until it was filled. The heads were then stacked. The header was more popular in the South but the binder continued to be a favorite in the North where threshing was done from the shock.

In the seventies the nomadic harvest hand originated. He came to bind on station and later to shock or care for headed grain. Like birds of passage, these wanderers began on the Oklahoma line in June and moved northward as the grain ripened, finally ending the season amid the frost of Dakota or Canada.

The straggling settlers of Civil War times threshed the harvest from their little patches with the flail. As their acreage increased they threshed it by allowing the horses or cattle to tread it out. In some places a little treadmill cylinder was used after a settler's crop increased. This threshed the grain but did not separate it from the chaff. The chaff was separated by winnowing or by using a fanning mill after such a machine was available in the seventies. In winnowing the wheat was poured from a little height onto a canvas or into a large vessel while a gentle breeze blew the lighter wheat and chaff away.

In the seventies the acreage was large enough to warrant the use of the complete thresher and separator.[4] The first threshing machines were manufactured by J. I. Case or Buffalo Pitts. The outfit was made up of three units, a separator, a horse power, and a trap wagon. On the move between jobs each unit was in charge of a member of the permanent crew of three. The owner had charge of the separator, the most expensive unit. His team served as wheel horses. It was customary for the neighbor whose farm was next to

[4] In the older settled regions the threshing machine had been in use for some years.

be visited to supply the lead team of four horses required to move the separator.[5]

In Brookings County, Dakota Territory, in 1873, one of the first machines in the state, a J. I. Case agitator separator, a Woodbury mounted power, and a trap wagon, threshed 15,000 bushels in three months. The homesteaders changed work, and crews were constantly assembled from a territory stretching over thirty miles. It was necessary for the hands to camp in the straw-pile at night for it was obviously impossible to entertain them in the dugouts and equally impossible to daily traverse the distance to their homes. When it grew colder the floors of the little dwellings were covered with straw and the men slept indoors.

The mounted power for one of these machines consisted of five long levers called "sweeps" which like spokes of a wheel, radiated from a central hub. This hub was attached to large cogwheels. Five teams of horses attached to the sweeps, traveled in a large circle exerting the force which was transmitted from the cogwheels to long "tumbling rods" with knuckle joints to the separator some rods away. The power was anchored to the ground by long stakes.

The driver stood on a square platform above the giant cogwheels of the power, around which the horses moved. His was no easy job for the horses had to be kept at a steady gait. In cold weather it was tiresome indeed to stand throughout the day in the sharp wind. Ordinarily the farmers for whom the threshing was done furnished the horses. Thus horses as well as men exchanged work during the threshing season. In addition to the driver two other men composed the machine crew. The second man "tended" the separator. Oil can in hand, in a great cloud of dust, he watched the sieves, felt of the pinions, and in general kept the machine in order. The third man "fed" the machine. Taking each bundle in the hollow of his arm, he spread it out into a thin golden band which was caught between the whirling teeth of the cylinder and the concave and torn into

[5] *Lennox Independent* (Anniversary edition), Lennox, South Dakota, October 25, 1934.

A HORSE–POWER THRESHING MACHINE

Courtesy of the Nebraska State Historical Society.

FENCE CUTTING IN THE HOMESTEADER–CATTLEMAN WAR

At the Brighton Ranch, Custer County, Nebraska, 1885. Courtesy of the Nebraska State Historical Society.

shreds. At the other end of the machine a stream of straw poured over the elevated stacker engulfing the man who tramped about in an endeavor to stack it. As the perspiring stacker tramped about in the cloud of mounting dust, his face was soon as black as a negro's. The three members of the thresher crew shifted their job somewhat with the following schedule. The first man would feed the machine while running out about one hundred bushels of oats. The second man would then step onto the feeding platform and relieve the first feeder who would tend the machine. A little later the man on the horse power would feed the machine while the second took his place, and so on.[6]

Two men were kept busy sacking and weighing the yellow stream of grain which flowed from the machine. After wheat growing became extensive the straw was considered a nuisance and was disposed of by a boy who, with a horse attached to each end of a long pole, dragged it away from the machine to be burned.

Suddenly in the midst of the day's work a crash would cause the men to run, seize the horses' bridles, and stop the machine while repairs were made. This was a welcome relief to the hired hands. On these occasions the young fellows had a wrestling or lifting match and the air was literally full of jokes.

As grain growing on a large scale came into vogue, improvements in threshers advanced. An engine on wheels replaced the mounted power in the seventies, relieving the horses of the neighborhood from an odious task, and the separator roared and rattled like a modern machine. Whereas in the earlier day the grain had been taken from the shock and stacked in a stack-yard preparatory to threshing, the process was now done in the field directly from the shock. The machine moved into the field and "set." Teams hauled the grain to the separator. Nomadic hands to a large extent began to supplant the old exchange system. This was particularly true of the threshing done early in the season for there was no chance for an exchange of labor.

[6] *Ibid.*

By 1880 the straw-burning engine [7] was a success and was used in the North. By 1885 the traction engine had been introduced. This was a great saving. Before that time it was necessary to bring in all the teams from the field stopping everything while the horses were used to move the engine and separator to a new "set" in the ever-expanding acreages. A crew of twenty men was idle while the horses worked. With traction engines, moving was done without extra men or teams, and when the machine reached the new position bundles awaited its devouring maw.

The little patches before the Civil War were sown by hand. The sower placed a rag on a pole to serve as a mark at the end of the field, and, taking half a sack of grain in a sowing pouch suspended under the arm by a strap across the shoulder, he walked straight toward his marker scattering the seed with his hand as he went. On arriving at the end of the field he moved the marker preparatory to the next "through," and replenishing his supply of seed, returned to the other end. Often an attempt was made at covering the seed by dragging a brush harrow across the field.

When larger fields were cultivated in the seventies, the broadcast or end-gate seeder came into use. This simple machine consisted of a hopper fastened to a board in such a way that it could replace the rear end-gate of a wagon. The hopper was filled with grain and a chain, properly geared, connected with the hub of the back wheel. The chain ran a revolving mechanism which flirted the seed in sprays ten or twelve feet from the wagon on each side. One person drove to the mark while a second with shovel in hand kept the hopper filled from the loose grain in the front of the wagon-bed. A large field was rapidly sown by this method. Afterward it was necessary to harrow it to cover the seed. The great

[7] With the straw-burning engine three men were required for an engine crew. It took the full time of a fireman to fire and draw ashes. A water hauler supplied that item and the engineer had charge of the engine. A sixteen horse power threshed from 1,000 to 1,200 bushels a day. See Hamlin Garland, *Boy Life on the Prairie* (New York, 1899), Chapter XIII.

trouble with the end-gate seeder was that it sowed unevenly. In spots the grain was too thin and in others too thick. This was especially true when the wind blew as it almost always does in the spring on the plains. Then, too, unless the ground was moist the grain would not come up well. To offset these disadvantages the seeder, a long narrow box-like affair, twelve to sixteen feet long, was mounted between two wheels. Tubes from the bottom of the box conducted the seed down into shoes which burrowed into the loose dirt and deposited the grain to the desired depth beneath the surface in uniform rows in the moist earth.

During the sixties and early seventies there was little improvement in corn planting over that of Indian agriculture. After the field had been plowed and harrowed a contrivance resembling a four-runner sled was pulled across the field. A man rode it and the weight made little furrows about four feet apart. The entire field was rowed out in this fashion and then just before time for dropping, the sled was driven over the field crosswise in such a way as to form a checkerboard. The soil was then ready for the "droppers." Boys and girls walked along digging their bare toes into the cool moist dirt, dropping three or four kernels at each intersection. After they got used to it they could walk along at a steady gait dropping the grain swiftly and accurately. Behind them came two skilful hoe men with light hoes covering each hill at a stroke.

By the late seventies the Deere "rotary drop" corn planter was used in a limited way. It had two seats, one on each side of the axle, to lighten the load on the horses' necks. The driver occupied one place and the dropper the other. The latter dropped the corn by a lever.[8] Such a planter was hired in the seventies and eighties at ten cents an acre. The wire check rower was first advertised in western farm papers about 1880. With this machine a wire was stretched from one end of the field to the other. About every four feet there was a knot or ball on the line. The planter was driven down the

─────────

[8] *Nebraska Farmer*, February, 1878, p. 48.

wire and the knots jerked the dropper. This is essentially the same planter that is used widely today.[9]

John Deere, a blacksmith from Vermont, settled in Grand Detour, Illinois, and there on the frontier in 1837 made a steel share for a plow out of a band saw blade. It was revolutionary and made him famous. A large, heavy, walking plow of the John Deere type with a steel share was used for breaking in the earlier years. The sharp steel blade cut the thick, tough roots of the prairie sod. By the eighties large red wheeled plows, capable of turning four furrows at a time, were used on the border. A disc gang plow was advertised in one farm paper as early as 1877.

Corn cultivators went through a similar evolution. At first a one or two shovel walking plow pulled by one horse was used. It was necessary to make a "round" in order to cultivate one row. A little later a two horse cultivator with wheels was perfected. It straddled the row and cultivated a whole row at a "through" or two at a "round." As early as the Civil War period, riding cultivators were used in a limited way. A contest between the Buckeye, Bradley, Sucker State, Peoria, and other makes of cultivators was held at Weponsit, Illinois, on June 18, 1864. The Sucker State won. It is doubtful, however, whether any of these found their way to the trans-Missouri-Red River territory until the boom years of the seventies. Many older farmers, reared in toil and educated in the school of hard knocks, disdained to use a riding machine if the old walking implement did the work just as well. It was thought to be evidence of slovenliness or laziness to sit down and to work at the same time. A new generation held no such ideas and gladly took up any machine that eliminated hard work.

During the preëmption and early homestead period, hay was cut with the scythe and raked by hand. In Brown County, Dakota Territory, in 1877 the first settlers, three men and a woman, cut

---

[9] A man in Holdrege, Nebraska, invented a sod corn planter. There were two rolling coulters which cut through the sod in front of the sled-like shoes allowing the grains of corn to drop into the sod.

thirty tons of hay with a scythe and put it up with home-made wooden forks and a home-made horse rake. But very soon each community had a mower. Douglas County, Kansas, had mowing machines in 1855. For two decades after that it was customary for the newer settlers to hire someone to cut hay for them. The price of a Buckeye mower in 1872 was $123 and a rake cost ten dollars. The owner of a mower charged five or six dollars a day for cutting. It was customary for a man to ride out on the unoccupied land of the prairie with his mower and cut a swath around the patch of hay he wanted. This act laid claim to the land laid out, and others respected it. The rake of this time was a revolving wooden implement drawn by a horse and operated by a man walking behind it. In the eighties the riding self-dump rake appeared.

Haying time was in many ways a pleasant season. It was a time when farmers exchanged work as in threshing season but it was not accompanied with the same rush and nervous tension. Neighbors came from their lonely fields to exchange help and to enjoy one another's company while stacking hay. The wives occasionally came to help with the cooking and incidentally relieve the monotony of lonely cabin life. The merry chatter and congenial association made haying an occupation which the pioneer anticipated.

The invention of barbed wire was perhaps as revolutionary as any other invention in the period. The fencing problem was acute on the prairies. In the eastern part of the plains area, rail fences and hedges had been used extensively. As the frontier crept westward away from the timber region in the seventies, there was an imperative need for a standard type of cheaper fence. Much experimenting took place. Considerable smooth wire was used but there were objections to it. It was expensive; it contracted in cold weather and expanded in hot; and animals learned to push through it with impunity. Therefore, taking a leaf from nature's scrap book, the inventors began to work upon the idea of a thorn wire with properties similar to the thorn hedges which worked so effectively. One early company manufacturing barbed wire, was known as the Thorn

Wire Hedge Company. A number of men developed the principle of placing spools or other devices carrying sharp points, on the smooth wire. Barbed wire was first manufactured in quantities at DeKalb, Illinois. Strangely enough two men at the same town began to perfect the successful type of barbed wire about the same time. Mr. J. F. Glidden, a farmer, made his first wire in 1873 and sold the first piece the next year. Jacob Haish was a lumber dealer and building contractor who was cognizant of the great demand for lumber for fencing. He had sold Osage orange seeds to his customers and foresaw the great fencing problem. At first he thought of growing the prickly Osage orange plants and of weaving them into a smooth wire fence when they had developed. Finally after several experiments, he came to the conclusion that iron barbs should be fastened on strands of smooth wire and these twisted into a single wire. When he showed his invention to a friend he was told that Joseph Glidden was working on the same idea. Both men secured patents in 1874 [10] and DeKalb became a great barbed wire manufacturing center. At this time the principal manufacturer of smooth wire was the Washburn and Moen Company of Worcester, Massachusetts. Noticing large orders for smooth wire coming from DeKalb, they sent a representative to investigate. This led to a consolidation of the Glidden interest with the eastern firm; but Haish refused to sell. Later the Haish interests and the American Steel and Wire Company which had taken over Glidden's patent [11] entered into a bitter controversy and litigation which involved enormous expenditures.

Barbed wire was advertised in Kansas and Nebraska in the late seventies and became common within a few years.[12] The price declined rapidly after it went into the hands of big manufacturing concerns and soon it was within reach of the homesteader.[13] Barbed

[10] Mr. Glidden's invention actually ante-dated that of Haish.

[11] An excellent discussion of the invention of barbed wire is given in Walter P. Webb, *The Great Plains* (Boston, 1931), Chapter VII.

[12] *Nebraska Farmer*, May, 1879.

[13] In 1874 it sold at $20 a hundred pounds, in 1880 at $10, in 1885 at $4.20, in 1890 at $3.45, and in 1897 at $1.80 a hundred. W. P. Webb, *op. cit.*, p. 310.

wire greatly hastened the agrarian conquest of the plains and sharpened the conflict between the herder and the agrarian, finally wreaking the rancher's doom.

The invention of the windmill was a boon to mankind for it transferred the drudgery of daily pumping from the over-burdened pioneer to the eternal winds of the plain. What was probably the first windmill in the region west of the Missouri River was one built at Lawrence, Kansas, in 1855. It was used more for manufacturing than for pumping water, however. The great use to which windmills were put on the prairies was pumping water and before long, according to Walter Prescott Webb, the windmill tower was "the unmistakable and universal sign of human habitation throughout the Great Plains Area." The first windmills were manufactured the year the Kansas-Nebraska Act became a law, in 1854. The windmills manufactured at that time were designed by Daniel Halloday, a mechanic of Ellington, Connecticut. After a time, seeing there would be a great demand for them on the plains, the windmill interests moved their factory to Batavia, Illinois, and there in 1862 the manufacture was begun on a larger scale. The main use to which mills were put in the sixties and early seventies was pumping water for the railroad locomotives. The mills were built on the European plan of furnishing a large amount of power. Most of the wheels were from sixteen to thirty feet in diameter while the ordinary farm windmill today is eight or ten feet. It was not until the late seventies that it became a common fixture on the prairies. The windmill and barbed wire invaded the plains hand in hand chronologically. So important is the windmill today on the plains, a region of never-failing winds, that in some small towns nearly every home has one.[14]

On account of the larger fields and lack of obstructions, machinery came into use in the West more quickly than in the country east

[14] *Ibid.*, pp. 336–341. The writer remembers having camped in a small western Kansas town late in the evening. The next morning he was astonished at the large number of windmills. Without moving from the camp ground, he counted some three dozen.

of the Apalachian Mountains. Travelers from the East in the eighties were astonished when they saw the station platform and the prairie around it covered with bright new machinery. In fact the people bought too much machinery. There was a tendency, as soon as the homesteader received his patent, to mortgage the farm in order to buy machinery. Farm papers admonished their readers not to borrow money to buy machinery which would be worn out before it was paid for. Nevertheless this is what many did; and hundreds of homesteaders finally lost their claims as a result of their lack of forethought.

In connection with the machine revolution there arose an interesting type of agriculture known as bonanza farming. Bonanza farming began in the Red River Valley in 1874, spread to other parts of Dakota, and was practiced to a limited extent in western Kansas and Nebraska. The first bonanza farm was started by Mr. George W. Cass, president of the Northern Pacific Railway, together with a prominent member of an express company, Mr. Benjamin P. Cheney. Real estate was a drag on the market. The company had failed to sell its lands in small lots, and so these men bought eighteen sections from the company. The tract was later increased to 12,240 acres. Mr. Oliver Dalrymple, an extensive wheat farmer of Washington County, Minnesota, was selected to manage this huge farm. He was a talented business man and had practiced law in his younger days. He reduced farming to mechanical precision.

The first four or five years sixteen-inch, single walking plows were used as on small farms; but by 1879 the double gang plow, drawn by four horses, replaced the single plows. A brigade of seven or eight to twenty of these would move across the field at once. They would travel about twenty miles a day each plowing five acres. Twenty such plows would plow a section in a week. A brigade of a dozen binders in line was superintended by a field foreman on horseback. A wagon hauled twine, water, tools, and so forth, and an expert was at hand to help in any emergency. The day harvest

MACHINES IN BONANZA FARMING

This picture of binders at work on the Dalrymple farm is only one section of a panoramic view which includes a dozen more machines. Courtesy of the Great Northern Railway.

closed, threshing began. By that time the first grain cut was well cured and ready for the threshers.

Each year new land was put under cultivation. As these farms increased in size they were organized into divisions over which a superintendent was placed. Each division was sub-divided into units or stations placed in charge of foremen. New equipment alone for the Dalrymple farm in 1878 was thirty-eight plows, thirty-five harrows, seventeen seeders, twenty-seven binders, fifty-two wagons, and five threshing machines. In 1879 four hundred men were required to do the threshing on sixteen units. Twenty-one threshing machines were in use. Of course, very few of these men were kept the year around. The company endeavored to become self-sufficing as far as possible. It raised its own supplies. Meat, vegetables, and stock feed, were produced on the farms. Blacksmith shops and harness shops did the repair work.

These farms were a good investment for years because of the increase in the value of the land and because it was free from weeds. After forty years they were broken up almost entirely. Nevertheless in the seventies the movement proceeded rapidly. By 1880 there were eighty-two farms in the Red River Valley more than 1,000 acres in area. A large number of these ran from four to six sections. The movement was just getting started by 1880 for the census of 1890 showed 232 farms that exceeded 1,000 acres. Truly a farm in Dakota was not considered a bonanza farm until it contained over a thousand acres.[15] In 1890 there were 930 which ranged in area from 500 to 1,000 acres. These, although not classed as bonanza farms, were nevertheless extensive and were a special frontier development.

The government allowed a man under the homestead, tree claim, and preëmption acts, to secure three quarter sections. Then by buying adjacent sections from the Northern Pacific Railway whose

[15] For bonanza farms see *Collections*, State Historical Society of North Dakota, Vol. III; also J. H. Shepherd, *Quarterly Journal*, University of North Dakota, Vol. XIII.

grants extended for a distance of fifty miles back from the main line, one could establish a sizable farm. Keenest competition existed at times for coveted quarter sections needed to fill out a block for an extensive farm. Races to the land office to secure the desired land were frequent during the boom days. Strategy was used to gain possession of land sought. Needless to say, the ordinary home-steader was not able to secure one of these large farms. This was for the man who brought a little money with him and could, by exer-cising his governmental rights and perhaps by investing the money he had received from the sale of a place in the old home state, secure a big farm. It was only natural that there should arise a tendency toward large farms in view of the general conditions of the time.

At the beginning of the decade of the seventies two men and six work animals using two fourteen-inch plows, could plow five or six acres a day. At the end of the decade one man with a gang plow could cover as much with four animals. By 1885 a man regularly drove four-horse teams. If a man had fifty acres of field grain he had to have a $235 binder to cut it. He used it only the five days necessary and it remained idle the rest of the year with his money tied up in it. In order to secure the maximum benefit he prepared as quickly as possible to cultivate a hundred acres on each quarter section and to cut it with the same binder. The interest on the in-vestment was about the same whether he cut fifty or a hundred acres, and the depreciation was but little greater. Improvements were being made so rapidly that a machine, no matter how little worn, was soon rendered useless or wasteful when compared to some later perfected model. It was then good economy to utilize machinery to its utmost capacity every year. This meant large farms.[16]

Other improved and labor-saving devices appeared to lighten the burden of the farmer. The old-fashioned square lantern with its candle within was displaced by the kerosene lantern. This was a boon indeed to the man who worked by artificial illumination both

[16] *Ibid.; Collections*, State Historical Society of North Dakota, Vol. III.

in the morning and evening during the winter months. A machine to shell corn was invented during the later pioneer period.

Labor-saving devices for women were introduced slowly. There was a tendency for the homesteader to buy new machinery to till broad acres and build new barns to house more stock and grain, while his wife went about the drudgery of household life in the old way in a little drab dwelling overshadowed by the splendor of machine farming. The earliest improvements came in the Civil War period when crude washing machines and wringers made their appearance.[17] The original washing machine while some improvement over washing on the board, was not a magic contrivance. The wringer was no doubt more successful and efficient than the machine. The sewing machine began to come into general use in the eighties. Its coming was not an unmixed blessing for it brought in its van a plague of agents who pestered the people in an endeavor to convince them of the superior merits of their respective machines. The New Home, the White, and the Singer, were some of the outstanding makes.

The invention of pumps was a great boon to the farm woman. At first she carried water from a spring or water barrel. Later, when a well was dug, a pulley with its chain and a bucket on each end simplified matters somewhat, but the invention of the pump was the greatest boon to the lady of the house. The first pumps were made of wood, but later those of iron manufacture displaced them. The windmill with its free lift of water made life even more comfortable. Illumination at first had been by means of grease dish or candle. In the seventies this gave way to the kerosene lamp. It was a tremendous improvement but the never-ending chore of filling kerosene lamps and cleaning sooty chimneys added another burden to the already overloaded housewife.

The preparation of meals was at first over a fire in a crude fireplace, while the utensils consisted of a teakettle, a Dutch oven, a skillet, a large iron kettle, and a coffee pot. The coming of the

---

[17] See advertisements in the *Kansas Farmer*, 1865–1867.

kitchen range with its oven and reservoir was a blessing to the frontier woman. Organs came into use during the frontier period and an occasional piano was seen. Rag carpets, a great improvement in frontier days, were displaced gradually by factory manufactured carpets. For the most part, however, the machine age did not greatly help woman. She continued to operate the churn, carry water, and run the washing machine—if she were fortunate enough to have one —and do her other work without the aid of horse power which her more fortunate husband began to apply in his harvesting, threshing, and planting.

CHAPTER XXII

THE GRANGE

THE FARMERS attempted to organize at a very early period. On March 5, 1862, the Kansas State Agricultural Society was organized in the hall of the House of Representatives at the capitol. During the legislative session in 1863 the society met every week while the legislature was in session. The farmers took a leaf from the Methodist crusaders and called their sessions A Farmers' Class Meeting.[1] In Nebraska, county agricultural associations were organized in the territorial period.

By all odds the most important factor in rural life during the seventies, however, was the Grange. Although this organization was national in character, it found its most effective support in the frontier and post-frontier regions. The founder of the organization was Oliver Hudson Kelley, a clerk in the agricultural department in Washington, D. C. He was sent on a trip through the southern states on public business and, seeing the unfortunate condition of the people there and appreciating the need for organization of the farmers with its resultant benefits, began to plan an organization for the purpose of uniting all the farmers of the nation in one vast union. He enlisted the aid of a few friends among the government clerks who were interested in the problems of the farmer and spent several months planning and perfecting the farmers' organization which made him famous. Mr. Kelley was a Mason, and Masonic methods were copied extensively in the new agrarian order. The ritual and constitution were completed on December 4, 1867. For some months the organization, which Kelley called The Patrons of Husbandry, existed largely on paper and consisted in actual

[1] *First Report of the State Board of Agriculture* (Kansas, n.d.), p. 14

membership of a handful of government clerks in the city of Washington, who met in solemn conclave from time to time. Kelley then resigned his position and devoted his time to perfecting and promoting the organization. For some years he made little progress in enlisting interest in his project. At first he made the mistake of trying to establish local units in the cities of the West. Finally, almost penniless, he turned to the rural regions and by the greatest exertion gained a foothold there. The movement swept the frontier and post-frontier states like a prairie fire.

The first local grange in Kansas was the Hiawatha grange in Brown County, which was formed in April, 1872. Until December, 1872, there were only nine granges in the state. The first state grange meeting took place at Lawrence, on July 30, 1873; at that time there were 409 organized local granges. In February, 1874, sixty counties had 975 granges with a membership of 27,000. By the first of April it increased to 1,200 granges with membership exceeding 30,000. The organization flourished on the raw frontier. Nebraska and Kansas furnished more grange members per 100,000 population than any of the other commonwealths.[2]

The first granges in Nebraska were founded about the same time as those in Kansas and one was organized at Yankton, Dakota Territory, in December, 1873.[3] By October, 1875, the movement reached its crest with fifty-three granges in Dakota Territory.[4]

[2] Number of grangers per 100,000 population in the region of the largest membership of the Order:

	Kans.	Nebr.	Dak.	Ia.	Minn.	Mo.	Ind.
August 2, 1873	353	694	107	741	355	166	93
October 18, 1873	526	763	242	763	394	315	163
March 1, 1874	847	1,010	364	775	478	603	513
September 1, 1874	1,064	1,190	433	806	549	658	680
January 1, 1875	952	1,042	361	735	490	649	667
October 1, 1875	293	508	341	452	441	613	498
July 1, 1876	571	568	143	382	271	974	375

Solon Justus Buck, *The Granger Movement* (Cambridge, 1913), p. 58.

[3] *Yankton Press and Dakotaian*, December 18, 1873.

[4] Harold E. Briggs, "The Development of Agriculture in Territorial Dakota," *The Culver Stockton Quarterly* (Canton, Missouri, January, 1931), pp. 34-35.

The reason for the great strength of the grange on the frontier, no doubt, was because of the straitened financial circumstances of the pioneers. The frontier was always poverty-stricken. That, added to the general depression which broke upon the country in 1873, ground the pioneer between two millstones, first, that of appreciating currency owing to the policy of specie resumption, and, second, the ordinary frontier shortage of cash with its accompanying borrowing at high monthly interest rates. These prepared a seed bed of discontent which readily bore fruit when the grange idea was presented.

The objects of the frontiersmen's special hostility were the railroads and the middle-men. Within a short time they devised means to control these agencies which were making life miserable for the farmer.

At first the settlers looked with the greatest anticipation to the coming of the railroad—in fact they could not be restrained from giving away vast sums in land and voting bonds to induce the railroads to come into the vicinity. Great celebrations were given to welcome the opening of new lines. After a few years, the drunkenness of the first enthusiasm having worn off, the citizens in a sober mood of reflection saw where they had duped themselves and had played into the hands of the corporations. Before long the companies which had been the dearest objects of their courtship, turned to objects of hatred. Discrimination, high rates, stock watering, together with sharp practices and the general attitude of the railroad managers toward shippers, led to organized opposition. The so-called "granger legislation" resulted.[5] The great influx of population in the seventies also brought competition and a surplus of crops which had to be shipped long distances. The profits were devoured by high freight rates. On the other hand, the extremely high price of machinery was boosted by the transportation rates from the factories in the older states. The farmers were furthermore at the

---

[5] A. E. Paine, *The Granger Movement in Illinois* (Urbana, 1904), p. 336.

mercy of the middle-men who also became special objects of their hatred. The sons of toil had no organization through which to deal with the manufacturers directly and furthermore they always had to buy on credit. This enabled the retailer to hold the farmers' trade even though he charged high rates.

The grange brought together the isolated farmers, welded them into a powerful unit with bargaining power, and in a short time, made of them a force to be reckoned with. Furthermore, the grange advocated a "pay-as-you-go policy," educating its members to save a sum before purchasing and thus escape the clutches of the money lenders and middle-men.

The organization of the order was interesting and effective. The national organization, known as The Order of Patrons of Husbandry, and presided over by a grand master, authorized minor groups known as granges. The state grange was presided over by a state master; and the lowest unit, the local grange, was presided over by the master.

When the organization was finally complete there were seven degrees. The local grange had four degrees:

First Degree: Laborer (man), Maid (woman).
Second Degree: Cultivator (man), Shepherdess (woman).
Third Degree: Harvester (man), Gleaner (woman).
Fourth Degree: Husbandman (man), Matron (woman).

The fifth degree was a state organization composed of the masters of subordinate granges and their wives who were matrons. The past-masters and their wives were given honorary membership. The degree was known as Pomona or hope. The sixth degree was composed of masters of state granges and their wives who had taken the degree of Pomona. Past state masters and their wives were honorary members. The seventh degree, known as Ceres or faith, consisted of members of the national grange who had served one year, had applied for membership, and had been elected. Subordinate grange officers held office for one year, state, two years, and national, three years.[6] The officers of the respective granges were addressed as "Worthy."

Three major lines of activity occupied the time of the Patrons of Husbandry—educational, business, and social. The educational feature was manifest in several ways. An effort was made to encourage all members to read and study the problems of the farm dweller so that they might not be imposed upon by the city man. It further encouraged the study of soil tillage, crop production, and animal husbandry. Programs which shed light on the problems of the farmer, started him and his wife to thinking and reading, and inspired them to seek more knowledge and improve themselves culturally, were offered at the regular monthly meetings.

The Kansas state grange sent out a leaflet from headquarters giving the titles of the programs to be carried out each month.[7] The program for the year 1889 gives some idea of the activity of the order along educational lines in that year:

January—Report of the State Grange committee on needed legislation.
February—Taxation and transportation.
March—Oat and corn culture—variety of seed, preparation of ground, etc.
April—Kitchen garden—how best made, how best kept, as a factor in household economy.
May—Small fruits and flower garden—kinds, culture, plan, etc.
June—The dairy—cows, food, care. The milk and manner of manufacturing cheese and butter.

They furthermore urged educational reform for the benefit of the farmers' children. Among the reforms asked for were: First,

[6] The officers of a grange, whether national, state, or subordinate, consisted of and ranked as follows:

1. Master	5. Asst. Steward	9. Ceres
2. Overseer	6. Chaplain	10. Pomona
3. Lecturer	7. Secretary	11. Flora
4. Steward	8. Gate-Keeper	12. Lady Asst. Steward

Two offices were always filled by women. *Constitution and By-Laws of Kansas State Grange.*

[7] *Kansas Grange Program for 1889* (Leaflet in Kansas State Historical Society Library).

better educational facilities and privileges; second, agricultural and practical education in the common schools, and an inspiration which would give the young people a greater love for the occupation. As a result of this new force in agriculture which swept the state like a cyclone, a movement to reorganize the State Agricultural College was launched and carried to fruition. The college was changed in 1873 from an institution giving an ordinary arts and science course to that of applied science in agriculture and mechanical arts.

As a result of the grange educational program savored with politics, the report of the Kansas committee on needed legislation recommended at one time that all money larger than the penny and the nickel, be made of paper and that $50 per capita be printed. This was closely akin to the greenback movement which flourished on the frontier at about the same period.

The national grange inaugurated a system of crop reports and published and distributed hundreds of thousands of tracts among farmers urging the need of keeping up with the times. The state grange sent out deputies and lecturers to disseminate information on agricultural topics. The subordinate granges paid the bills and were expected to reap the benefit. The results were marked. There was a freer social intercourse, a higher respect for the opinions of one another, and a more careful attention to personal appearance. One pastor in the post-frontier region wrote of a remarkable change in the conduct and general outlook of his congregation. Frequently there was an increase in demand for books and papers. In one community where only one paper was received before the organization of a grange, the subscriptions jumped to thirty.[8] Grange libraries were established in some localities. Farmers contributed to papers more frequently and the movement for farmers' institutes greatly advanced.[9]

Organization brought a sense of power and a desire to take advantage of the new-found strength to save money by coöperative

---

[8] This incident occurred in the post-frontier but illustrates what no doubt took place a little farther west.

[9] A. E. Paine, *op. cit.*, pp. 377–379.

buying and selling. Coöperative buying apparently was first tried
with considerable success. The local grangers sent their orders with
the money to the state grange which bought in carload lots from
the manufacturer. At first it was difficult to find a manufacturer who
would deal with the grange, for middle-men naturally tried to prevent the manufacturer from selling directly to the consumers. Since
the manufacturers had contracts with local dealers, giving the latter
a complete monopoly of sales in a given district, they naturally felt
that it meant ruin to lose the trade of these dealers. Manufacturers
certainly were not to be blamed for hesitating to break away from
long-established business connections to chase the pot of gold at the
rainbow's end. But finally the grangers made contracts with certain
manufacturers, who far from suffering from lack of sales, found
themselves utterly unable to supply the demand. The grangers
effected great savings for some time. Reapers, for which the retailer charged $275, were secured by the grangers for $175. Threshers costing $300, were bought for $200. Wagons, selling locally for
$150, were obtained at $90. Sewing machine prices were reduced
from thirty to forty per cent. On fifteen hundred machines the saving was as much as $30,000.[10] The saving probably averaged about
thirty-three and one-third per cent for a few years.

Failing to prevent the manufacturers from selling directly to the
grange, the middle-man tried to exterminate the new competition
by price-cutting. For a while local dealers sold at lower prices than
the goods could be procured through the grange. In Kansas the re-
tailers supplied agricultural implements and other necessities at
prices varying from thirty to forty per cent lower than usually
charged. Naturally this venture, so successful with implements,
was carried over into groceries, dry goods, and other supplies.

Montgomery Ward and Company of Chicago was organized in
1872 as the original wholesale grange supply house.[11] In the early
years coöperative buying probably saved the purchaser as much as

[10] Edward Winslow Martin, *History of the Grange Movement* (Chicago, 1874),
p. 477.
[11] *Kansas Grange Bulletin*, May 10, 1872.

twenty per cent of the cost of the previous purchasing price. Later there was a call for local stores inasmuch as a saving could be effected only by buying in large quantities and storing the goods in country or town. As a rule these coöperative schemes for selling were not as successful as the buying projects. Live stock commission agencies were established at the live stock markets,[12] elevators were bought or built, and mutual insurance companies were chartered. Very few of these enterprises succeeded permanently, although it is said that in Iowa the grangers had control over two-thirds of the grain elevators in 1874.

Eventually the grange lost control of most of these establishments. The grangers were many times untutored in business ways. Often they hired someone to manage the business who was dishonest or who did not take the interest in the enterprise that a private individual would, so that in time, the business failed. At Greenwood, Nebraska, an elevator failed and cost the stockholders twelve times as much to get out of the business as it did to get into it. Another Nebraska grange began manufacturing cultivators and failed. Still another shipped grain by steamboat but, lacking warehouses, suffered loss.

Another form of coöperation was for county and subordinate granges to pass resolutions to hold their hogs thirty days unless offered a certain price.

Possibly the most lasting benefit was the social activity which was generated by the Patrons of Husbandry. The humdrum monotony of farm life on the frontier in the sixties and seventies was deadening in its effect on the people. Isolated and with scant means of travel, the settler and his family had to remain apart from his fellow men; social life was stagnant. The women, who are more dependent upon social life than are men, were especially cursed by this isolated life. It kept them at home doing the daily rounds of toil

---

[12] *Yankton Press and Dakotaian* of December 18, 1878, reported that the agent of the grange at the Chicago stockyards had sold $200,000 worth of stock for the Iowa grange.

almost constantly while their husbands were called by duty to go to town or to some other place where social intercourse was possible. Woman's constant routine of toil and isolation was broken only by an occasional wedding, funeral, or visit. The grange abolished this stagnation. The regular meetings of the grange brought the people together twelve or more times a year. New friendships were formed, old ones strengthened, and the discussion of the common problems of their vocation gave them courage and made for progress. Furthermore, the grange promoted social relaxation and pleasure through association as a legitimate human need. Occasionally in the long winter evenings an oyster supper was arranged by the leading members of the subordinate grange. The women brought big kettles or wash boilers and each family brought milk. The oysters and crackers were purchased from the order's fund. Songs, debates, recitations, essays, and other forms of entertainment often accompanied the oyster stew and coffee. Discussion of political and religious questions was strictly forbidden by the constitution of the order. Grange meetings were usually held in school-houses but occasionally a grange built a substantial hall for its own use. A few miles north of Topeka stands a large stone building built by the local grange in the eighties. A commodious barn, tennis courts, and other facilities show that it remains a social community center to this day.

In the summer at a time which would least interfere with the crops, they held the annual picnic which was looked forward to for weeks. Often a central location was selected and all the granges within a large area united in this event. Contests, speaking, visiting, games, and a huge basket dinner, characterized these picnics. Every young man who had a top buggy had it polished for the use of his lady fair, and those who did not own a rig patronized the livery stable at the nearest town. Some doubled teams with friends, built a Bowery wagon out of a wagon-box, and with a four or six horse team rode away in splendor. The picnic ground was usually along some stream in a shady grove. Early in the morning the various granges met at prearranged rendezvous and traveled together, joining other granges en route, until there was one vast procession. The different lodges were led by great banners carrying the motto of the home unit. Some columns were preceded by bands. To the isolated farmer who saw those long lines of carriages joining into one mighty column, it was an inspiration indeed. Probably no other social force has arisen in American life which has been more helpful in raising the rural folk to a higher plane of living, in inspiring courage and self-confidence, and in relieving the stark loneliness of the isolated farm family.[13]

[13] Hamlin Garland, *A Son of the Middle Border*, pp. 165, 166.

CHAPTER XXIII

READIN' AN' 'RITIN' AN' 'RITHMETIC

AMONG certain groups of Kansas, Nebraska, and Dakota emigrants it was truth as well as poetry that

> They came to plant the common school
> On distant prairie swells.[1]

When these settlers touched the soil of the new land schools sprang up as soon as there were children to attend. The first party of emigrants reached Lawrence, Kansas, on August 1, 1854, and the first school, a free one, opened five months later, in January, 1855. On March 7, 1857, the Quincy High School was established. Topeka was settled late in November, 1854, and early the next summer a school was opened. On January 2, 1856, the Topeka Academy was established.[2]

Samuel C. Bassett reached Buffalo County, Nebraska, with a colony on April 7, 1871. At that time but four claims had been filed at the land office and no railroad land had been sold. The county had only recently been organized. The colony lived in railroad cars until they could build homes, and eight days after they arrived, while yet living in these temporary rolling houses and before any of the group had filed on homesteads, a meeting was called to consider the organization of a school district. At a meeting held on April 22, school district officers were elected and a tax voted to build a school-house. In less than three months a term of school began in the wing of a private house just completed.[3] So it was that over the

[1] John Greenleaf Whittier, "The Song of the Kansas Immigrant."
[2] Richard Cordley, "Address of Rev. Richard Cordley," *Transactions*, Kansas State Historical Society, Vol. III, pp. 227, 228.
[3] H. G. Taylor, "Influence of Overland Travel on the Early Settlement of Nebraska," *Collections*, Nebraska State Historical Society, Vol. XVII, pp. 152, 153.

rolling prairie, volunteer movements arose even before there was legal provision to aid. Without a murmur and before the settlers had built themselves comfortable homes, they sacrificed to provide for their children.

It must not be taken for granted, however, that all the settlers were of the same mold as the Massachusetts people who reproduced their New England culture in Lawrence and Topeka, and that all were as energetic and progressive as the Free Homestead Colony of which Mr. Bassett was a leading figure. On the contrary there were not a few in Lawrence and Topeka who, having less education than the New Englanders, were careless or prejudiced against learning. The more illiterate townspeople felt their inferiority; this erected a barrier between the two groups. On the prairies in the sixties and seventies as a rule brawn and nerve were more respected than brains and culture. Often men felt themselves sufficiently educated if they could read some, write a crude hand, and "figger." Among some groups, much instruction militated against success and made "sissies." The essence of success was the accumulation of much money or property. Rich people could be identified who could not even write their names. On the edge of the prairie frontier a person with a meager college experience had at times to be tactful about it to avoid being dubbed "stuck up" or a "smart aleck." Many parents often withdrew their children from school on slight pretexts feeling that they had learned enough.[4]

The first schools were usually subscription schools although, as noted above, Lawrence, Kansas, had a free school. In a subscription school the teacher taught for what he could get and "boarded around" at the homes of the parents of the pupils. The tuition charge was from a dollar to a dollar and a half a month for each child. In the small towns where there were the beginnings of the modern grade system, the primary rate was one dollar a month, the common English branches one dollar and a half, and the higher branches, corresponding to our early high school years, two dol-

---

[4] Stuart Henry, *Conquering Our Great American Plains*, p. 173.

lars. In these schools of the fifties the plan was to have three terms a year. Each was of three months' duration with a vacation period of two weeks between terms. Teachers were hired for one term only, thus rendering their tenure even more unstable than in the small schools of today. This tended also to destroy the efficiency of the school since a pupil might have three teachers in a given year.[5] At a later time when the number of pupils increased, the teacher was paid by the school board at a rate of twenty-five to seventy-five cents a month per pupil. In other places the teacher was paid by the day and "boarded around." The wages ran from seventy-five cents to a dollar a day.

The building of the school-house in any neighborhood was an outstanding event. The erection of this building was a date from which occurrences were reckoned—as happening before or after the school-house was built. This structure was frequently built before a regular organized district had been formed and before any taxes were available for this purpose.

There was great difficulty in agreeing to the location of the school-house. Often considerable contention and bad feeling was aroused in a neighborhood over the exact location of the citadel of learning. Near Superior, Nebraska, five or six men had worked one-half day on a dugout when another citizen asked them to move it one-half mile farther west. They agreed to accommodate their neighbor and started working again in the new location. Another neighbor then requested them to move it one-half mile farther west so it would be close to his place. They moved to accommodate him. This process was continued until they had moved four times and were two miles away from the original location. People were not always so accommodating and frequently there was trouble. In one place in northeastern Kansas the eastern section of the district wanted the school near them and the western part also wanted it. Finally the district was divided and a school-house erected in each vicinity.

[5] Not many places, however, were fortunate enough to have more than a term or two each year.

Even then it was with the greatest difficulty that they could decide where the structures were to be located. In McPherson County, Kansas, the patrons on the south side grumbled because the school-house was located too far north. When a house moving outfit came through the country, a crowd took advantage of the opportunity one night secretly to move the house of learning one mile south. The next morning the astonished pedagogue and his pupils were surprised to find the building gone.

These school-houses, built before money was available from the public funds, were often coöperative enterprises. Each man furnished so many hewed logs of a given length if the house were to be of logs, or a given number of loads of rock if it were to be of that material. Then at a bee the house was built. If the building was to be a dugout or sod structure, as most of them in the western two-thirds of the prairie states were, the men of the neighborhood brought their tools and constructed it in a day or two. A collection was taken up by public-spirited citizens for the purpose of buying window frames, windows, and doors. In the fifties and sixties the windows consisted merely of holes in the walls as there were no window sashes nor glass.

In Potter County, Dakota Territory, when the school board declined to provide a school-house, against the public will, a group of the children abetted and helped by older people, made the rounds of the neighborhood and called the settlers to a meeting at an appointed place for the purpose of providing a school. One settler near the center of the township donated the use of the ground and the settlers came and held a building bee. In a few hours' time a serviceable sod school-house and stable were erected.

Various settlers donated money for the necessary lumber and hardware. The boys plowed the strips of sod and laid up the walls while the men directed their efforts, sawing wood and finishing the building. The bed was taken from a wagon, and planks placed on the running gears formed a flat car arrangement for hauling the sod squares. At noon a table cloth was spread on the prairie and set with good food by the mothers and sisters. Within a week the school-house, eighteen by twenty-two feet, was finished. Home-made desks and furniture sufficed. The teacher gave his services. All that winter he drove twelve miles to teach young people who were eager to learn; and for this he never received a penny.

Graft, unfortunately ever present, found its way into the handling of school funds. When the school fund functioned and there was opportunity to bond the district, the early settlers occasionally used the bonding method for their own advantage. They voted bonds to run over a long period so that the settlers who should come later would bear the larger part of the expense. The majority of the little handful of settlers who voted for the bonds had teams, and as a matter of course secured the job of hauling the lumber forty or fifty miles. This was in reality a profitable arrangement for the early settler. A sod house would have been more in keeping with the spirit of the law and in harmony with the financial resources of the country. It seemed hardly right at a time when the whole population lived in dugouts or sod houses, to vote bonds for an expensive frame school-house which would be paid largely by later comers.

Often the first schools were held in one room or one corner of a settler's home. The first temple of learning in Alliance, Nebraska, was a tent. One man from Kansas spoke of having school in a cellar. It was walled up and enough windows put in to give the necessary light.

The school-houses in the eastern part of the states and along the streams farther west, were built of logs in much the same manner that those of Ohio, Illinois, and Iowa, had been built during the previous half century. The roof was often made of branches and sod and the whole structure built as a community enterprise. The logs were chinked with blocks and pointed up with clay in lieu of mortar. A long broad board rested on pegs inserted in the logs along two sides of the room. This formed a steep desk. The seats were rough slabs of wood from the sawmill or hewn logs with pegs put in for legs. These seats and desks around the room were for the older pupils. The little ones had benches in the center of the room. There were no backs to any of the benches. The teacher was fortunate to have a rude desk and chair. The dirt floor was dusty in dry weather and muddy with pools of water from the leaking roof for three days following a rain. There was a slab or puncheon recitation bench in front of the teacher. At one end of the room was a large fireplace or stove, and at the other end were the door and window. The community with a school having panes of glass was fortunate indeed. In these first schools there was not the faintest suggestion of a blackboard. There were no maps, no globe, and the nearest dictionary was often miles away. The rural school had no library. In the better schools a typical library was one contributed by the patrons and consisted of a Bible, hymn book, history of the Indian Wars, an almanac, and a few old schoolbooks brought from the East by the settlers. A wooden pail accompanied by rusty cup or dipper stood in the corner. Some of the big boys were permitted the great privilege of going after the water, a job which the proud independent frontier boy would have done sulkily if ordered in a servile manner to perform. Some of the little children were given the privilege of passing the water. All drank from the same dipper. The children had to be watched to keep them from pouring water back in the bucket.

The children furnished their own books and what a motley array of tools for the cultivation of knowledge! The lack of uniformity in textbooks was the bane of the frontier pedagogue. The parents brought the old texts from their former homes in the East and often in a class there would be three or four different kinds of geographies or readers. This caused an utter lack of uniformity and impeded progress. As early as 1861 the Nebraska territorial commissioner advocated a law making books uniform throughout the territory. Some of the favorite books in use in the seventies were: Webster's, McGuffey's, and Worcester's spellers, McGuffey's and Hilliard's readers, Ray's *Mental Arithmetic*, Montieth and Mc-

Nally's geography, and Clark's grammar. Spencerian penmanship was the standard and in the earlier days it was executed with a goose quill.[6]

There were no examinations in the modern sense of the word. The teacher knew where the pupil belonged without any of these improvements. When a child could easily read the fifth reader through he was ready for the sixth reader. The child started in at the first of the book each year until he could read it and then passed on to the next. As time went by and new improvements were made, the slate came into vogue. When there was need for erasure the boys spit on the slate and rubbed it off with their coat or shirt sleeves. The girls, a bit more dainty, carried slate rags. These had to be wet innumerable times and insured frequent promenades to the water bucket, a pleasing break in the monotony of school.

With progress in the town school and on a later frontier, blackboards were introduced. These were made of plaster or boards painted black. A package of chalk and a rag or sheepskin eraser accompanied this improvement. The town schools took considerable pains to make the school-room attractive. The second Nebraska City school, in 1856, had the desks and seats painted in contrasting colors of blue and white. White window curtains gave a touch of daintiness to the room. This was a private school, however. At Brownville, Nebraska, a private school issued a weekly paper in manuscript form and according to the local newspaper it was well done. The articles written by ten-year-olds would have done credit to older heads according to the editor of the Brownville paper.

It was customary for the settlers to pad the school census in order to receive a larger share of the territorial school fund. Sometimes

[6] According to the third annual report of the Commissioner of Schools (for 1861) the following subjects were taught in Nebraska to the number of pupils indicated:

Alphabet 173	English Grammar 239	Mental Arith. ..311
Orthography ..1,390	Composition 111	Algebra 15
Reading 1,248	Rhetoric 11	Geography 285
Penmanship 610	Vocal Music 61	History 21
Nat. Philosophy ..11	Geometry 4	Latin 4
Chemistry 1	Astronomy 5	Written Arith. ..507
Physiology 26	Bookkeeping 2	

the names of married children in an eastern state were turned in. This bit of dishonesty was defended on the ground that the children needed a school.

There was a territorial law in Nebraska which required a seven months' session of school each year, but this was widely ignored. According to the Hall County statistics of 1876 seventy-three per cent of the children attended school and twenty-seven did not. Only twenty-one districts out of forty-seven which had schools, ran for six months. The average number of months was five. At that time there were in that county twenty-nine frame and seven sod school-houses. The statistics for Seward County, Nebraska, in 1871, showed that there were only twenty school-houses in the county at that time, of which six were frame, seven sod, three dugouts, and four log.[7]

A description of what the county superintendent found as he visited the schools will give an idea of the general physical condition of the schools in that year. In district twenty-five he found a sod house fourteen by twelve, only two small seats, no desks, no table, no blackboard, and no place to put away books. In district twenty-four he found a dugout, rude but comfortable, with board benches, a board writing desk around the room, and a blackboard. In district one he found a log building, rude and uncomfortable, poorly furnished with slab benches and a board desk around the room. Many of the school-houses he mentioned had dirt floors and a few seats made of rough boards.

The life of the early school-teacher was far from pleasant in many respects. He had to board around at the homes of his pupils, staying longest at the homes with the largest number of children. These as a rule were the poorest and least comfortable of the lot. There was no privacy in the little sod house crowded with the parents, their numerous brood, and occasionally the circuit rider or

[7] County Superintendent's Annual Report for the year ending April 1, 1871. Seward lies in a rich agricultural country not more than eighty miles from the Missouri River, adjoining the county in which the state capital is located.

some other visitor for good measure. A teacher who taught near Tecumseh, Kansas, told of one large family who always fed him on corn-bread and home-made molasses. He dreaded this arc of the boarding circle but was forced to endure it, for the family was sensitive and, having a large number of children, was expected to contribute to the teacher's living. He often drove several miles to his home over the week-end in order to avoid staying with one of the patrons.

The number of men and women in the profession was about even. The West tried to entice teachers trained in the eastern colleges or academies for this work. This was hard to do on account of the low wages offered. Enough educated people came West for the purpose of homesteading to furnish a considerable number of teachers. Many times a young girl homesteaded far from neighbors and taught school to secure needed funds for making a home. A typical lady teacher of the seventies wore high shoes, a long skirt, a tight waist, long sleeves, and a high neck. A neat white apron protected the dress and gave a professional touch; her hair was coiled high on her head.

She was the school janitor, wending her way across the prairies at an early hour in order to build the fire of green cottonwood. Sometimes the larger boys did this for the teacher. Some who had fallen a victim to the teacher's winning personality, occasionally stayed to help her sweep the dusty floor. The wages varied greatly but ran between ten and fifteen dollars a month in the sixties and twenty and thirty in the seventies. One teacher speaks of having received his board and a dollar a day for every day he taught. Another received seventy-five cents a day. Sometimes the teacher was promised a salary which he never received; the fund might have given out and the patrons were too poor or too dishonorable to fulfil the contract.

The schools, although conducted in small buildings, were nevertheless not small. The crude little school-houses of Nebraska in 1871 had an average of seventeen pupils each. Seventeen pupils in a school-house twelve by fourteen with no busy work or equipment is a test of anyone's managerial and disciplinary ability. The scenes portrayed in *The Hoosier Schoolmaster* were reënacted in many a prairie mansion of learning. Five or six of the boys from eighteen to twenty years old, weighing 160 to 175 pounds, ganged up on the teachers and whipped them as fast as they arrived. They bullied the little folks and broke up the school. In some districts teachers lasted only a week or two and the school board in hiring a teacher, looked to his brawn more than to his brains. The community assumed an attitude of expectancy, waiting to see how the new pedagogue could handle the situation. Once licked by a man proficient in the fistic arts, the school settled down to business. Sometimes a mere girl or a puny little male like the Hoosier schoolmaster by use of strategy and nerve, walked off with the load where stronger ones had failed utterly.

As compared to the teachers in the older states it must be admitted that those in the new country were only fair. There was an attempt to induce normal-trained teachers to come to the plains, but the prosperous, successful teacher could hardly be expected to leave his position for the West where terms were short and pay none too certain. As a rule the earlier teachers in a given community were homesteaders who had a better education than their neighbors.

At Adams, Nebraska, the first school was established in 1863 after this fashion: John Adams had four children to go to school. A neighbor of his had been a student at the Zanesville Academy in Ohio. Mr. Adams made a contract with this man to teach his children in a front room of his house for board and room from Monday to Friday and a three-year-old heifer to freshen soon. The equipment consisted of one long wooden bench, one splint bottom chair with a red and white knitted "tidy" over the back, a cross section of cottonwood log for a stool, a walnut stand table, a home-made bedstead and feather bed from Pennsylvania covered with a crazy patch quilt, a clock on the mantel, and two winter bouquets made of tickle grass dipped in green and purple dyes. For their work the children had one slate, two McGuffey's readers, a Bible, and a copy-book. Soon the neighbors' children joined and they had a school of nearly a dozen with this meager equipment.[8]

Here and there were to be found people with considerable education who had come West to secure a farm of their own. These, either through the requests of their neighbors or through their own desire to make a little money with which to improve their claim, taught school during the winter months.

Obviously it was impossible to supply the region with people educated in the East, and as schools increased it became more difficult to get well-educated teachers. Strange as it may seem, in Kansas there were no statutory qualifications required of county superintendents until thirty years after the creation of the office. Under these circumstances it is not surprising that the loosest standards for the certification of teachers existed. Each county granted certificates and the standard was determined wholly by the county superintendent. The superintendent, like other county officials, itinerated. Teachers' examinations were advertised to be held on certain days at different places over the county. Sometimes they were held in a school-house, sometimes in a store, sometimes in the superintendent's home, and again in a church. Often these were special examinations and of a most perfunctory nature. The young lady who taught the first school in Cloud County, Kansas, was examined orally. There were a few questions in arithmetic, grammar, and geography, the reading of a paragraph from a newspaper, and the signing of her name. It is to be doubted whether some of these superintendents dared to ask any very profound questions lest they should not know the answers themselves.

In 1864 Kansas made some progress toward correcting this abuse by requiring the county superintendent to designate a particular time and place in the spring and autumn of each year for a general examination of teachers. Even then special examinations were per-

---

[8] Mr. Adams was an early settler and had a comparatively comfortable existence as compared to the later settlers.

mitted on payment of a dollar. One man related that in 1867 in a certain Kansas county two school girls stepped into the superintendent's office and asked for certificates. The superintendent asked them some simple questions that a primary child should have known and said, "Now girls, if you will make a real nice bow, and say 'Thank you,' I will give you each a certificate for twelve months." That same year special examinations were prohibited by law. Throughout the homestead period on the prairies it was quite regular for a bright student finishing the elementary rural school to go to the normal institute, take the examination at its close, and if successful, teach pupils of the same grade he had finished in the spring. Teachers of this kind, although possibly well-grounded in the work they taught, had little general knowledge and information to transmit to their pupils.

It must not be inferred that all applicants received certificates. Frequently nearly half of the examinees failed to certify.[9] Owing to the great need for teachers, however, it was almost necessary to ask simple questions so that the required number of teachers could secure certificates.

In Dakota Territory in 1877 four kinds of certificates were granted. A special certificate was valid for three months, a third grade for six months, a second grade for nine months, and a first grade for a year. Frequently owing to the shortage of teachers, a special certificate was issued to an unqualified person for a period covering the duration of the term to be taught. As time passed examinations grew more rigid and formal. One Kansas county report of 1873 shows that a two day examination was held at the schoolhouse in the county seat. About sixty questions were written on the blackboard. Paper was furnished for the candidates.[10]

The superintendent of Seward County, Nebraska, received two

[9] Of the 102 candidates examined in Seward County, Nebraska, in 1871, seventy-four received certificates. In September, 1870, in Iola, Kansas, half the applicants failed.

[10] Of the forty-four examined, six received first grade certificates, twenty-seven received second grade certificates, and eleven received none.

hundred dollars a year for his salary in 1871. The presiding elder on visiting the home of the superintendent of one county, found that he lived in a part sod, part dugout dwelling. Some of the children were hurried off to the neighbors to borrow dishes before the visitors could eat dinner, for it appeared there was not an earthen plate or cup in the home.

In all the prairie states teachers' institutes were started in the sixties. At first these were held by the state superintendent in Kansas and the territorial superintendent in Nebraska. One was held in each senatorial district. These were from two- to five-day institutes; even this was too great an undertaking for the state superintendent. Later laws provided for county institutes presided over by the county superintendent and such other capable professional assistance as he could secure. The length of the institute gradually increased until in the eighties some lasted several weeks. The teachers were obliged to attend this institute. Here the superintendent had an opportunity to select the best teachers.

One of these institutes, held in 1873 in Lone Tree, Nebraska, was reported in the *Grand Island News* and is instructive as to the content and nature of such meetings. The sessions opened at 8:45 o'clock in the morning and at 1:30 in the afternoon. In the morning the day was begun by a minister with song and a prayer. The minister then discussed such topics as "The Teacher's Work" and "Preparation for the Teacher's Work." In these talks the minister emphasized the importance of stressing the moral and spiritual in teaching and of inculcating in the child a reverence for the Most High. Every teacher, the clergyman emphasized, should have Christ for his model. After the devotional and spiritual hour the technique of teaching was presented. According to the reporter, "Arithmetic received very thorough ventilation from the Fundamental rules to Square and Cubic Roots." Then followed lessons in botany, grammar, reading, geography, and school economy. Certain evenings were given over to lectures, debates, readings, music, and sociables. Essays on school government, compulsory education, and other important questions were read. At this institute sixty-nine teachers from seven counties attended.

The report of institutes in Dakota Territory shows that they were similar. For six hours or more each day one subject after another was considered. A few minutes interval occurred between subjects and a recess of fifteen minutes was allowed in both the afternoon and the evening. The superintendent together with visiting superintendents and visiting professional talent, taught classes and gave instruction in methods and school law.

As has been stated there were no formal examinations in the school-room, but there were various kinds of stimuli toward scholarship and advancement in school which are taboo today. Prizes were offered for the highest standing in a given subject. In arithmetic, geography, or reading, the winner was determined at a public examination and exhibition on the last day of school. This was a splendid opportunity for the teacher to show off his work to advantage. The county superintendent or some other man of influence was chosen to conduct the examination and award the prizes, which as a rule consisted of books. Prizes were often awarded to the best speller who was determined by the old head-mark scheme; the pupils stood in a line and when a person missed a word the one who spelled it correctly had the privilege of advancing above him. The one who stood at the head of the line when the lesson was over received a head-mark and took his place at the foot of the class the next day. In due time if a person missed few words he would advance to the head of the class and receive a head-mark. The one having the most was rewarded at the close of school.

During the intermissions the children played various games which required little or no playground equipment. Drop the handkerchief, hide and seek, black man, and King William, were favorite games with the smaller children. The older children played ball with a string ball, shinny, and crack the whip until accidents ruled it out. The type of ball was usually one-, two-, or three-old-cat or work-up. The boys and girls enjoyed vigorous exercise. Killing snakes or luckless rabbits, skunks, or badgers that happened their way, was entered into with zest. In most places prairie dogs or gophers abounded. Snaring these animals or drowning them out was a favorite pastime. In some places the boys and girls had their recesses at different times. In order to save a few feet of lumber the outhouses were built together with very poor partitions between them. This brought about an unwholesome atmosphere and tended toward moral declension.

On the last day of school in the rural sections it was customary for the patrons to come in, bring baskets of food, and after the closing exercises, have a large picnic dinner in the school-house or nearby. Sometimes a medicine man attended one of these gatherings, doing his tricks and disposing of his wares.

In some places contests between different schools were arranged at various times during the year. Spelling was the principal subject in these contests. Prizes in the form of a map or picture, were offered to the winning school.

Other types of school found in the small towns and better settled frontier, were the penmanship and the singing school. A good penman or musician went into a community and advertised for students. The price for instruction in penmanship was about $1.25 for a term of three months. Singing schools were organized on a similar plan. In 1873 the *Yankton Press and Dakotaian* advertised a course of twenty lessons in singing school for two dollars.

The territories had scarcely been thrown open to settlement when colleges were started. At Lawrence, Kansas, Charles Robinson promoted a college to be located on Mount Oread, the forerunner of the Kansas University which stands on that well-known eminence today. Settlers at Manhattan, Kansas, immediately planted a college which later developed into the Kansas State Agricultural College. Nebraska kept pace with her sister to the south. The first general assembly provided for three institutions of higher learning: Simpson University at Omaha, City Collegiate and Preparatory Institute at Nebraska City, and the Preparatory Institute and Nebraska College at Fontenelle. None of these ever came into actual existence. The element of land speculation and booming the country in certain vicinities called forth their projection.

What is claimed to have been the first college west of the Missouri River was College View situated on a bluff of the Elkhorn River. It was begun in 1856 and finished in 1859. The Congregational church built a college known as Nebraska University in 1857. It lasted for sixteen years and came to an end during the panic of 1873.

The Brownville College at Brownville, Nebraska, was apparently a project begotten of community spirit and speculation in an endeavor to build up Brownville. It was incorporated by legislative act on February 9, 1857. The capital stock was $100,000 with shares of $25 each. In 1858 the college board asked the territorial delegate to obtain a donation of ten thousand acres from Congress for the erection of a suitable building. This evidently was not successful. The medical department of the college opened February 22, 1858. The faculty consisted of five teachers, three of whom held the degree of M.D. Of these, one was professor of anatomy, a second was professor of the practice of medicine, and the third was professor of *materia medica*. A man with an A.B. degree was professor of chemistry and another man, probably a local lawyer, was professor of medical jurisprudence. One of the doctors was the dean of the medical department. The whole course consisted of forty lectures and cost $5 per scholar or twelve and one-half cents per lecture. It was not expected that all who attended would do so with the idea of becoming doctors, but all were urged to attend in order to support the school, and it was felt the lectures would do everyone good. This plan shows the lack of technical instruction.

It must be admitted that a good many of these early colleges were projected to draw settlers or were planned by overoptimistic pioneers. The colleges at Lawrence and Manhattan were rescued from oblivion by the state, which made them over into state institutions. Most of these early colleges failed to materialize owing to the failure of the town in which they were situated or because they were premature and lacked a population to support them at this time, when the prairies, only a few miles west, were covered with buffalo.

The Congregational church planned a number of academies. These grew and became strong enough to branch out into the collegiate field. Finally as state schools developed and the spirit of denominational training declined, the number of these also diminished. Of the Congregational schools of Nebraska one developed into a permanent college, Doane College at Crete. The Methodist conferences each founded colleges but in time these were abandoned until only a few remain today.

The earliest school laws of Kansas provided for the election in each district of an inspector whose duty it was to examine all applicants proposing to teach in the county common schools. He was given unlimited power to issue and revoke teachers' certificates. A certificate issued by one of the inspectors was good anywhere in the county in which it was issued. When the office of county superintendent was created, that of inspector was abolished and the authority transferred to the county superintendent.

In Kansas and Nebraska the school district is the local unit in school government and management. Each district is virtually autonomous and through its board, appoints teachers and provides a school building and equipment for the district. In the Dakotas in accordance with a law of 1883, the county is divided into school townships. Like the smaller unit in the sister states to the south, each school township has three officers (director, clerk, and treasurer); but unlike them several schools may be built in one district according to the needs of the community.

CHAPTER XXIV

THE CHURCH AND THE FRONTIER

THE EARLIEST CHURCHES west of the Missouri River were the Christian, Presbyterian, Methodist, Congregational, Baptist, Catholic, and Episcopal. The Methodists, as usual, were on the ground first, entering Kansas shortly after the territories were opened. Reverend William H. Goode of the Northern Indiana Conference, received his appointment to Kansas on June 3, 1854, and entered the territory July 5. He passed through that territory and into Nebraska, visiting the settlements as far north as they extended. A Methodist minister preached the first sermon in Omaha, August 13, 1854.[1] This was probably Mr. Goode. Returning to the East, he reported that there were five hundred families in the two territories. He recommended the establishment of four circuits, two in Nebraska and two in Kansas, and the organization of the territories into one district with a presiding elder or superintendent of missions who should travel at large, make further explorations, and employ preachers as the occasion demanded. The report was accepted and carried into effect that fall within six months after the passage of the Kansas-Nebraska Bill.

The first conference session was held in Lawrence in October, 1856, when 1,138 members were accepted. Of these 302 were from Nebraska. In four years' time the church grew from nothing to an annual conference with six districts, fifty-seven appointments, and 2,669 members. The growth under the efficient frontier organization was phenomenal. One minister who attended the annual

---

[1] "Omaha's First White Boy," *Omaha Herald*, February 21, 1932. It must be remembered that missions had been established on the plains years before settlement by the white man. This chapter deals with the church beginnings following permanent white occupation.

conference at Leavenworth in 1860, had traveled from Nebraska on horseback, a distance of two hundred miles. He spent three weeks away from home, one week going, one coming, and one at the conference.[2]

What is said to have been the first local church organization in Nebraska was the Christian Church at Brownville,[3] organized in 1855. About the same time the Presbyterians founded a church at Bellevue. In Lawrence, Kansas, the Puritans from Massachusetts soon established their church. The congregation met in a sod building thirty by fifty feet. The seats were made of logs split in half with the tops smoothed and with pegs driven into the ends for legs.

The first sermon in Bismarck, Dakota Territory, was preached under these circumstances: One Sunday morning as the players were gathered around a poker table in a gambling house a stranger appeared, and, before there was time for an explanation, he mounted an unused table and began to read the Bible. The first impulse of the crowd was to stop the disconcerting noise with a bullet, but they decided to allow him to go on until he tried to stop the game. He attended strictly to his business, however, and won the respect of the gamblers. At the close of the impromptu meeting the men took up a collection of about forty dollars in poker chips. The proprietor in presenting these to the minister explained that they represented money and he could "play them in" or "cash them," just as he chose. He also offered, in case the preacher wished to gamble, to take a pistol, and see that things were "square." The minister declined to gamble but cashed the chips.

In the rural communities it was customary to meet in a private home. All the worshipers in a given neighborhood crowded into a little cabin, dugout, or sod house for services. Frequently the meeting place was rotated from home to home in the neighborhood. The

---

[2] In 1862 the Bishop, en route to the Nebraska Conference, held at Bellevue, rode the last five miles on a hayrack.

[3] The Reverend Pardee Butler, ardent Free-soiler, who was placed on a raft by pro-slavery men at Leavenworth, was a Christian preacher.

women wore sunbonnets, the men overalls. When a minister of the Gospel was not available, one of the congregation read the Bible and closed the service with prayer.

Although many of the settlers had come from a Christian environment, and it is not to be supposed that only the ungodly came West, there seemed to exist in some parts of the new settlements a spirit of apathy if not acual hostility toward religion. Many expected to make money and return to their eastern homes. There were few mothers and wives to provide moral anchorage to the large male population. This temporary citizenship with no home check on conduct, tended to create a careless and Godless attitude. In Kansas it was often said in the seventies, "There is no Sunday west of Junction City and no God west of Salina." Sunday to a great extent was a day of pleasure and business. The Reverend Reuben Gaylord complained that in Omaha, in 1856, a correct moral sentiment had yet to be created and that there were few to aid in doing it. Likewise when Colonel and Mrs. N. S. Babcock arrived in Fillmore county, Nebraska, in 1871, they found nothing in their part of the country to distinguish Sunday from any other day of the week. In some communities the day was an occasion for a community dance, the calls resounding until morning. Christians were scarce. When people heard that a family was religious it was thought that the head of the household must be a minister.

Many unusual places were used for church services. The first Sunday-school in Lawrence was held in a little native lumber shack about ten feet square. Rough boards laid on nail kegs formed the seats. In Union County, Dakota Territory, the First Baptist Church of Big Springs was organized in a sod stable. Many times the first service was held under the shade of a friendly tree, or on the prairie under the open sky without so much as a leafy bough overhead. At other places a large tent was used to shelter the worshipers. Carriage houses, blacksmith shops, barns, store buildings, and even drug stores, were used for Gospel meetings. The first sermon in Yankton, South Dakota, was preached in a store. The pulpit provided for the Presbyterian preacher was a whiskey barrel turned on end. When public buildings were completed, they were generally used for gathering places. The dining room of a hotel served admirably for a community assembly. The court room of the county seat was available for services. School-houses were used widely. When the railroads came, the depot was frequently the place of worship.[4]

The Methodists are more easily traced than other churches because of their great activity and the ample records left. The well-known character, the circuit rider, although more familiar than the other itinerant ministers, had his counterpart in most of the other denominations which made any real headway on the frontier. The work of the Methodist circuit rider as herein depicted, is fairly representative of the traveling ministry of the other denominations. The preparation for the ministry was quite simple. For example, when the Reverend Charles Wesley Wells was seventeen, and without special training, the Methodist Episcopal church gave him an exhorter's license. He preached occasionally and in a few years was given a local preacher's license. He spent a great deal of time preaching locally and came to feel he should give his full time to the ministry. He was admitted on trial and was sent out on a circuit. After his entry into the ministry he continued to study the common branches and the English language together with certain other conference studies.

A conference was divided into districts under the supervision of a presiding elder. In 1871 J. B. Maxwell was presiding elder of the Beatrice district in Nebraska. There were eleven circuits and stations in the district, each under an itinerant minister or circuit rider. Each circuit rider had a number of appointments on his circuit. In early days these were more numerous, but later a smaller number made for greater efficiency; in the seventies there were from four

---

[4] The Reverend C. W. Wells preached for seven years on six circuits in the Nebraska Conference and did not have a church building until the eighth year. He had a parsonage a considerable part of the time, however.

to six appointments on the circuit.[5] If a man had six appointments, he could, by riding hard and preaching three times on Sunday, manage to preach to each congregation every two weeks. When an appointment grew to the size of a station it received the constant services of a minister. A station preacher could enjoy the comforts of home instead of riding through storm and cold. The station preacher had to spend more time in reading and study so as to be able to preach a new sermon to the same congregation each Sunday; but he had more time in which to do it. This was before the days of luxurious traveling on passes or clergy certificates, and the circuit rider was obliged to furnish his own transportation. Occasionally an impoverished minister walked to meet his appointments. The Reverend Mr. Evans of the Eagle City Mission in 1858 left Lawrence on foot for his circuit one hundred miles away and continued thus to make the rounds of his circuit which was two hundred and fifty or three hundred miles in circumference.[6] A few others were prosperous enough to be able to drive light rigs. Probably the great majority, however, rode horseback with their few belongings in a saddle bag.[7]

The motto of the itinerant preacher was: Never miss an appointment. Week in and week out the tireless rider sped. The weather, winter or summer, did not deter him. Many times drenched with rain, or half-frozen with cold, the sturdy messenger of the Gospel was undaunted. The long weary rides, the raging torrents to ford,

[5] In the fifties the number of appointments sometimes ran as high as twenty. In 1869 the Wood River, Nebraska, Mission circuit consisted of a straight line of appointments from Silver Creek Station, just west of Columbus, to Gibbon Siding, ten to twelve miles east of Fort Kearney, embracing all intermediate points and three places west of Grand Island.

[6] At Ulysses, Nebraska, an impecunious minister on a hundred mile circuit traveled the whole year of 1872 on foot. At the end of the year he had 140 members, a gain of 116 during the year. Nathan Taylor, *Diary of Rev. Nathan Taylor for the year 1858 and 1859*, MS (in Kansas State Historical Society Library), May, 1858.

[7] In the eighties a minister on the ranching frontier met much hostility. Reverend O. T. Moore, a temperance worker of Red Willow County, Nebraska, was advised by his presiding elder to arm himself. Getting permission from the authorities he made it a practice to preach from the pulpit with a revolver in his pocket. A co-worker had been beaten nearly to death and he had to choose between backing down and daring the whiskey men to carry out their threat of violence.

the diversity of fare, the cold sleeping quarters, the crowded homes visited with their lack of comforts, all tested the physique and the mettle of the minister. The Reverend J. B. Maxwell on one occasion in company with two brethren, was traveling across country in a spring wagon on his way to a quarterly service eighteen miles distant. In the late afternoon they encountered a terrific rainstorm. They were thoroughly drenched but decided to continue to the appointment. When about three miles from the place they came to a swollen stream. Almost as soon as the horses stepped into the water they began swimming. The darkness was intense. The horses, swept on by the rushing waters, failed to strike the exit and found themselves facing an abrupt bank. They then turned downstream upsetting the wagon in the ten feet of water with the presiding elder under it. He was alternately under and above water until at last, exhausted, he grasped a clump of weeds; his two companions who had safely reached the bank came to his rescue. The horses were drowned and the elder lost his satchel filled with his manuscript sermons, books, and clean linen. He went on to his appointment without dry clothes in which to appear.

In other instances the man of God waited on the prairie for hours until the torrent subsided. Many nights were spent on the lonely prairie under the open sky. At noon the traveler unhooked his horse, and man and beast ate a frugal meal by the wayside. Much of the minister's travel was made over the uncharted plains. Sometimes in the sixties he covered sixty miles without seeing a house. The settlers were hospitable. Company was welcomed in a land where people were hungering for fellowship. The minister enjoyed this fellowship and social intercourse. As he ate at their table, slept in the same room, talked with them of the Christian way, mingled around the family altar, both pastor and layman were refreshed. The parson made himself welcome by becoming a part of the family and helping with the chores and work. He thought nothing of pitching hay all afternoon and preaching at night. If he were staying a few days in a home while holding a revival meeting, he took his exercise on the woodpile and kept the fuel box replenished. He encouraged the children to secure an education and brought courage to the parents and older people. The lady in whose home he stayed provided the best food the larder afforded while the minister was present.

At the time of his regular visits he performed various pastoral duties. The poor and the sick were visited, a funeral or memorial service preached, or a marriage solemnized. Perhaps a church quarrel had arisen over some problem, either real or imaginary. It was the duty of the minister to untangle the knotty skein. At Oskaloosa, Kansas, the Reverend James Shaw found the church had become divided over the question of instrumental music and he had to use his skill as a diplomat to smooth over the trouble. On another occasion when a man had left his wife the preacher was called to reconcile the two. Other misdemeanors of one kind or another had to be straightened out by the traveling preacher. He had ever to be ready to help raise his own salary or to lend a hand at building or maintaining a church if one existed.

The Reverend J. A. Mattern of Medicine Lodge, Kansas, was a good example of the foregoing. When assigned to Medicine Lodge in the late seventies, he found few Methodists there. He wanted to build a church but the parishioners were poor. He was not discouraged, however. It was arranged to burn a kiln of brick to make the walls. In this activity he made a full hand, shoveling the clay into the mixing machine, piling the brick into the kiln, helping to keep up the fires at night, and finally making a most industrious hod carrier. He worked all week and preached on Sunday. This industrious humble attitude won him many friends among the rough frontiersmen.[8]

Revival or protracted meetings lasting three or four weeks, were held each winter at the station churches which usually had buildings. The appropriate time for such a meeting was after the corn was shucked and the wood gathered for winter. The hour of meet-

[8] T. A. McNeal, *When Kansas Was Young*, pp. 129-130.

ing was announced as "candle lighting time." The bare room with its plain hard wooden benches was but poorly illuminated by three or four kerosene lamps which lighted a space around the rude pulpit and the big stove, leaving the distant corners in the deep shadow, a haven of refuge for the unconverted. When it was nearly time for the meeting to begin, one of the deacons acting as a sexton, made the rounds, turning up the lights which had previously been turned low to save fuel. Everyone from the surrounding country was there. Families, cold from the ride in the chill winter weather, paused by the big stove to warm before assuming their accustomed seats.[9]

The men sat on one side of the house and the women on the other. There was no organ and frequently few hymn books. It was the custom for the minister to read slowly two lines of the hymn, pause while the congregation sang those two, then read two more, and so on until the hymn was sung. The minister or song leader used a tuning fork before starting to secure the correct pitch. The strong men and lusty women sang with all their might. In this whole-hearted singing strong lungs counted for more than fine expression. There were no solos unless a song was chosen which no one except the leader knew. The prayers, though unpolished, were earnest and solemn. The congregations were appreciative and enjoyed the sermon despite rude benches or rough cottonwood planks laid across from chair to chair.

The minister, like the well-known Peter Cartwright, preached with a fiery eloquence that made the prairies ring. His sermons were more famed for their exhortation to higher living than for their scholarship or fine theology. A home in paradise was held as the reward for faithful living, while the retribution for the wicked, the awful gaping maw of an eternal, burning, fiery abyss, was so vividly pictured that sinners cried for mercy. These followers of John Wesley upheld a stern code of morals and social relationships. Dancing was strictly prohibited; sharp dealing and dishonest practices were dealt with summarily.

[9] E. J. Wiggin, *Impressions of Early Kansas*, p. 36.

The Methodist church had a pastoral limit of only two years and usually the ministers were transferred to a new circuit each year. Of the thirty-nine stations and circuits listed in the minutes of the Nebraska Conference for 1869, only seven were reappointed to the same places in 1870. Of the one hundred appointments in 1878, only twenty-six were sent again to the same places the following year.[10] This shows a growing trend toward longer tenure. All during the frontier period it was the lot of the itinerant to move to a new field on his return from the annual conference in the spring. He placed his goods on a wagon and frequently drove 200 miles to his new charge, stopping at night at the homes of those who would take him in.

The presiding elder had no easy task to perform. In 1871 the Beatrice, Nebraska, district extended from somewhere east of Beatrice three hundred miles west to the boundary of the state. Most of the circuits were in the central and eastern part of the state, however. It was the duty of the presiding elder to visit each circuit for the quarterly meeting. In 1871 these meetings in the Beatrice district required every week-end from December 9 until March 2 with the exception of Christmas. When this round was over the next quarter's appointments began. The presiding elder had a quarterly meeting nearly every week-end in the year. The number of meetings was often decreased by holding a joint camp-meeting of two circuits. The presiding elder was transferred by the bishop every second or third year.

If the circuit rider was overworked, he certainly was under-paid. In each appointment on the circuit a steward was entrusted with the responsibility of raising the minister's salary. A certain portion supported the general officers; the balance was given to the local minister. If the steward did not do his work well or the minister was unpopular, the amount raised was small. Generally in new fields the preacher received about $50 a year missionary money from the

[10] *Minutes of the Nebraska Conference*, MS, Nebraska Wesleyan University, 9th Session, pp. 18, 19; 10th Session, p. 10; 11th Session, p. 17; 12th Session, p. 30.

East. Had it not been for this, the minister would have gone hungry. In 1861 the average amount received by each preacher in the Nebraska Conference was $228. Of this the largest amount was $495 and the smallest $28. According to the report rendered at the third annual session of the Northwest Iowa Conference by Presiding Elder James Williams of the Dakota District, the ministers of Dakota, during the conference year 1873 to 1874, received an average of less than $300 which included an allowance for house rent. The fixed salary was oftentimes very unsatisfactory for various reasons. Not infrequently the preacher obtained less than half of the stated salary. It was a general practice to pay him in kind. He took flour, corn, hay, meat, dry goods, and groceries. The Reverend Charles Wesley Wells did not receive more than $30 in cash throughout the entire year of 1876. During the harvest of 1874 he drove a four-horse team to earn money to support his family. The Baptist missionaries although better paid, received only from $400 to $600 a year.

Of all the activities carried on by the Methodist denomination, the camp-meeting was no doubt the most interesting. Probably the first one held west of the Missouri River was at Lawrence in 1855, although they became numerous in the last half of the decade. The camp-meeting originated on the frontier in the Great Revival of 1800. The first ones were held in the forests of the border region between North Carolina, Tennessee, and Kentucky. The earliest efforts were union meetings conducted by the Presbyterians, Baptists, and Methodists. In a few years this type of meeting became an accepted institution in the Methodist denomination. An ideal spot for such a gathering was on the banks of a wooded stream where there was ample shade, water, and pasture. The ministers left the camp arrangements to a layman called the camp superintendent. A large oval clearing was made in the forest and the trunks of the fallen trees were hewn flat on one side. These were arranged in rows for seats. A rail fence was then built through the middle of the oval. This separated the men from the women. At one end of the clearing a platform covered with boughs was used for the speakers. Each congregation or community furnished its own tent. A large congregation sometimes found it necessary to have more than one such tent. There were also family tents, and many lived in covered wagons.[11] These dwellings ordinarily were pitched in a circle around the place of meeting. Vehicles of every possible description from the most modern buggy to the ox wagon, were drawn up in the grove. Hundreds of horses were tied in the woods. At night the encampment was lighted up with lanterns, lamps, and camp-fires. Three meetings were held each day, 9, 2, and 7 o'clock. The camp-meeting continued for one or two weeks. The whole neighborhood abandoned everything except the most necessary work and assembled to spend the time together. An eating tent was established to serve those who desired such an accommodation. The sound of a trumpet or bell called the congregation together at the appointed hour for worship and meals.

In the earlier years these meetings were supported by the joint efforts of two circuits. As membership grew, one circuit could manage such a meeting. In 1867, however, the Nebraska Conference recommended that one meeting be held annually in each district and that the several stewards in the district purchase a permanent camp-ground in a central location for the annual meeting; the expense involved was to be apportioned to the several circuits and stations of the district. This, however, did not prohibit circuit camp-meetings from being held as formerly wherever circumstances demanded them.

These meetings indeed were happy occasions where the lonely pioneers, parched and thirsty from lack of spiritual drink and hungry for social intercourse, met and mingled with Christian friends for a spiritual and social feast. The cares of life were laid aside for a few days. Shut in from all the world, the sweet spirit of God held sway.

[11] Mr. Wells tells of going to camp-meeting in a "herder box." He placed a cloth top on it and took a ladder along with which to get in and out of his improvised tent. When the meeting was over all he had to do was hook up and drive home.

A CAMP-MEETING OF THE SEVENTIES

Courtesy of the Review and Herald Publishing Association.

And yet it was difficult to shut the world out, for the devil crept in with all his wiles. The huckster, the drink peddler, the politician, the irreverent rowdies—all had to be contended with and conquered.

Presiding Elder Nathan Taylor of the Lawrence, Kansas, district wrote in his diary of a meeting which was nearly broken up by commercialism:

At this meeting we were anoyed with a few fellows of the "Basor sort." The brethren had unfortunately permitted a man making no pretention to Christianity, to erect and keep a boarding tent on the grounds without throwing around him the necessary restraints and placing him under requisite restrictions. Hence feeling himself at liberty to persue his own course, he fixes up a "bar" directly oposite the pulpit, brings forward his cigars—Lemonaid &c and goes into a regular retail business opperation. Well here we were with the Devil in our midst, under the sanction of the Church, and of course drinking Lemonaid & smoking cigars soon became the order of the occasion. By a little management, however, we were enabled to keep this unfortunate state of things within controlable bounds. Our brethren at this point were taught a lesson by this unintentional blunder, they will never forget.

Then, too, there were those trouble makers who clandestinely brought for sale some liquid of a stronger character than lemonade. These illicit liquor dealers as a rule were barred from the grounds, but the thirsty ones knew where to find the desired goods. It must be remembered that there were dozens of persons who came not from religious motives but for the purpose of looking on, who simply accompanied Christian members of the family. Some of these were harmlessly uninterested. Others were truly "fellows of the baser sort." These exhausted the genius of their imagination in inventing means of deviltry and aggravating, scurrilous, and annoying tricks. Some gambling appeared occasionally. Horse races were sometimes arranged. Again eggs were thrown or a meeting disturbed. The culprits were dealt with in different ways. If the ministry could not handle the case, they appealed to Cæsar.[12]

Usually the meeting began on Friday with services at three o'clock

[12] Officers of the law.

in the afternoon and in the evening. The order of the day was almost uniformly as follows: The tin horn hanging in the preacher's stand was blown at sunrise when it was expected all persons would rise. Half an hour later it was blown again for family worship. Then breakfast was prepared and eaten. At eight or nine o'clock the horn sounded for prayer meeting in the several church or community tents. At ten, the blast announced the preaching services. At three, and again in the evening, the congregation convened in the assembly. On Sunday morning occurred the love feast [13] or testimony meeting; the presiding elder preached at the eleven o'clock hour. At the close of the sermons invitations were offered for those convicted of sin to come to the mourners' bench, or, as it was sometimes said, to come forward for prayers. A few benches immediately in front of the preacher's stand were designated the altar or mourners' bench. The success of the minister or meeting was measured by the number who came forward. The penitents sat on these benches or knelt. The congregation sang songs of invitation and penitence such as "Come ye sinners, poor and needy"! The ministers then talked and prayed with the mourners.

Although these prairie meetings were not the scene of hysterical phenomena such as "jerking," "losing strength," and other excesses which marked the great camp-meetings of the Appalachian forests, yet there was a marked tendency toward emotional worship. At the mourners' bench there was great excitement, struggling, pleading, weeping, and shouting when a mourner found glory. Occasionally someone who struggled and agonized in such a manner even swooned and was carried to her tent; but such cases were rare enough to be noted as news.

The love feast was also a happy occasion. As the saints rendered their testimony, shouts of victory filled the air and reverberated among the trees and far out onto the prairie. Elder Nathan Taylor described one meeting where the worshipers enjoyed a happy occasion:

[13] Sometimes called a "speaking meeting."

The sermon was followed with singing and prayer, during the exercises the power of God came down among the people, Sinners cried for mercy, Saints rejoiced and shouted aloud the high praises of the Lord of Hosts. The songs and shouts of the Lord's redeemed continued for several hours.

Victories were won over besetting sins. Mr. John Speer told of a camp-meeting in which the great Jim Lane, border warrior, general, and senator from Kansas, made a public disavowal of the tobacco habit. Mr. Lane spoke and, after his earnest exhortation, the minister continued the meeting. Eventually he turned his attention to the vice of tobacco, warning the people against this habit. This seemed to move Lane visibly and he reached in his pocket, drew out a long twist of dog-leg tobacco, and gave it to the preacher. As the minister took this evidence of full consecration, new inspiration came to him and he exclaimed,

Glory to God! This great man, who has led the hosts of his country in battle, stood upon the forum of the capitol, and in the serried ranks of war, has given up his last idol, and surrendered his heart to the Lord. We will cast this vile weed to the four winds of heaven!

And suiting the action to the word, he flung the dog-leg far into the bushes surrounding the camp. Then in spontaneity, the whole audience shouted the song, "Praise God from whom all blessings flow."

Large crowds gathered at these meetings. Sundays witnessed the largest attendance of the whole session. In the very earliest days on the raw frontier, as many as a thousand persons were reported present on some Sundays.[14] At a state camp-meeting held near Lincoln, Nebraska, in 1872, there were three or four thousand present.

[14] The editor of the local paper gave the following report of a camp-meeting held in the vicinity of Iola, Kansas, in August, 1869: "Last Sunday was, especially, a 'big day'—many persons coming from miles around to witness the ceremonies. Iola sent nearly half its population. Geneva and Humboldt were also well represented, and, in fact, people from all portions of the county were there. It seemed to be a place of general resort, at which a regular reunion was the order of the day. . . . Throughout the entire day the woods were thronged, and the utmost propriety and decorum prevailed."

Frequently the monotony of camp life was varied. A couple were married, or a rain caused a break in the usual routine. At a camp-meeting southwest of Red Cloud, Nebraska, in the seventies a heavy rain-storm saturated the ground so that the place of assembly was unfit for use. The presiding elder, with the local itinerant and a few of the other brethren, went on a buffalo hunt. The company had a very exciting hunt and killed enough buffalo to supply the entire camp with fresh meat for over a week. The circuit rider reported that the meeting closed with good results.

The success of a meeting, of course, was measured by the number of people converted, backsliders reclaimed, and new members joining the church. As the meeting drew on, occasional baptismal ceremonies took place in the nearby stream. A fair proportion of those who joined the church in the exciting prayer seasons, remained with the religious body and the experience bore fruit in their lives. Others, returning to the old environment like the swine in the Good Book, went back to their former state of life and were fit subjects for the renewed labors of the saints at the next season's camp-meeting.

At the close of the meeting the campers filed out in a line around the circle of the tents, the ministers leading the way; the company broke ranks and everybody shook hands. It was a sad occasion, for hearts had been knit together in Christian fellowship and never again would the same group be present at a like gathering. The hand of the grim reaper would snatch some away, the ministers would be shifted, and the same scenes could never again be reënacted.

The camp-meeting, as mentioned above, replaced the regular summer quarterly meeting in a given circuit. In the winter the meetings were held in buildings of some kind. The meeting began on Saturday and lasted over Sunday. This gave occasion to a good many "basket meetings." People from the various churches came to quarterly meetings bringing their lunch and staying for several sessions. In the summer months frequently arbor meetings or grove meetings were held in the timber near some little creek. This type of meeting was particularly necessary where there was no church building.

The first Methodist preachers in Dakota were sent there by the Iowa Conference in 1860, but not until the early seventies was the Methodist work well established.

It must not be thought that the Methodists were the only religious influence on the frontier. Although they were more numerous than the others and their organization was especially fitted for frontier work, it must be remembered that the United Brethren held camp-meetings and sent out circuit riders. The Congregational church, although not so well fitted by organization for frontier work, was very influential and its members became very numerous in both states. Now and then the Episcopal and the Catholic churches were seen doing their missionary work. The Baptists, although not quite so spectacular as some, ranked numerically with the Methodists, and silently developed one of the strongest Protestant bodies.

Some of the smaller churches made an impression on the frontier far out of proportion to their numbers. The Seventh-day Adventists traveled from place to place, pitching their gospel tents, holding meetings for a period of six weeks, organizing a church, and moving on to the next town.

The Reverend John McNamara, an Episcopal missionary, recalled the evolution of a meeting house in a certain rural section in Kansas. At first preaching was held at the crossing of a creek, where the people stood or sat. A little later the meeting place was moved to a grove where log seats had been hewn. Still later a log church was contemplated. The heads of families gathered and the preacher drew up a constitution for the society. On an appointed day the group assembled at a spring and debated the size of the proposed structure and the material to be used. It was decided to construct a log building sixteen feet square. Each man was to cut and hew on his own place three logs and have them drawn to the spot determined upon. In addition to this, each was to give $2.50 in money to procure a door, windows, flooring, and plaster for the room.

The building problem was not so simple in an urban community. As a rule the church was built on faith and it took some years to pay the debt. The leaders organized and did their best to help pay for the church and furniture. The Ladies' Sewing Circle offered its services to the many bachelors in frontier towns, sewing on buttons, and repairing the gentlemen's clothes. Again, this organization, or others, held church fairs and festivals. The fairs seemed to have consisted mainly of a sale of useful articles such as lace, or other fancy work, cookies, and other edibles. The festival was an institution of harmless entertainment. There were a number of stands or places of amusement. People paid for entertainment at each place. For example, at one stand the young men paid ten cents to see "what a young man hates." This collected a number of dimes for which the victims had the privilege of looking at a small mitten in a pasteboard box. Then there was a rustic well like Jacob's Well where a fair Rebecca drew for the thirsty—not water, but lemonade. Confectionary and ice cream stands lured the money of others into the church coffers. An art gallery at which pictures were displayed was another humorous feature. A fish pond offered the angler a catch for a piece of change. A brass band or orchestra played for the guests. There were also strange and ludicrous hoaxes. At the Methodist festival in Beatrice, Nebraska, in August, 1872, there was advertised a grand bridal scene. When this scene opened, two couples marched into the midst of the company. The people thought a wedding was to take place. Suddenly the party pointed at an object at the rear of the rostrum. A horse blanket was pulled aside and a bridle was seen hanging on a nail. Often a cake was announced as a prize to the handsomest girl. The audience was allowed to select this person at so much a vote. Ordinarily several candidates were nominated and a few complimentary votes given by their friends. Finally the competition confined itself to candidates from different neighborhoods, cliques, or factions. Sometimes such a contest drew as much as a hundred dollars.

The ring cake was a type of lottery. In this scheme a gold ring was baked in a cake. The cake was sold by the slice. Usually there was a large grab sack, where for five cents a grab, one was likely to pull forth a most ridiculous toy to the accompaniment of great shouts of laughter from all present. One scheme to pair off the young people was the necktie partner arrangement. Each man received a necktie at the door. Then followed a hunt for the fair seamstress who made it. When found, she became the partner and recipient of the swain's attentions for the evening. A church sometimes conducted as many as two or three of these festivals a year. Frequently considerable sums of money were taken in. At Omaha the Congregational church in 1857 took in over six hundred dollars at their first church fair, four hundred dollars of which was profit. As a rule these affairs cleared from fifty to seventy-five per cent.[15] Frequently churches ran stands at the Fourth of July celebrations or at fairs.[16] The Episcopal and Catholic churches had no scruples against having dances to raise money, but the Methodists and others raised their money by what they considered less harmful methods.

In 1865 just at the close of the War a rather remarkable entertainment was given by the Presbyterians at Fort Scott, Kansas. Mr. J. R. Morley and Mr. C. W. Goodlander sponsored this rare treat for the little frontier community. The program was a combination show, the first part a circus, the second a minstrel show and vaudeville, and the third a railroad wreck or tragedy. The entertainment was held in the city hall. The showmen spent days making lion heads, elephant trunks, imitation horses, and other paraphernalia. The lion head was a huge affair made of wire covered with a buffalo skin. Two men formed an elephant. The elephant became quite shaky and one of the leading men of the show asked the ring-master

---

[15] The Presbyterian church at Beatrice in 1871 made a profit of $167 out of a gross income of $180.

[16] At the Fourth of July celebration at O'Neill, Nebraska, in 1882, the Catholic Church made between $150 and $200 with their dinner, stands, and bowery dance.

why the elephant was like the Confederacy. The ring-master did not know and he was told it was because the elephant was falling to pieces. The elephant collapsed amid the roar of the audience. In the railroad wreck the engine blew up making everyone think that the house would go to pieces. The show took in $700 for the church treasury.

In various places the Methodists and Presbyterians had a mite society which met once a week for luncheon or other social intercourse; each member contributed a mite before leaving. The money was used to build the church or afterward for painting and redecorating it.

The donation party was a social hour conducted to raise the money for the minister's salary. Sometimes it was held at the minister's home and at other times at a school-house or other building where a fair or festival was held in connection with it.

Frequently a wood bee was held. The brethren came together and drew up a great pile of wood which was given to the preacher as partial payment of his salary. On certain occasions such as Easter, Christmas, or special days, programs were held. Occasionally a church or Sunday-school picnic was arranged.

The Protestant churches were very strict in the regulation of the personal habits of the members as well as their general conduct. Liquor and tobacco were banned.[17]

[17] The Methodists condemned tobacco as a filthy habit, an expensive indulgence and a debilitating influence on mind and body. Therefore, the Nebraska Conference resolved that no minister be received on trial without his pledge not to use tobacco. They further resolved that no minister would be received into full connection who persisted in using it; that all ministers should teach these principles by precept and example. They "resolved, third, that in the future we will neither recommend or support by voice or ballot men for position in state or army who are not temperance men. Resolved, fourth, that during the coming conference year we will Preach at each of our appointments one sermon on the subject of temperance—and make war with King Alcohol both in the pulpit and out of it. Resolved, fifth, that we will give our hearty coöperation to all the noble actors upon the human platform of temperance Praying God's blessing to rest upon their labours until the last inebriate is saved from his wallowing in the gutter." *M. E. Church Reports*, Second Session, Nebraska Conference (M. E.), March 26, 1862, p. 10.

The Congregational Association of Nebraska also placed itself on record squarely against liquor and tobacco.

In spite of these resolutions and the teaching against the use of the "filthy weed," many lay members used tobacco and it was customary for them to sit, chew, and spit, while the minister preached in the school-house or sod house.

CHAPTER XXV

THE COMING OF THE IRON HORSE

EVERY PIONEER looked forward to the time when the railroad would come through the country, and everyone wanted it to come through his town or near his farm. Naturally the settler was ready to assist in securing this superlative benefit.

The first train to reach the Missouri River was the Hannibal and St. Joseph Railway which ran across northern Missouri between these two points. The first iron laid west of the Missouri River was put down on the Elwood and Marysville Railroad in Kansas. This stretch of road, now a part of the St. Joseph and Grand Island line of the Union Pacific, extended westward from St. Joseph toward Marysville. The first train was run on this road in April, 1860. The earliest road of considerable length was the Kansas Pacific which ran from Kansas City westward. It was begun in September, 1863, and reached Denver in August, 1870.

A Pacific railroad was hastened by the Civil War. Neither Congress nor the people imagined that the commerce and travel of the United States demanded a trans-continental railroad. The country was not ready for such a project as a business enterprise; but the War had accustomed the North to such a lavish expenditure of money that the necessary outlay for a connecting link between the East and the West seemed less terrifying than before. There was also some murmuring and rumor of a Pacific republic. Then, too, in case of a foreign war the isolated coast would prove to be a weak point in our defense. The opinion of the day valued the Pacific Railroad as a military necessity. This railroad, known as the Union Pacific, was chartered in July, 1862.[1] Ground was broken on De-

---

[1] A. D. Richardson, *Beyond the Mississippi*, p. 602.

cember 2, 1863, near Omaha. The Kansas Pacific and the Union Pacific received the same congressional aid—namely, 12,800 acres of land and $16,000 in government bonds per mile completed.[2] In Nebraska 6,499,376 acres of land had been granted to the railroad before July 1, 1880. A large acreage had likewise been granted in Kansas.

Ordinarily the road was given each alternate section for a distance of five miles on each side of the railroad right-of-way. The railroad was compensated for land already taken by settlers, by receiving an additional grant farther west where the land had not been filed upon.

Congress passed the act giving the Northern Pacific a right-of-way across Dakota (Lake Superior to Puget Sound) on July 2, 1864. Its grant was similar to that of the other railroads. It was to receive the odd sections of the public domain within a limit of twenty miles on each side of the track in the states and within forty miles in the territories with an indemnity limit of ten miles on each side of the primary grant as compensation for any land already settled. This gave the company a strip varying from sixty to one hundred miles wide depending upon the locality—whether in a territory or a state.

The matter of land grants to the railroad was destined to cause much friction between the railroad company and the settlers in certain places. An example of this was the violence in Allen County, Kansas, and the adjoining counties. Squatters had settled on the land. Some of these were too poor or for some other reason, had delayed filing on the land. Meanwhile the government granted this land to the railroad which sold it to innocent third parties in the East or elsewhere. When the buyers attempted to take possession of their purchases the squatters refused to move, declaring that

---

[2] For the mountainous sections the Union Pacific and Central Pacific received more—$32,000 or $48,000 per mile; the Atchison, Topeka, and Santa Fe was granted for each mile 6,400 acres consisting of the alternate sections in a strip ten miles on each side of the track. The Kansas Pacific received a grant of $16,000 in bonds and 12,800 acres per mile which amounted to the alternate sections for twenty miles on each side of the track.

they had settled there in good faith and that it was illegal to grant this land belonging to the Indians to the railroad. Furthermore, they argued, the railroad had not fulfilled the conditions of the contract by which it received the land and therefore all railroad land should be taken from the corporation and given to the settlers. Other late-comers, encouraged by the determined stand of the squatters, took possession of unoccupied railroad property. They formed the Settlers Protective Association of the State of Kansas, the members of which were usually called the Leaguers. Each member paid an annual fee which was used to promote the interests of the whole. Growing in boldness, the Leaguers attempted, by intimidation and threats, to drive buyers away from railroad land which had never been occupied. Those who had bought railroad land accordingly organized the Anti-leaguers. The Leaguers built small structures that could be pulled by horses. These shacks were moved onto a piece of land and the jumpers took possession during the night. The League hired clever lawyers and kept the cases in litigation for several years while they farmed the land and harvested the prairie hay which grew so luxuriantly there. The long litigation was unsuccessful except for the few Leaguers who had squatted before they knew the railroad had been granted the land. During this war blood was shed. The railroad, of course, was always glad to sell the land; the third party was usually more successful in winning the suit than the railroad was.

The advent of the railroad on the prairies hastened the settlement of the plains. Whereas some of the older states were raw frontier countries for a score of years, many prairie counties became well settled within a period of two or three years. The older frontiers were subject to hardships and privations for a decade. Schools and churches were years in coming. On the plains these institutions developed quickly with the continued waves of migration. Naturally the land nearest the railroad was occupied first and only gradually was settlement made farther and farther away from the magic iron bands which stretched across the plains.

Another kind of friction was that which arose over the payment of taxes. It has long been a favorite pastime of the American people to load onto the railroads and other corporations a tax sufficient to pay for as many of our public conveniences as possible. The railroads no doubt deserved this, considering the amount they received from the public crib. The emigrants swarmed in, settled the government domain, and started organizing local governments and building schools. The homesteads were not yet patented and therefore not subject to taxes. The taxes from the railroad were expected to provide a fund for the needed improvements. On the other hand the railroads maintained that the lands granted to them should likewise be tax exempt until they were patented. The railroad policy was to patent the lands only when they had been sold. During the early seventies this controversy was a constant source of friction between the railroad companies and the settlers. Before the settlers had long been blessed with the railroad they were cursing the institution which they had solicited with so much pleading.

Nevertheless the coming of the railroad was immediately and ultimately a great boon to the settlers. It furnished much work for which the settlers secured real money. Large numbers of men with their horses and mules were needed to do the grading. Tons of stone were necessary for bridges and piers. Millions of ties were sought and great quantities of cordwood were consumed by the locomotives. Food for men and animals found a market at good prices. Mr. Michael Sweeley of Nebraska, sold 1,200 bushels of sod corn in 1871 to be used by construction workers. He was paid one dollar a bushel. A paying market rose for the great quantities of prairie hay which grew so profusely and could be had for the labor of cutting it. Mowing machines were expensive, however, and much of the hay was cut with scythes and raked with home-made rakes. Ultimately the effect of the railroad was as though the manufacturer of the East, the fruit grower of Florida and the Pacific Coast, the coal dealer of Illinois, and the lumberman of Wisconsin, had moved into the same county with the settler. They became his neighbors in terms of the cheapness and facility of exchange of his products with theirs.[3]

Early rates were high but at length these were reduced. In 1866 the rate was ten cents per mile per passenger. This later dropped to seven cents and then to five cents; by 1900 it had fallen to two and a third cents per mile.

The history of the Union Pacific is one of the most romantic of the railroads which cross the plains. It was the first to connect the two oceans by bands of iron and since the rapid advance surpassed anything in previous history of speed of construction, there is a halo of romance and interest woven about it. The work was accomplished with an astonishing rapidity. A train of cars accompanied the track layers and a perfect system of work was carried out. Six strong men on each side of the track grasped an iron bar and the word was given, "Up!—forward!—ready!—down!" When these words of precaution were ended another twenty-eight feet was added to one of the iron rails which were soon to bind the two oceans. Mr. Richardson, the noted correspondent, gave this description of the laying of the Union Pacific:

We found the workmen, with the regularity of machinery, dropping each rail in its place, spiking it down, and then seizing another. Behind them, the locomotive, before, the tie-layers; beyond these the graders; and still further, in mountain recesses, the engineers. It was civilization pressing westward—the Conquest of Nature moving toward the Pacific.[4]

Many of these early railroads were built along stage routes. As the iron highway pushed into the new country the stage ran from the end of the railroad on to its next destination. From time to time

[3] J. H. Ager, "Nebraska Politics and Nebraska Railroads," *Proceedings and Collections*, Nebraska State Historical Society, Vol. XV, pp. 36–37.

[4] The Union Pacific went forward with increasing rapidity. The following table gives the number of miles built each year:

1865 .... 40 miles		1868 .... 425 miles
1866 .... 265 miles		1869 .... 105 miles
1867 .... 245 miles		(four months and ten days)

The great railroad wedding, the uniting of the Union Pacific with the Central Pacific, occurred at Promontory Point, Utah, May 10, 1869.

the railroad extended its service to a point at or near the end of the line. The stage then made that point its near terminus, ever shortening its race across the prairies. As the railroad expanded, large towns grew up here and there. These were the bases of operations or base construction camps. Such a town became a buzzing place of business with a population of three to six thousand inhabitants, a crowded city with enormous warehouses, banks, stores, and other places of business. Men had large tents equipped with a bar, billiard tables, and gambling devices. These, moving along with the construction camps, minted money for their owners. Other types of amusement of an even more questionable nature were going at full blast. Newspapers fulfilled their purpose and apparently found good patronage.[5] The streets were filled with freight teams starting out into the beyond. Stage teams left at regular intervals.

In a few weeks this scene shifted, this varied life faded, leaving only a little station, stock-yards, water tank, and a few forlorn dwellings, a mere shadow of the day when it had bloomed in all its prosperity and iniquity. North Platte was the terminus of the Union Pacific during the summer of 1867 and had a population of about three thousand. A few months later the terminus was moved to Julesburg and at the autumn election only sixteen votes were cast to bring the county seat to North Platte. The whole population had deserted to Julesburg. This point remained a busy one for some days or months and then the population moved on to a new construction headquarters. Instantly the bloated town was reduced by ninety per cent and became only another little dead village along the line. Some railroads built by starts and spurts, giving the effect of a great measuring worm reaching out rapidly for a time and then pausing before another stride. In this way some of the cities grew to considerable size. The cattle trade, coming at that time, aided in this building process.

[5] On the Kansas Pacific the *Railway Advance* was published in 1868. A paper published at the terminus towns of the Union Pacific was called the *Pioneer on Wheels*. It was printed and published from a box car and was useful in supplying the camp with news of the outside world.

The early railroads, although a splendid improvement, were indeed primitive and slow in comparison to our present trains. The first engines burned wood and the coaches were heated by a wood fire. At the lonely little station a man pumped water with a horse-power arrangement. All overland trains were armed with guns loaded and ready for use. The tracks of some of these early roads were so rough that the bell on the locomotive would ring of its own accord.

Even in the days of the slavery struggle before the Civil War the railroad question occupied a prominent place in the minds of the settlers. It is not to be thought that such leaders as Governor Charles Robinson of Kansas, were engaged entirely by the slavery problem. As early as 1857 Governor Robinson was chairman of a meeting which was trying to secure a railroad for Lawrence, his new home. During the years following the Civil War there was great excitement over the building of railroads. It was a matter of deep concern to the settlers whether or not a railroad built through the country and whether or not a town secured a railroad.

Wide-awake editors continually drilled their readers on the necessity of leaving no stone unturned in an effort to secure a railroad. Great mass meetings were held. Speakers urged on the people the necessity of doing everything possible to secure the coveted prize. The newspapers were filled with news concerning prospective lines. Counties and towns vied with one another in an effort to get lines built through the vicinity. The citizens of a town sent committees to meet the railroad officials and urge them to build through the town designated. The railway usually had a good route selected and probably would have built over it without the lure of bonds; but the people did not know exactly where the company intended to build. Judicious negotiations with different counties and towns along the selected route usually resulted in the citizens' voting bonds as an inducement to the company. After a mass meeting of the citizens a verbal vote was taken. If favorable, the next step was to sign petitions to be submitted to the county commissioners calling

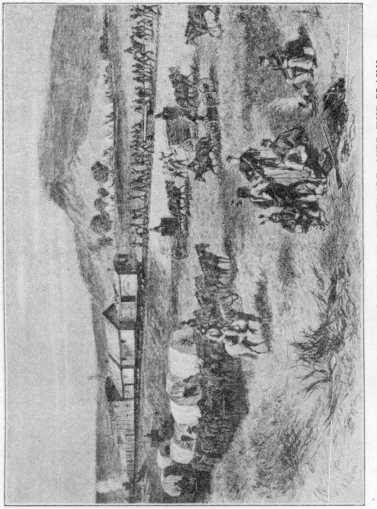

THE NORTHERN PACIFIC BUILDING WESTWARD OVER THE PLAINS

From a drawing by A. R. Waud, *Harper's Weekly*, 1875.

for an election on the proposed railroad bonds. The county commissioners set a date for the balloting.

In the meantime a hot campaign ensued. The towns through which the road would pass usually strongly favored the bonds. The towns of the county and the districts farthest from the road objected to the project. A terrific forensic battle occurred between the time of publication of the notice of the election and the date of polling. Papers in different towns in the county were bitterly arrayed against each other.

In Gage County, Nebraska, the paper in the town to be most benefited presented the following arguments for voting bonds for constructing the road:

1. The railroad would not come unless the bonds were voted.

2. The railroad would open up the country, establish manufacturing, and draw trade to the towns near it.

3. If a railroad did not come the towns would lose their trade to towns along railroads.

4. Farmers could not have profitable markets until the railroad came through.

5. The lands of the county would lie unimproved until a railroad came.

6. The necessity of teaming all supplies forty or fifty miles was ruinous to all classes.

7. The railroad would add one-half million dollars of taxable property to the wealth of Gage County.

8. A railroad pays so much taxes that it would lighten the load for others.

9. The interest on the bonds would be more than paid every year to the county treasurer by tax on personal property of the railroad.

In answer, the opposing party claimed that voting bonds would not change the intentions of the railroad, that the company would be just as apt to come through whether the bonds were voted or not, and that this was only a ruse of the railroad company to secure money. It was argued that there was not enough property in the county, even with the railroad, to warrant the bonds. Furthermore, there was not enough benefit to warrant the cost. In spite of this the bonds usually carried, for the voters were driven on by fear that if the bonds were defeated the road would build elsewhere, thus helping some rival town or county. Jay Gould, one of the prominent officials of the Union Pacific Railway, made a speech from the rear of his private car at Columbus, Nebraska, threatening to make grass grow in the streets of the town because of the antagonism of the people in not voting bonds.[6]

Numerous instances occurred in which once-flourishing towns died through quarreling with the railroad. These incorrigible towns were quietly strangled by the great corporations because they failed to coöperate. In some cases the railroad did not build through the town. In other cases the depot was located a mile or two away from the town leaving the promising little municipality stranded. After some time a new town was built around the station. The citizens of Ladore, Kansas, failed to come to terms with the Missouri, Kansas and Texas Railway. As a result the railroad built through Parsons instead of Ladore. Not long afterward the people of the little town placed their houses on rollers and moved them to Parsons, leaving the once promising town to die.

Usually the bonds carried. Some counties voted bonds several times to secure different railroads. If one railroad was a good thing several would be better, and the county seats aspired to become railroad centers. Lyons County, Kansas, voted $200,000 to secure the Missouri, Kansas and Texas through Emporia in 1867, and in 1869 voted a like amount to the Santa Fe. In addition to land grants by the national government, bonds voted by the county, city, or voting precinct, the people encouraged the railroads by gifts. Some gave the land for a depot in order to secure its location on or near their place of business or farm and to obtain the benefit of the increased valuation of their property because of it. Again, the landowners in a certain township agreed to give a railroad a right-of-way and other land provided it would build where they wanted it. The one or

[6] Cass G. Barns, *The Sod House*, p. 131.

two citizens who refused to donate were bought out by the others who visited each landholder.

Men who were wise residents of older communities, became engulfed in the mad swirl of mob psychology and voted bonds recklessly, forgetting that a time of reckoning would inevitably roll around. Many of the great fortunes in the East were gifts from communities in the West. In many cases the gifts of the people living along the route amounted to more than the cost of the railroad.

The companies usually made conditions favorable to the communities voting the bonds, but as a rule these conditions were violated, often by agreement of the people themselves. The usual plan was for the railroad to agree to issue stock to the community voting aid, but this was finally returned to the railroad for promises never fulfilled. The representatives of the people who engaged in these transactions, were not dishonest men but simply boomers. Frequently the transaction was made in the following manner: A private car was uncoupled in a town and soon the rumor was easily noised abroad by some interested party that the company was thinking of building machine shops to employ thousands of men. Perhaps the official did not say a word but allowed the citizens to concoct the story to suit themselves. As a result of two or three such visits the people often turned over their stock to the railroad company for one dollar.

Voting bonds became such a mania in the newer states that legislative restrictions were found necessary to prevent the people from giving away their heritage. Yet in spite of the terrible experiences in bond voting, the settlers often evaded the law. For months they conspired to gain control of their valuables so as to give them away.[7]

The railroads usually outmaneuvered the settlers. An example of this was the ruse worked by the North Western Railway at Pierre, Dakota Territory, in 1879. Four families had settled at that point. A covered wagon came from the East and camped for some time

[7] Kendrick Babcock, "Provincial Peculiarities of Western Life," *Forum,* September, 1892, pp. 91, 92.

in the neighborhood. The occupants had been sent out by the railroad but kept that fact hidden and stated that they were looking for a location for a large stock ranch. They said the site was an ideal location for a ranch and began to make offers to the squatters. The settlers, however, held off and the company resorted to stratagem. It sent the civil engineer to a vicinity nearby to lay out a site for a depot, side-tracks, and other terminal needs. The rumor was then spread that the terminus would be there and a bridge would be built across the Missouri at that point. This ruse proved successful. The settlers sold out in order to secure a location as quickly as possible and as near to the new town as they could. The railroad then made Pierre its terminal and with its usual generosity gave each squatter a lot in the town.

In numerous instances companies built roads for the sole purpose of extracting bonds from the community. The contract called for the bonds at the time the first train ran over the track or when the road-bed was ready for traffic. In some instances cheap narrow-gauged railroads were built to fulfil the letter of the law. In other cases the bonds were delivered in accordance with the terms and the first train was the only one over the track. Large grades across the country today bear mute testimony to the gullibility of the railroad-hungry pioneer.

There was great rejoicing when the locomotive drew the first train over the newly laid track. There would be no more weary traveling by coach-and-four from town to town, no more exasperating delays in teaming freight from distant points. A solution to the outstanding problem had been solved. The whistle of the locomotive was a welcome sound. One of the fondest dreams had come true. Frequently the opening of the railroad was accompanied by a great celebration. A large number of the citizens of a town loaded onto flat cars and into coaches and traveled to a large town where the linking of the two by iron was celebrated by eating, drinking, smoking, and speech-making. Sometimes great barbecues, parades, and band music, accompanied these first rail excursions. The young people, sitting on box cars with ties for seats, enjoyed these rides better than a pullman today.

A citizen described the completion of the Elwood and Marysville Railway as "celebrated by the most ardent wide-spread and all prevailing inebriety ever attained in the state." The train of cars that carried the celebrators to the picnic ground was made up of flat cars well calculated to carry the festive party. According to the narrator it was composed about equally of men and barrels. The cars were decorated with green boughs and the seats were constructed of planks set crosswise in the cars. The engine was gaudy with all the colors of the rainbow. The passengers and barrels jostled and jerked as the engineer ran the train at a high speed over the rough track.

In later years the railroad laid out the new towns and named them before the question of inhabitants was taken up; so it became the great builder of states, counties, and towns.

Railroad fares were high in the frontier times. However, the railroads handed out passes freely. Political leaders of both parties received them. Whole conventions and legislatures were bought by the railroads. In 1890 the Populists declared that the office-holders were bought by passes; yet they themselves accepted these gifts. One sheriff applied to the railroad company for a pass. He was turned down twice but on persisting at the third request he was asked what service he had rendered the road. He replied that he had done nothing except fail to arrest its agents when they tampered with witnesses in court. He received a pass without a murmur.[8]

Great conventions were made possible by this free transportation. It did not cost much to hire a hall, and a frontier convention afforded the leaders in the community an opportunity to pour themselves out in talk. Many desired to make speeches, and oratory flowed freely. There were stockmen's conventions, wheat growers' conventions, agricultural meetings, and various others. The leaders of the people fed at the crib of the railroads, hence were favorable to them, making corrective legislation well-nigh impossible.

[8] Cass G. Barns, *op. cit.*, pp. 133, 134.

CHAPTER XXVI

PLEASURE AND PLAY

THE PIONEER like his prairie predecessor, the Indian, was a great visitor. The whole homestead frontier was poverty-stricken, yet they enjoyed visiting one another. And visiting with them was no fashionable after-lunch call for the purpose of saying, "How-do-you-do" and showing one's fine clothes. A visit was of several hours' duration. The lonely settler looking out the window some Sunday morning, might see a neighbor coming across the prairie in his big wagon and soon the whole family unloaded and came in to spend the day. All were ragged. The wives knew the circumstances of one another and it was not offensive for the visitor, more blessed than her neighbor, to bring a few pounds of white flour, some butter, eggs, meat, or other eatable. This was welcomed and all had a good time. Neither age, wealth, nor position made the least difference. After a day's visit the two families separated, to remember the pleasant occasion for days.

One of the first types of social diversion in a new community was the bee. It assumed many forms. In the timber country a house-raising was popular. The logs were hewn and made ready for the structure and a house-raising was announced for a given day. The neighbors came from far and near to lay up the walls ready for the rafters. This work was so common in those days that the qualifications of each settler were well-known throughout the community, and a sort of informal division of labor was effected. There were corner men, skid men, scorers, and hewers, each taking his part as a matter of course. The man whose house was being constructed had nothing to say about it except to indicate the location. The day's work closed with a feast which the neighborhood women prepared while their men raised the house. Then the crowd dispersed with many expressions of good wishes.[1]

A bee might be occasioned by the misfortune of some family in the neighborhood. Perhaps the husband had died, or was sick, disabled, or behind with his work because of the loss of a horse or oxen. Someone went around and assembled the neighbors to help with the worthy cause. Sometimes it was husking corn, sometimes plowing, hauling wood, or planting crops. No one thought of pay. A suggestion of that would have been heartily resented. In some places the husking bee was a custom. This New England custom apparently was not general throughout the great West; its broad acres of corn had to be tended in a manner which was in sharp contrast to the little New England patches which could be disposed of at an evening's entertainment. At a "huskin'," the neighbors went to a home, sat in the barn, husked the corn, and shelled it by rubbing a cob on the ear. After two or three hours of this activity, the group went to the house for a good supper. Men, women, and young people, then played all sorts of games and told riddles. An occasional public project such as building a school-house, church, or bridge, also brought the neighborhood together in good fellowship.

Of all frontier amusements, dancing continued to hold first place. In the towns every new building that went up was the signal for a dance by way of dedication. This was accompanied by the little brown jug and a feast. This custom known as "house warming" was varied by the Methodists who ruled out the dance and liquor, but enjoyed a good meal and games. In more religious communities everybody played authors. Dances were the universal indoor amusement, however. They were held on every holiday, when a new ferry boat was brought into service, in celebration of the election of successful candidates, when a new bridge was built, when a couple were married, on the occasion of the first trip of each steamboat of the season, and on any other occasion for which an excuse could be

[1] Albert Robinson Greene, "In Remembrance," *Kansas State Historical Society Collections,* Vol. XI, p. 484.

found. They were held in homes, barns, stores, restaurants, court-houses, hotel dining rooms, and even on the prairie.

A man in Buffalo County, Dakota Territory, went to a place about ten in the morning and found the family just arising. The ceiling bore marked evidence of a dance the previous evening; there were marks on it made by male dancers. It was the custom for a gentleman to swing his lady around and kick the ceiling, then swing her around and kick the ceiling again, keeping perfect time to the music. Many were expert kickers. One dancer could not kick any higher than the wainscoting but just the same he was considered a good old sport.[2]

In the growing cities a certain degree of sophistication began to show itself soon. The dances were given due notice in the news-papers where they were called reception parties, cotillion parties, fancy hops, social parties, or simply balls. These dances, even in the towns, frequently lasted from early in the evening until daylight. The editor of the *Brownville* (Nebraska) *Advertiser* in noticing a dance, said:

Bright eyes sparkled with pleasure and fair cheeks glowed with the excitement of the quadrille. Sociability prevailed and the "golden hours on angels' wings" rapidly flitted away, and not until the East began to kindle were we warned of its being time to start on the homeward path.[8]

With the young people dedicating each new house, a week hardly passed when there were not several dances in the rapidly growing towns. Dancing schools were proposed in the larger towns even be-fore high schools were built.

January 1, 1857, at Lecompton, Kansas, a New Year's ball was given by the United States officers on the prairie. The ladies all wore mackinaw shawls and overshoes and at the end of every cotil-lion ran to the fire to warm their noses. The supper was served in a

[2] *Buffalo County History*, p. 13.
[8] January 14, 1858.

tent. In the morning holes were cut in the ice of the Kaw River so the ladies could wash their faces.

At Lawrence a ball was held in honor of the local military unit, the Kansas Rifles. Hunters, members of the military company, were dispatched far and wide to secure game for the supper. The ladies used their greatest skill in preparing the feast. The big event was held in the old Free State Hotel, on November 15, 1855. Five hundred people of all ages, sexes, and shades of political opinion, were present. The sumptuous supper was eaten at nine o'clock and the young people danced until three the next morning. A rosette was awarded to the man who had secured the most game, and a cake baked by the ladies, went to the second most successful.

In the towns masquerade or dress balls were held. Many unique and interesting costumes were contrived. One man in Barton County, Kansas, knocked both ends out of an apple barrel and used it as the principal part of his costume. He arranged straps to hold it up under his arms and pulled a hat box over his head and shoulders to hide him completely. On the top of the box was a layer of cotton to represent foam and behind was a handle; the whole costume represented a mug of beer. At a masquerade ball in Wichita, Kansas, in 1872, fifty appeared in masks. The costumes for the most part had been secured from Kansas City. Among the costumes were: A Spanish cavalier, goddess of liberty, Satan, Buffalo Bill, clowns, a baseball, Indians, a Vermont Yankee, a Quakeress, Red Riding Hood, a Scotch lassie, a French count, and many others.

At the larger towns even in the earliest times, expensive food was served. In White Cloud, Kansas, the refreshments at a December dance were cake, candies, peaches, cherries, figs, raisins, champagne, claret, blackberry brandy, and other drinks.

On the rawer frontier the dances were, if anything, even less formal and more hilarious. It was a true leveler in which staid matrons, grave gentlemen of years, and little children, all mingled. Women brought their babies and tried hard but often without results to quiet them before participating in the evening's amusement. The children screamed in unison with the violin as impatient mothers crooned nursery songs. In spite of the cries of the wakeful babes the dance went gloriously forward.

The violinist, a local celebrity, opened the dance by mounting the little platform or box provided for him and, with the air of a full orchestra, looked about on his audience and drew his bow with skill. The instrument emitted a sharp note. This was the signal for the gentlemen to select partners. T. A. McNeal described one of these dances for us: [4]

In the spring of 1879 I witnessed my first frontier dance. A new store building was to be dedicated with a dance.

There was room for three "sets" of four couples each to dance at once and the musician and caller was Dume Evans. Just what "Dume" was a contraction of I never knew. His music didn't appeal much to even my unpracticed ear, but his unique and poetic improvisation as he "called" to his own fiddling impressed me more than the movements of the dancers. When the "sets" were full Dume's fiddle and also his voice came into action. He always sang in a droning monotone, keeping time also with his foot.

The opening was always the same.

"S'lute ye pardners."

"Jine hands and circle to th' left."

"Right hand to yer pardner an' gran' right and left."

By this time his eyes were closed and his voice had risen to a sort of rhythmic wail.

"First couple lead to the couple on the right."

"Lady in the center an' three hands round; min' yer feet fellers, don't tromp on her gown."

"First lady swing out and second lady in, three jine hands and circle ag'in.

"On to the next couple, hoe it down; jine hands three and caper aroun'."

"Third lady to center; give your honey a whirl, lead to the next with your best girl."

"Grab your honies, don't let 'em fall, shake your hoofs and balance all."

[4] T. A. McNeal, "When Kansas Was Young," *Topeka Capital*, May 9, 1923.

"Ringtailed coons in the trees at play; grab yer pardners and all run away."

It was sometimes difficult to secure music. A good fiddler was in constant demand and his talent proved a real gold mine. Mr. J. C. Hallam of Richland County, Dakota Territory, reported that he made eighty dollars playing for dances during the fall and winter of 1880. For lack of a fiddler, dances were known to have been held with only the hum of a Jew's harp for music. At Niobrara, Nebraska, in 1874 a dance was reported in the local paper as having had a big drum, a little drum, a fiddle, a pitch fork for a triangle, a keg of beer for company, and considerable noise for variety. In other places it was possible to secure a sizable orchestra for dances. In the small towns brass bands were organized at an early date. The Bohemians and Swedes were great musicians and managed to form musical organizations at a very early time.

Since the men always outnumbered the women three to one on the frontier, the young men traveled up and down the creeks for miles seeking partners for their dances. The advent of a new family into a community was always an important event and doubly so when an attractive young lady formed a part of it. The young bachelors soon wore a path to such a home. In the end all but one came away dejected, explaining that they had "got the mitten." A girl of ten years and a grandmother of eighty were eligible to the ball so as to equal the number of the opposite sex, and even then it was always necessary for a number of men to take the part of ladies. In that case they wore a handkerchief on one arm to indicate that they were "ladies." In Box Butte County, Nebraska, some settlers took stock of their prospective neighbors and found only seven men and not a single woman living within a radius of twenty miles. They had traveled fifty-one miles from the town of Hay Springs and had seen only one woman.[5]

[5] Grace L. Johnson, *Pioneering in Box Butte County*, MS, Nebraska State Historical Society Library.

If possible these country dances were held in a cabin which had a board floor; if not, it proceeded just the same on a dirt floor. They had to stop occasionally and sprinkle the dirt to keep down the dust. One pioneer recollected seeing a man and his wife dancing barefoot on a dirt floor with the dust flying high. If any of the older men had a good pair of boots, the boys tried to borrow them to dance in. A collection was taken up to pay the fiddler and each man was supposed to contribute twenty-five cents. It mattered not if someone was short of cash and did not contribute anything.

The fiddler began with four good strings and often ended with only two or three. With his instrument he ground out such tunes as "Fisher's Hornpipe," "Arkansas Traveler," "Devil's Dream," "Leather Breeches," and "Golden Slippers."

The frontier dance, if less graceful than the more cultivated art in the hands of a dancing master, certainly was filled with activity and enjoyment. The very building shook with the energy of the dancers. There was little regard for time or tune as the unpolished swain grabbed the delicate woman and rushed her over the floor with the tenderness of an animal of the wilderness of which he was a part. The dance went on with an abundance of hilarity and animation which entirely compensated for the lack of dignity and formality. With all constraint removed, the entire night was spent in merry-making.

These dances were punctuated by drinks. The longer the evening's program lasted the more hilarious the group became. Finally some young blood, having visited the whiskey jug a little too often, started a row which became a near riot when he was joined by other well-saturated participants. The *Dakota City* (Nebraska) *Herald* reported such a row. A young man, who had worshiped at the shrine of Bacchus once too often, threw a gingerbread missile at the head of a fair lady. She became very angry and her gallant defender had to show his loyal devotions by whipping the gingerbread thrower. The party ended in a fisticuffs and a knock-down. The Oakdale, Nebraska, *Pen and Plow* noticed this displeasing custom:

About the only disagreeable thing connected with our dances in this western country is drunkenness indulged in by the disorderly. Some young men never dare go to a dance except when under the influence of liquor. . . . Some very sensible men are so keenly alive to their natural inability to go through the movements and etiquette of the dance, that they oil up and limber up with a few well-timed horns.

The *Winfield* (Kansas) *Courier* noted the same thing in that community:

One of the roughest gatherings that ever met in Cowley county to chase the scratch of cat-gut round the room assembled at Hoerneman's on Little Dutch creek last Monday night. About sixty persons were present; crammed into a room some fourteen by twenty feet in size, in the centre of which two sets in cotillion were compelled to "all saschey." The honest sons and daughters of the soil were there in their plain garbs; widows and widowers in whom the blaze of passion had burned the carbon of life to a cinder, were there trigged by art to hide nature's truth; chins were there that showed the eider down of tender teens, and the heavy hand of time's reproach; the tender maid just swelling with the truth of nature's possibilities, and the mother holding the unweaned offspring to her bosom were there. The polished gentleman of travel, who speaks five languages correctly and fluently, and the tobacco chewing bummer who could not speak one, were there; the mild and harmless, the swaggering and armed, and the "gay young man from town" were all there. To set the meaner elements of that heterogeneous mass well in motion whisky was introduced. In a little while it could be smelled in the air, upon their breaths and clothes, seen in their eyes, and noticed in their "balance all," and down the throats of half the party. Even the cat-gut caught it, and slewed among the minor and major keys in reckless disregard of "tone." Halters to teams were cut, whips stolen, the road strewn with fence posts, three or four fights ensued, pistols drawn and bedlam mirrored. We have told enough; numerous other things happened that won't do to tell.

The dances were varied occasionally. There was the so-called calico ball. As a matter of fact a calico dress and sunbonnet was the proper dress for any occasion on the prairies in the seventies. At a calico ball, the lady made a calico dress and a necktie to match it. The men were given a bunch of neckties and asked to choose one without seeing the lady whose dress it matched. In this way the partners were selected. This same method of selecting partners was often used in church festivals and other social occasions.

But dancing was not the only entertainment, albeit it was the chief amusement in most frontier localities. The Methodists and other religious organizations looked askance at dancing. Then there were some who either did not care to dance or were not particularly interested in that form of amusement. In communities where the dance was taboo a very good substitute could be found in the play party. In the standard play party the young people went through certain floor work similar to the dance but without instrumental music. In place of this the young people sang: "Miller boy," "Skip to ma lou," or other appropriate songs.

At other more staid gatherings such games as ring-around-the-rosy, drop-the-handkerchief, and paying forfeits were popular, as was also "Old Mother Wobble Gobble." In this game all were seated in a circle around the presiding official. He began by reciting a rhyme: "Old Mother Wobble Gobble, pray pity you; Old Mother Wobble Gobble, do as I do." At the conclusion of this inspiring rhyme the leader proceeded to distort his features, or do some other ridiculous thing. The rest of the group were to imitate the bell sheep. This led to much amusement. Those who were unable to comply forfeited some personal belonging such as a ring, handkerchief, or necktie.

Forfeits were redeemed in the following manner: Someone held the object to be redeemed over the head of the one who adjudged the forfeit, saying "Heavy, heavy hangs over your head; what shall the owner do to redeem it?" Then the judge who was seated in the circle asked, "Fine or superfine?" The person holding the object answered, "Fine," if it belonged to a man or "Superfine," if it belonged to a woman. The penalty was pronounced. One popular sentence was to pick three cherries with Hannah Francis Doe. Whereupon Hannah came forward blushing and the gentleman would kiss her three times very methodically.

The lyceum, or literary society, was a regular winter activity. It was held weekly or semi-monthly. In the country school-house this program started very early in the evening. It was not unusual to hold it at six-thirty. The association had a constitution, by-laws and officers. The programs listed recitations, songs, dialogues, debates, essays, some extremely grotesque representations, and tableaux. So strong was the urge for literary societies that lyceums were held in frontier towns under the open sky before there were any houses for a meeting place and at a time when ninety per cent of the settlement was men.

A newspaper representing a community news sheet was an outstanding feature of the program. The editor combed the community for amusing incidents. While the paper was being read some began to look glum; some faces would spread with crimson. These little arrows darted out from the paper in all directions, striking here and there to the amusement of the group. Although there was not the least ill intent in anything that was written, at the close of the meeting different members could be heard saying, "If they don't stop that paper, I shall quit coming." And yet when the next meeting occurred they returned and thoroughly enjoyed the jokes on the rest of the crowd. Sometimes the editorial privilege was abused. The *Wichita Astonisher* and the paper of the nearby Park Township, *The Blunderbuss,* were criticized as containing too much personal abuse.

The pioneer farmers always attended court for the gossip and entertainment it afforded. They traveled miles to attend this show. The majority of the literary programs were filled with debates in which the noisy harangues were patterned on the speeches of the small town lawyers which had been heard at the court sessions. Ordinarily the subject for debate was chosen two weeks or a month ahead and was debated by two or three on each side; but in some instances as many as eight or ten took part on each side. In that case the chief disputants chose the additional debaters. Since the debaters had no source material at hand, their arguments were chiefly unsupported assertions made in a vehement manner. The hearers probably received little information, but the speakers learned to stand before an audience and developed a certain ready wit which was enjoyed and applauded by the audience.[6] In the seventies the subjects of debate had grown more practical than they had been in the sixties. Typical subjects were: "Resolved that farming does not pay." "Shall capital punishment be abolished?" "Resolved that the statesman is worthy of more honor than the soldier of the United States."

In the sixties and early seventies spelling schools were popular. Young and old attended these gatherings held every week or every second week at the school-house during the winter months. Sides were chosen and the school-teacher or some other competent person was selected to "give out" the words. Two systems were used. One called "chase the fox" was built on the principle of head-marks. Each time a speller received a head-mark it registered a point for his side. At the close of the evening, tallies were counted and the side having the most was acclaimed winner. In the other system, the "spell down," the pronouncer alternated between two lines of standing spellers. When one missed a word he was "spelled down" and took his seat. Whoever stood longest had "spelled down" the crowd and won the contest for his side. Occasionally one school would challenge another to a dual meet. Each school rallied its best spellers. Delegations were there from the schools represented. They applauded their champions and sang school songs at appropriate intervals. A participator in these good times in her youth, said that after the spelling was over the teacher and students boarded the lumber wagon and started homeward, making the prairies resound with their songs and cheers—cheers for Golden Valley school, or Number Ten, or perhaps Pleasant Hill.[7]

A spelling school at Marysville, Kansas, has been described in

[6] Lewis F. Crawford, *Rekindling Campfires* (Bismarck, North Dakota, 1926), p. 276.

[7] Mrs. J. W. Wheeler, Wabaunsee County, Kansas, personal interview, October, 1931.

some detail.[8] After the corn was husked and the hard farm work done, one school invited five other schools to a contest which was anticipated for weeks ahead; school-houses gleamed as night after night the contesting schools prepared. McGuffey's spelling book was learned completely. Parents pronounced words by the page to their children at home. Children spelled every Friday afternoon at school and practiced dialogues and declamations at noon. Those who could not spell so well prepared parts to play, sing, or present in dialogues. When the eventful night finally arrived, each school chose its spellers and wrote each name on paper. These were placed in a box from which they were drawn one at a time. The spellers took their places as selected in long lines arranged around the dingy school-house wall. A disinterested person was asked to "give out" the words. Three generations attended this event. By guess of page the starting side was learned. The spelling continued until only one was left standing. She received a book as the prize. After a recess the musical and literary program began. There were "pieces" by little tots, songs, readings, violin solos, and other selections by the older ones. When finally the group broke up, the songs of the schools and the jingle of the sleigh-bells made the prairie merry as the crowd wended its way homeward.

In the later seventies with the advent of black-boards, ciphering matches became the popular amusement. Each neighborhood had its champions which it was ready to match against all comers. School-masters were tried out in this way. As more and more skill was displayed addition and simple problems gave way to square and cube roots.

The singing school, although a commercial enterprise, was a social function, a place where young people got together. Probably young gallants who had little interest in singing and could not carry a tune, attended these merely for social purposes.

In the fifties and sixties before the settlers could afford buggies

[8] John G. Ellenbecker, *Old Time Spelling School* (Marysville, Kansas, 1922), not paged.

the young couples went horseback riding on the prairie. At Lecompton, Kansas, as many as twelve or fifteen couples rode out of town together. Ordinarily each person had his own horse; the ladies rode side saddles and dressed in riding skirts which had shot in the hem to hold them down and insure modesty. Joy riding in a lumber wagon drawn by oxen, or later by horses, was a common type of amusement. In the winter the wagon bed was partially filled with hay where the couples sat, covered with lap-robes. The bob sled drawn by horses with sleigh-bells was a luxurious and elegantly equipped conveyance. The jingle of the bells could be heard in the still crisp winter air for a mile. The *Nebraska City News* of January 14, 1860, in commenting on the good sleighing, spoke of the gay time the lads and lasses were having. The editor recorded that the men were very rigid in collecting "toll" every time a bridge was crossed. The bridges were few and the same one was crossed a half dozen times in a single evening.

Shortly after settlement had passed its early stages of hardship and little luxuries began to creep in, a livery stable was erected and the most affluent young gallants hired buggies to take their ladies riding over the prairies. These prairies with their level plains and gentle slopes appeared as smooth as a floor, but they were hard to ride over in a vehicle. In certain parts of the country the dirt was swept away from the roots leaving the grass standing in bunches and making a rough surface. A day's jolt over the prairie left a person lame and sore. Nevertheless the family that could afford a buggy took rides in the cool of the evening; and the young man took his lady fair to some farmer's home where they procured a drink of buttermilk or cold spring water.

Before long it became customary for every young man to procure a buggy when he reached the courting age. When he secured a new buggy it was regarded as a sign that he was interested in some member of the fairer sex. It was more or less a rule that a young couple interested in each other must go somewhere together. The little houses did not invite visiting in the presence of younger children and the young lady's parents. They chose a church and went on Sunday nights whether either one was interested in the particular denomination or not. If they did not go somewhere there was little excuse for their being together. During stormy weather or when there was a lull in the social activities of the community, the young men had difficulty in finding an excuse for being in the company of their ladies.

When the minister read the announcements the young fellows listened intently for possible opportunities to become escorts. Many young men attended Sunday-school zealously because they knew the girls would be there; and in a day of limited social activities this became an opportunity for social outlet. With all the inquisitiveness that only a frontier or isolated small community can have, everybody took a lively interest in the affairs of a couple. If the couple went together oftener than a few times the girl obligated herself to the young man. If the friendship broke up after a few weeks or months, there was always the embarrassing question: "Who got the mitten?" In case the young man were dismissed, he usually sat in an obscure position on a back seat until the embarrassment wore off; then he sallied forth seeking new worlds to conquer.

Love-making on the frontier was rapid work. Marriageable girls who had any inclination whatever toward getting married, were soon sought out and rushed to the altar. At Lawrence, Kansas, in the fifties a man died leaving a widow of eighteen in the autumn. She was quickly wooed and married again by February. In the first few years of territorial rule no doubt there were a number of irregular marriages entered into which were not recorded since laws regulating and recording marriages were not provided immediately. One such irregular marriage took place at Hog Thief Bend, Nebraska, where a wedding party gathered for the nuptial ceremony. The crowd waited but the Methodist circuit rider who was to perform the marriage was delayed at the crossing of a neighboring river. The guests arranged for the sheriff of the county to perform the ceremony. The mother of the bride objected but everyone else said it was all right and she gave in. The ceremony was accordingly performed, the pigs and turkey were eaten, and the puncheon floor rattled under the feet of the dancers until sunrise. Two days later, the river having receded, the circuit rider arrived and insisted that they should be remarried according to the forms of the church. This was done.

Apparently most of the weddings were civil marriages performed by the justice of the peace or the county judge. Sometimes these accommodating officials took work or produce for the fee in lieu of cash. Occasionally there was an elopement but this breach of Victorian etiquette was comparatively infrequent. The frontier with its freedom of association and informal conduct produced more divorces per capita than the old home state; and yet the breaking of the marriage contract was less frequent than it is today. In a land where a person's every public and private act was so open to the public eye, infidelity was discouraged and social irregularities were curbed.

After the ceremony was performed the couple usually went to the home of the bride for the wedding feast. Sometimes this was given in a hotel and ended with a dance. A wedding was accompanied by fun-making and amusement on the part of well-wishers in the neighborhood. Though the wedding were kept a profound secret, the news usually leaked out and soon the street surrounding the house where the bride and groom were staying was filled with a crowd of serenaders. The discordant sounds, produced by an orchestra of drums, tin pans, horns, sleigh-bells and every other noise-provoking contrivance, continued until the bridegroom came out and offered to treat. The editor of the *Nebraska Advertiser* gave this story in the editorial column of his paper:

They Took Him. A few evenings since, an unearthly noise, caused by beating tin pans, empty oyster cans, ringing cow bells, shooting fire crackers, playing on the "Pigaree" and such like instruments was heard in our quiet city. The cause was soon ascertained. Billy Hoblitzell, some weeks ago, concluded that it was "not good to be alone"—especially as cold weather was approaching—took to himself a "better half"—has been staying "out home"—maybe to fool the boys until they would forget—fixed his house in town this week—moved in—boys wide awake —after him—"trotted him out," as above described. Finale—oyster treat at Hugh Baker's Saloon.

In that day as in our own, friends frequently gave the bride and groom a parting salute in the form of a shower of onions, old shoes, and other odds and ends.

A necessary formality of frontier life was the "infair" which took place the day following the wedding. It consisted of a visit of the bride and groom, the bride's folk, and perhaps others of the wedding party, to the home of the parents of the bridegroom. An extended honeymoon was out of the question but sometimes the happy couple loaded up a grist and drove gaily across the prairie to the mill, camping along the way and while awaiting their turn. Or perhaps they took a two or three day trip to the county seat to buy a few articles for their meager housekeeping equipment.

In September, 1855, the young men of Lawrence, Kansas, gave a social entertainment. Nearly one hundred watermelons were served for refreshments. Taffy pulls were held in the winter at the homes or at the country school-house. Sorghum, when boiled down thick enough to pull, made satisfactory taffy. Young men and their partners took delight in pulling this delicacy.

Surprise parties were quite the fashion in certain communities. Often a load of merry-makers made their way across the prairie to some lonely cabin. The "whoa, haw, gee!" of the driver was the signal which aroused the early retiring family from their slumbers. Soon the visitors alighted and there was a splendid scene of merry-making.

Certain special occasions received more than passing notice. The Fourth of July was always celebrated with fervor on the frontier. The people welcomed an opportunity to break the monotony of frontier loneliness. As the years passed the program varied some-what from that of preëmption days.[9] The occasion became less formal; the prayer was omitted and the toasts, speech-making, and formal music, were greatly abbreviated. In their place the ball game, horse race, sack, wheel-barrow, donkey, and foot races made their appearance. A parade of the militia, a band concert, and a dance in the evening, usually formed part of the program. At different times and places such events as catching the greased pig or climbing a greased pole or a tub race in the river, were conducted. A home-made merry-go-round pulled by one horse or mule, furnished amusement for old and young. In the eighties skating rinks, ice cream saloons, and balloon ascensions, enjoyed great popularity.

At Concordia, Kansas, in 1870, a table seventy feet long, was filled with diners four times. There were plenty of good things to eat. In some places anvils were fired; and the tremendous noise reverberated through the woods. In some places on the occasion of the first Fourth of July celebration a flag-pole was erected, dedicated with a formal program, and a flag spread to the breeze above the verdant prairie. Sometimes friendly Indians were invited to participate in the program of the day. These dusky denizens of the wild with their varicolored blankets against the background of their white tents and the green grass, created a picturesque scene.

Barbecues were popular in the earliest years of settlement. In 1870 the Indians had threatened the settlers of Jewell County, Kansas, who had assembled, organized a military company, and built a sod fort made of turf walls four feet thick and seven feet high. On the Fourth of July the soldiers decided to celebrate. One committee was sent to construct an arbor. The second group of soldiers went on a buffalo hunt to secure fresh meat, and a third went to barbecue the meat after it was brought in. The ladies furnished bread, pies, cakes, and preserves. Thus was the first Fourth of July celebrated in Jewell County.

The first Fourth of July celebration at Blue Springs, Nebraska,

[9] See Chapter IV, "River Cities of the Fifties," pp. 74–75.

was held in 1859. For two months before the holiday everybody who passed was invited to come to the celebration and to bring his skillet. In good American style these pioneers appointed committees to make the arrangements. A committee of three was appointed to catch catfish during the three weeks prior to the celebration. By the Fourth these men had over a thousand pounds of large catfish penned up in the mouth of a nearby creek; stakes had been driven across the creek above and below to form a pen. Another committee of three built a brush canopy and secured boards at a sawmill for a forty foot table and for a dance platform. A large pile of logs was gathered from the timber for fuel. The promoters sent to Brownville, forty miles away, for a two hundred and fifty pound hog which furnished an abundance of lard to fry the fish. A corn crusher was improvised of sheet iron. There was much good corn-bread even though the meal was not grated fine nor bolted. There was a sumptuous repast of catfish and corn dodger with a little white bread which a few had brought for dessert. On the afternoon of the third, people began to come. By the next day there were one hundred and fifty people. They came walking, riding in ox wagons, and any way they could get there. The ladies were dressed in sunbonnets and plain dresses. There was but one silk dress in the whole crowd; some of the men were barefoot. The flag was run to the top of a pole seventy feet high; the Declaration of Independence was read; and after a sumptuous meal had been served, the fiddles, brought from over an area of eighty miles, were tuned up and the dance began. This lasted until broad daylight of the fifth, when the settlers wended their way back to their lonely homes, thinking of this bright event, an oasis in the desert of dreary frontier life.

People sometimes came as far as one hundred miles to celebrate. One man spoke of having walked twenty-four miles to join in the festivities and was glad to be able to go. At Ainsworth, Nebraska, in 1882 a twenty-foot flag was offered to the community having the largest delegation. The celebration was centered about the depot and the dance held on the platform.

Washington's birthday was usually celebrated with a party or dinner and dance. Valentine's day was celebrated by an exchange of valentines. The drug stores were headquarters for such goods. Many fancy ones with lace on them were to be had.

Thanksgiving was celebrated in a more religious fashion. A church service was held in the forenoon and in the afternoon a great feast was enjoyed. Settlers went into the unsettled region to the West and returned with an ample supply of game for this feast.

Christmas was celebrated with little ado. There were few presents but a program was arranged. There was, of course, little opportunity to secure an evergreen Christmas tree on the prairie so another tree was decorated with strings of pop-corn and other home-made decorations.

Lodges were early organized on the frontier. Members of the various fraternal and benevolent societies formed local units of their order in their new homes.[10] These organizations were mutually beneficial and offered a vent for the social proclivities of the citizens of the small towns.

At Fort Scott, Kansas, in the fall of 1859 during a lull in the Jayhawker warfare, the young men of the town, feeling the need of something to relieve the monotony which contrasted to the stirring times just experienced, decided to organize a Sons of Malta Lodge.[11] This organization provided opportunity for much pleasure during the winter. Apparently the chief reason for this order was the fun of initiating new members. Once a man had gone through the ritual and made himself the victim of members of the lodge, he was anxious to get his money's worth at the expense of a friend. In this way nearly every man in town had joined and been initiated before spring.

[10] Among the more prominent orders were Masons, Knights of Pythias, Independent Order of Odd Fellows, Sons of Malta, Good Templars, Sons of Temperance.

[11] The Sons of Malta was organized in the early fifties following the failure of General Lopez's invasion of Cuba, and was formed for the alleged purpose of taking revenge on his enemies who prevented his successful invasion of Cuba.

In the initiation ceremony the officers and members, dressed in black dominoes and masks, gravely sat in an imposing array. In the center of the room was a table on which there was a skeleton. Two men dressed as soldiers guarded the skeleton. One soldier walked one way on one side of the table while the other walked in the opposite direction on the other side. The first degree was very solemn. The victim was brought in unblindfolded before this august assembly and impressed that the step he was about to take was a very serious one. After this he was taken out and the room was cleared for action. The novice was then blindfolded and brought in before the grand master to answer a number of questions. Among others he was asked if he would lie in wait and steal in upon Cuba if he were going to attack it. If he answered in the affirmative the recorder announced through a large trumpet: "He lies and steals; let it be recorded." The other members repeated it in a solemn voice. Then the grand master said: "Try his marching qualities." The victim was then marched around the room and every object imaginable was thrown in his way. Finally they made him climb a ladder and mount a box. While standing there resting from his exertions, the initiate listened to a lecture on the importance of knowing how to swim in case he got shipwrecked on the way to Cuba. At the close of this he was told there was a large tank of water before him and that he must jump in and show his aquatic ability. The "tank" was a large tarpaulin some twenty feet square, held by the members. As the new member jumped, his fellows tossed him as high as the ceiling several times. On one occasion a man weighing two hundred and fifty pounds and another weighing one hundred and twenty-five pounds came up for initiation at the same time. The larger man was so big that the men could not throw him very high and when the little man came next he was thrown so high that he struck the ceiling and broke his arm. The victim, after initiation, was told he had passed through the ordeal so well he was eligible to a seat of honor. He was escorted to a chair and seated. This seat of honor was a soaking wet sponge about the size of a half bushel.[12]

In the spring of 1860 a spectacular formality was carried out. A torchlight procession marched around the fort and across the parade ground several times, before proceeding to the center of the parade ground. Each member carried a roll of paper. The grand master explained that the work of the lodge had been accomplished and to prevent the outside world from obtaining the deep secrets of the order, they would burn the records. He lighted his roll and threw it on the ground. All then marched solemnly around the fire casting their rolls into the flames. The records were destroyed.

In addition to the ordinary lodges two orders peculiar to the farming community were organized; namely, the Patrons of Husbandry and the Anti-Horse Thief Association. The former has been given special consideration in another chapter. The latter was organized to provide protection against horse thieves. In time it developed certain social features such as school-house programs, oyster suppers, and picnics.

Families assembled and played euchre, seven up, and other card games. Sewing circles, temperance societies, and church societies abounded. Many musical instruments were brought from the East and sometimes two or three persons wandered about town serenading various individuals. In the fifties soda fountains were advertised in the river towns and, no doubt, became social centers for couples.

Reading matter was very scarce and everything readable was hungrily devoured by the more intellectual. Almanacs and patent medicine pamphlets, each with a loop of string fastened in one corner, were issued by the medicine companies and dispensed at the stores. These were hung on a nail in the corner or behind the stove. Usually they were gaily colored—green, yellow, or blue, and made elaborate use of the signs of the Zodiac. Piles of these almanacs were

[12] C. W. Goodlander, *Memoirs and Recollections of the Early Days of Fort Scott* (Fort Scott, Kansas, 1900), pp. 51–55.

to be found on the counter of the general merchandise establishment or drug store each spring. The almanac was free but the "Healey's Bitters" or "Allen's Cherry Pectoral" which were said to purify the sluggish blood after the inactivity of the winter months, sold for one dollar a bottle. No doubt its alcoholic content did make many parched pioneers feel young and vigorous. Much of the reading matter consisted of proverbs and aphorisms, many of which doubtless came from *Poor Richard*.

Amateur theatrical societies were formed in many towns. At Wichita, Kansas, a home talent minstrel troupe, called the Frontier Minstrel Troupe, was organized when the town was only a few years old. The plays in these frontier dramatic presentations were usually of the Shakesperian variety. *The Merchant of Venice*, *Othello*, and *Macbeth*, were popular. In one instance a frontier troupe presented a play featuring the Bible character, John the Baptist, and in the process of the show brought in his head on a platter. To secure this effect a living man's head was made gory by a liberal use of beef blood. Just how the body of the man was hidden from view while the head was being carried in on a platter was not mentioned in the report.

At Fort Scott, Kansas, at an impromptu act produced by a club, a man stuck the handle of an old-fashioned feather duster down the back of his neck and, with blanket and other impromptu arrangements, danced a scalp dance. His brother, just from the East, sat interestedly watching the terpsichorean triumph when with a dash he was neatly scalped. His wig had been taken off leaving his head bald as an egg. This took down the house. With howls of delight the men rolled off their chairs.

In the eighties the first phonograph in the vicinity was the source of considerable interest and amusement in Buffalo County, Dakota Territory. The owner, Mike Dillon, gave a number of shows at the various school-houses of the county. The "talking machine" was one of the great wonders of the period.

CHAPTER XXVII

THE PRAIRIE TOWN

AS TOWN PROMOTERS journeyed from place to place selecting town sites, many new towns were laid out. The great majority of these prospective towns never materialized. On the other hand, certain spots grew into towns almost without promotion. In the sixties and early seventies the location largely determined the success or failure of the enterprise. Towns were usually located on rivers or creeks, for there seemed to exist an idea that it was impossible for a city to grow great without a river. Rome was on the Tiber, London had its Thames, Washington was graced by the beautiful Potomac; therefore, Eden City must be located on some sort of stream. This ideal was strengthened by the benefits which naturally came to a town built in this favorable spot. The best natural location for a prairie city was at a place where a trail crossed a stream. The man who in an early day had settled at such a point, reaped a harvest from his wise choice. He might build a ferry and collect toll from the passer-by. Furthermore, owing to the general scarcity of fuel, a stream with its fringe of forest and its water for camp purposes, made an inviting camp site. Even though it was impossible for the settler to build a ferry, the location was still a desirable one. At certain times heavy rains made the swollen stream impassable for days. As a result, a numerous company gathered on the banks waiting to cross. This brought prospective buyers to the door of the settler. If he were enterprising, he set up a blacksmith shop and small outfitting store. In time others, seeing the advantages of the spot, settled nearby to enjoy the potential prosperity. In this manner, either by plan or natural growth, a little town developed. Among the towns which grew in this manner were Marysville, Kansas; Elkhorn, North Platte, Beaver Crossing, and Milford, Nebraska. Some towns were located at the junction of two trails. Tecumseh, Nebraska, was situated at the crossing of the Nebraska City, Marysville, and Fort Riley Trail and the Brownville and new Fort Kearney trails. Other towns grew up at railroad junctions or crossings. Junction City, Kansas, Norfolk, Nebraska, Orient Junction, South Dakota, and Minot, North Dakota, illustrate this fact.

In some cases the owner of a grist-mill found a suitable spot for his mill and set it up. This formed the nucleus of a town. He, or others, established stores to serve the people who drove miles to get their grain ground. The following were cities of this kind: Crete, Nebraska, and Enterprise, Kansas. In a few instances towns were formed around deposits of natural mineral resources which drew people. A notable example of this is Lincoln, Nebraska, which attracted people for hundreds of miles to this Mecca for a much needed substance—salt.

When the railroads came through the country many of these towns were connected by railroad lines. Those which were omitted, in time withered away until today their former glory is remembered only by a country store and post office or perhaps only a farming community. When the railroad built into Phelps County, Nebraska, it missed the town of Phelps Center. A new town was established on the railroad and the people in Phelps Center were offered lots free if they would move their houses from their old homes or build on the gift lots. In this way Holdrege was built up. A large proportion of the houses of Polk, Nebraska, were moved from the little inland town of Arborville which lay four miles out of the line of construction of the railroad.

The towns in the central and western part of Kansas and Nebraska, and in Dakota Territory, were for the most part planned by the railroad. These were more or less arbitrarily placed six or eight miles apart. In later times a junction of two railroads or the building of some establishment started new towns.

The origin of the names of the towns and counties is a matter of interest. There were several different classes of names. The first class represented personal names of national heroes, particularly presidents and Civil War generals.[1] A second class represented personal surnames of early settlers and prominent local and railroad men. The larger number of towns in this class probably were named for railroad men. Especially in the western two-thirds of the prairie area, which was unsettled before the coming of the iron horse, the railroad established the towns and named them as it saw fit. Even section bosses were permanently honored in this manner.[2] A third class consisted of names carried from the old home in the East or the Old World. Under this class came such names as York and Lancaster Counties in Nebraska [3] and Chautauqua [4] and Bourbon [5] Counties in Kansas. A few names were derived from local geography or peculiar characteristics; that is, names descriptive of localities. Among those from this class were Great Bend, Silver Lake, Galena, Neosho Rapids, and Oak Valley in Kansas, Table Rock, South Bend, Wood River, Big Spring, and Willow Island in Nebraska; Badland, Crystal Springs, Coulee, Slim Buttes, Cedar Canyon, Castle Rock, and Grand Forks in Dakota Territory. In South Dakota are found a very large group derived from Indian names; Kansas has eleven counties whose names are derived from the Indians, and Nebraska five. In Dakota Territory a number of counties especially in that portion which later became North Dakota, were named for French or half-breed French and Indian trappers or employees of the fur companies. Among these is Rolette County named after Jean Joseph Rolette, an employee of the American Fur Company. Pierre, South Dakota, owes its name to French influence. A few names were coined. Ohiowa, Nebraska,

---

[1] Over one-half of the counties formed in Kansas following the Civil War are named after Civil War heroes.

[2] The Burlington had an alphabetical system of naming its towns.

[3] Counties in Pennsylvania.

[4] A county in New York.

[5] A county in Kentucky.

was settled by emigrants in about equal numbers from Ohio and Iowa. They accordingly coined this name. Kanorado and State Line in Kansas indicated the close proximity of these towns to the Colorado and Kansas boundaries. Mohall, North Dakota, was named after M. O. Hall, an early homesteader. In Bourbon County, Kansas, five towns located within an area of two square miles formed one town of five hundred inhabitants; it was appropriately called Uniontown. A number of cities received the given name of individuals. Examples of these in Nebraska are Merna and Lillian, named for the daughter of the first postmaster in each instance. In Kansas, LeRoy, Iola, Isabel, and Florence are examples of this class. In Dakota such names as Vesta, Vera, Alice, and Alfred are representative of this group.[6] A number of towns were given Bible names: Abilene in Kansas; and in Nebraska, Bethany, Salem, Lebanon, Bethel, Alpha, and Omega. Banner and Garden Counties in Nebraska represent in their names the hope of their promoters. During a dry season in western Nebraska a little town was founded. People were meeting together to pray for rain. In casting about for a name, a preacher, who was also the first postmaster, named the town Rain.

There was a tremendous town boom in the seventies and eighties just as there had been in the pre-Civil War migration. Again town companies were formed. Once more lots sold at fabulous prices. Now as before, towns grew up like mushrooms. In the first two years' growth of Wichita, Kansas, five hundred and nineteen buildings were erected.[7]

In the eighties as migration moved westward the same thing occurred. In September, 1880, the first load of lumber was hauled to the sight of Hillsboro, Traill County, Dakota Territory. In

[6] Other Christian names in Nebraska were: Elwood, Edison, Earl, and Max.
[7] From the summer of 1870 to the summer of 1872. The editor of the *Wichita Vidette* on January 12, 1871, expressed himself thus: "There is no use talking, we need money here now, Wichita has enough brains, she's gorged with them. We wish we could influence some capitalist who has plenty of the 'needful' to emigrate our way, he need not know enough to tend to his own business, there are plenty here will do that for him."

November the town contained three hundred residences, a school-house, a church, two elevators, and a bank besides the usual business houses where sixty days before the spot had been covered with waving prairie grass.[8]

Garden City, Kansas, had a similar boom in the eighties. The streets were thronged with horses, wagons, buggies and ox teams. Long lines of people stood waiting to get their mail. The railroad ran its trains in two or three sections a day, pouring out a flood of home-seekers into a virgin region. The prairie adjacent to Garden City was dotted with ever-changing groups of tents and covered wagons, the temporary homes of the emigrants waiting to file on land. Although there were many rooming houses and hotels, they could not accommodate the large crowds. During the boom days Garden City had nine lumber yards. Lumber was hauled in all directions to improve homesteads. One day in 1886, one hundred and twenty-nine loads were taken from one of these local lumber yards. There were thirteen drug stores and two daily newspapers in the thriving town. The flourishing city erected a few posts on main street and mounted coal-oil lamps on them for illumination. The same spirit of unbounded optimism flourished that had existed a quarter of a century before in the pre-War rush. The editor of the *Winfield Courier* breathed this spirit of optimism into his pages:

We would say to all men everywhere, who contemplate coming west to engage in business of any kind, come to Winfield. No better or more desirable place can be found in the state of Kans. Situate on one of the most beautiful and romantic streams imaginable, on as pretty a site as could well be selected, built up with neat substantial, and some even elegant buildings. The county seat of one of the richest counties in Kansas. Composed of a class of people, who, for energy, enterprise, are not excelled. And for morality stand head and shoulders above most people in the state. Containing within herself and surroundings all the elements necessary to build up a large and prosperous city, Winfield is

[8] Hallie Farmer, "The Economic Background of Frontier Populism," *Mississippi Valley Historical Review*, Vol. X, p. 410.

AN EMIGRANT CAMP OF THE EIGHTIES
Near Pawnee Rock, Barton County, Kansas. Courtesy of the Kansas State Historical
Society.

destined, at no distant day, to become one of the most desirable locations in the west.

The prairie town of the seventies and eighties was a forlorn-looking institution. The typical town consisted of a handful of rude one-room shacks made in the cheapest possible manner. Fairbury, Nebraska, might be selected as a typical town of this period. The traveler from the East overlooked the valley of the Blue River and beheld a group of about a dozen houses nestling in the valley. On the first floor of a two-story building there was a store. The *Fairbury Gazette* was printed on the second floor. Prairie grass grew luxuriantly in the streets. There were not enough buildings around the public square to mark its boundaries. On the west side were three one-story structures. The best was the office of the county clerk and the board of county commissioners. The second was the pioneer store and also served as the home and office of the proprietor who was justice of the peace. On the north side of the square were two similar buildings. One was occupied by a man engaged in the sale of Hostetter's Bitters; the other was the post office and drug store. On the east side there was only a store; and the south side was vacant. The south half of the court-house square was used for a ball ground. A pile of lumber lay in the yard of one of the residences on the corner of the square. This had been hauled from the nearest railway forty-five miles distant. The Otoe Indians, whose reservation was nearby, camped on the public square on their way to their annual buffalo hunts.

Great Bend, Kansas, was described as consisting of several dinky little houses along one side of a road which had been created by the passing of many wagons. A large proportion of the crudely constructed shacks bore the sign "saloon," "dance hall," or "billiards and pool." Occasionally in front of covered wagons or tents one saw open camp-fires surrounded by men in broad-brimmed hats, varicolored shirts, and pants tucked into high-topped boots.

In its earlier years Abilene, Kansas, was described as

a very small dead place, consisting of about one dozen log huts, low, small, rude affairs, four-fifths of which were covered with dirt for roofing; indeed, but one shingle roof could be seen in the whole city.[9] The business of the burg was conducted in two small rooms, mere log huts, and of course the inevitable saloon, also in a log hut, could be found.

The settlers lived "in dugouts or mere hovels constructed of poles and dirt." Their poverty was extreme. A grassy street was vaguely indicated and a small prairie dog village occupied the middle of the scene. One place housed a tiny post office, a court room, and the office of the register of deeds. For months a plank served as a railroad station.

Hay Springs, Nebraska, in 1886, was a little hamlet of one hundred inhabitants housed in rude shacks built of native lumber. The business section consisted of three saloons, three stores, a makeshift hotel and a church-dance hall combination shed. Saloons were prominent in nearly all frontier towns and drunken brawls were frequent. The local paper at Iola, Kansas, in one issue in 1869, reported three rough and rowdy experiences of drinking men resulting in disturbances and shooting. The newspaper editors implored the local government to subdue these wild outbreaks. The *Frontier* of O'Neill, Nebraska, urged that "shooting off firearms indiscriminately on our streets should be prohibited" and again the Oakdale *Pen and Plow* of March 8, 1879, commented: "During the past winter the report of guns and revolvers, and the whizzing of bullets sent on foolish errands became so common in the town that no one thought of protesting against it." In some instances large parties seized sticks and engaged in a general free-for-all mêlée. In Winfield, Kansas, such a battle originated over a misunderstanding between a brewer and another citizen. Several advances were made

---

[9] After a rainstorm at Beatrice, Nebraska, in 1872, the editor of the local paper stated that very few houses there were proof against water. Leaky roofs, leaky windows, leaky chimneys, and leaky parts generally caused great discomfort; the cellar walls caved in. Among the dugouts on the river front the rain had played havoc by undermining the dwellings and ruining them.

on the brewer by a militant party but he repulsed them. Finally the besiegers entered the back door and the battle was concluded on the prairie. All members of the parties returned to their work after the armistice.

At Chanute, Kansas, thirteen saloons were in operation during the seventies. Gambling was as open as the sale of groceries and long after the town started, the gambler's cry of "Keno!" was the last thing heard at night and the first thing heard on waking in the morning.

The arrival of the train or the stage was always an affair of prime interest. In addition to seeing the puffing iron horse or the dusty coaches which always bore a deep fascination, there was the chance to see the crowd, the possibility of meeting someone from the old home state, the opportunity of learning the latest news from back East, or of seeing the drummers, always interesting characters; and, of course, the chance to get acquainted with any new settler. The children at Garden City, Kansas, took baskets of goodies such as pies, cookies, boiled eggs, and milk, to the train to sell to the immigrants. On one occasion a newcomer grabbed a basket from the hand of a lad. This led to a fight between the townsmen and the immigrants; one immigrant was killed in the affray. The towns of an agrarian community, as a rule, were peaceful as compared to the cow towns or mining towns in which a long season of privation and hardship was followed by levity and intemperance. In the farming communities the saloon more often was a drowsy unoffensive little place where the majority of people drank moderately. It was a sort of drug store where people went to get whiskey or bitters. It was thought that the medicine found there was proof against snake bites, chills, and other ailments. Furthermore it was a medicine easy to take, and some were terribly afraid of any kind of real or imaginary frontier ailment. A sufficient number visited these places frequently enough to keep the dead little towns in a lively condition at least part of the time. These celebrations rarely ended in an orgy of death as did those in the cow towns. Moreover, the normal farming town was ordinarily not a scene of brothels and shameless debauchery such as the cow or boom towns were.

As the town developed, the wild lonely spirit of the prairie was reflected in the somber architecture and in an absence of houses distinguished in form and color. There was a deplorable lack of the esthetic. The rows of plain houses were scrambled along the streets in a manner that suggested a clash between the various edifices. Paint, when used, was a dreary lead color. The walks often ended abruptly before a mud hole, and a population without overshoes tracked mud and dust over the wood surfaces. The interiors of the business places were not designed to welcome or please. They were dirty and cluttered with large cuspidors on a dirty floor that was uninviting to the woman who in that day wore a cumbrous train which mopped up the filth.

The homes were usually of the one-room variety, though in the later seventies four-room frame buildings became a familiar sight. In the single room dwelling a blanket or cloth curtained off the sleeping quarters. The morning ablutions were performed at the well or at the wash stand near the water bucket by the door. Bathing was an almost unknown practice. The cottage was scantily furnished. A cheap chromo, a motto, possibly a dreary old family portrait adorned the walls. Furniture was plain and limited, since in migrating all but the well-to-do had left their belongings in the old home.

The sanitary conditions in these new towns were far from satisfactory. The ground where the horses were tied to the hitching racks around the square and along the street in front of the stores, became veritable cess pools of filth. This drew flies and created a vile odor. Furthermore the absence of sewage disposal also made for unpleasantness. Nearly everyone had a horse. Piles of refuse from the barn increased the discomfort. Hog pens added to the medley of smells. The editor of the *Wichita Eagle* spoke his mind on this matter:

MAIN STREET IN A KANSAS BOOM TOWN

It was called Empire City. Courtesy of the Kansas State Historical Society.

A fair sample of what we may expect in the way of variety and kinds of smell, and the different thicknesses of the stratas, was given last Saturday, when it was a little warmer than any previous day this spring, with a stiff breeze blowing from the south. Pedestrians on Main, Market and Water streets, anywhere north of Douglas avenue, were regaled with oleaginous olefiant, concentrated and moist, with the quintessence of putrifaction. Oh! was the exclamation of those who, according to size, had their olfactories saluted while plodding nose high in the different stratifications. Many differed as to the resemblances but a tall man who was sitting on the sidewalk said, as he got up and passed through them with his nose, that there were two hundred and forty distinct and odd smells prevailing there and then; this confirmed all dissenting reports. All, however, agree that some sanitary measures are needed, and heavy fines should be imposed on those who will throw slops, old meats and decaying vegetable matter at their doors or on the street.

The cows were herded in a town herd on the prairies, but often hogs, chickens, and horses had the run of the town. Irate women chased the pigs and chickens away, only to have them return and play havoc with the family garden.

The sheriff was the chief officer of law enforcement. He was inclined to endeavor to keep deviltry at a minimum but closed his eyes to much unsavory conduct.

The growing prairie town was peculiarly susceptible to fires. The frame houses which were erected as soon as the owners could afford such structures were very inflammable. Furthermore, in many cases hay-covered stables sheltered the family cow and the horse. Stacks of hay placed in various parts of the town furnished food for these animals and added to the fire hazard. Careless smokers, or ignorant children at play, were enough to start a conflagration that would ruin the town in a few hours. Alliance, Nebraska, was established in 1888. In a period of eleven months, between August 1, 1892, and July 3, 1893, the young metropolis suffered three disastrous fires.

After the horse is stolen the barn is locked. After a town had passed through such a fire calamity, the city fathers usually drew up rules for fire prevention and provided for a method of fighting fire. The normal practice was to rally all the able-bodied men. At Great Bend, Kansas, after a fire, the town council authorized a local wagon builder to make a four-wheeled wagon to be drawn by hand. A local carpenter was engaged to build two sixteen-foot ladders, and the council sent to Kansas City for two dozen leather buckets, each having a capacity of about three gallons. In case of fire everyone was supposed to grab a bucket and get busy. Gradually these loose organizations were systematized. At Wichita, Kansas, the fire-fighting organization was called the Hook-and-Ladder Company. They had a captain and a secretary and solicited members. Those who could not join as regular members could become honorary members on payment of twenty-five cents a month. It was the great ambition of every boy to help put out a fire. Whether the members of these companies served merely for the honor of serving their home town or for the gifts that a grateful property owner might bestow in gratitude for the protection of his property, can only be conjectured.

The editor of the *Wichita Eagle* noted in 1873 that the company in practice made a three block run, scaled a three-story building, and got their buckets passing up and down in an astonishingly short time. Wells or shallow cisterns were dug and pumps installed at the street intersections of the business district and elsewhere. In cold weather these pumps often froze, leaving the city almost unprotected at a time of greatest danger inasmuch as the poorly constructed houses necessitated heavy firing to keep them comfortable. Volunteers were invited to hasten to the blaze at the sound of the bell, to grab a bucket and dash to aid the regular force. On their return home the firemen stopped at one of the town pumps to quench their thirst.

At Fremont, Nebraska, shallow cisterns were placed in the business section. In due time an improved fire fighting apparatus was introduced. This consisted of a pump operated by man power, which drew the water from these cisterns and forced it onto the fire through a hose. These force pumps, known as mud suckers, were mounted on a four-wheeled vehicle and pulled about by hand. The pump was operated by a ten-foot handle on each side similar to those on a hand-car. The firemen and citizens supplied the power. The cart was also supplied with many leather buckets which hung from the sides of the truck. The residential section remained without protection except such as a bucket brigade could give.

In 1874, at Iola, Kansas, the editor of the county paper suggested as the beginnings of a fire department adequate for the town, a hook-and-ladder company with six ladders, six hooks, the same number of axes and twenty-five pails. As early as 1869, Topeka had a Silsby fire-engine manufactured in Schenectady, New York. Huge cisterns were located in the center of the principal street, Kansas Avenue. As there was no long hose, the water was pumped from the river into the nearest cistern and relayed from cistern to cistern by the short hose. Within two and a half minutes the engine could be fired up, run several blocks, and throw a stream of water.

A new town was often endangered by prairie fires. The editor of the *Niobrara Pioneer* [10] in his issue of September 23, 1875, urged: "Fire-breaks are now in order. It has been suggested, and we second it, that our people get together on a still day next week and burn the grass south of town to insure us against the terrific fires which occur here every year. The property in town now is too valuable to allow neglect."

The town of Sykeston, North Dakota, was nearly destroyed. The morning was calm but by noon a terrific wind came up from the West. The fire started west of Eureka, miles away, some time before noon and in four hours despite the efforts of all the available men it had reached Leola. The women and children had been warned to leave town and go North. They started with their extra clothing tied in sheets but the wind was so strong that they were unable to carry it and care for the children. After the fire was over, only the court-house and a few other buildings remained standing.

[10] Niobrara, Nebraska.

The water supply was another age-old problem. Some towns like Boston, of Puritan Massachusetts, were blessed with a spring from which the citizens could secure water. Others, not so favored, had to dig for this life-giving element. The town well was one of the first improvements, since a proven water supply was sure to draw settlers. This was located in an accessible place. In some of the promising young towns in the western part of Kansas and Nebraska, the pump was operated by a windmill and the public tank was kept full for the thirsty stock. Emporia, Kansas, deservedly famed as a progressive little educational city, was greatly handicapped in its early years. Water had to be hauled in barrels during summer and winter. It was the opinion of some that the man who first found water saved the town.

At Pierre, South Dakota, a well near the river supplied water; a man with a tank wagon hauled it to customers on a route. He filled barrels at the various places every morning at a charge of ten cents a barrel.[11] In due time a growing town dug a reservoir in the side of a neighboring hill or mounted a supply tank on a tower; this established a gravity system which conducted the water through pipe-lines to the homes of the residents. Ice was delivered daily from ice houses where it had been stored after it was cut from the river in the winter. An advertisement in the *Yankton Press and Dakotaian* in August, 1874, stated a liberal supply would be furnished for two dollars a month.

The first telephone was a novelty and an astonishing phenomenon; it was inconceivable that the human voice could travel through solid wire. The first telephone was a pay station in some business house used for communication with a neighboring metropolis or county seat. In a few years the more prosperous business men installed private telephones.

The grassy streets became a quagmire in rainy weather and a

---

[11] Huron, Aberdeen, and Redfield, South Dakota, were supplied in the same manner. No doubt this custom was very general in the prairie towns.

broad strip of dust in summer. The only crossings on the streets were stepping-stones. Horseback was the nearly universal mode of travel. Single buggies were used by the gallant young swains to escort their ladies to the various entertainments. On a holiday occasion the three-seated spring wagon was popular. It was not uncommon for the occupants of the back seat to be spilled when the wheels struck the stepping-stones which stuck up prominently. Livery barns with a large assortment of horses and vehicles for hire, supplied the means of transportation for the townsman who had no horse and buggy. The trotting horses and the splashing mud were a constant menace to the finery of the ladies in rainy weather. Impromptu horse racing down the city streets caused concern and annoyance. One editor suggested that ditches be dug across the streets to prevent fast driving and racing on the streets. Runaways were frequent occurrences and formed one of the main items of news in the local papers.

The inhabitants of a frontier town were always inquisitive. This is not strange when one considers their isolated condition. The newcomer was eyed curiously. What was his name? What was his business? Was he married? What was he going to do here? The people hesitated not at all to pry into a person's private affairs. A half dozen idlers constituted themselves a livery stable forum and caused respectable citizens no end of annoyance by their prying proclivities. The benches or chairs in front of the stable, stores, and possibly the blacksmith shop, commanded a strategic view of all events. These places were occupied by patient watchers who sought to catch every stray bit of local scandal and hearsay. These observations were compared and conclusions drawn which were painful and annoying to upright respectable citizens. At first the exigencies of frontier life placed all on an equal plane. The highest and the lowest associated together on equal terms. Gradually before the town was old, however, a few more prosperous citizens began to consider themselves in a higher class. The local weekly paper then exhibited items like the following: "Mrs. John Smith entertained at a small but select party Monday afternoon." [12]

The one universal amusement like that of the older generation was dancing. The initial feature of the evening was the polonaise or grand march in which all took part. Some of the fashionable dances were: Money Musk, Virginia Reel, the Fireman's Quadrille, Cut the Pigeon Wing, polkas, mazurkas, and the lancers. Frequently there was a dearth of musicians. At one dance a Jew's harp was the only instrument played during the first part of the evening. Later this was supplemented by a mouth organ and an accordian.[13] In other places there were bands. These were the subject of considerable civic pride. They played at Fourth of July celebrations and gave concerts occasionally. The band rode about town on a wagon prepared for its use, serenading the citizens. As the town grew a board of trade or business men's club was organized for mutual coöperation and helpfulness in forwarding the interests of the growing metropolis.

The food of the town resident was somewhat better than that of the homesteader although it lacked the perishable necessities. At first fruit could scarcely be obtained. Vegetables were grown in private gardens or secured from farmers when in season. The butcher killed a beef once a week in summer and fresh meat was obtainable only on Saturday. Oysters and ice cream, although not unknown, were still in the category of the unusual.

[12] Harry P. Simmons, *Under the Kerosene Lamp* (York, Nebraska, 1922), pp. 162–164.
[13] Mrs. Emma Porter, *Marshall County News*, Marysville, Kansas, February 27, 1931.

CHAPTER XXVIII

ALONG MAIN STREET

HOTELS were among the most essential institutions in a new country. Sometimes they grew up naturally to fulfil the need at a given place. At fords where travelers were forced to wait while swollen streams receded and at boat landings or termini of stage lines or railroads, hotels and boarding houses sprang up. A fast growing settlement presented a golden opportunity for the hotel keeper. Again hotels were built to draw emigration. They were public improvements like parks or school-houses which were erected by the town company and which stood as proof of the town's permanency. Then, too, the less needy settlers preferred to locate where they were sure of finding a place to stay until their own homes were habitable.

The more permanent and lasting hotels, however, were those which were built to supply a definite demand. These frequently began in very humble circumstances and grew with the need. Often such a business was started in the rudest of surroundings. A tent, sod house, dugout, log structure, or rude lumber building sufficed. At Lawrence, Kansas, two intelligent Massachusetts women operated an open air boarding-house. They laid rough boards across some logs for a table. Around this make-shift arrangement they and their boarders took their places on wash tubs, kegs, and blocks. This was the first boarding-house in that famous town. A little later the "hay tent" made of poles and prairie hay was opened as a boarding house; the guests sat on beds, boxes, trunks, and other improvised seats. Not far away a large tent served as a hotel. The tent had two apartments separated by boxes. One was for men and the other for women. Straw on the ground served for beds. In the fifties everyone when traveling was expected to "find" his own bed clothes. Buffalo robes were suitable and were universally used for bed blankets. The guests were kept awake the greater part of the night by noisy discussions concerning the slavery question.[1]

In 1854 a traveler reported having stayed in a caravansary for immigrants. Its walls were sod; its roof, cloth; and its carpet, prairie hay. The newer buildings were arranged with an office, kitchen, and dining room down stairs, and one or two large rooms upstairs. Beds were crowded close together in them—so close that one traveler said the air was so foul that he slept in his wagon.

Mr. John McNamara, an Episcopal minister, told of his experience in one of these houses. At bed time he was shown to a large unfinished room upstairs. There were no partitions, no lath, and no plaster. The floor boards were laid temporarily with cracks between the planks. Blankets were supplied but in insufficient numbers to serve the large crowd. There were no beds. Each man seized a blanket and hung onto it while he took off his hat, shoes, and coat which he used for a pillow. Twenty-nine men retired in one large bed. Some of the later arrivals took extra blankets off the sleepers. The night was very cold and the sleepers awoke and went on conquests. Finally someone took a blanket from a man who did not relish the joke. This started a row, and a general reckoning ensued. By that time all were so chilled that sleep was impossible, and conversation lasted until morning.

A Dakota hotel of the boom period of the eighties, was described as a primitive wooden structure. The walls of its rooms were brown building paper fastened to upright scantlings which partitioned it off into little cubicles occupied by the guests. An unstable bed, a wash stand, bowl and pitcher, and a chair were the only furniture. The dim light from the smoky kerosene lamp revealed the hay-filled

[1] In Brookings County, Dakota Territory, in 1879, the Pioneer House was partitioned off into rooms by army blankets; at Aberdeen in the same territory, a large circus tent was used as a hotel until the proprietor built a structure of sod thirty by fifty feet with three foot walls.

pillow on the bed and the other features of the dingy room. The door was flimsy and the "catch" out of order.

In steamboat days some of the best hotels were old steamboats which had served their day as transportation vehicles. Without engines and boilers they were towed up the river to congested spots where, tied to the wharf, they became luxurious hotels for the emigrants. John J. Ingalls, who had been persuaded to buy stock in the little town of Sumner, Kansas, and had noticed a picture of the magnificent hotel on the lithograph, was disappointed when he found a building whose floors were destitute of carpets and its walls bare. One traveler left the record of a rooming establishment which had a special room for the married people. It had one large bed so arranged that a lady could go to bed at one side, the husband next, then another husband, his wife, and so on. In this way several families were accommodated while they erected their own dwellings.

At meal time a dinner bell was rung or a man beat a gong which produced such a clatter that it could be heard throughout the straggling settlement. The hungry guests hurried to partake of the meal. The dining room was ordinarily the most spacious in the settlement and was used not only for dining but also as a place of assembly. Politicians declaimed there, the first church services were conducted in its bosom, civic gatherings and even funerals were held there. In such a room Abraham Lincoln addressed the citizens of Elwood, Kansas, in 1860, and spun yarns by the glowing stove. A wash room at one side of the dining room provided facilities for the morning ablutions. The equipment consisted of a bench or two with buckets of water and tin basins. The roller towel, wet from end to end, provided the unsanitary accompaniment to this public utility. A favorite story of the West pictured a patron complaining to the landlord about the towel, whereupon that worthy with an air of authority squelched the patron with "There's twenty-six men used that towel before you and you're the first one that complained."

A boarding house is seldom blessed with a reputation for good food. If reports are accurate, the early hotels were no exception to the rule. The price was high and the food was indifferent. One boarder spoke of the meals of long strips of side pork swimming in grease, pickled cabbage, pickled cucumber, dried apple sauce, and biscuit. Another spoke of the eternal hog meat and biscuits. Still another complained of the bread, bacon, and very black coffee served without milk or cream. One man mentioned that the guests were cheered when a steamboat arrived bringing a supply of bacon, dried apples, and a keg of molasses. When travelers pulled up to one hotel and asked the proprietor if they could stay all night he replied: "Yes, if you can put up with darned hard fare." The travelers in reminiscing expressed thankfulness for the corn-bread, molasses, and coffee, and the comfortable beds of prairie hay.

Rates ran from three to eight dollars a week for board and room, depending upon the traffic, the location of the house, and the date.[2] At rush points rates were the highest. After supper there came the dip into the bowl of wooden tooth picks and the selection of cigars. In some places a cigar went with the meal. Frequently there was a bar at one end of the dining room where the guests liquored up a bit and then, lighting their cigars, they gathered around the stove for the evening's discussion. The dining room was the bar room, the smoking room, whittling room, standing room, coughing room, spitting room, reading room, and writing room.[3]

In Buffalo County, Dakota Territory, Mike Hileman and his wife conducted a hotel for many years. Mrs. Hileman was a famous cook and the table was always loaded with good food prepared in an appetizing manner. Mike was an old soldier, an Andersonville

[2] At Columbus, Nebraska, an establishment advertised: "80 cents will pay for stable and hay for a span over night, and for supper and breakfast at J. B. Senecals, etc." Oakdale (Nebraska) *Pen and Plow*, March 9, 1878. In the rush times in the eighties one hotel in Dakota Territory charged two dollars a day for accommodation. Later this was reduced to one dollar a day. A common schedule of prices in Dakota Territory was:

Feed for a horse ..	$0.25
A meal	.25
Stay over night ..	.25

[3] John McNamara, *Three Years on the Kansas Border* (New York, 1856), p. 67.

prisoner, and never failed to entertain his guests with an endless fund of information and anecdotes on all subjects and suitable for all occasions. The hotel office was the general headquarters of the "Old Home Town"; and wit, speculation, and imagination were given wide range. The winter evenings produced tales that would have taxed the ingenuity of Baron Munschausen, Jules Verne, and even Ananias himself.[4]

In the summer the idle frequently pitched horseshoes or played ball near the hotel. In the afternoon the crowd gathered on the veranda to hold their powwow. Land agents "blew up" the country to strangers and sounded them out on possible deals. Once a victim was cornered his escape was well-nigh impossible.

During the rush seasons the floors, tables, and every other available foot of space, was utilized as sleeping quarters and the enterprising hotel keeper became prosperous. One hotel keeper whose house was located on a stage line and who had the stage business reserved to him, cleared $1,800 in six months.

The names of the hotels were in no way distinctive. Many were called after the name of the proprietor or owner. For example, the Eldridge House opened at Lawrence, Kansas, on January 1, 1859, was said to be the best hotel west of the Ohio River. It was the beginning of the second growth of hotels and varied from the ordinary frontier type. It was built of brick at a cost of $75,000. Others carried the word "hotel" in their title such as "Pioneer Hotel" or "Bean's Hotel." Some few, however, did bear entirely distinctive names. An example of this was "The Roaring Gimlet" in Hastings, Nebraska, or "The Drovers Cottage," a cattleman's hotel at Abilene, Kansas.

The finest room in the hotel, if it were a two story structure, was the one directly above the office; it was warmed by the stove pipe. This was given to the judge or the visiting official.

The proprietor was often a burly, coatless gentleman attired in

---

[4] Unfortunately the prairie hotel has not been immortalized as was the stage coach tavern in Longfellow's "Tales of a Wayside Inn."

red woolen or hickory shirt, or other plain attire, who sought to care for his guests as well as possible under the rude circumstances. He was informally friendly but inclined to sympathize little with the criticism of his establishment. A visitor at a South Dakota hostelry in the eighties found the keeper a rude, unkempt, barefoot woman. Some of these hotel keepers were very eccentric. In the eighties a guest at the Campbell House, in Dakota Territory, left a call for a 2:00 A.M. train. The landlord sat up in order to make the call good. When called at 1:30, the traveling man said, "I've changed my mind, general, I guess I won't go." "But I guess you will," said the landlord waxing wroth. "Get up and dress and hike for the train or I'll blow your head off." The guest was soon on his way to the station.

One day a real estate man from a neighboring town drove to the little town of Clifton in Sully County, Dakota. Unhooking his horse on the prairie grass opposite the little hotel, he fed the animal and sat in his buggy eating his lunch. The hotel keeper noticed him but said nothing. A few days later the agent brought a lady client of his to town and took her to the hotel for dinner. When he called for the bill it was twice the amount it should have been. When questioned, the hotel keeper reminded him of the time he stopped near the hotel before. When he remonstrated that he had not eaten there, the proprietor said, "Well, it was here for you and if you didn't eat it, the fault wasn't ours." The real estate man paid rather than cause a scene before his prospective customer.

The hotel usually had certain conveniences for the public such as stables and feed-yards. A typical advertisement of a Dakota hotel reads:

Elk Point House, Elk Point, D. T. The undersigned having leased the above named house, and fitted it up warm and comfortable, is now prepared to wait on the travelling community, and all who may favor him with patronage. Good stabling, with plenty of corn, oats, and hay. A. L. Edwards, Proprietor.

In addition to this a hack and baggage line was often run for the convenience of the guests. This was not necessarily operated by the hotel management. It transferred passengers and baggage from depot or stage station to the hotel or from station to station.

In the sixties the commercial traveler or drummer made his advent on the prairies. He was a hail-fellow-well-met, and in addition to educating the merchants of the town in the new departure of buying goods, he enlivened the community and brought a touch of the outside world to the young men. He was always ready for a frolic and was heartily welcomed by the hotel keepers and the crowd that "hung out" there.

The saloon on the raw frontier was crude indeed. The shelves were ornamented by soiled decanters, dirty glasses, and a few boxes of cigars. In the corner sat a few barrels with spigots in them. The proprietor, slightly inebriated, wore no coat and was not easily distinguished from the other denizens of the place. Perhaps a card table had been improvised by laying planks across a whiskey barrel. A fiddler and other loafers hung about drinking, swearing, and whiling away their time. In boom days these saloons became more pretentious, affording the most attractive furniture in town, including a chandelier supporting four kerosene lamps. Degraded women frequented these places, dancing, drinking and furnishing pleasure for the large group of men uprooted from the routine of domestic life in the East and thrown out into the rugged life on the plains.

The frontier store was a general merchandise house in the true sense of the word. Every thing was kept from a needle to a wagon and from a cathartic pill to a keg of whiskey. At the "Old Pioneer Store," established in 1858, on the Santa Fe Trail in Kansas, over $12,000 worth of whiskey and probably $400,000 worth of merchandise were sold within two years. During the same period $15.20 worth of Bibles were sold. Not all frontier stores, however, did as large a business as these outfitting stores or houses located at strategic points.

Ordinarily the merchants were men of some means who came West, took up homesteads, and utilized their capital in the establishment of merchandise concerns. They visited their claims frequently enough to prove up on the land. The store might be kept in any type of building from a tent or a dugout to an ample frame structure. The third house built in Omaha was a sod dugout used for a grocery and saloon. After a short time the growing prairie town came out of the ground; one-story frame buildings were constructed with square fronts projecting above them like sign-boards; each was painted in a different color and gave the place the atmosphere of a carnival.

A traveler described the typical grocery store as a structure ten by twelve or smaller with a row of rough board shelves holding a few items. The stock of goods included saleratus or soda, salt, flour, coffee, tobacco, and liquor. The more pretentious stores carried a correspondingly larger and more diversified stock of goods. Vinegar was made by placing acetic acid in a sugar barrel of rain water colored with burned sugar.

Frequently the storekeeper and his wife and children lived in the rear of the store near the stock of calico, sheeting, blankets, pins, needles, buttons, smoking and chewing tobacco, cigars, lamp wicks, hinges, nails, dishes, boots, powder and lead, baking powder, and many of the provisions sold in grocery stores today. Dried vegetables and fruit were kept, but there were no fresh vegetables, fresh fruits, nor canned goods.

Liquor was plentiful and as a rule before trading, the merchant took the customer down into the cellar or into the back of the store for a drink. This drink gave the customer an appetite for business and stopped any dickering on prices. Whiskey was often kept in a tub or barrel and the customer drank from a tin cup.

Barter was conducted on a large scale. In 1871 a prairie merchant inserted the following advertisement: "Furs and hides taken at highest cash prices at the O.K. Clothing Store." The articles taken in trade by one general merchant in the seventies included old copper, rags, eggs, chickens, butter, furs, hides, sheep pelts, corn, vegetables, tallow, lard, rabbits, quail, and hogs. During the winter of 1871–1872 the firm sold $4,793.05 worth of furs and hides alone, During the same winter from November 21 to January 6, seven hundred and sixty-five bushels of corn were taken in trade. In the earlier days buffalo robes were a regular item of trade at four dollars each. In 1872 more than one thousand tanned robes were exchanged for goods at one local store.

Fortunate indeed was the merchant who could secure the post office for his place of business—not that the government contract brought a large income, but his store became the central rallying point of the town. In a Dakota boom town of the eighties the arrival of the post was announced by raising a flag on a high pole. This brought men and women pouring in from miles around for news from the eastern world. In a short time a large crowd had gathered. The sack was poured out on a counter or in a box and the storekeeper, that is to say, the postmaster, mounted on a dry goods box, picked up the mail piece by piece and read the inscription to the crowd. Each claimant cried out, "Here!" in response to his name. Sometimes two-thirds of the mail was distributed in this way.

Some postmasters used this occasion for making comments regarding the pieces of mail they were handing out. A woman's handwriting on a letter addressed to a young man received the postmaster's special notice to the delight of the listening crowd and the annoyance of the single man under fire. Such an entertainment, while wholly beyond the expectations of the United States Government mail department, was nevertheless highly entertaining and enjoyable to the community. The pieces of mail which remained were left in a box on the counter and those coming in later were allowed to pick out their own.

The earliest boxes were made by partitioning an empty cracker box into little pigeonholes. This was fastened to the sod wall by pegs or nailed onto the flimsy frame building. At a later time a few standard boxes were provided. Some of these with locks were used by the newspaper editor and other important men of the town. They walked into the place without so much as looking at the postmaster, unlocked the box, and left with a bundle of mail; the common folks were obliged to give the number of their box or their name and wait while the clerk looked through the mail.

There was much complaint by the newspapers that subscribers failed to receive their papers and that the exchanges were often weeks late although the editors were on direct mail routes. One editor complained that the papers were jumbled into a few little pigeonholes or were piled upon a desk, box, or barrel, amidst boots, hats, bridles, horse collars, and other coarse wares, to await the call of subscribers. The store where the postmaster distributed cheese and codfish as well as mail, became a popular establishment in the right hands.

Certain social features also attached themselves to the country store. The loafers gathered around the roaring red-hot stove and with heels high, chewed tobacco, talked religion and politics, whittled, and ate cheese and crackers. The lonely prairie dweller, although ordinarily too busy to stop and idle away much time, was nevertheless glad to enjoy the pleasant association before beginning the long, tedious journey back to his isolated dwelling.

Many customers came from long distances and had to be accommodated for the night. In warm weather they camped out, sleeping under their wagons; but in the winter months they sat around the fire visiting until bed time and then spread their robes on the floor and slept.

In the earlier years groceries were not considered a very profitable business. Many men who kept groceries sold them at cost in order to bring trade for the other goods. Gradually stores grew up which dealt in groceries alone. Some advertised their business as wholesale and retail establishments. In the modern sense of the word there was little wholesale trade until retail stores developed further out on the frontier. At this early day, however, several settlers would send one team, and purchase a wagon-load amounting to several hundred dollars. The buffalo hunters and trappers on the plains brought in wagon-loads of buffalo hides and tallow to exchange for their supplies. That was the wholesale trade. Occasionally an enterprising merchant would buy up a herd of hogs and drive them to a larger town where the packing industry was beginning to develop. In due time this business gravitated into the hands of the stock buyer.

The amount of business at one of these stores was astonishing. In 1857 a consignment of six hundred stoves was landed on the levee at Lawrence, Kansas, at one time. In 1888 a small store advertised in the local paper: "Crockery—A carload of Red Wing crocks just arrived at the Red Front. Five thousand gallons for sale." In the flood tide of emigration the business of a store increased by leaps and bounds in a single season in spite of a ten-fold increase in competition. Mr. Joel Hull launched a merchandise business at Lowell, Nebraska, with the arrival of the railroad on July 3, 1874, when there were only forty-seven persons in the vicinity. Before August 1 the sales averaged over one hundred dollars a day and the demand was so great that in September he laid in a stock of thirty-three thousand dollars' worth of goods all bought on credit. At times he had barely enough to pay the freight bills. Trade increased to two hundred dollars and then three hundred dollars a day. A considerable part of this was in flour and meal of which two or three cars a week were required. He was a very busy man with seven clerks. Meanwhile this lucrative traffic had attracted others and seven general merchandise stores had been established in town. From July, 1872, to July, 1874, Mr. Hull sold $130,000 worth of goods at a clear profit of $13,000, exactly ten per cent of his sales. Money was free in the West at that time in spite of the panic. Every night and every day was a "hot time in the old town," Sundays included. Mr. Hull bought buffalo hams with the skin on at three and three-fourths cents a pound and sent them to Chicago where they brought from ten to twelve and a half cents a pound. He sent over four tons of this meat to the East. Not every storekeeper, of course, was fortunate enough to share in the profits occasioned by the slaughter of the buffalo.

The ordinary small town store in the strictly homestead section was more quiet. People who lived in town went to trade armed with a basket of generous dimensions; delivery wagons were unknown in the earlier times. The visitor from the East was atonished at the large number of stores, "fitting out houses," "outfitting establishments," other places of business, and the relatively small population of the town. One storekeeper in the eighties advertised flour and coffins, a rather strange combination.

The drug store of frontier days was more truly an establishment dispensing medicines than its modern successor which handles everything from soda water and sandwiches to silk hosiery and rubber goods. The proprietor was supposed to be an apothecary who knew how to mix various chemicals and prepare the correct formulas for various remedies. Alcohol in some form or other formed a prominent ingredient in his medicines. The frontiersmen felt that whiskey was equally potent for snake bites and dispelling social gloom. If there were no regular bar in town—which was seldom—whiskey for medicinal purposes could be obtained at the drug store. Another concoction known as Hostetter's Bitters was supposed to remedy various ailments. This was little more than a vile brand of whiskey.

Meat was seldom sold in the general merchandise store. Town dwellers secured their fresh meat at the butcher shop. The butcher secured game from the homesteaders and hunters and butchered beef raised on the ranches and farms. As the towns grew, more pretentious butchering was done at a slaughter-house on the outskirts of town. In the smaller places butchering was done in home fashion. One butcher, standing by his block, was described as wearing a colored wool shirt with sleeves rolled up above the elbows, trousers tucked into high-topped, high-heeled boots, a broad brimmed hat covering the back of his head—a typical cowman retailing the range product off the block.

T. A. McNeal, the veteran editor of the *Kansas Farmer*, called for the town barber when he arrived at Medicine Lodge. He was informed that the tonsorial artist was at the livery stable. Supposing the latter had wandered over there during a lull in business, Mr. McNeal decided to call him back to his work. When he inquired at the horse hostelry he was confronted by a large man who said, "You are looking at the barber right now." He was doing his regular chores at the livery stable; leaning his manure fork against the barn, he conducted his customer to a little room, a boarded off corner of the stable. The equipment consisted of two ordinary chairs. The future editor sat in one while the barber took lather from an antique cup and stropped his razor vigorously on his boot-leg. Putting his foot on the chair behind his customer he bent the victim's head back on his knee and proceeded to shave him. Another newcomer on the prairie upon inquiring for the barber, was told that he had gone out into the country to plaster a house but that he would be back in a day or two. Professions and crafts were not rigid on the frontier. One individual might be capable of performing the work of any one of a half-dozen trades or professions as well as an ordinary member of these crafts.

Every town had a blacksmith shop. The frontier blacksmith was no mere cobbler nor makeshift workman. He was a mechanic who could make new machinery or skilfully repair the most intricate machinery then in use. He could make a complete wagon or put in spokes in a wheel that had broken. Most of his work consisted of shoeing horses and oxen and sharpening plows. For fuel the blacksmith used oak bark or charcoal burned at home.

Harness-making was another trade which appeared soon after the horse became a popular means of motive power. The harness-maker made and repaired harness and shoes. One of the chief attractions in his place of business was a large assortment of buggy whips.

Equally important was the livery stable. When the rural dweller became prosperous he "put up" his team in the livery barn while he transacted his business during the middle of the day or overnight. Tenders fed and watered the animals, thus saving the owner the trouble of carrying grain and hay and also affording him a certain luxury in that it relieved him of the care of his animals while in town. To have the hostler take care of the horses when the weather-beaten son of toil arrived in town and to have the team brought out to him when he was ready to leave, was an appreciated service although it could be afforded only occasionally. Those living in town who had no horses could hire a rig and team to drive out into the country. Land agents provided their prospective customers with livery rigs. A stranger in town desiring to make a business trip could secure transportation at the livery barn. The highest tribute a young man could pay to a desired young lady was to give her a ride across the prairie on a moonlight night in a livery rig. Telegrams giving notice of the death of relatives in the East were delivered by livery messengers.

Nor was the livery stable without its social side. The office of the barn was a forum for the loafers. A hot stove made it comfortable and enabled travelers to heat bricks or stones for foot warmers on lonely trips across the frigid, wind-swept prairie. In the evening the stable man entertained his cronies at checkers or cards. During the summer days horse-shoe held sway. News was disseminated from this center also. The answers to the questions, "Who is the stranger?" "What is he doing here?" and "Where did the sheriff go in that hired conveyance last night?" were all answerable at the livery stable. The livery barn was also an information center. The liveryman could tell the stranger all about the country, where the most desirable claims were, which trails were best, where to cross the various creeks, and how best to get to an isolated place.

The land hunter, loan agent, or other prairie traveler ordinarily took a driver with him for the price was no higher. The liveryman preferred to send a driver for experience had taught him that it was to his advantage to care for his property even though it cost him the driver's wages. The customer preferred a driver also, for in case of an accident, the liveryman attempted to collect for the damages. Fifty miles was considered a full day's work for a team.

A LIVERY STABLE OF THE EIGHTIES

South Thirteenth Street, Lincoln, Nebraska, 1882. Courtesy of the Nebraska State Historical Society.

The price varied. If business was rushing, it was high. If times were slack the proprietor went about seeking business at cut rates. Ordinarily the rate was five dollars for a day's drive anywhere within a range of fifty miles. Often a number of land seekers would drift together at the hotel, form a party, and hire a two or three-seated spring wagon or surrey. The liveryman charged a much higher rate for such an outfit, but the cost was small for each individual. In the boom period there were many livery stables with well-filled stalls and full equipment and there was business enough for all. Frequently proprietors named their establishments cleverly. In Ottawa, Kansas, one was called "The Hotel d'Horse." However pleasant such an establishment may have been for horses, it was an institution to be endured and not enjoyed by man; its unsavory smell caused the fastidious to give it a wide berth.

Of the luxuries to be had in a prairie town the eating saloon was one of the outstanding. The countryman who wanted to enjoy a little luxury went to one of these for a meal while in town. Fresh oysters were served during the winter months. In the summer ice cream was made. Soda pop was first sold on the prairies in the late sixties. Other "eats" tempted the speculator or city man, but the poverty-stricken homesteader was compelled to eat his lunch or subsist on crackers and cheese while his more fortunate neighbors ate at the hotel or eating saloon.

Of all the city people those who incurred the deepest enmity of the farmers were the grain and stock buyers. It was against these in particular that the horny-handed sons of toil rose up in rebellion in the move for coöperative marketing during the seventies and eighties. The farmers considered these men dishonest and in too many instances they were correct in their analyses. It was customary to discuss stock-buying transactions in the ever-present saloon and to drink freely until the proper condition was reached before striking a bargain.[5] By hook or crook the crafty buyers cheated the farmers of their produce. One trick was to inform the producer

[5] Cass G. Barns, *The Sod House*, p. 138.

that a hog had died in the yard before it was weighed and hence the owner had to take the loss. Hogs or cattle were frequently under-weighed when bought from the farmer and over-weighed when sold to him. One dealer, before weighing a flock of sheep he had sold to a feeder, ran them through a creek. When later fed and shipped to market, they weighed less than when the feeder bought them from the dishonest stock buyer. This deal was considered good busi-ness and had the sympathy of the yard hands and other dealers. The farmers had no scales; it was easy to manipulate the scales so that a farmer was defrauded of five or ten dollars on a wagon-load of hogs.

The coal and grain dealers were in little better standing. It was charged that they weighed loads of coal too heavy when they sold to purchasers. It was said that a man, having weighed his wagon, went into the coal yard but decided not to take any coal; when he weighed the empty wagon on the way out the dealer neglected to note whether he had a load or not and charged him for 800 pounds of coal. The grain buyers faced one other charge in addition to short weighing. The elevator proprietor bought Dakota wheat as grade No. 2 or 3; the Minneapolis grain brokers, after storing it a few months and allowing it to bleach, sold it at a grade or two higher than the producer had. This continued fleecing by both the local dealer and the big interest at the central grain market, finally drove the farmers into rebellion and eventually bankrupted or drove out of business the more corrupt dealers.

CHAPTER XXIX

THE PIONEER NEWSPAPER

THE PIONEER NEWSPAPER was a pioneer in the true sense of the word. The printing press preceded all other institutions of civilized life. A spirit of speculation and optimism pushed it along ahead of the post office, the jail, the school, and the church; the newspaper was on the ground waiting to print the news when there should be any; it awaited the coming of the first stores to advertise their goods and it awaited the coming of subscribers to make it a permanent profitable undertaking.

In the forefront of the great exodus from the East came the speculators and town builders. After a town was laid out residents had to be attracted. One of the most desirable means of attaining this end was by subsidizing a newspaper. Having secured a mouthpiece which might very appropriately be named the *Herald, Advertiser,* or *Bugle,* the town was ready to sound its own praises to the waiting world. Nearly every paper in a new community was a trumpet for a town company, promoting the get-rich-quick schemes of the proprietors.[1]

Dr. George W. Brown was hired to establish the *Herald of Freedom* as an organ to represent the New England Emigrant Aid Company rather than as a newspaper to represent the community. The *Kanzas News* of Emporia, Kansas, a predecessor of William Allen White's famous organ, was started with a paid list of 1,200 subscriptions, three hundred from each of the four town fathers. The

---

[1] Herbert Flint, *Journalism in Territorial Kansas,* MS, Master's Thesis, Kansas University Library, Vol. II, pp. 434–440; Thomas E. Thompson, "Early Days in Old Boston," Kansas State Historical Society *Collections,* Vol. XVI, p. 480.

citizens of Atchison agreed to donate four hundred dollars to get Dr. J. H. Stringfellow to found the famous *Squatter Sovereign* of "Bleeding Kansas" days. A townsite company sometimes subsidized a publisher by erecting a building and deeding the lot to him; at other times a cash bonus was paid. The newspaper thus became the great publicity agent in the settling of the frontier.[2]

As a rule very few of the early settlers could afford to subscribe to a newspaper. A paper was so rare that it was passed around until some of the lines became illegible before it was finally discarded. Although the news was weeks or even months old, this link with the outer world was eagerly sought. Yet the papers did find subscribers; and therein lies the second motive which prompted men to be in the van of civilization and establish papers before there was a buying public on the plains—the possibility of securing subscribers in the East.

All eyes were turned on Kansas and Nebraska in the late fifties; prospective emigrants, after choosing the particular place where they expected to come, subscribed to its paper and devoured its columns. The historian reading one of these early papers cannot help but notice that the editor was publishing his paper for eastern readers almost entirely. The columns were filled with long and glowing accounts of the climate which was the most healthful to be found anywhere, of the richness of the soil, the mineral resources, the prospects of locating the Pacific Railway in that section of the country, the new brick or stone hotel going up, or other improvements which could be of interest only to outsiders. This was devoured with the greatest zest by those who had been bitten by the wanderlust bug in the East. Groups sat around the stove in the country store discussing the wonderful land of opportunity in the golden West. The *Kansas Weekly Herald* of December 29, 1854, carried this item:

[2] Flint, *op. cit.*, Vol. II, p. 440. Mr. Flint well remarked that the trail of the town company led to the door of practically every printing plant established in the territories before the great land booms which made proof advertisements a gold mine.

Still they come. Every week brings us more new subscribers, and the cry is still they come. This week we have added thirty-six names of paying subscribers to our subscription book. Our thanks are especially due to Mr. T. J. Fain, for 20 cash subscribers at Unionville, Tennessee. We hope many of our friends will go and do likewise.—Thus far we have met with great encouragement, equal to our most sanguine expectations.

The first number of the *Kansas Weekly Herald* was set up and issued on September 15, 1854, and on February 9, 1855, it reported a circulation of 2,970. Dr. George W. Brown's paper at Lawrence grew rapidly, making him prosperous in a few months. It was said to have had 8,000 subscribers in 1856. The Oakdale, Nebraska, *Pen and Plow* gave the following as its aim: "The leading object of the Pen and Plow is to call the attention of the emigrant East to the upper Elkhorn Valley as a desirable field of settlement and investment."

The third motive which led the printer into the wilderness was the hope for the future. The spirit of optimism gripped the newspaper editor along with the other early settlers. The owner of the press set it up and threw in his lot with the intention of rising or falling with the town. He had visions of his town becoming a great city with himself as editor of a metropolitan daily; or of his becoming a great financier through the riches he had gained from the sale of lots in the town which he "puffed" in every issue of his paper.

The first paper published in the sod-house era in Kansas or Nebraska, the *Kansas Weekly Herald* of Leavenworth, was printed on the river levee before a house had been completed. The first issue, dated September 15, 1854, informed its readers that:

All the type of the present number of the Herald has been set under an elm tree in the city of Leavenworth. Our selections have been made, our editorials written, our proof read, sitting on the ground with a big shingle on our knee for a table. Think of this, ye editors, in your easy chairs and well furnished sanctums, and cease to grumble.

The editors lived in tents, carried wood, built fires, cooked their own meals, and slept on prairie hay on the ground. A rousing log fire before the press constituted the only semblance of a hearth. Shortly afterward the press was moved into the first house in Leavenworth.

The *Huntsman's Echo* of Wood River, Nebraska, was established in 1860 at a point a few miles east of Fort Kearney on the Mormon Trail. Overland travelers wondered at the publication of a newspaper in an isolated log cabin one hundred and fifty miles west of Omaha. The editor complained that nearly every day buffalo trampled the townsite, destroyed his garden, played havoc with the growing corn, and in general made a nuisance of themselves. This sturdy paper existed for some months on the cutting edge of the frontier where civilization met savagery in mortal combat.[3]

The first paper at Omaha was the *Omaha Arrow*. The editor had his headquarters in Omaha, but the paper was printed in Council Bluffs, Iowa. At that time the Omaha Indians still occupied the townsite and charged the proprietor and other settlers ten dollars each for the privilege of building houses there. The editor began his work amidst the rudest surroundings. He made his editorial bow to the public as follows:

Well, strangers, friends, patrons, and the good people generally, wherever in the wide world your lot may be cast, and in whatever clime this ARROW may reach you, here we are upon Nebraska soil, seated upon the stump of an ancient oak, which serves for an editorial chair, and the top of our badly abused beaver for a table, we purpose editing a leader for the Omaha ARROW. . . . There sticks our axe in the trunk of an old oak from which we purpose making a log for our cabin and claim.[4]

In many instances the first issues of a newspaper were printed in the older settled country, antedated, and given the caption of the town where they were alleged to have been published. The first paper published in Nebraska was the *Nebraska Palladium* issued at Bellevue but actually printed in St. Mary's, Iowa, July 15, 1854.

[3] *Omaha Nebraskian*, April 28, 1860; *Huntsman's Echo*, spring and summer of 1860 *passim*; in 1870 there were seven newspapers published in the sparsely populated region of Dakota Territory.
[4] *Omaha Arrow*, July 28, 1854.

Three newspapers were published in Lawrence, Kansas, during the first week of January, 1855; each claimed to have been the first in the field. The *Kansas Tribune* claimed to be the first paper because its editors, John and J. L. Speer, had come to Kansas in the preceding September. They had collected much information about Kansas, printed the first number at Medina, Ohio, on October 15, and dated and headed the paper Lawrence, Kansas. The *Herald of Freedom* had also printed a number at the office of its editor, Dr. George W. Brown, at Conneautville, Pennsylvania, September 21, dated it October 21 and captioned it Wakarusa, Kansas Territory. Dr. Brown claimed that his was the first paper at Lawrence. His second issue was printed at Lawrence, January 5, 1855. The third paper, the *Kansas Free State* was published at Lawrence, January 3, 1855. Naturally the field was crowded and there was some hard feeling.

All three newspapers were printed in two buildings which did not even have roofs for several weeks. On his arrival Dr. Brown unloaded his material on the open prairie and began to construct a building. He took his seven typographers out to cut trees. The boards of which his printing establishment was made, were green and soon warped and shrank. The other office was equally crude with rough furniture. There was no roof on either establishment during the entire fall and until after Christmas.

The editor ordinarily did not confine his time to the business of running a paper. Frequently lawyers published newspapers. At Iola, Kansas, two practicing attorneys edited the *Neosho Valley Register*. They advertised, "If legal assistance is desired, call at the *Register* Office." Mr. J. E. Johnson, one of the editors of the *Omaha Arrow*, was a Mormon who lived in Council Bluffs and engaged in several kinds of business simultaneously. He practiced law, ran a blacksmith shop, was an insurance agent, and carried on a general merchandizing business, in a successful attempt to support his three wives and their dependent relations. Often the editor was the mayor of the town, one of the town company, a practicing attorney, and the holder of a preëmption claim or homestead. Almost all of the editors appear to have taken homesteads or bought out claimants. One issue of a prairie newspaper informed its readers that the senior editor had been "so busy gathering corn, fighting prairie fire, building winter quarters for his livestock, etc. that we have had nearly nothing from his pencil for this number."

There was a certain frontier informality about publishing a newspaper which did not necessitate regular publication. The editor of the *Nebraska Enquirer* gave his agricultural pursuits as an excuse for his delinquency:

We are late with our issue this week, but hope our patrons will excuse us, as we have been compelled to take the time that should have been devoted to the paper in harvesting our wheat—thereby providing against the necessity of going to bed hungry during the inclement weather of the coming winter.

The *Wichita Vidette* made this retort to criticism of its irregularity:

OUR PAPER—There has been a great deal of inquiry made at our office, as to when we issued the paper. We wish to state to those who are concerned, that we issue it sometimes on Thursday's and sometimes on Saturday's and in all, a little more regularly than we receive our pay for Ad's.

In pioneer days not over half the paper was printed at home. The rest of it, known as the patent "outsides" or "insides," was printed in Chicago, St. Paul, Sioux City, or elsewhere, and shipped to the prairie newspaper office. The newspapers were similar. Usually there were four eight-column pages. The patent insides were secured for about the actual cost of the paper and printing. The ready print companies made their profit from the one hundred inches of advertising which they reserved.

When severe storms tied up transportation facilities and the patent insides failed to arrive, a small edition was sometimes printed on the job press. During the great Dakota storm of 1881 there was no train service for weeks, and the papers "came out" with their

A FRONTIER NEWSPAPER OFFICE

The *Broken Bow Republican*, Nebraska, 1886. Courtesy of the Nebraska State Historical Society.

diminutive editions on brown store wrapping paper or wall paper. These legalized the land office notices and other legal advertising.

The first newspaper establishments were far from imposing. Often the press had been hauled over the prairie by ox teams. At Emporia, Kansas, on the date of the first issue of the *Kanzas News*, there were only three buildings—a hotel, a store, and a third building used for a store and dwelling. The type for this first issue was set up in one of the hotel bedrooms and it was printed in a room which was afterwards used as a parlor. Other hardy progenitors of the thriving press of prosperous towns of today, were published in dugouts.

The portion of the paper printed at home was set up by hand and the press was turned by hand. The type had to be inked with an old-fashioned hand roller, and a lever was yanked to make the impression. The job press was kicked by foot.

Many of the newspapers were printed on the army press. This was a small press which could be lifted by a strong man and was easily transported across the prairie. There was a cylinder of approximately one foot in diameter on the top of a frame work. A crank ran the type back and forth under the cylinder. A paper could be started with one of these old second-hand presses on a capital of one hundred and fifty dollars. The larger papers were printed on a Washington hand press.

The editor called his office his sanctum. It became a gathering place for those who wanted news from the papers. One editor complained that people rummaged through his desk and read his exchanges before he had finished with them. Some papers, he objected, never came back and others were so soiled or worn as to be unfit for preservation. He therefore scolded through the editorial columns.

Certainly these pioneer newspaper offices were rude establishments. T. A. McNeal, dean of Kansas editors, described the office of the *Medicine Lodge Cresset* in 1879:

When I entered the *Cresset* office on that windy March day, Iliff, the editor, was seated at a pine table. In front of him lay his "45" revolver, fully loaded. He filled my imagination of what "Jim Bludso" of the *Arizona Kicker* ought to look like. His hair, black and coarse as that of an Indian, fell down over his collar. His eyes, black and flashing, looked out from under bettling brows with hairs stiff and wiry and as long as the ordinary mustache. His dress was in keeping with his appearance. Around his neck was a red bandana handkerchief. His dark gray woolen shirt, flaring open slightly at the throat, revealed in part the muscular neck and hirsute breast. He wore the leather "chaps" common to the cow man of that day, and his pants, stuffed in his boots, were held in place by a belt well filled with loaded cartridges. A woven rawhide quirt hung from his left wrist. The heels of his boots were ornamented with savage-looking spurs. He was booted and spurred and ready to ride. But he was not just then thinking of the range. He was engaged in writing a most vigorous editorial.

The interior of one of these crude printing offices was described by one who visited the first one in Kansas.

A visit to the printing office afforded a rich treat. On entering the first room on the right hand three "law shingles" were on the door; on one side was a rich bed, French blankets, sheets, table cloths, shirts, cloaks and rugs all together; on the wall hung hams, maps, venison, and rich engravings, onions, portraits, and books; on the floor were a side of bacon carved to the bone, corn and potatoes, stationery and books; on a nice dressing case stood a wooden tray half full of dough, while crackers occupied the professional desk. In a room on the left, the sanctum, the housewife, cook and editor lived in glorious unity, one person. He was seated on a stool, with paper before him on a piece of plank, writing a vigorous knockdown to an article in the Kickapoo *Pioneer*, a paper of a rival city. The cookstove was at his left, and tin kettles all around; the corn cake was "a-doing" and instead of scratching his head for an idea as editors often do, he turned the cake and went ahead.[5]

The editorial "puff" was common in the early days. It varied from the editor's calling attention to an advertisement in another column to an out-and-out boost of the advertisers' goods. It was customary for the people to bring presents in the form of produce to the newspaper office. The editor acknowledged these "first fruits"

[5] Flint, *op. cit.*, Vol. I, pp. 27, 28.

and gave the donors a "puff" in the next issue. There were no stations nor distinctions in rank in that frontier society. The editor of one paper announced: "Judge Bost's wife brought a crock of most excellent butter last week. It just suits." Another editor spoke of two different people who had brought messes of lettuce. People brought honey, tomatoes, watermelons, wild plums, and other products of the soil to offer on the altar in the newspaper man's sanctum.

Three young unmarried men [6] were printing the *Marysville* (Kansas) *Democratic Platform*. The income was meager. The printing office building was a one-room, one-story, cheap affair. All three publishers slept in one bed in the loft and batched in the office, cooking on a heating stove. The bed was a tick of straw laid on the floor boards of the attic and the food was principally lye hominy made of corn from a crib near at hand. Someone presented the editors and proprietors with a head of cabbage. Editorial appreciation was expressed for the very acceptable gift. Mr. Sol Miller, for so many years editor of the *White Cloud Chief*, took occasion to tease the boys:

The Marysville *Democratic Platform* gives an extended notice to a citizen who presented its publishers with a head of cabbage, which looks like making a good deal of fuss over one cabbage for a paper that already has three cabbage heads.

Agricultural products were not the only things taken to the editor, however. The butcher shop sent beefsteak, and a store presented the newspaper man with an axe. At Wichita, Kansas, the editor of the *Eagle* spoke of having received a barrel of apples and a can of oysters from a local merchandise house.

When the paper eventually had to depend on the immediate vicinity for its support, the editor struggled to keep the wolf from his door. Notices appeared in the editorial columns frequently. The hungry editor offered to take potatoes, corn, molasses, cabbage, flour, meal, fruit, or any other food stuffs that a farmer produced.

[6] One was Mr. Edward C. Manning. E. C. Manning, "In at the Birth and—," *Transactions*, Kansas State Historical Society, Vol. VII, p. 202, footnote.

Wood, oats, wheat, cane, bran, and shorts, were also acceptable on subscription fees or on past accounts. After enumerating a long list, one editor offered to take almost "any other variety of produce except babies." The editor of the *Nebraska Advertiser* expressed it in this fashion:

Bring them along. A good many of our farmers complain they are too poor to take the "Advertiser," unless we take "garden truck" and the like. In other words, as a clever old farmer said to us one day last week: "Money I have none; but if you will put your labor against mine, we can trade. I have chickens, butter, eggs, pork, potatoes, onions, etc." Look here, my good friend, that is just what we want. We have a wife and five boys to feed, clothe and take care of. We need all these articles you mention. We have to pay cash for them. If you have them, and wish to become a subscriber, or if any of you who are already subscribers, wish to pay in that kind of currency, all we have to say is "it suits." Bring it along. If you shoot a fine buck, send us a portion, 'tis good as gold. Or if fortune smiles, and two, three or four good fat turkeys fall before the unerring aim of your rifle, send us one—rather have it than silver,—yea, upon such do we delight to feed.

At a time when most of the subscription money was paid in wood, turnips, butter, squash, and corn, it required real managerial ability to secure enough money to buy paper and ink. It is small wonder that a newspaper occasionally skipped a week. The principle source of cash revenue was in printing the proceedings of the county commissioners, the delinquent tax lists, and the government notices with regard to homestead and preëmption entries. It is then not surprising that the frontier journals had a tremendously high birth and death rate. An item in one paper in 1858 stated: "The Wyoming Post has gone under.—This is the sixth Nebraska newspaper discontinued for want of patronage since last spring."

During the boom of the eighties newspapers were founded with the aim of running them only during the few months of lucrative business while the homesteaders were "proving up." By Federal law each homesteader had to run his final proof notice six times in the paper nearest to his land. For this a fee of six and a half to ten dollars was charged, depending on the conscience of the publisher and the strength of competition. Since contests could be printed in any paper in the county there was greater competition and the price was lower. The price for these averaged five dollars. [7]

The boom period brought in proofs in whole counties within a few months of one another resulting in a golden harvest for the publisher. When he had garnered in the "sheaves," he moved his little press in a spring wagon to new frontier a little farther west.

During the final proof rush in the Dakotas when the Big Sioux reservation was opened, E. L. Senn put in about thirty presses at different spots to secure the proving up business. He hired men to run the papers at scattered post offices of strategic importance.[8]

One figure often to be found in the print shop of a local newspaper, was the tramp printer or "typographical tourist." He usually was adept at his business and could fill various positions. He was, however, most adept at doing his duty at the dinner table. He had a store of jokes and knew how to "crack" them at the expense of others. His life, though one of hardship, was nevertheless so fascinating that once started it was almost impossible to separate him from the nomadic life. He would decide to quit and settle down, but the wanderlust spirit would grip him and he would be off again. A little lonesome at times, homesick to be back East, or hungry and ill, after a good night's rest in some barn or by a haystack, he set out light-hearted on his way, and, whistling a merry tune, was soon himself again. Sometimes he went several days without food. Then

[7] By the term "proof notice" is meant a published statement that the homesteader had faithfully lived up to the government rules, was expecting to give final proof of this, and receive a patent from the government which would give him full ownership. It was a notice to all who knew the situation to "speak now or forever hold their peace" before the final act of the ceremony was performed. By a "contest notice" is meant a declaration on the part of an individual that a homesteader had not lived up to the rules, had forfeited his right to the land, and that the filer of the contest notice proposed to file on that claim. It was sometimes better policy to run this in a paper published in a far corner of the county so that the original homesteader might not become aware that his claim was contested until he had lost it to the "jumper."

[8] In Sully County, Dakota Territory, nine papers were published during the final proof days. Only two are published there today.

when a good meal came his way he filled stomach and pockets. In the frontier days when the railroads were new and trains irregular, the railroads were not so particular about extra passengers and the country was filled with drifters of every craft. The tramps had a code of signs and signals learned while passing over the road. These marks could be seen on fence posts, barns, or wherever they were visible to the passing eye. By these he could tell whether the place he was approaching would receive him kindly or not, whether the dog was cross, whether there was a wood-pile in the back yard on which he would be set to work, or a manure pile to be moved in the pleasant environment of the corral. The Weary Willie usually was successful in steering clear of these difficulties, but when caught, he worked. Sometimes newspaper men hoped he would come, for he was needed and was usually a good hand. He would work through the rush for a bottle of booze and a restaurant meal. If he was given money, it went to the saloon. The country printer could usually learn from the tramp printer, for new ideas were hatched in his fertile brain or stored there as he roamed over the country. Walt Mason was one of these traveling typos.[9] From the point of content papers were very characteristically different from the ordinary newspaper of today. The editorial was overdeveloped; the editor of a first-class journal frequently used the Horace Greeley style of telling news in a personal way; that is, by saying "we believe a certain way," and so forth. Editors were very contentious, wrangling back and forth through their columns, shooting darts of sarcasm and irony at one another. Some of them, like knights who had built up reputations, rode about ready to throw down the gauntlet to any editor who could stand the shock of the joust. Consequently they were always having a tilt with someone. E. W. Howe said they imagined they were buzz saws and often tried to prove it. There was a large amount of feature material; as much as one-fourth of

[9] Henry Allen Brainerd, *History of the Nebraska Press Association* (Lincoln, 1923), Book II, pp. 37–42; William Allen White took him in at Emporia, Kansas, and gave him the opportunity which made him a national figure.

the reading material was of that character. Such headings as these appeared: "Pearls of Thought," "Things Wise and Otherwise," "The Scrapbook," "Choice Poetry," and "Select Tale." Occasionally there were articles on farming or household economics. Such columns as "The Garden and Kitchen" appeared. An agent elsewhere, either paid or unpaid, sent in whole columns of material. One of these correspondents was almost sure to be located at the territorial capital to inform the people what was taking place when the legislature met.

Newspapers were very informal in their portrayal of events, and the most personal items were treated in a manner that would be considered a discourtesy today. A wedding was reported in detail with a list of all the presents from album to towels. When the protracted meeting in the church produced results, the editor rejoiced that certain old hard and crusty sinners had succumbed to the spiritual onslaught of the hosts of righteousness.

Dancers were noticed in the most personal way. A detailed description was given of their beauty, grace, and charm. The *Kansas Weekly Herald,* of Leavenworth, gave a description of the third dance within a week:

Among the most beautiful women there assembled was Miss E— W— who was conceded by all to be the "observed of all observers." There is something pleasant, striking, and impressive in the appearance of Miss W—. She resembles nothing earthly we have ever seen, or unearthly that we have imagined, except it be the *beau ideal* of a Hebe. The most luxuriant tresses, of the most silken texture; eyes bright and radiant as the stars in the azure sky; cheeks of rose, lips of carnation, and a skin white and polished as—what shall we say, not marble for that is hard—not snow for that is cold—not satin for that sounds like a man-milliner comparison—like nothing that we ever saw before, or we verily believe shall see again except in her. Then her figure! by Jove it is matchless! All the elasticity and bounding animation of the child, with all the rounded beauty of contour of the woman. Arms that might serve as models to the sculptor, hands that look as only formed to play with flowers; and feet that seem almost too small to bear the beautiful figure in which she excelled all other ladies present.

The early newspapers were printed on rag paper and contained no pictures or cartoons with the possible exception of a small wood-cut here and there among the advertising. A much larger portion of the paper in those days was covered with advertisements than now. There were a large number of lawyers' cards, numerous notices of general merchandise establishments, restaurants, hotels, and other places of business. Occasionally someone would write up a catchy advertisement which would attract the readers' attention by means of heavy head-lines which on first sight appeared to be news. For example, the *Neosho Valley Register* of Iola, Kansas, carried this advertisement:

THE INDIAN WAR

19TH KAN CAV'Y

Has been completed and equipped without requiring all the people of Allen County to enlist, the undersigned have concluded to supply the wants of those who remain with all kinds of Furniture. . . .

Another announced in big black letters, WAR IS DECLARED, and below, the reader was informed that a certain mercantile estab-lishment had declared war on high prices. These ads, clever enough at first, became monotonous when run for weeks. The *Huntsman's Echo* baited its reader with the following advertisement:

AN ACCIDENT

Whilst in Omaha the other day, we were startled by a cry in the street of—stop thief! stop thief! . . . We rushed out and saw a "peaker" with a huge load of goods, making off in hot haste with a whole train in his wake, reechoing the shout. The man in the lead being very heavily loaded, was soon brought to, and upon asking the cause of the fuss, was informed that he was suspected of having stolen the goods with which he was so rapidly making off. The fellow laid down his load and gave vent to the following exclamations:

"You d——d fools—you are as soft as toadstools and green as squash! Think I'd be such a ninny and simpleton as to spend my time stealing goods when I can buy them so cheap at McGeath's! Why, a fellow would be a blamed fool to steal under such circumstances."

The crowd dispersed, and we ran down to McGeath's to see, and went away satisfied the "peaker" was right.[10]

Probably half of the advertising was from the town in which the paper was established. The editor who ran an advertisement for an eastern magazine received the periodical free as his pay for the advertisement. This plan of taking part or all of the price of the advertisement in trade was practiced widely. The man who advertised his wares expected the publisher to take one-third to one-half the price in goods advertised. The merchants always marked their goods higher than they were worth when such an arrangement was made. In later years the newspapers expected a big sum for an advertisement of a circus. As much as one hundred dollars was demanded. Patent medicine furnished a large portion of advertising. Many patent medicine concerns in the East sent expert salesmen to make contracts for their advertising.

In addition to that found in the papers there was considerable outdoor advertising. The citizens of Wichita, Kansas, one morning found the words "The Green Front has it" placarded on all the walks, store boxes, posts, and other places on Main Street. The newspaper noticed this by stating that it had caused great speculation among the townsmen but that all might rest assured that the particular thing which the Green Front had was not contagious; people would find out the meaning by calling at the Green Front store.

Poor communication service caused no little annoyance to the newspapers and readers. The *Nebraska Advertiser* complained that it had taken fifteen days for some letters to be delivered from Nebraska City to Brownville, a distance of twenty-seven miles. In July, 1856, the editor of the same paper gave very complimentary credit to the "Uncle Sam" line of steamers which regularly brought the papers from Cincinnati in sixty days, and from St. Louis, Omaha and

---

[10] "Peaker," a nickname for the gold hunters on their way to the Pike's Peak region; *Huntsman's Echo*, June 14, 1860.

Council Bluffs, in thirty days. The editor sang a song of joy at these great and wonderful improvements that had come to pass:

> Wonders sure will never cease,
> While works of art do so increase.

With the arrival of the railroad and the telegraph in the sixties, news traveled faster, but even then national news was often not received until the patent insides from the East carried it.

There was very little local news. Runaways, always frequent, were a popular tid-bit. Social items, church or school news, marriages, sporting notices, theft, murder, and other law violations were the chief news items. Even a dog fight was accorded space in a Clay County, Dakota, paper in 1873.

The majority of the earlier papers no doubt had a subscription list of one or two thousand. The price was usually two dollars a year. As a rule traveling agents went through the East taking subscriptions. Some Kansas territorial papers had as many as forty agents. To spur on the agents it was customary to offer certain prizes in addition to the regular commission. Dr. Brown of the *Herald of Freedom* was also one of the proprietors of the town site of Emporia, Kansas. He offered as a first prize in a subscription contest one share of ten lots in the town. Other prizes consisted of a lot in Lawrence, one in each of several other towns some of which have long since been defunct, and twenty dollars in money as a last prize.

In some instances there was decided competition for subscriptions. At Aberdeen, Dakota Territory, two papers, the *Dakota Pioneer* and the *Aberdeen Pioneer*, were printed by the same press and issued on the same day. Each wished to secure the subscriptions from the little town of Frederick, twenty-six miles north. The *Dakota Pioneer* was the first off the press but the team which was to carry the paper north was delayed and did not get started until the *Aberdeen Pioneer* was well on the way. Naturally the team which arrived first would get the most subscriptions. The two teams started after nightfall for the midnight race across the prairies. The *Dakota*

Pioneer team lost its way and its rival reached town first, long after midnight, and retired to rest and start early in the morning. The venders of the *Dakota Pioneer* arriving somewhat later "made hay while the sun shone" even though it was in the wee hours of the morning, and proceeded from house to house arousing the occupants from their slumbers and signed up everybody before the other representatives appeared on the scene.

Sometimes newspapers were produced under queer circumstances. In the fall of 1858, *The Cricket* of Holton, Kansas, was established by Thomas G. Watters who possessed neither type nor press. The articles were written in ink and cartoons of political events were illustrated with colored pencils. This little manuscript newspaper was continued for about two months.

The *Railway Advance* was published near the end of the Kansas Pacific Railroad as it pushed across the plains. It styled itself "Official paper of the Buffalo Country." Its local column was headed "Buffalo Chips." [11]

The original pioneering instinct shown by the newspaper continued to orientate its course. The press preceded the railroad, moving into new towns by ox teams; this position in the van of progress has been maintained through the years. The editor stood at his post forming public opinion, leading progressive movements, ferreting out graft, offering inducements to railroads, and urging the citizens to vote bonds for their construction, pleading for law and order, for a new jail, for adequate fire protection, for laws to keep the pigs from the freedom of the city and for many other important civic improvements.

The editors on the whole were a capable group issuing papers comparatively free from errors. Usually they were outstanding men who fearlessly expressed themselves freely on all questions. As a result the pioneer editor was a stormy petrel. Violence against his person or property was much more common than today. The

[11] The Kansas State Historical Society has one issue of this paper published June 23, 1868, at Hayes, Kansas.

newspaper in frontier times was much more of a personal message of one man, the editor, to his subscribers than it is today. The reader today seldom knows who wrote the editorial, nor does he care, but in the days gone by, the reader ardently agreed or violently disagreed with the message from the pen of the editor. Oftentimes strong feelings were aroused and editors were horse-whipped or in other ways maltreated. The editor of the *Barber County Mail*, [12] a certain Mr. Cochrane, gained the ill-will of a party of people who ordered him to leave town. When he refused to comply, the crowd decided to tar and feather him. Since tar was non-existent in Kansas and sorghum was plentiful, it was agreed to use sorghum instead. They filled a keg of this thick molasses with sand-burs and plastered the nude body of the luckless editor with the mixture and then rode him on a rail. [13] Sometimes an editor raised a party of friends in his defense and the community was torn by dissension.

The newspaper editors have probably furnished more political leadership than any other class of people, not only in their constant molding of public opinion, but also in furnishing leaders. In Kansas the press gave us such great names as Senator Preston B. Plumb, Governor John A. Martin, Governor and Senator Henry Allen, Representative Victor Murdock, William Allen White and above all, Governor and Senator Arthur Capper. In Nebraska such names as J. Sterling Morton, Secretary of Agriculture in President Cleveland's Cabinet, Governor Robert W. Furnas, and Governor Samuel McKelvie represent the long line of distinguished newspapermen. In North Dakota Senator H. C. Hansbrough ably represented that state in Congress.

The newspapers grew with the country and probably did more to civilize and raise the standards of a crude frontier than any other secular agency. The editor stood in the forefront of the battle, wielding mighty blows for better citizenship, good government, reform of abuses, and development of the country's resources.

[12] Medicine Lodge, Kansas.
[13] From T. A. McNeal's account in the Kansas State Historical Society *Collections*, Vol. XVII, p. 616, footnote.

CHAPTER XXX

THE PIONEER DOCTOR

THE MEDICAL PROFESSION played an important part in the development of the frontier not only professionally but also politically. In Dakota Territory the first governor was a physician. [1] In Kansas during the hectic days just preceding the Civil War the outstanding Free-state leader who later became first governor of the state, was also a doctor. [2] In the very early days of settlement the sparseness of population and the poverty of the people which deterred them from calling for professional services, starved out the doctors and they were compelled to turn to other tasks to mend their fortunes. Speculation offered its get-rich-quick allurements, and politics, offering power and civic prestige, tempted them from their chosen work. The doctor usually had a claim and many times was active in real estate transactions and political campaigns. Among the early doctors in Dakota Territory, one forsook medi-

[1] Governor William Jayne was born in 1826 at Springfield, Illinois. He was graduated from the University of Illinois and the Missouri Medical School. During his practice of medicine in Springfield he became the family physician of Abraham Lincoln who appointed him governor of Dakota Territory in 1861. Arriving in Yankton in May, he started the government functioning and returned to Illinois for the winter. He resigned the governorship in 1863 and returned to live in Springfield where he occupied many positions of honor and made a fortune. He returned to Yankton for the Golden Jubilee.

[2] Charles Robinson was born at Hardwick, Massachusetts, in 1818. He attended Amherst for a year and a half and later studied medicine under a doctor at Keene, New Hampshire. In 1845, in coöperation with another doctor, he opened a hospital at Springfield, Massachusetts, where he practiced medicine until the lure of gold led him toward the setting sun amidst the hordes of forty-niners. In a clash between squatters and vested interests he led the squatters and, although arrested, was elected to the legislature. Returning to Massachusetts, he became the agent for the New England Emigrant Aid Company and as such became one of the outstanding leaders of the anti-slavery forces in Kansas during the half decade of controversy prior to the Civil War. He was elected the first governor of Kansas in 1861.

cine for law; another who arrived in 1865, went into the Indian service; and a third was able to eke out an existence temporarily by serving as chief clerk of the legislature. During the first decade not a single doctor had been able to sustain himself solely by his practice.[3]

Where settlement came in with a rush there was an abundance of practice. Frontier newspapers and land advertisements always proclaimed the climate as most salubrious, invigorating, and healthful. It was stated that illness did not exist, but facts contradict these assertions. In the fifties Lawrence, Kansas, was one vast hospital of sick people. Cholera, typhoid fever, the ague, pneumonia, pleurisy, smallpox, and other diseases swept scores of people into eternity. At Kansas City in 1855 within two hours' time ten young men died victims of cholera. During the height of the epidemic a nurse reported that sleep was almost impossible as the sound of making rude coffins was heard at all hours of the night and day. From Omaha in 1857 the Reverend Reuben Gaylord wrote that there was still much sickness among the people, that it was different from anything the physicians had seen, was very obstinate, and did not readily yield to medicine. Diaries and letters of the time speak volumes with regard to the lack of health. Page after page portrays the deplorable conditions. With physical sickness and loss of loved ones and friends came heart sickness and a longing for the old home.

Such diseases as cholera, smallpox, typhoid fever, and diphtheria came in epidemics wiping out whole families and striking every neighborhood. Cholera struck quickly. The victim, apparently well in the morning, was suddenly taken ill and died in agony in less than twelve hours. Friends and neighbors feared to touch the afflicted lest they be stricken. Smallpox, although less feared, was deadly in its effect. Diphtheria took a heavy toll of the children. Hardly a family in a stricken area escaped unharmed and some lost every child. In Jerauld County, Dakota, in the year 1883, the Lawton

---

[3] Doane Robinson, *History of South Dakota*, Vol. I, p. 479. It must be remembered that Dakota Territory settled slowly during the first decade of its history.

family, consisting of a husband, wife, and five children, took ill with diphtheria. They lived in an ordinary claim shack and the neighbors shrank from visiting them because of the deadly contagion. A young man went in, cared for the living, and buried the dead. Five died and were buried a short distance from the shanty. Only the wife and one little girl survived. In 1880, South Dakota with a population of 99,000 had two hundred and twenty-four deaths. In 1920 with advanced medical knowledge, and modern conveniences and with six times the population, the deaths from this disease were only thirty-eight.

The causes for these diseases were germane to the hardships of a new country. In the absence of wells the first few years, the water was supplied from springs, sloughs, or water holes. Frequently these were contaminated, spreading death. Then, too, the common drinking cup in the home, the school, the stores, and the public square, spread disease once it appeared. Disease germs lurked everywhere in the sod house or dugout for the dirt floor could not be scrubbed or disinfected, and an attempt at sweeping, or children playing on the floor, raised dust which contaminated the air, the dishes, and the food. Paucity of sunshine and the presence of vermin such as bedbugs, fleas, and insects, carried germs and infections. Lowered vitality caused by improper clothing, exposure, and unbalanced rations, resulted in much sickness also. Salt pork, dried foods, corn-bread and other food lacking in vitamins and minerals, caused scurvy or so weakened the individual that he fell prey to various diseases. Settlers searched the woods and prairies for "greens" and many new and strange weeds were used. No doubt many of these were detrimental to health. Frequently badly-chosen dwelling places together with crowded quarters in dark, unsanitary dugouts, sod houses, or too well-ventilated shack or log cabins, promoted disease.

Of all the diseases, no doubt malaria, or the ague, carried off more young people than did any other ailment; while pneumonia accounted for the greater part of the deaths among older people. The ague, although not the most deadly, was the most prevalent disease on the prairie frontier. It was so common that people felt it was almost normal. There were many theories as to its cause. One was that the disease was caught while following the plow turning the virgin soil. The soil was very rich and was said to emit gases which poisoned the system. Other people held that the dew was responsible for the ague. It was correctly observed that the young who went out in the morning to catch horses and oxen for work, contracted the disease more readily and it was thought that the wet dew and dampness of the valley was the cause of it. Some children were not allowed out of the house until the dew dried off. Although it was not known at that time, the germ was carried by the mosquito which thrives in damp valleys, swamps, and low ground.

The sick person was afflicted by intermittent chills and fever. The attack began with a chill shortly after sunrise and lasted an hour or two calling for the use of all the blankets obtainable. The shaking and shivering was checked only by the fever, terrible headache, and delirium lasting for a period of from two to eight hours. Then came a devitalizing sweat. A period of temporary recovery followed, only to be succeeded in a day or two by a repetition of the first attack. Some fevers came every day while others occurred every second day. Still others came every third day. In valleys or marshy land hardly a person escaped. Whole families—father, mother and children—were down at once, stretched out on hay-covered floors or improvised pallets. For months these intermittent attacks continued. Whole communities were in this condition.

Numerous remedies were used widely. Some of these no doubt were prized because of their alcoholic content. A large number were patent medicines concocted to gather the loose change of the gullible and unwary. Among the widely advertized remedies were Dr. Easterley's Fever and Ague Killer, Ayer's Ague Killer, Osgood's Callagogue, sarsparilla, and calomel. Many considered quinine the best remedy.

A sallow complexion accompanied this ailment. It was pitiful to see the large number of pale-faced pioneers in any frontier gathering. When a newcomer asked one of the older settlers if he considered the climate healthful, he answered "Yes, perfectly healthful." When asked what it was that made the people so yellow, he replied: "That's nothing; we only have the ager."

Another common ailment was a complaint known as bilious fever. No doubt it was a derangement of the digestive system due to poor food.

There were no window nor door screens and the mosquito and disease-carrying house-fly gained admittance to do their deadly work. Outdoor toilets and other unsanitary conditions permitted flies to infect a whole colony with typhoid fever and start an epidemic where the houses were close together. A score of people were sometimes carried away in one community by this scourge.

There were few doctors and they were not well trained. A common school education was required for entrance to the medical school. At the end of a two-year course the candidate was granted the M.D. degree and began the practice of medicine. A man with this preparation had the best training obtainable. No doubt many practiced with little or no training since there were no restrictive laws for a number of years after the territories were opened. In Nebraska the first law regulating the practice of physicians was passed in 1880 and provided that after June 1, 1881, all practicing physicians should register in *The Physician's Register* at the office of the county clerk. All physicians beginning practice had to be graduates of a reputable medical school. Those who had practiced for two years before the law took effect were permitted to continue even though their training was deficient.

In a work which occasioned long weary rides, great fatigue, and hardship it is small wonder that the doctor frequently took to drink. On the frontier the man who did not drink was an exception. Perhaps the doctor undertook an operation or delivery while intoxicated. Sometimes he kept on operating after the patient had died.[4]

[4] Cass G. Barns, *The Sod House*, pp. 248–250.

In Dakota the first law affecting physicians was passed by the first territorial legislature and dealt with the liability of a practitioner. It made the physician guilty of a misdemeanor if he poisoned a patient while intoxicated, if the patient's life were endangered thereby. If the patient was killed by the poison the physician was guilty of manslaughter in the second degree.

No doubt many men who had been around doctors and learned something of medical lore, practiced without any theoretical classroom training. In Turner County, Dakota Territory, in the seventies when there were no regular physicians west of Yankton, A. B. Sage who had been in the employ of a doctor in the East and had gained considerable knowledge and experience, came West and secured medical books and a case of homeopathic remedies. He served the community very acceptably, continuing practice the remainder of his life. One settler mentioned a certain doctor who although not a certified physician had been an orderly to a doctor in the Civil War; having read and picked up some medical training he had some knowledge of medicines and diseases. Many settlers called on him. Certainly there was not a great deal of learning among the profession in frontier days; even the most learned physicians were still bleeding people for fevers.[5] Nothing was known about preventative medicine; the physician relied almost wholly on internal medicine.

In 1862 a certain Dr. William Browner became the physician of Jefferson County, Nebraska. It was said that he used one panacea for all ills whether coughs, colds, mumps, measles, or fevers; namely, "August Flower Bitters."

Even with the ease of entering the profession, practitioners were scarce. In Antelope County, Nebraska, in 1877, when the settlement was eleven years old, there were 1,500 people, two flour mills, two sawmills, six post offices, nine stores, five lawyers, three preachers, and only one doctor.

[5] Doane Robinson, "The Pioneers," South Dakota Historical *Collections*, Vol. XII, p, 143.

The physician sometimes set up practice in a tent and nailed his shingle "Physician and Surgeon" to a nearby tree. Usually he took up a homestead and spent part of his time on it. As the little town grew he took an active part in its development, investing in real estate, promoting the voting of bonds for a railroad, and in other ways boosting the community. His office was frequently in one room of his dwelling and was equipped with a bell of peculiar tone. When the doctor was downtown and a call came, his wife rang the bell. It could be heard all over the settlement.

One of the chief drawbacks to the practice of medicine on the frontier was the long distances to be traveled at all hours of the day or night. The irregular hours, broken rest, and hardships of travel, combined to wear on the physician's health. The humane man who loved his work and desired to help humanity, never refused to answer a call. He rose from a sick bed to minister to the needs of others lest they perish for the lack of care. At the hour of midnight in the winter an imperative knock sounded on his door. Aroused from sleep the physician hastened to harness a team of wild horses and quickly the buggy sped on its errand of mercy. It rolled over the prairie to a lonely cabin twenty or thirty miles away. Often the winding prairie trails grew dim or were entirely obliterated under the swirling snow as the cutting wind blew a gale and the air was filled with icy particles which made the mercury hide in the bulb. Sometimes the doctor accompanied the messenger. Again he was obliged to find the elusive home himself. Arriving at his destination with a few instruments and appliances he was expected to be able to handle the case whether it was fracture, contagious disease, pneumonia, gangrenous infection, gunshot wound, or childbirth. There was no trained nurse in white to prepare the patient or help with the instruments and dressings. If the patient·was passing through a crisis the doctor watched by the bedside during the passing hours. When the battle was a losing one he became clergyman as well as doctor and nurse, and cared for the spiritual needs of his patient as he crossed the great divide from which no man returns.

The doctor's wife literally kept the home fires burning. A lighted lamp in the window was a beacon to the cold and weary physician as he returned to his home late in the night.[6] Perhaps then as he prepared to rest from his long fatiguing trip another knock came, an imperative duty to face the cutting gale on another night ride. A doctor's life was hard then. In some instances a doctor living on his homestead put up a tall pole and hung a lantern on it at night to help him find his way home. Many times the doctor slept only while going to or returning from a professional call. He slept soundly on the back of a pony or in the buggy as the horses found their way home unguided.

In his practice the prairie doctor had no clinical thermometer nor stethoscope. The use of serums, antitoxins, and the taking of blood pressure were unknown.

The pioneer country doctor did his best work in the case of accidents. Accidents were numerous owing to the nature of life on the frontier. Gunshot wounds were almost a daily occurrence. The doctor was called upon to cleanse wounds, amputate limbs, take out bullets and arrows, and in other ways save life in cases of dangerous wounds. Often these operations were performed with crude instruments in crude surroundings. The first amputation in Labette County, Kansas, was performed by means of a bowie knife and carpenter's saw. The patient was soon in good health.

In 1858 Judge W. W. Brookings of Sioux Falls, Dakota Territory, while locating town sites got his feet wet in crossing a swollen stream and froze them severely in a blizzard which followed. For lack of attention mortification set in, and as a last resort his legs were amputated to save his life. Without anesthetics and with no other instruments than a large butcher knife and a small tenon saw, the work was done. The patient, lying on a bed of buffalo robes in a floorless cabin without the comforts of the sick room, survived the

---

[6] James Grassick, "The Pioneer Physician," *Quarterly Journal,* University of North Dakota, Vol. XIII, pp. 244–246.

shock of this harsh surgery, regained his health, and became one of the state's foremost citizens.[7]

At Brule River, Dakota Territory, Thomas Watson was shot through the back in an Indian raid. The point of the arrow, imbedded in the flesh upon the shoulder, was almost through above the collar-bone in front. It could not be drawn back because of the metal point which projected on each side of the shaft. This case called for one of the earliest surgical operations in Dakota. The shaft was cut off close to the man's body and Mr. James Fate removed the point with a razor, a silver penholder and some camphor. He made an incision over the arrow point and pulled it through. The silver penholder was used as a syringe.[8]

Many other crude operations were performed on kitchen tables by coal-oil lamp, on barn doors laid across carpenter's horses, or inverted wagonbeds, and under other strange conditions. One country doctor told of operating for appendicitis on one occasion. He had never seen an operation for this malady but recognized the ailment from having read about it in medical journals. He knew he must operate but had no time to go to town for anesthetics. Without anesthetic he put the patient on the kitchen table and operated while a farm-hand held the kerosene lamp. In the midst of the surgery the farm-hand began to shake so violently he let the lamp chimney fall and break. There was no other and the doctor finished his work by the flickering light of a smoking flame. The man made a quick recovery. The same surgeon operated on a man injured by a threshing machine. He laid the man on the grass on the shady side of the stack and took care of the emergency case.

Doctor Emerson of Winfield, Kansas, was called to operate for an abdominal tumor. The one-roomed house was not sanitary and the doctor improvised a table under a tree by placing wagon sideboards across two barrels. Hunting up an old tea-kettle, he scoured

---

[7] Doane Robinson, *History of South Dakota*, Vol. I, p. 168.

[8] M. B. Kent, "Historical Sketches of Union County, South Dakota," *South Dakota Historical Collections*, Vol. X, p. 516.

it inside and out with sand and water. He boiled water and cloths in the kettle, making all the necessary preparations. One woman gave the chloroform while two others brushed flies away with branches of trees. The patient recovered as quickly as though in a modern hospital with the best of care.

The pioneer surgeon did the best he could with what he had at hand. Sometimes he had to repair to the woodshed or shop to fashion a crude instrument of wire or old iron. It was always necessary to watch not only his own work but the work of his assistants who were usually friends or neighbors of the patient. It was not uncommon for the friend administering the chloroform or for the one holding the lamp to faint. Sometimes these incidents delayed the work so that the patient began to regain consciousness before the operation was completed.

No nurses were to be had in frontier days. When an accident or sickness visited a family the neighbors came in to sit up with the sick. Frequently people lay ill for weeks and the neighbors took turns. It was customary for the lodges to send two members to sit up with a sick comrade. When this became irksome the lodge hired individuals. In time this developed into sick and accident benefits.

Many herbs and home remedies were used for medicinal purposes. Usually a kind of tea was made by boiling the roots of certain shrubs. Wahoo root tea was said to be good for rheumatism; ginger tea was used for chills. Liberal doses of sulphur and molasses were prescribed for the ague and scrofula. Pennyroyal tea was also widely used. Snake root tea was used to make the patient sweat. Polk root, generally thought to be deadly poison, was covered with whiskey which was later taken; this was supposed to be a boon to the rheumatic. Slippery elm was used as a physic.

In the eighties a bolt of lightning struck a man in Turner County, Dakota Territory, badly burning one leg and the side of his body. The nearest doctor, twenty miles away, was called. He applied poultices made of all the sour milk in the neighborhood mixed with clay. The man soon recovered consciousness and lived.

A little girl in Buffalo County, Dakota Territory, had a disease of the bone in her arm.[9] Doctors at that time called it "white swelling." There was no doctor in the county so a young man, a student visiting there, treated it as best he could. Lancing the sores, he put pure carbolic acid in to burn out the proud flesh. Large pieces of the bone worked out. Finally the sores healed up and the child regained her health. Blue vitrol was also inserted in wounds to heal them.

Remedies for snake bite were as numerous as they were peculiar. One plan was to tear a chicken apart while alive and place a piece of the meat on the wound. Another treatment was to pour turpentine over the wound and give enough whiskey to the patient to make him drunk. Taking whiskey was a favorite remedy. It was thought the whiskey neutralized the virus of the snake. Poison ivy was treated by placing the victim in a hog wallow or other mud hole for ten or twelve hours after which the poison was completely gone.

The following advertisement from the Sioux Falls, Dakota Territory, *Democrat* of August 26, 1859, gives some idea of the wide claims for certain patent medicines on the market and no doubt widely used at that time:

J. L. CURTIS' Original Mamaluke Liniment! A sovereign remedy for man and beast. It is confidently recommended to the afflicted as an infallible remedy for the following diseases to-wit: Burns, Cramps, Pains in the Joints, Sore Throat, Frosted Feet, Rheumatism, Erysipelas, Spinal Complaints, Lumbago, Old Sores, Cuts, Bruises, Swellings, Sprains, Pains in the Back or Sides, Headache, Cutaneous Affections, Ague Cake, Bites of Insects, or Reptiles, Salt Rheum, Mange, Cracked Hands, Tetter, Dysentery, Diarrhoea, Cholera Morbus and Cholera.

J. L. CURTIS' Syrup of Sassafras! for Consumption, Bronchitis, Croup or Hives, Colds, Coughs, Asthma, Hoarseness, Difficulty of Breathing, Spitting of Blood, Purifying the Blood, Whooping Cough, etc. To all those who are afflicted with any of the diseases for which this is recommended no difference how trifling it may appear, don't delay, but get a bottle of J. L. Curtis's Compound Syrup of Sassafras, for it is

---

[9] Tuberculosis of the bone.

certain to give more relief in a short time than all the Sarsaparillas and other compounds the stomach could bear. It costs only 25 cents per bottle, and every family should be supplied with it at all times, as by so doing many a dollar and much suffering could be saved to them.

A certain Mr. York in Deuel County, Dakota Territory, in 1875 was away trapping. While he was gone his wife, needing medicine, walked fifteen miles and drew her child in a cart all that distance.

Maternity came often to the sod houses. The children were sent to a neighbor's, the doctor was summoned, and the neighbor women called in.[10] With a doctor from fifty to sixty miles away, the baby often came before he arrived. The neighbor women were always ready and helpful, caring for the mother and child with a degree of skill in the art of mid-wifery. After the baby was born the women frequently had to return home to care for their numerous brood while the husband of the mother had to act as nurse, doctor, washwoman, cook, and friend.

Many sad stories of sickness and death on the prairie make pathetic chapters in the winning of the plains. In 1854 Mr. Augustus Wattles of Lawrence, Kansas, returning home from Fort Riley on a late afternoon in October, saw a settler's cabin with a white cloth fluttering from a pole. Wondering if it was a signal of distress, he drove to the house and found a sad sight. An old man about sixty years of age lay on a bed unable to help himself. He told this story. In the spring he with two sons, aged twenty and twenty-two, had arrived from Maine. The father was a carpenter and ship-builder. It was planned that the young men improve the claims while the older man worked at his trade; but there was no lumber in the country and no settler for whom to build a house, so all three set to work and put in a small acreage of corn. Then one son became ill with the ague; the other went to Fort Riley for medicine at the time when the cholera epidemic was most virulent. Three days after exposure at the fort the son died of cholera. Father and son sorrowfully fashioned a coffin from the boards of their wagon-box

[10] Cass G. Barns, *op. cit.*, pp. 248–250.

and buried him with only the service of their own loving hearts and hands. The following day the second son was stricken and after two days of extreme suffering he also died. The sorrow-stricken father without assistance, dug a grave as best he could, placing boards in the bottom in the form of a coffin, and then carrying the form of his loved son to the brink, he descended into the open grave and lowered the body to its resting place, covered it with a sheet, arranged the boards over it as a cover to the make-shift coffin, and using his little remaining strength laboriously filled the grave; he had barely energy to creep back into the house where he expected to die alone. Mr. Wattles arrived in time to rescue him; the next day he placed the man with his belongings in his wagon and cared for him in his own home throughout the winter. In the spring he took the bereft father to the steamboat landing on the Missouri River and he started his long lonely journey back to the old home. It is not known whether he ever reached there or not.[11]

The pioneer felt that the doctor's fees were excessively high. In 1862 the *Nebraska Farmer* stated that the customary fee was fifty cents a mile for his ride and one dollar a visit in addition to high prices for his medicine and prescription. The *Farmer*, representing the settlers' interests, urged the people to give the professional group *"a tremendous letting down."* The common doctor bill for one trip was from fifteen to twenty-five dollars. It was not unusual for a doctor to lead a colt or calf back to town as payment for his bill. One woman mentioned that they gave the doctor a heifer calf on a thirty-five dollar bill but had nothing with which to pay the balance. Finally she thought of her feather bed and give it to him. No doubt the reason the doctor's fees bore so heavily on the people was because very few of his calls resulted in his receiving anything and hence the ones who could or would pay bore the brunt of the burden.

Early day dentistry was as crude as medicine. It consisted princi-

[11] Mrs. O. E. Morse, "Sketch of the Life and Work of Augustus Wattles," Kansas State Historical Society *Collections*, Vol. XVII, p. 295.

pally of pulling aching teeth. This was usually done by the physician who sometimes pulled the good tooth and left the aching one. One man recalled his painful visit to an early dentist's office in a garret over a store. There was no ceiling nor finishing, simply the rafters and boards overhead, with numerous holes and cracks between the shingles, which made a good place to count the stars when the dentist placed him in a common chair and hung his head over its narrow back. The dental workman placed his instrument around the tooth and pulled with all his might. Suddenly the instrument slipped off and the patient's head which was near the side of the building, flew back and hit the rafter in the slanting roof with a tremendous thump. Again the operator closed in on the stubborn tooth and this time lifted the patient from the chair. The dentist finally called a doctor and the medical man held the patient down while the dentist pulled the tooth. In the sixties in the towns dentists advertised painless extraction of teeth by running a current of electricity through the tooth while it was being extracted. Circuit dentists appeared later staying in each town a few days. One could count on the dentist's being in his town once a month and thus work accumulated over the month. After working in one town he journeyed to the next appointment. The equipment of these itinerant dentists was of necessity meager and their work was done crudely. One man spoke of visiting a man said to be a dentist, who had the patient lie down while the dentist, a big man, sat on him. He procured a pair of forceps and after some pulling and tugging succeeded in extracting the offending tooth. As time went on the more technical work of making false teeth and other replacements was effected.

The eyes were taken care of in a way even more haphazard than the care of the teeth. Peddlers traveled through the country carrying a quantity of spectacles. Those with failing eyesight tried on spectacles until they found a pair which improved their vision and in this crude way selected a piece of merchandise which few people today would think of procuring without examination by a specialist.

CHAPTER XXXI

LAWYERS AND LEGAL PROCEEDINGS

LAWYERS were apparently more numerous on the frontier than members of any other profession and they were more versatile than any other. Lawyers were found doing carpentry work, editing papers, running sawmills, laying out towns, running stores, teaching school, and in various other ways taking an active part in the development of the frontier.

No doubt the very low requirements for entry to the profession accounted for the large number of lawyers. The custom of the time was for a young man to gain a knowledge of the law through apprenticeship. A young man with a desire to become a lawyer, would seek a connection with a practicing attorney and keep office for him. He swept out the office, cleaned the cuspidor, and did the other menial tasks. In the meantime he was supposed to acquaint himself with the meager library of his patron and become familiar with trial procedure, attend court, learn the knack of pleading cases and filling out legal papers. In this way the apprentice in time became acquainted with the leading lights of the profession, and after a few months appeared before the court for admittance to the bar.

Most of the early attorneys on the prairie frontier had received such training in the semi-settled region just east of the border. Minnesota, Iowa, Missouri, Illinois, Wisconsin, Michigan, Indiana, and Ohio, furnished the bulk of them. These half-illiterate men, having practiced law in a state, were readily admitted to its practice in the territories. As soon as possible a new crop of equally indifferent practitioners was admitted to the bar. Apparently the more thriftless and least successful eastern practitioners came West. A successful man with a good practice had all to lose and nothing to gain by emigrating to a point where he would again have to build up a business. The first laws in regard to qualification for the bar required a man to be twenty-one years of age, to give satisfactory evidence of good moral character, and to pass an examination before a judge. Inasmuch as the judge was ordinarily innocent of any close acquaintance with true legal training, the examination was merely perfunctory. Anyone in the adjoining states having a desire to enter law, went into the territories, was admitted to the bar, and returned to his new home ready to aid the courts in the administration of justice.

It is small wonder that John J. Ingalls, fresh from New England with a brand new legal training, wrote to his Massachusetts father that he had gained the reputation of being unsurpassed by any jury advocate in his part of the territory. He modestly attributed his success not so much to personal merit as to want of ability among the general run of practitioners:

I can hardly say whether I am really prospering here or not. Everything depends on the future. Our firm does a large amount of business both in the courts and in the way of tax paying and money loaning and land transactions generally. . . . I suppose our legitimate business [law business alone] will foot up between three and four thousand dollars this year. . . . I . . . think I have the reputation of not being surpassed at least by any jury advocate in Northern Kansas. My success is not so much attributable to superior personal merit as to the want of ability among the practitioners generally. A more ignorant, detestable set of addle-headed numbskulls and blackguards I have seldom met.[1]

The actual process of admission to the bar was as follows: Upon the application of a candidate a lawyer would propose the appointment of a committee to examine the applicant. The judge appointed the committee with himself as chairman. Upon reception of the report, which was usually favorable, the judge made a speech to the

[1] John J. Ingalls, letter to his father, October 7, 1860. Kansas State Historical Society *Collections*, Vol. XIV, p. 119. General Sherman, who had no legal training, was admitted to the bar in Kansas in the late fifties on the strength of his having a fund of general information.

applicant similar to the charge given by the bishop in an ordination service of the church. Among these words of instruction the judge advised the young man to study and conduct himself as becoming one of the profession. The court then adjourned to the nearest saloon to have a drink at the expense of the new lawyer. A North Dakota attorney recalled that he had seen a "class" of business men and farmers arrayed in court to be "sworn in" to practice the profession of the law, many of whose members could not give their oath in correct English, or explain the difference between the statutes and Blackstone's *Commentaries*. The principal object of this, he added, was to avoid jury duty that took a man far from home.[2]

That there were some great lawyers on the frontier there can be no doubt, but they were either the well-trained Easterners who came West to follow Horace Greeley's sage advice or they were men of great native ability who cultivated their talents and became self-made lawyers like Abraham Lincoln.

The first few months or years before the country was well settled were lean ones for the attorney. With few people there was little business. The young lawyer frequently slept in his office to save room rent. One early member of the profession built himself an office of rough green cottonwood lumber. The cracks were unbattened and the building was unplastered. He made a bunk of the cottonwood lumber, furnished it with a mattress of prairie hay, and covered it with blankets brought in his covered wagon, making it up in the daytime in such a way as to give it the appearance of a sofa. If it rained and blew in from one side at night, he moved his bed to the other side until the wind changed. When winter came he filled in the space between the studding with brick, using a kind of alkali clay for mortar. In such a humble way one of the outstanding lawyers and state builders began his practice, turning his hand at anything he could find to do, working at the carpenter's trade, teaching school, and farming. The poverty of the profession was shown

[2] F. W. Ames, "The North Dakota Bar of the Pioneer Days," *Quarterly Journal*, University of North Dakota, Vol. XIII, p. 249.

by the fact that when the lawyers from one town traveled to the county-seat they sometimes carried their food with them to eat during the court session and slept in the hayloft of the livery barn.

With the rush settlement there was much need for legal talent, for the frontiersmen were a boisterous, lawless lot. Fights, brawls, and tragic deaths were frequent. Scores of men were killed in drinking brawls or disputes over land or debts. There were also frequent prosecutions or suits for setting prairie fires.

The first lucrative cases were those dealing with land claims. This was known as land office practice; some of the old preëmption claims needed attention. But the lawyers' greatest prosperity came with the homestead law and particularly in the boom years the lawyers did a "land office" business. These land cases taxed the lawyers so that they had all they could do to care for them. A North Dakota member of the bar said he had "known the work of some officers to yield from $300 to $1,200 a month the year around." [3] This kind of practice required no legal skill but consisted merely in helping claimants prove up and in settling claim disputes. There were "contests," and claims of one homesteader against another as to whether the law had been complied with. These cases were tried before the Register and Receiver of the United States Land Office and were decided by him. Reverse decisions were appealed to the United States Commissioner at Washington, in which case the lawyer made out the brief and sent it to Washington. A large number were appealed.

In connection with this public land business there was a branch of practice known as professional claim-jumping. In this business a claim-jumper watched for any delinquency on the part of the settler, and for a given sum pointed out the opportunities to "contest" or "jump" a claim. This business developed a higher class of service than the ordinary land office practice. A claim-jumper was, of course, very unpopular with the homesteaders. [4]

[3] Ibid., p. 250.
[4] Ibid.

The lawyer's close connection with the consummation of the settler's homestead right, placed him in an admirable position to act as a loan broker. The counsellor was usually able to secure money from a friend or business connection in the East. As a rule the legal man charged his client ten per cent commission for securing the loan and added it to the expense of proof. In the end the lawyer posing as a friend had exploited the farmer and added to his burden for some time to come. This, no doubt, explains the intense antagonism of the rural dweller toward the learned counsellor at law.

The land office lawyer, having covered his territory briefly but prosperously, passed quickly to the next frontier. After a few such experiences he was ready to start a bank or embark on some other capitalistic enterprise. Some settled down to the humdrum practice of the frontier in post-land-office days. There was still sufficient litigation. This seems to have shaped itself largely around the business of collecting debts. One paper of 1873 remarked: "In view of the fact that the custom of putting everything in the 'wife's' name has become so common we think it would be well to let the wife do all the business, and then we would know who the responsible persons are."

In the fifties before government had been organized and legal procedure had been definitely established, it was customary to collect in a rather summary fashion. The creditor and one or two of his friends would meet the debtor and make a final demand. If the money was not produced, they would take the unpaid-for article back to the shop of the creditor. The debtor, out-numbered and out-armed, had to yield. Disputed accounts were left to referees. Although much business was done on credit, obligations were met promptly. Sam Wood, a lawyer of Lawrence, Kansas, was once employed by a widow to collect a debt of twenty-five dollars which she had loaned to a certain man. Mr. Wood waited until he knew that the man had the money on his person and then demanded it when he met the debtor on the street in the midst of a crowd. The man, after pretending not to have the money, finally became bellicose and said, "Sam Wood, if you get that money before I get ready to pay it, just let me know." Immediately the lawyer had the fellow down on the ground, reached into his pocket, secured his wallet, and handed it over to a spectator to count out twenty-five dollars. The wallet with the remainder of its contents was returned to the owner. Such direct action, while effective, sometimes caused disputes and bloodshed which were later taken up in the courts and dragged through months and years of litigation. Criminal lawyers then began to develop in the larger centers and on occasion were called to the remote regions to carry on their work.

Another common type of work which developed after the homesteader acquired title to his land, was the mortgage case. Farmers mortgaged their farms in order to improve them, to buy stock, or after an adverse year, to buy seed. Later they bought quantities of machinery.

In the days of the virgin prairie, court week or court days loomed large on the calendar of the little county-seat, competing with fair or circus days for local interest. People came in from miles around to see the show and hear the lawyers plead their cases. It was indeed a great spectacle for all except those who had to pay the fiddler. After the case had been settled in court the whole trial was gone over around the glowing stoves of the country stores, hotels, and rural school-houses. To a society suffering from a lack of entertainment, court days were beautiful isles in an uninviting ocean. These seasons brought a pleasant interruption to the dull prosaic prairie life. They brought trade to the merchants, and they brought news to the local paper.

In the early days there were no court-houses and the first sessions were held in various queer and unusual places. Frequently court was held in school-houses, sometimes in stores or saloons, occasionally in homes, and in some instances it was called in the open under the shade of a tree. On one occasion a justice of the peace in traveling across the prairie with one litigant, met the second, court was called, and the justice proceeded to adjust matters. Judgment was rendered there on the open prairie. At another time court was held in a hotel. The floor for this occasion was covered with sawdust to a depth of six inches, doubtless to accommodate the inveterate tobacco chewers.

The sheriff, like other professional men of his time, knew little about his chosen profession. He was butcher, auctioneer, barber, farmer, or other plain citizen by calling, knew little about detective work, and on the whole was very inefficient.[5] Only the more resolute and fearless sought such a dangerous office, and hence oftentimes certain counties had sheriffs well-endowed by nature, if not by training, to perform this hazardous work. Such an individual was cool, brave, and tireless in his search for criminals. He went after his man no matter how desperate he was, nor how great the obstacles. He broke up gangs or drove them out of the country, reducing crime to a retail status at most.

There were many quarrels with a quick appeal to guns or knives. Horace Greeley reported an instance in Kansas in 1859 in which a party of gold seekers returning to the East, claimed that the ferryman was trying to charge them an outrageous price. Perhaps they did not have the money. A quarrel ensued and the party fought it out with the ferryman. The latter was killed but not until he had killed or wounded five of his assailants.

Other occasions for bloodshed were drunken revels, boundary disputes, disputes over the ownership of land or chattels, counterfeiting, thievery, and occupational disputes over the control of the public domain. In the latter instance the cattleman tried to keep the homesteader from appropriating the public domain and thus depriving him of his range.

One scheme at Fairfield, Nebraska, a little more original than the ordinary run of crimes, was that of forging or faking abstracts. The leaders were Brown, Drumm, and Reid. Their scheme was worked in this fashion: Brown would select a piece of land to which he had no claim whatever, and deed it to Reid. He, in turn would convey

[5] The same inefficient system exists to this day, a frontier trait not outgrown.

it to a henchman, and so on. After a number of transfers it was deeded to Drumm and he went East with the bogus title to sell the land for whatever he could get. He acted as the selling agent and traveled on counterfeit money made by the gang.

Another type of thievery caused many amusing prosecutions of the early homesteaders for taking timber from the railroad and the speculators' lands. In one instance it was taken, so they said, "for fear it would be stolen." As a rule it was impossible to convict the perpetrator because of the unwritten law among the settlers that timber on the land of non-residents really should belong to the homesteaders who were braving dangers and suffering hardships to build up the country to the profit of the speculators.

Many of the members of the frontier bar were as eccentric and picturesque as the circuit riders, their contemporaries in the church. A large wardrobe of the latest fashions was not necessary to success. In fact such an outlay would have had the opposite effect. Even the judge was frequently indifferent to what would be considered good taste in dress in a more civilized country. It was said of a certain Judge Allen A. Bradford that, "He was a large bodied man, and always wore a dirty coat; large headed and never knew a shirt collar; large hearted, he had not learned the value or uses of shoe strings." One of the most prominent lawyers, and a former mayor of Omaha, wore a red flannel shirt. One striking character by the name of T. M. Marquett was described as having long hair and beard, wearing coarse shoes, frayed and worn, but when he was arguing a legal question, the spectator forgot his crude dress and mannerisms.

The border lawyer did not like hair-splitting arguments, nor quotations from authorities of ancient vintage, nor citations from outstanding decisions. He liked horse-sense, eloquent speech, and strong, if crude, rhetoric. The judge likewise disliked fog-raising disputations which would cloud the issue and drag out the case. He knew very little law but preferred to do business on the basis of equity. Here again direct action came into play.

A trial over a speak-easy or "hole in the wall" was being conducted. The first witness, a prosperous farmer, swore he had been served drinks at the place but did not know what he was drinking. No amount of questioning could bring him to admit that he had bought and drunk either beer or whiskey. At that stage of the game the judge broke in with the exclamation: "Mr. Sheriff, take that witness to jail and keep him on bread and water till his memory gets better." This seemed to have a wonderfully exhilarating effect on the witness whose mental powers visibly improved till in a short time he swore positively as to the nature of the drink furnished him by the defendant.[6]

Judge Miller of the probate court of Douglas County, Kansas, was at one time trying a case in a replevin suit for a calf worth $3.75. The trial dragged out until on the afternoon of the third day the judge, growing weary, brought the proceedings to an abrupt close with the announcement that he would pay for the calf himself.

Little formality was evidenced at a frontier court session. Occasionally during a heated argument two attorneys resorted to fisticuffs. At other times a lawyer and a judge or two lawyers became so anxious to settle some difference that court was adjourned while they went out to reach a decision in a rough and tumble fight. When the court got dry, the judge adjourned that august body while everybody went across the street or to a nearby saloon to drink and talk a while. Lawyers drank heavily and sometimes a judge or lawyer when drunk was more dignified than when sober.

Citizens did not always know correct court usage. One jury of a criminal case, having been given full and elaborate instructions from the court, and after having deliberated for a period of several hours, returned to inquire whether the prisoner had plead guilty or not. When set right on this important question they soon handed down a verdict of acquittal. At another time a jury was out at the close of the day. The sheriff was instructed to notify the judge when the jury had agreed. Later in the evening the judge in his room

[6] Cass G. Barns, *The Sod House*, p. 148.

at the hotel heard the resounding tramp of feet on the stairway leading to his room. On coming out he was met by the sheriff bringing the twelve men, good and true, to render the verdict there in the hotel. The judge ordered a counter-march and the verdict was read in the court room with due formality.

It was well-nigh impossible to convict a prisoner of a misdemeanor no matter what the law, if public opinion was against the law. It was particularly hard to secure convictions in liquor cases although the people all knew that the saloon-keeper was violating regulatory laws.

The frontier bar worked hard. They furnished their own transportation and the judges rode over their immense districts at their own expense. Justice was crude and summary but there were few complaints of delay, and the costs were low. One judge in 1868 left home on Sunday evening, drove his team eighty miles and held court on Monday during which he sent two men to the penitentiary with the aid of a grand jury and trial jury. He also cleared the docket of twenty-seven civil cases and reached home at Tuesday noon. The bar worked twelve hours a day then.

CHAPTER XXXII

TURBULENT DAYS IN COUNTY AFFAIRS

IT WAS only natural that the founders of a town were anxious to secure any advantage that might be had to guarantee the growth and development of the child of their labor. Among the things which would assure the permanent existence and growth of a town was the possession of the seat of the state or county government. At first the desire for this plum was prompted by economic motives. Those who owned real estate expected to profit. As the struggle dragged on over a period of months and years a second lesser motive appeared. Towns in the rival communities swelled with local patriotism and pride of achievement until their citizens felt the air was purer, the soil more fertile, the natural advantages in every way more desirable, than in the neighboring vicinity. When this spirit overcame two rival communities, nothing could be done until one or the other had triumphed.

In the vast majority of counties in Kansas, Nebraska, and the Dakotas, these county-seat quarrels occurred. Many of these disputes were harmlessly settled at the ballot box. Others became the occasion of interminable quarrels, bloodshed, and the loss of life. In some instances whole communities were pitted against each other in civil strife.

The earliest counties were organized when there were very few settlers. One old settler remarked that "the conditions were ideal for the organization of a county, inasmuch as there was an office for every man." In Cuming County, Nebraska, at an election in 1858 the two contestants were West Point and Dewitt. West Point received twelve votes and Dewitt seven, making a total of nineteen votes in all. Many of these counties were organized by a handful of settlers in a dugout, or in a little shack,[1] and the place decided upon for a county-seat was little more than a spot on the prairie. Nebraska Center when named as the county-seat of Buffalo County consisted of but one dwelling, one store building, and one warehouse. In Harlan County, Nebraska, three little towns competed for the county-seat. One writer said of them: "Republican City and Melrose each had a store, hitching post, and a clothes line, while Alma had only her buffalo skull."[2] At first the home of the county officers was designated as the county-seat, or the various county officials each had their offices in their homes. In other places the records were carried from place to place and business was done at certain towns or other convenient centers—a kind of itinerating county headquarters.[3]

In what is now Neosho County, Kansas, the county attorney held his office at New Chicago,[4] the county superintendent of public instruction was to be found on his farm in East Lincoln; the probate judge was located on his farm on Big Creek. The probate judge attended his alleged office one day a week—Saturday. If he was wanted in the meantime it was necessary to hire a livery rig and hunt him up. One arrangement, however, which facilitated matters, indicated the irregularity with which business was carried on. The judge kept a number of signed marriage license blanks and some lawyer or store-keeper was verbally authorized to fill in the necessary details if a couple applied.[5] Furthermore, specialization had not reached its later development and oftentimes a man with good sense and an ordinary amount of talent, functioned in several capacities. Record is left of a man who served as county judge, holding court at the noon hour; he

---

[1] The election for the organization of Nuckolls County, Nebraska, was held under a large elm tree on June 27, 1871.

[2] A. T. Andreas, *History of the State of Nebraska*, Vol. II, p. 961.

[3] In Jefferson County, Nebraska, the county business was done at two different towns and at the homes of the county officers. The county records were carried around in gunny sacks.

[4] Now Chanute, Kansas.

[5] Judge Leander Stillwell, "Address upon the Opening of the Neosho County Courthouse," Kansas State Historical Society *Collections*, Vol. XIV, pp. 184–185.

taught school during the day, and in the evening worked on his farm.

It was inconvenient and inefficient for the local officers to be scattered here and there over the county because they could not attend to business properly. On one occasion in Neosho County, Kansas, a lawyer wanted to prevent a horse thief from being extradited and went to see the judge several miles away. He met the judge on his way home from another town and persuaded him to sign a writ of habeas corpus. The judge told the lawyer to go to his office, get the official seal and make the paper legal. This shiftlessness which saved the thief's life and miscarried justice was the result of the irregularity and informality with which business was attended at that time.[6]

In the early years of organized county government the revenue from taxes was very small and the salary paid to officials was likewise meager. In Adams County, Nebraska, the county clerk's salary was three hundred dollars a year, and the probate judge received seventy-five dollars a year. The first court-house in that county was a log structure sixteen by twenty feet, with a shingle roof, four windows and one door, a floor, and ceiling of building paper. According to the contract all the material except the door and windows was to be furnished by the county; the contract was let for the work for thirty dollars; the building was to be ready for occupancy in ten days.[7]

Speculators tried many ways to secure the county-seat for their town. Frequently a man would offer a tract of land with the provision that the county-seat be built on the tract. In Fillmore County, Nebraska, a man offered to build a court-house at the

[6] In Polk County, Nebraska, the county offices were conducted in the homes of the officers. The county clerk bought a safe. It was too big to go through the door of his log house so it was set outside the door next to the wall where it served its purpose for two years.

[7] In Holt County, Nebraska, in 1878 the county funds were kept in a receptacle hollowed out of a cottonwood board in the sheeting of a shingle roof dwelling house. This was the only safe vault and bank in the county. *Nebraska History and Record of Pioneer Days,* Vol. I, No. 7, p. 4.

cost of $2,500. Another man actually built a large hall on his land and offered it for a court-house if the county-seat were located there. The profits which accrued from securing the location of a county-seat were immense. A section of land at the government price was usually eight hundred dollars. Counting eight lots to the acre there were 5,120 lots in the town. One hundred dollars a lot was a reasonable estimate of the selling price in the East. If all went well, the founders secured over a half million dollars for a staked area on the prairie which at most did not cost over three or four thousand dollars. Since the expected profits were so great there was a temptation to risk a considerable sum in order to secure the seat of government and guarantee the sale of the lots. Some men went so far as to buy a large portion of the lots in two or even three rival towns, knowing that should any one of them secure the prize their investment would pay well.

County-seat wars differed, but there were certain characteristics common to all. Both towns in the contest exhibited a complete lack of honor, a disdain for truth, a disregard for common honesty, and a willingness to stoop to any corrupt practice. One factor which abetted this graft and pollution was the loose way of conducting elections. Formalities were waived and elections were conducted with little or no regard to the propriety of the occasion. These elections were frequently held in the shade of trees or in the dugouts of settlers. Elections were frequent and heated. Fist fights, mob violence, and even bloodshed, accompanied some of them. Minors were habitually allowed to vote.

At the first election in Thayer County, Nebraska, in 1876, sixteen ballots were cast. The voters were supposed to register before voting, but this rule was waived; the voters registered when they arrived and then cast their votes. The polls were closed when the officials thought everybody had voted.

Erastus Beadle gave a vivid picture of the first election in a precinct near Omaha, Nebraska:

Our German neighbor and his man came along about eight o'clock when we armed ourselves with our revolvers and bowie knives and taking the trail in Indian file started for the polls. The Judges of the election had not arrived. we here first learned we were entitled to two constables and two justices. . . . About half past nine the judges arrived and one notary public to swear them in. Two McArdles and a McQuin were the judges one of them could not write his name had to make his mark in signing his affidavit. The notary public and the old man McArtle were appointed clerks of Election one of this number had to have a deputy to write for him and still he had to keep the poll list. The Ballot Box was an old sugar box imported from Omaha for the occasion. it was tied together with a string and a hole cut in the top with a table knife while the judges were at breakfast. . . . At last the voters were sent out doors and the breakfast dishes and all was shoved up to the door and I had the great honor of casting the first vote that was ever cast in the pappillion district. . . .

The first election in Franklin County, Nebraska, was held near a settler's dugout under a large cottonwood tree. The ballot box was a cigar box. There were two factions, and when the voting was over, the judge took the ballot box under his arm and went into the brush to count the votes.

There were a few outstanding issues which caused great excitement and corruption. In the early days the question of slavery caused much fraud, trickery, and bloodshed in Kansas. The location of a county-seat, the voting of bonds for a railroad or other enterprise, or a vote on prohibition in certain communities, were all productive of great excitement. Otherwise the political activities of a frontier community were quite calm and composed. The occasion of the first election in Jefferson County, Nebraska, was made into a gala affair. Indeed it was more like a picnic than an election. Contests in wrestling, foot racing, horsemanship, and marksmanship, were arranged. Speech making added to the day's activities. After several days the proposition to organize the county was declared unanimously carried with a total of seventy-five votes cast although it was alleged that there were not over forty actual settlers in the county. This overflow was due to the voting of stage drivers, freighters, and others who arrived a day or two later and were allowed to vote.[8]

Mr. John Turner of Boone County, Nebraska, also testified to the general nature of the elections in the seventies. He observed that one or two men strolled in, voted, and sat down to regale the crowd with stories of their prowess and exploits in the early days. At noon, with little ceremony, the judges and the others adjourned to eat. One man sat on a backless chair, one on a wood box, one on the stove, and still another lay sprawled on the floor. The poll box was located on a dry goods box. The backless chair was a great luxury on this occasion. In some places saloons were closed on election days, but in spite of this precaution some of the citizens became hilarious by sundown.

When an election on a vital issue was held, all the devices of the Irish ward heelers were brought into play. At Milford, Nebraska, in 1872, the question of voting bonds to aid the Midland Pacific Railroad arose. Milford and Seward were strong rivals. Owing to the rains, the rivers and creeks were at flood tide at election time, and the two cities put forth every effort to get the voting population across the turbulent waters. At Seward the people turned out en masse and built boats, rafts, and other craft to carry voters over the river and creeks to the polls. The people at Milford afterward laughed at them, saying they had only a few planks for a raft at one place and a couple of sorghum pans at another; yet they won the election. A man in the saddle carried messages to settlers and urged out the voters. Men had their teams out taking voters to the polls. At dawn the next day a cannon at Milford boomed out the joyful news of the defeat of the bonds. The townsmen got out their anvils and celebrated.[9]

Various unfair schemes for carrying an election were used.

---

[8] Charles Dawson, *Fairbury News*, March 14, 1912.
[9] Blacksmith's anvils were loaded with powder and fired. The report made a terrific noise.

Stuffing the ballot box, that is, one man casting a large number of votes while the judge was not looking or through the connivance of the judges with one faction or the other, was a common practice. Certain persons known as "repeaters" cast ballots a dozen or more times for different men who were not at home on election day. Other men known as "manipulators" so manipulated the votes of a certain precinct as to get the number necessary for their purpose. This was the epoch before the Australian ballot; more or less bogus tickets circulated at every election. Sometimes tickets containing double negatives were secretly circulated in a precinct bitterly opposed to bonds or the removal of a county-seat. These, of course, were rejected; sometimes a few votes turned the tide for or against a certain project. Frequently the ballot box was spirited away or the tally sheet stolen. In that case the votes of the precinct were thrown out. In a bitter county-seat contest, oftentimes the two factions stationed men at each other's polls to insure fairness. Under these circumstances votes were commonly bought and sold.

In Gray County, Kansas, in the seventies there existed in Ford precinct a secret organization called the Equalization Society, composed of seventy-two members whose sole object, as shown by their constitution and by-laws, was to sell their votes in a solid block to the aspiring county-seat which would pay the most for the votes. The money derived from the sale was to be divided equally among the members who were bound by oath to vote solidly for the town to which the sale was made. The punishment for the violation of this oath was death. According to the record, T. H. Reeves, a leading Cimarron manager, made a bargain just before the election with the Equalization Society; it was to receive $10,000 for its vote for Cimarron as the county-seat. In order to make the contract binding fifteen outstanding citizens of the aspiring county-seat gave a bond binding themselves to the payment of the ten thousand dollars. The organization duly cast its seventy-two votes and sent a committee to Cimarron to collect the money. They were told they should get nothing; the town had the votes and the bond was a forgery.[10]

For the purpose of nominating party candidates and organizing the local political machines, caucuses were held. At these meetings in school-houses or the humble dwellings of the settlers, each candidate passed a box of cigars around. The meeting was barely started before the air became so blue that one could scarcely recognize his neighbor. It was necessary to raise the windows and let the smoke out before doing business. Candidates jumped up on the platform or desk and talked loudly. They were bound to have admirers whether they had any real message or not. The demagogue found a full supply of agrarian grievances for an effective text for his oratorical powers.

So bitter did county-seat struggles become that they not only broke up neighborhoods but divided churches and plunged families into strife. If one of the many corrupt and bloody county-seat contests must be taken by way of illustration, the choice of Howard County,[11] Kansas, is ideal. Three towns tried for the county-seat. Perhaps the most promising aspirant was Boston, a little hamlet of a half dozen store buildings and not a tree on the town site. By means of a bonus the little town had induced a rather disreputable newspaper man to establish a paper. The town, it was subsequently learned, was located on an extremely dry spot. Two wells each eighty feet in depth were dug, both of which were as dry as powder. Drilled wells put down here and there were equally arid. A small spring nearby, a branch some distance away, and rain barrels set under the eaves to catch the rain water furnished the supply for the young metropolis. The public well in the center of the town was kept supplied by volunteer water haulers who, like rogues, clandestinely hauled the water from the branch under cover of night. This was kept secret lest the rival

[10] T. A. McNeal, *When Kansas Was Young*, pp. 182, 183.
[11] Howard County was divided into two counties, Chautauqua and Elk, in January, 1875.

towns benefit by the knowledge. All the propaganda and publicity proclaimed Boston a well-watered city.

The other two contestants were Peru and Elk Falls. At the first election held early in 1872, Peru won the decision. Petitions for a new election were circulated. At the second election the returns were clearly so fraudulent at all points that the board refused to canvass the result. After a number of spirited elections the contest was only between Elk Falls and Boston. At the final election Boston won, and when the result was announced, the whole county flocked in to Boston to celebrate. After a huge dance and supper, the morning found the town without a drop of anything to drink.

But alas there is many a slip 'twixt cup and lip, and Boston was not destined to win so easily. Elk Falls went into the courts and secured an injunction forbidding the transfer of the county records. The county clerk had moved his office to Boston the night the votes were counted and that office functioned there for several months. It soon became apparent that Elk Falls would not surrender the county-seat. The district judge was known to own lots in Elk Falls. Boston attempted to give him town lots to secure an unprejudiced decision. The judge, however, was different from some others of that day and refused to accept bribes from both sides.

Boston grew impatient and desperate. Collecting her adherents from the surrounding country one morning in the winter of 1874, one hundred and fifty heavily-armed men made a raid on Elk Falls. In less than a half hour they had all the county records and property except the treasurer's iron safe loaded in wagons and moving over the prairie toward Boston. The sheriff organized a posse and demanded the immediate return of the records and the surrender of the perpetrators of the theft. The town laughed at them and warned the posse to stay at a safe distance from the new court-house, for a large number of Bostonians were just itching to shoot their arch enemies. For many days and nights a state of war existed. The county property was guarded constantly by grim gunmen. It was soon seen that Boston had injured her cause by taking things into her own hands. The records were again loaded into wagons and spirited away into another county where they remained hidden pending the arrangement of final settlement. A number of the leading citizens of Boston were arrested and kept under guard by a sheriff's posse but this availed nothing.

Eventually an agreement was reached with Elk Falls whereby her citizens were to coöperate with those of Boston in securing a decision of the courts on the legality of the elections; the records were to be returned, and the prisoners released. The case, arranged by the contracting parties, awaited the action of the supreme court and the citizens sat down to count the cost. During the months of the war the business of the county had suffered severely. Half the taxes had been collected and the county treasurer seized this favorable opportunity to embezzle the county's money and leave. In the fall of 1874 the citizens, tired of the interminable wrangle, voted to divide into two new counties. This was done and neither of the competitors was successful in securing a county-seat. In a few years there was not a house on the site of Boston and the population of Elk Falls in 1930 was only 255.[12]

In Spink County, Dakota Territory, a war raged intermittently for some years. Old Ashton was the county-seat and when the railroad missed it, a campaign was waged to change the seat of government. In the first election four towns were rivals for the honor: Old Ashton, Frankfort, Redfield, and New Ashton. None was able to secure the necessary two-thirds vote required by law. In the autumn of 1884 twenty leading men of Redfield, among them a banker, a preacher, some lawyers and some other business men, united in the strictest secrecy to invade Old Ashton some dark night, seize the records, and take them to Redfield. According to the Ashton version the returns of the election had been altered to

[12] Thomas E. Thompson, "Early Days in Old Boston," Kansas State Historical Society *Collections*, Vol. XVI, pp. 479-487, *passim*.

show that Redfield had really won. With shovels, picks, crowbars, and a few guns, the attacking party, for the most part masked, took possession of the safe and records, loaded them in drays, and took them to Redfield. The raid was made on Saturday night and the preacher filled his appointment as usual Sunday morning.

The plundering expedition caused great indignation in the other towns contending for the county-seat. Three hundred armed men under command of the sheriff marched to attack Redfield. The Redfield forces parleyed and held their enemies at bay without actual bloodshed. Meanwhile the defenders sent a telegram to the governor for a company of militia and also sent two men to Milbank where the territorial court was in session, to apply for an injunction against the record retrievers. They chartered a locomotive to carry the messengers at fifty miles an hour from Redfield to Watertown and then there followed a forty mile midnight ride across the prairie to Milbank. Returning with a temporary writ from the judge, the sheriff was properly impressed and withdrew his forces. In the meantime a militia company from Fargo arrived to maintain order. When the case came into the courts a permanent injunction was denied and Redfield was humiliated. The preacher was tried but the case was dismissed.

Redfield then took a new tack. She pushed a bill through the legislature providing for the relocation of county-seats by a majority vote and proceeded to build a splendid court-house which she donated to the county. In the spirited campaign, Redfield was declared the winner by forty-five votes. When the little county jail was loaded on a moving truck and hauled to Redfield, the fighting preacher rode astride the peak of the roof entering the new county-seat in triumph.[13]

The struggle for the county-seat in Hamilton County, Kansas, is fairly representative of another type of county-seat quarrel. The original seat of government was Kendall by virtue of a proclamation of the governor. Although the first continued to exist, a

[13] Edwin C. Torrey, *Early Days in Dakota* (Minneapolis, 1925), p. 149.

second county-seat was established at Syracuse by a fraudulent election at which the remarkable miracle of polling 1,178 votes was executed by a little village of less than five hundred inhabitants. Another election located the county-seat at Coolidge, but, like the popes of the Great Schism in the Church,[14] the two existing county-seats continued to function. The three towns, Syracuse, Kendall, and Coolidge, became prosperous, but lived under the blighting curse of a county-seat struggle. For some years the people lived under a triple government, one located at Syracuse, another at Kendall, and a partial one at Coolidge at different intervals. Some of the records were kept in each town. There was a county treasurer at Syracuse, one at Coolidge, and a deputy at Kendall. There were two probate judges "marrying and giving in marriage." This chaotic condition increased the indebtedness by leaps and bounds and produced a ruinous state of affairs destructive to business and an obstacle to progress.[15]

In Gray County, Kansas, occurred the last of the really bloody county-seat wars of western Kansas. Three towns, Ingalls, Cimarron, and Montezuma, were striving for the county-seat. A. T. Soule, a millionaire of New York, became interested in Ingalls and attempted to make that very small new town the county-seat. He thought to turn the tide by means of his great wealth. During the campaign prior to the election, his agents were prodigal in the use of his funds for corruption. Soule's checks for $100, $500, and

[14] The Great Schism in the Catholic church, lasting from 1378 to 1415, came about as the result of an attempt to displace Pope Urban VI by another pope. Urban refused to be displaced and as a result two popes held office for a number of years. Finally a general council was assembled and the two popes were deposed and a third elected. Instead of solving the problem, this only magnified it for the two refused to be displaced and the third continued to reign. Thus, the church was divided against itself in a triple schism. Three different popes, each claiming to be the genuine and only representative of Christ on earth, stoutly maintained their official prerogative. Each pope appointed bishops and inferior officers. Each group of appointees declared the other false. Sincere Christians all over Christendom were at a loss to know which officers they should employ to perform their sacred rites. Thus all Europe was divided into three camps, each supporting a different pope.

[15] J. S. Painter, "Southwest Kansas," *Transactions*, Kansas State Historical Society, Vol. IV, pp. 281–282; H. N. Lester, "Colonization of the Upper Arkansas Valley in Kansas," *Ibid.*, p. 264.

other sums were freely dispersed throughout the county. He proposed to build a railroad to Montezuma and persuaded that town to withdraw as a contestant. He and his agents imported to the county a crowd of "toughs" for the election. A dramatic incident in the struggle occurred in January, 1889, when a wagon with ten or twelve armed men concealed in the bottom of the wagonbed, drove from Ingalls into Cimarron, halted at the court-house, and made the clerk hold up his hands while they took possession of the county records. The news of their visit spread and a battle soon followed. The streets were spattered with blood as several were killed and wounded. In the meantime the county records were safely hustled out of town. Three or four of the Ingalls invaders were captured by the Cimarron men. The sheriff into whose custody they were given, was an Ingalls partisan and immediately released the captives. A company of militia was hurried to the scene, order was restored, and the curtain was lowered on this final bloody scene in the history of Kansas county-seat struggles.[16]

In Buffalo County, Nebraska, the county records at Gibbon were loaded into a farm wagon at night and moved to Kearney where they arrived at two in the morning; the county-seat was spirited away.

In McPherson County, Kansas, there was a struggle between McPherson and Lindsborg. In the election McPherson received a majority of the votes, but Lindsborg hated to submit to her enemy and kept some of the records. A group of McPherson men went over to Lindsborg and asked the men guarding the papers to step out and talk it over. While they were talking a McPherson man put the papers into a spring wagon and drove off before the act was discovered.

In Sully County, Dakota Territory, the first commissioners located the temporary county-seat at Clifton in 1883. A six-ton safe was procured and a little shack was built over it in such a

<hr/>

[16] T. A. McNeal, *op. cit.*, pp. 182–185.

way that the back part of the safe was part of the court-house wall. In reality, so far as records were concerned, the safe was the court-house and the shack was a place for the county officers to sit. Everything was stowed in the safe each night. In 1884 at an election held to determine the permanent county-seat, Onida, Clifton, and Fairbank contested for the honor. Each town imported voters and used other illegal means to secure the decision. According to the ballots Onida won. In view of the probability of corruption in the election the contest was carried to the territorial court and the judge issued an order declaring Onida the permanent county-seat. Upon receipt of this, the Onida men, armed with the order, proceeded in force to Clifton and, rolling the safe upon a heavy wagon, hauled it to Onida. Soon the Clifton men obtained a court order annulling the first one and they proceeded to load the safe on a wagon once more and restore it to its original location. Onida, undaunted, got a third order annulling the second and once more the safe was rolled back to Onida. On arrival they took the wheels off the safe and hid them so the safe could not be moved without a derrick. The wheels lay hidden for three or four years and, the excitement and contention having died down, the county-seat remained at Onida permanently.[17]

Such internecine turmoil as this led the *New York Tribune* to burst out:

The news that another county-seat war has broken out in Kansas has found its way to New York by telegraph. Kansas is again in the saddle. Once more a four-mule team is attached to one of the court houses and it is going across the prairie on a fast trot.

The existence of the western Kansas court house is at best transitory and uncertain. The golden morning sunlight floods it in Pottawatomie City, but its lengthening evening shadow falls across the streets of Little Paradise Valley. One day the stray swine of Occidental City seek its hospitable shade, the next some predatory calf in Big Stranger bunts open the back door and eats a deed and two mortgages while the register is

[17] S. A. Travis, personal interview, July 10, 1935.

taking a nap. Today we mark it in Grand Junction with a new front door painted yellow, and the gable end blown off by the last tornado, but tonight a band of determined men will come from Rattle Snake Crossing and haul it away with a yoke of oxen, with the mayor and city council of Rattle Snake pushing on the end of the court house. The Kansas court house is the "Wandering Jew" among public institutions.[18]

Strategy as well as brute force was used in these struggles. In Allen County, Kansas, a mortal struggle ensued between Humboldt and Iola for the seat of government. Humboldt was located nearer the south edge of the county than was Iola. An astute doctor and politician of Iola, who was a member of the legislature, promoted a harmless looking bill giving the next county to the south a six-mile strip of territory and then dividing that county into two new counties. This cut Humboldt's throat effectually by drawing the line in such a manner that a large part of Humboldt's supporters were thrown into the next county, giving the majority to the newer town of Iola.[19]

Although in most cases a county-seat dispute was merely a selfish quarrel for personal gain, in some instances these contests were justifiable. For example, the first county-seats were located along the rivers and oftentimes the rivers formed the county boundaries. It was therefore natural for the later settlers to wish the seat of government moved to a central location. At other times the population of certain districts decreased and the court-house naturally followed the shift of population.

In Ramsey County, Dakota Territory, this literally occurred. The county-seat was originally located at Devil's Lake. A substantial frame court-house was erected and the town flourished. Several stores, dwellings, and a hotel sprang up but the railroad passed through Creel City which developed rapidly at the expense of the older town; business gradually drifted to the new location. Finally the county-seat was moved to the new town and the

18 T. A. McNeal, *op. cit.*, p. 186.
19 A similar scheme was attempted in Faulk County, Dakota Territory.

court-house was cut in two and hauled over on wheels.[20] The name of the new town was changed to Devil's Lake.

As a rule the county-seat war was futile. The fact that it was a county-seat did not make a town. The advantages derived did not compensate for the lives lost, the bitterness engendered, the property destroyed, and the expense involved. For many years one county-seat in southwestern Kansas had only fifteen inhabitants. Two others did not have more than seventy-five each and the best block in town would not have brought enough at auction to pay for the funeral expenses of the men whose lives were sacrificed in the early bitter struggles.[21]

In some cases the pioneer, swept on by an unbounded enthusiasm, carried the organization of counties beyond the populated area. Kearney County, Nebraska, including several of the present counties south of the Platte in the vicinity of Fort Kearney, was organized January 10, 1860. In 1860 one hundred and eleven votes were cast, in 1864 only sixty-one, and in 1865 only sixteen. In 1866 the organization was allowed to lapse; it was reorganized in 1872. The coming of the Union Pacific Railway attracted the settlers across the river to that artery of transportation. Buffalo County, in the same state, apparently was organized about 1855 or 1856. It was inhabited by a migratory class of citizens; the land was unsurveyed and was not opened for settlement. If these migratory persons held office, they kept no records of administration. The county became disorganized in 1867 apparently because all the county officials moved on west into Wyoming taking all record of the county government. The county was reorganized in 1870.

In Kansas, Wallace County was organized in 1868, but most of the settlers who lived there in 1868 had abandoned the county and

[20] In Box Butte County, Nebraska, the court-house was located at Nonpariel. When the railroad missed it the county-seat was moved to Hemingsford. Owing to drought and hard times the latter town declined and a third contestant, Alliance, a railroad town, stepped in and took the prize. The court-house, a two-story building weighing twenty tons, was placed on railroad trucks and moved twenty miles by rail.

[21] T. A. McNeal, *op. cit.*, p. 186.

the few remaining brought action to set aside the organization. This end was attained by action of the supreme court in 1875. Several of the fifteen counties organized in western Kansas in the seventies abandoned, or tried to abandon, their old organizations and form new ones. The main object of these efforts was not accomplished; namely, to get rid of old fraudulent debts. These old debts had been saddled on the counties by unscrupulous promoters and grafters. A whole group of counties was "worked" by these swindlers. A few stories of the fraud committed in these counties will give the reader an idea of the graft that prevailed.

In the summer of 1874, Barber, Comanche, Ford and Ness Counties were organized.[22] The law required that a county should have six hundred voters before organizing. There was not a quarter of that number in any one of these counties. A sparsity of inhabitants was no obstacle to the conscienceless organizers, however. The census enumerator secured old hotel registers and copied a sufficient number of names to meet the legal requirements. The names of hundreds of men who lived in other states and had never been in Kansas nor contemplated migrating there, were duly recorded as citizens of that sparsely inhabited region. Barber County probably had not more than one hundred inhabitants. Of these, practically none were permanent residents [23] and consequently had little interest in thwarting the perpetrators of the wholesale steals.

Immediately upon organization these self-appointed organizers and officials began to exploit the infant country. The new board of county commissioners issued $25,000 in warrants to a party to build a court-house. This sum was issued to him before he had furnished even a brick or nail. When no attempt was made to fulfil the contract no legal action was taken. In a second attempt to build a court-house, the board proposed to vote bonds to the amount of $40,000. The few honest citizens rallied enough votes to block this move,

[22] Kansas.
[23] These temporary residents possessed large herds of cattle which they were grazing; but they did not expect to remain permanently in the county.

but the commissioners issued the bonds and then by an act of the legislature, put through by the leader of the gang who had been elected the first representative of that county, they issued funding bonds to cover the debt. And still no court-house was erected. Then the looters organized a railroad corporation known as the Nebraska, Kansas, and Southwestern. It never had any existence except on paper. A bond election was held. The looters were alleged to have secured enough votes and $100,000 in bonds were issued. There was never a single mile of road constructed. The bonds finally passed into the hands of an English capitalist, a member of Parliament. The tax-payers of the county afterward tried to cancel this debt. It was carried through the supreme court, but the county lost and for a half century the later settlers paid interest and principal on these fraudulent debts saddled on the county while it was yet inhabited only by prairie dogs and coyotes.

The grafters voted script to build bridges over streams that carried no water except on rare occasions. Thousands of dollars were issued for the support of the poor and there being no poor, these promoters represented the scores of poverty-stricken citizens which were alleged to wear out a wretched existence in abject poverty.

Finally the few real settlers, aroused to fury by these indignities, proceeded to right things after the manner of the independent West. A vigilance committee was formed with the laudable purpose of hanging the plunderers. They captured them but unfortunately allowed them to say a few words before they swung from the cottonwood limb. The thieves utilized this opportunity and by smooth talk persuaded the vigilantes that if they were hanged it would do no good and might get the regulators into more trouble. On the other hand, if released, they promised to restore the plunder already taken and to leave the country forever. On these conditions the county clerk and commissioners were released. They departed, taking with them the county seal and warrant books. At the safe distance of a hundred miles, in Hutchinson, Kansas, they organized themselves into a board and proceeded to contract thousands of dollars of new indebtedness in behalf of the plundered county. Not a cent of the loot was ever recovered. For years the county endeavored by fruitless litigation to annul this indebtedness. A member of the vigilance committee was later heard to remark that if they had not been a "passel" of fools they would have hung the thieves and listened to what they had to say afterward.

A group of swindlers journeyed to the region of Comanche County, Kansas, and invited some buffalo hunters to assist them in their nefarious designs. One man, in a ten days' tramp over the country, and with the aid of a St. Joseph, Missouri, hotel register, secured the names of six hundred residents, although there was hardly an inhabitant in the whole region. A fraudulent election was held which placed the grafters in office and the returns were sent in to the state, thanks again to the St. Joseph hotel register. In all $72,000 in bonds were issued to build a court-house, bridges, and pay general expenses.

A second phase of the plan was that of organizing school districts and issuing bonds. Fortunately the attorney general stepped in and stopped this raid on the state school funds. One of the chief swindlers who had been elected to the legislature was expelled and prosecuted for his actions. The case was dismissed for lack of evidence. Not a thief was punished. The courts protected them and saddled the burden of debts on the subsequent settlers who had no part in their making.[24]

The proceedings in Harper County were similar. A gang of saloon loafers, thugs, and other desperate characters from Baxter Springs, Kansas, planned the looting of the county. By means of a Baxter Springs hotel register sufficient settlers were discovered and at the ensuing election the leader, a murderer, was elected to the legislature, and a suitable county board was selected from among his cohorts. Forty thousand dollars' worth of bonds were sold, for

[24] T. A. McNeal, "Southwestern Kansas," *Transactions*, Kansas State Historical Society, Vol. VII, pp. 92–95; T. A. McNeal, *When Kansas Was Young*, pp. 23, 24, 64, 65.

which these desperate characters received $30,000. From the viewpoint of the vast swindles of today it is astonishing that these comparatively honest thieves stopped at $40,000 when the plunder might have run into hundreds of thousands. It is difficult indeed to see why the courts held that the purchasers of these bonds at such large discounts were innocent purchasers, thus setting the court's seal of approval on these transparent steals. It is also hard to believe that the governor did not know when he consented to these organizations, that they were a huge fraud.

Indeed the governor was sometimes a party to such crookedness. In Dakota Territory in 1883 Governor Ordway and a few friends formed a ring to mulct the citizens in connection with county organization. The country was quickly filling with the rush of settlers during the boom of the eighties and there arose an urgent demand for county organization. The governor was supposed to appoint county commissioners upon receiving a petition from fifty legal voters requesting organization. When he received the petition he sent the customary notice of his appointments to the secretary's office but withheld the notification from the appointees themselves. Instead he handed the names to his representative who proceeded to the county to dicker with the appointees and deliver the commissions provided the prospective officers proved tractable.

The governor's agents would not deliver the commissions until the parties named had given definite assurance that they would locate the temporary county-seat where the governor wanted it. In the meantime the governor's agents canvassed the county for bids from various people for the location of the county-seat. When a satisfactory price was secured for the governor and his clique, the commissions were handed out and the deal consummated. In some counties the organization was held up for months. Petition after petition was forwarded in an effort to obtain an organization. Meanwhile the would-be county was without power to levy taxes for the support of any kind of government or schools. The settlers were obliged to travel great distances to do legal business and were without the protection of the law, either criminal or civil. This scheme, of course, did not permanently locate the county-seat but was the means of the governor's securing bribes from the anxious settlers. After the county-seat was located temporarily the battle began and election after election was held in the struggle between the various aspirants.[25]

[25] Captain C. H. Ellis, *History of Faulk County, South Dakota* (Faulkton, South Dakota, 1909), p. 44; L. C. Ochsenreiter, *History of Day County*, pp. 37–38; George W. Kingsbury, *History of Dakota Territory* (Chicago, 1915), Vol. II, pp. 1332–1335.

CHAPTER XXXIII

ITINERANTS

AS SOON as a thin line of settlement appeared on the prairie various itinerants appeared to take the settlers' small store of money.

First and most important was the circus group which was always a tremendous attraction in a new country. The circus had its own transportation, consisting of long wagons for hauling the tent poles, ordinary wagons for hauling tents and other equipment, and heavily-built cage-wagons in which the large animals were carried.

Old Dan Castello's "Great Wagon Show" competed with Cooper, Bailey and Company's "Great International Circus" and Grady's "American Circus" for business in Kansas during the early seventies. Grady's advertised forty-nine first-class performers among whom were four lady gymnasts and three great clowns. In addition there were a large number of trained horses. Admission was fifty cents for adults and twenty-five cents for children. A "grand free balloon ascension" and "grand procession" at ten o'clock in the morning provided a special inducement.

Cooper, Bailey and Company advertised as ten allied shows in one with one thousand animals and equipment representing an outlay of one million dollars. It was a two-ring circus and gave performances at one o'clock and at seven, with an admission charge of seventy-five cents for adults and fifty cents for children. Still another circus showing at Iola, Kansas, in 1870 advertised one hundred men and one hundred and ten horses. Some of the wagons were pulled by oxen.

As the circus moved across the virgin sod from town to town often members of the troupe stopped at the settlers' houses to secure food for man or beast or perhaps to secure a night's lodging. They gave complimentary tickets in exchange for these accommodations. One early settler [1] recalled that his parents played host to the strong man who juggled the cannon balls at the side-show, the bareback rider, and the fat boy who, although only sixteen years of age, weighed three hundred pounds. Storms, bad roads, and swollen streams made travel and the meeting of appointments extremely hazardous. Another early settler [2] remembered that one circus had a large number of horses drowned near his home.

In 1859 at Nebraska City the special attraction before the performance was "a terrific ascension on a single wire three hundred feet long, from the ground to the top of the flagstaff of the canvass." This show, Davis and Crosbies Great French and American Circus, performed three times daily and offered a change of program at each exhibition. The James Robinson Circus advertised a moral show, a giant, menagerie, museum, aviary, and a caravan when it showed at Yankton, Dakota Territory, in 1874. One traveler mentioned that in 1883 people from Valentine, a distance of 114 miles, attended the Robinson's Circus at O'Neill, Nebraska.

In a day when medical science was in its infancy and many people were filled with aches and pains from the rigors of frontier life, they were peculiarly susceptible to the wiles of medical quacks and the patent medicine vender. Sometimes these traveling medicine men went from house to house in a covered spring wagon selling the elixir of life. The salesman had the name of his medicine painted on the side of the wagon in glowing letters.

One such salesman, now gray with age, who sold Jo-He [3] Magnetic Oil a half century ago, earnestly told the author that the medicine was an excellent remedy for colds, scald head, piles, rheumatism, cancer, and croup. In one instance, the salesman said, a man with cancer was quickly healed, and was so well satisfied with

[1] J. Clarence Norton of Allen County, Kansas.
[2] Noah Ard, Elsmore, Kansas.
[3] The name was manufactured from a combination of the first names of the producers, Joseph and Henry. It was an oil from Texas.

the medicine and thankful for his cure that he accompanied the sales-man about the neighborhood recommending the medicine, thus caus-ing a large increase in his business. The remedy sold for seventy-five cents for a three-ounce bottle. The veteran salesman admitted that although he knew the medicine was good for the above-mentioned disorders it probably did not cure all the diseases that the pro-ducers claimed. He maintained, however, that it was a good gen-eral medicine for the ordinary run of ailments.

Two brothers of this man secured a recipe for a corn remedy which they manufactured and distributed. A few dollars were spent for the following items: A hundred salve boxes, printed labels, several bars of soft soap, and a few pounds of sugar. A small quan-tity of sugar was worked into the soap and the resultant mixture was placed in the boxes. The men then journeyed from house to house retailing the valuable corn solvent. The best of it was that it cured. In a day of hard cowhide boots and poorly fitting foot-wear, business was good for the corn remedy salesman.

Sometimes the salesman traveled with his wife. This brought a friendly contact and gave the lonely homestead a feminine contact with the outer world. At night the itinerant camped near a house to secure water.

The medicine show was another means of distributing some bot-tled panacea. This required more talent and clever talk. The man-ager of such a business had to possess native ability and polish. The medicine show ranged in size from a large ably directed troop showing in a tent to one man selling from his rig on the street. The aim was the same; namely, to gather a crowd by means of a free entertainment and then sell medicine, cheap jewelry, patent soap, or other luring goods at a very attractive price. The larger shows had a quantity of equipment and horses. The proprietors set up their tents on a vacant lot and, after advertising by singing or per-forming a few acts on the streets, they gave some evening exhibi-tions. Usually the medicine was of one variety—a panacea for all ills from ague to rheumatism. Sometimes, however, a show carried several brands of medicine or tonic.

Diamond Dick was a noted medicine showman, unique and striking in appearance. He displayed many diamonds in his make-up and wore long hair. After his well-trained troupe had presented a program of considerable merit, he began a very clever and successful sales talk. As many as five hundred to one thousand people attended one of these shows. Some of the well-known medicine sold in this way was Indian Sagwa and Wizard oil. After a few days' showing, the medicine man moved to the next town where more "suckers" were awaiting his luring bait.

Frequently a man and a woman, a man and a boy, or two men and a woman operated a medicine show. One attracted an audience by an exhibition of marksmanship. Railroad ties were erected for a background and various feats of marksmanship were performed. A number of potatoes were suspended by strings. The medicine man deftly shot the string and dropped a potato every time he put finger to the trigger. Then he put a potato on his head and repeated the words "Dead, dead, dead"! At the third word his consort shot the potato, splitting it wide open. The woman also flicked the ashes from the lighted cigar of the salesman as he sat calmly smoking some two rods away.

Hamlin Garland mentioned in his *A Son of the Middle Border* that one of his first contacts with the better things of the art of the world was through a patent medicine vender at the county fair. "Doctor" Lightner was selling his magic oil from a cart. This faker, a handsome fellow with long black hair and an immense white hat, was addressing the crowd while a beautiful young girl with a guitar in her lap sat in weary relaxation at his feet. A third member of the troupe, a very short plump man, was handing out the bottles. The future author listened while the trio went through their part in securing an audience for another sale of medicine. It was art to the country boy. The graceful hand of the "doctor" sweeping across the strings of the instrument, the clear ringing voice of the tenor, and the bird-like voice of the girl, although singing an absurd song, opened a new world to him. During the intervals between songs the "doctor" talked of catarrh and its cure and offered his medicines for sale.

Where there were two or more men, one man mingled with the crowd to jolly them along. Sometimes one man alone ran the show. Driving into town, he stopped on the corner and proceeded to do a few sleight of hand tricks such as sword swallowing, fire eating, or the impossible with a deck of cards. He then disposed of his medicine at "half price" or gave away cheap jewelry with each sale. These men went wherever picking was good, and wherever there was a crowd there was the medicine man. He visited last-day-of-school programs, Fourth of July celebrations, election assemblies, and county fairs.

Sometimes one of these street salesmen tried dishonest dealing. In the seventies a well-dressed, suave, loquacious young man drove into one of the towns in Barton County, Kansas. By his side in an open barouche sat a Negro banjo player. They stopped at a prominent corner and the Negro played and sang. Then the salesman told the assembled crowd about the things he was going to sell at a ridiculously low price. He sold various articles of apparent value. Then he began calling in all the articles he had sold, saying he would redeem them at double the amount he had sold them for. After more music, songs, and jokes he again commenced selling things to be redeemed—so the audience understood—at double what they paid for them. This time he got better prices for his goods, and, of course, made a much larger number of sales since all were thinking of the redemption of the articles. When he had sold as many as possible he whipped his horses and drove out of town with the money, leaving the purchasers to discover that the flimsy goods they had purchased with dollars were worth only a few cents. Such a person who preyed on the credulity of the uninitiated, was termed a "slicker."

Another trick illustrative of the same kind of dishonesty was worked by a sharper who drove into town with a candy bucket full of money, began to cry, "Money, money to throw away"! and promptly commenced to throw it away by handfuls. People gathered from every direction and started to pick it up. He then started to operate a gambling device which consisted of three boxes in which the stranger placed money and the people wagered on the device. For a time the crowd won fairly consistently but when the gambling moved along nicely, the gambler began to win more and more frequently, allowing certain ones to win occasionally to egg on the gambling. When the "slicker" was two or three hundred dollars ahead of the game, he put his paraphernalia down and calmly drove to the next town, leaving the citizens standing with their mouths open and their pockets empty. He had scattered a few dimes and quarters and had taken hundreds of dollars in exchange. Since there were no telephones or communication between towns, the gambler was able to win in town after town in fairly close proximity.

Hamlin Garland tells of a patent soap vender who, having fooled the crowd in a similar manner, picked up the lines to leave, saying that he had their money and they had the experience and so they were even. One horny-handed farmer grabbed the whip and struck the salesman across the face while a second pulled off his boot and used it effectively on the head of the swindler. The crowd held the horses until the officers came and took the crafty salesman into custody.

Sometimes a lone medicine seller would give a little show in a private home. The rumor that he would give some performances attracted a large crowd. One entertainer had a large cabinet built in such a way as to give fake spiritualist performances. Among other tricks he sat in a chair while one of the guests tied him securely to it. Two men then placed him in the cabinet. Another person, preferably a woman, was asked to step inside the cabinet and feel the cold clammy spirit hand touch her. The lights were extinguished. Presently the lady in the cabinet let out a shriek as something cold touched her skin; the faker called for lights. This revealed that individual bound hand and foot as when he was placed in the cabinet. His trick was to make his hand smaller than his wrist by muscular control, grab a wooden stocking darner, touch the highly excited individual with the smooth cold wood, and then replace his hand in the bonds. After the performance, medicines of various sorts were sold to the group which felt indebted to the entertainer and were in a more ready mood to buy.

In the earlier days Irish peddlers walked through the country carrying large packs of linens, socks, shirts, table cloths, handkerchiefs, needles, thread, thimbles, ribbon, cheap jewerly, and other trinkets. The Irishman was later displaced by the Armenian trader who dealt in much the same kind of gaudy goods and trinkets but who drove a horse and wagon. These men were well received, for the women liked to see the pretty things and it formed a link with the outside world.

People anticipated the coming of the silversmiths who repaired clocks and watches and sold jewelry. Since there was not business enough in the small communities to support a jeweler these men traveled through the country picking up the business. Often a clock would be out of running order for weeks because there was no one to repair it. Sometimes a bum or ordinary tramp who had a trade would come through the region and make himself welcome by fixing the clock or doing some other task requiring skill. More often these knights of the road asked for a hand-out or a place to sleep and were on their way as soon as possible lest their stay be made unpleasant by the invitation to work.

Of the various agents who called, probably the most detested were the lightning rod agents. They abounded during the summer months and the newspapers sounded a warning against these "swindlers." No doubt most salesmanship along this line was honorable, but enough of it was questionable to give it all a bad reputation. A Nebraska paper in 1884 reported that a swindle was

AN ITINERANT PHOTOGRAPHER

On the Loup River, Nebraska, 1886. Courtesy of the Nebraska State Historical Society.

worked by two men in that vicinity. The first man took orders to put up the rod as a sample in the community. The second put up the rod and asked the farmer to sign a note for $53 promising that a rebate of twenty dollars would be given when a third man, the inspector, came to look over the job. Needless to say, the inspector's visit was indefinitely postponed.

The fruit tree peddler was almost as cordially hated. The *Nebraska Farmer* warned the farmers against the "abominable traveling tree peddler," urging its readers to buy their trees at home. These nursery agents carried beautiful lithographs of apples, plums, cherries, and other fruits. The settlers, longing for trees and fruit like that in the old home state, were tempted to buy more than they could afford. The agent's commission was high and the trees frequently were a long time on the road and in poor condition when the farmer received them. No doubt a poor quality of goods was frequently delivered, for a company far away would be more likely to pass its inferior product to a buyer in the West than would the nursery near at hand which was anxious to establish a reputation.

Various canvassers made their rounds. Subscription books, with elegant bindings and gold-edged leaves, caught the eye of many who were hungering for knowledge on the intellectually starved frontier. A longing to have a pretty volume in the home or to give the children advantages which the parents never had, influenced others to part with their hard-earned cash. Redpath's *History of the United States* sold in the seventies for prices varying from five to twelve dollars, according to the binding. The illustrated family Bible was another popular subscription volume.[4] The Baptists, during the eighties, built a colporteur wagon for use in the Dakotas. The colporteur lived in this wagon and visited many small communities which had no pastoral help. In this way the church made contact with its members and distributed literature. When schools were established, the school supply salesmen began to ply their

[4] *Canton* (Dakota Territory) *Advocate*, October 24, 1878.

trade. They played the school board members against each other until map, dictionary, or chart was purchased for the uplift of the youth of the district.

Washing machine, sewing machine, and windmill agents were among the other callers in the rural regions. In the straggling towns as early as the fifties, hand organ grinders with monkeys followed the river "making the towns." Another familiar character was the scissors grinder who walked about town pushing a small vehicle and ringing a bell to advertise his business.

Traveling entertainers had visited the towns as soon as they were founded in the seventies, traveling in their own conveyance. Ordinarily there were only between one and five members to a group, but in 1872 a troupe of nine itinerated, stopping two or three nights in a town giving such plays as "Lucretia Borgia," "Rip Van Winkle," and others of like character.[5] Italian musicians, Jim Crow Rice who was a burnt cork artist, Blind Sam and his brother who were Negro musicians, the Andrews family of Swiss Bell Ringers— nine in number, and the DeCastro troupe of ventriloquists, jugglers, and comic actors were some of those who brought cheer and amusement to the lonely inhabitants of the little towns. In 1877 a ventriloquist traveled over the country giving an entertainment in which puppets acted and talked to one another. In 1871 a magician traveled from place to place in his own buggy, posting his own bills and giving two-hour shows. Certain "professors" journeyed here and there singing or training the people to sing. At O'Neill, Nebraska, a musicale was held after four days' practice. Two concerts were given with an admission charge of twenty-five cents each. Part of the proceeds was used to purchase an organ for the Sunday-school.

The standard price of admission for all entertainments was twenty-five cents and the school-house was the opera house. Towns on the main arteries of travel had frequent visits while those in more remote places famished for entertainment and in an effort to

[5] *Beatrice Express*, October 12, 1872.

stave off stagnation organized home-talent groups. The first show in Cheyenne County, Kansas, in 1885, was a magic lantern exhibition. The machine threw a dim picture three feet in diameter. Magic lantern shows, although poor in mechanical ability, were entertaining and educational.[6]

Probably the most picturesque of all wayfaring characters of the plains was the horse trader. As one man said "swapping was the sport of kings when horses ruled the road." In the days before the automobile, horse trading was the breath of life to many men. Horse traders and horse swappers existed everywhere and the art was cultivated widely, but the real artist, the one in whom perfection was reached, was the road trader.

The trader began his season about the first of May when the weather grew warm and there was grass for his animals. Oftentimes a man with his wife and family journeyed about all summer. The man drove ahead in a spring wagon; his wife and children followed him in a jolting covered wagon. Following the wagon were a number of worthless horses known to the profession as "snides." These animals, although good looking, were fit only for trading purposes. Worthless from the point of view of utility, a "snide" was, nevertheless, valuable as a trading animal. Men actually made a side line of supplying traders with "snides."

The first law with a horse trader was always to get something "to boot." It was generally understood that there were no honest men when trading horses. Traders were not haled into court as often as might be expected. A person beaten in a horse trade was not enthusiastic about advertising it. Then, too, horse traders were facile talkers. The trader was an actor who used his family as part of the scenery and as players in the drama. The family lent truthfulness to the story that the trader and his family were on the way to homestead. Just at the moment when the victim's suspicions were aroused the wife would interrupt with: "Now, you're

[6] The magic lantern was used as early as 1874. *Niobrara Pioneer*, October 27, 1874.

not going to sell Dobbin, are you, John? We raised her from a colt," or something in a similar vein. Sometimes even veteran horse traders succumbed to such deception.

The victim of a trade, upon discovering the worthlessness of the "snide," was usually willing to trade back at a loss. One trader had a beautiful horse which he would sell at a low price without unhooking him. When the horse was unharnessed and the large collar taken off a fistula appeared. The buyer naturally objected since the horse was valueless for legitimate purposes. The trader then replied that the buyer had bought the horse cheap, without guarantee and without asking that the harness be removed. The trader then offered to settle for twenty or thirty dollars and it was usually accepted. A "snide" of this kind might be sold several times a day and proved a veritable gold mine to the trader. A trader might be without a rain coat for himself, but he had a covering for his "snide." When another trader came along and bought him, the first trader mourned sincerely and actually offered a big premium to trade back.

Gypsy traders flourished. Their wives told fortunes, sold beads, laces, and fur coats. This helped the men, for they were not obliged to trade unless they had an opportunity to make a neat sum.

As a side line the peripatetic horse merchant had the running pony and the little pulling mare. A member of the horse trader's party made it a point to circulate about town and casually drop the remark that a boy out at the horse trader's camp had a fast pony and that he had a little money to bet on his horse. This was a challenge to the sporting blood of the town. The fastest horse of the town was matched for a three hundred yard race on a twenty-five or fifty dollar wager. The boy usually won the money. County fairs presented excellent opportunities for these races. In one instance before the regular races a queer-looking character rode around the track on a woe-begone nag that ambled along casually, apparently barely able to drag one foot behind the other. As the rider, in an attempt to secure speed, flailed the mount with a lath, the crowd began to hoot and shout in derision. At this the rider lost his temper and shouted back: "This horse *can* run. I'll bet twenty-five dollars he can." The challenge was quickly accepted, and a confederate appeared with a saddle, which when cinched, put new life into the sorry steed. He ceased dragging one leg behind the other, stepped out like a thorough-bred and promptly took the stakes.

Pulling contests were arranged by similar tricks. A representative of the trader would hang around the livery barn or dray stand. His little mare would be hitched to a buggy nearby. After a time the stranger would venture: "You wouldn't think that little mare could out pull your big team." Usually town pride, coupled with the hope of taking some easy money on a sure bet, caused the cash to be put up and a contest arranged. The trader always insisted that they hitch to a wagon scale, and the little mare, like the trained weight lifter, was pitted against the big team which was like the raw untrained man. Almost without exception the trained horse won the money.

Horse traders often sat and whittled for an hour at a time; then they would walk into the saloon and have a drink. Finally a deal was closed.[7]

The horse trader, like the other wayfaring peoples of the frontier, flourished also in the post-frontier but faded before the industrialism and urbanization of the twentieth century.

[7] B. F. Sylvester, "Hoss Tradin'," *Saturday Evening Post*, January 6, 1934.

CHAPTER XXXIV

PIONEER INDUSTRIES

MANUFACTURING in a new country is largely dictated by the immediate needs and the proximity to raw material. One of the most immediate needs of the settlers upon arrival was a house. Consequently the manufacturing of material for home building took the lead from the first. The New England Emigrant Aid Company was active in bringing mills for the settlers. Some of these could be used both for making lumber and grinding grist. When they were first established they turned out lumber and a little later, when grain was available, they were used to grind flour or corn meal. One writer of Manhattan, Kansas, observed that the arrival of the Emigrant Aid mill from Lawrence, drawn by twenty yoke of oxen, was a greater event to the citizens in 1859 than the arrival of the Union Pacific Railway eight years later.

Before the coming of the sawmill it was necessary to saw up logs by hand. The first "mill" at Yankton was of this character. Two parallel timbers were projected over the river bank. The log to be sawed was rolled out on these and two men did the work of sawing the rough lumber, one man standing above and the other below, working the whip saw. About five thousand feet of lumber were cut in this way. When sawmills were introduced, lumber was sawed "on the shares." A man cut his logs and hauled them to the mill; the owner of the mill and the owner of the logs divided the lumber and slabs [1] equally, thus settling the sawing bill. Often patrons had to wait several hours for their turn. In 1860, only six years after the first settlement, Kansas had one

---

[1] This is the waste portion along the edge of the tree which could not be worked into boards. It was used for firewood.

hundred and sixteen sawmills, employing four hundred and seventy-eight men; the annual production was valued at a million and a half dollars, placing this industry far ahead of any other in importance.[2] Nearly two-thirds of the employed labor was engaged in the lumber business at that time. Usually sawmills were operated by steam, although water-power was frequently utilized and occasionally a windmill.

The first machinery brought into Lincoln County, Dakota Territory, in 1868, was a shingle machine. Kansas had eight shingle-making establishments in 1860.

Other manufacturing processes for home building were the burning of brick and lime. Often two or more neighbors united, quarried a large pile of limestones, cut a good supply of wood, constructed a crude kiln, and took turns at firing day and night. Some families made their living over a period of years by burning lime. Brick-yards were very numerous in the fifties. Almost all of the river towns had one or more of these establishments. At Marysville, Kansas, the first bricks were made of mud and dried in the sun. Many of the brick buildings of the time were made of that kind of brick. In 1857 one firm was engaged in burning 168,000 brick for the Free State Hotel. The newspaper editor remarked that three or four brick-yards were needed in Lawrence. He gave the cost of production as: Labor—common yard hands, fifty dollars a month; fuel—four dollars a cord; clay—abundant. Brick at that time sold for $8.50 a thousand. As the years passed, there was a tendency for brick-yards to be located where materials were more favorable instead of each town having its own yard. In 1882 there were five brick-yards in Cass County, Nebraska, three of which each produced from five to six hundred thousand brick. A yard in Hastings, in the same state, in 1881 produced 1,100,000 brick.

---

[2] Exeeption must be made in the matter of gold mining which was conducted in that portion of Colorado which was a part of Kansas during the territorial period.

As the country became more populous the manufacture of certain food products grew in importance. As soon as agriculture developed sufficiently, grist-mills were in demand and by 1860 the value of the output of these mills was second only to that of the sawmills. In Nebraska the grist-mill output was about one-third that of the sawmill and in Kansas it was one-fifth.

Often a miller or mill-wright would let it be known that he was ready to receive an inducement to establish a mill in a certain place. The coming of a grist-mill was always a matter of great interest and importance. Frequently the town would give a good bonus in land, or other substantial aid, to the mill owner who could be persuaded to erect his mill in the town. Many cities of today can trace the beginning of their growth or prosperity to the time when the mill was established there. At Marysville, Kansas, a man was given seven shares in the town, each worth about twenty dollars.[3] The mill raised the value of shares to twenty-five dollars each.

Of the thirty-six mills in Kansas in 1860, or the seventeen in Nebraska at the same date, by far the larger portion were small water-power establishments grinding corn and flour for the settlers. Although a few prospered, most of them were custom mills and did their grinding only as the farmers brought in the grain and waited while it was made into meal and flour for the family needs. These mills ground the grain into a form suitable for home consumption and were not, strictly speaking, manufacturing enterprises. Often they were built in connection with sawmills and were equipped with "one or two run of stone buhrs and a hexagon reel." They ground more corn than wheat. Some charged a toll ranging from one-sixth to one-twelfth of the grain. Others ground the patron's grist for twenty-five to thirty-five cents a bushel. In the former case the customer got all the bran and shorts which his share of the grist made. These mills ran night and day and had a daily capacity of about three hundred bushels of wheat, or more

[3] To establish a sawmill.

of corn. The mill on the Republican River at Milford, Kansas, ran from 1866 to 1875 and only once was closed for a period longer than two weeks.

The exchange mill was a later development. It exchanged wheat for flour. From such a mill the producer usually received thirty-two to thirty-five pounds of flour for each bushel of wheat. The miller retained the lower grades and the by-products. The merchant mill, where grain was bought and the flour and by-products sold outright, was a post-frontier development. In early times the miller advertised for hogs and fed a great herd of them on the shorts from his part of the grist, thus turning his unsalable by-product into pork.

In custom grinding a man was expected to place his grist at the hopper and take his meal sacks to the spot where they were filled. Some of the small mills were primitive indeed. In Osage County, Kansas, a man made a set of millstones out of hard limestone. The mill was kept running constantly grinding corn for the settlers. In the early seventies Claus Rohwer built a horse-power mill at Fort Calhoun, Nebraska. He sent to Germany for buhrs and mill machinery. He made the power of wood entirely himself. It was carved by hand from logs felled on his land. The mammoth cog-wheel and the small one show evidence of skilful workmanship. The mill was operated in connection with the farm and was active mostly in the winter when farm work was not pressing. As a rule four horses furnished the motive power. It was arranged so that the horses could make their rounds inside the building, thus stormy weather did not halt the work. Coarse grinding of all kinds was done with the two sets of Rhenish buhrs.

Another item ranking high among the infant industries of the plains in 1860 was the manufacture of malt liquor. This was the fourth largest industry when measured in value of products in Kansas in 1860.[4] No doubt the citizens of prohibition-minded Kansas would have us think that this malt liquor was largely

---

[4] This item ranked sixth in Nebraska.

freighted across the prairie for consumption on the mining frontier in Colorado; and this was probably the case. As soon as crops were produced, the high prices in the gold fields naturally attracted the product there.

As early as 1858 a slaughter house at White Cloud, Kansas, received eight hundred hogs in one week in December. These were produced in Missouri.

There was a great demand by the plains travelers for wagons and carriages and their repair. It was only natural that establishments catering to this need should be listed high among the manufacturing interests. In 1860 the carriage, cart, and wagon manufacturing business in Kansas produced $65,000 worth of these commodities and employed thirty-five hands. Blacksmithing added another $15,500 and twenty-four hands.

In Nebraska the same year the manufacture of boots and shoes ranked third, only exceeded by lumber and flour. Thirty-four persons were employed.

Salt was one of the great needs of the frontier and naturally when beds of salt were found, the production flourished. Saline deposits existed near the present city of Lincoln, Nebraska, and led to the establishment of permanent settlement there. In March, 1853, one year before white people were legally entitled to settle in the territory, the Saline Manufacturing Company was incorporated. For some reason this company did not function; the first plant was constructed in 1862 by John Stanford Gregory at a cost of $8,000. He continued in this business until the railroads ran into Lincoln.

Mr. Gregory used both bench boilers and solar evaporators. As early as 1857 the optimistic frontier journal, the *Nebraska Advertiser*, spoke in glowing terms of the prospect of salt manufacturing in Nebraska and uttered the belief that "the day is only just in advance of us when Nebraska will furnish all this vast western region of country with that necessary article of consumption salt."

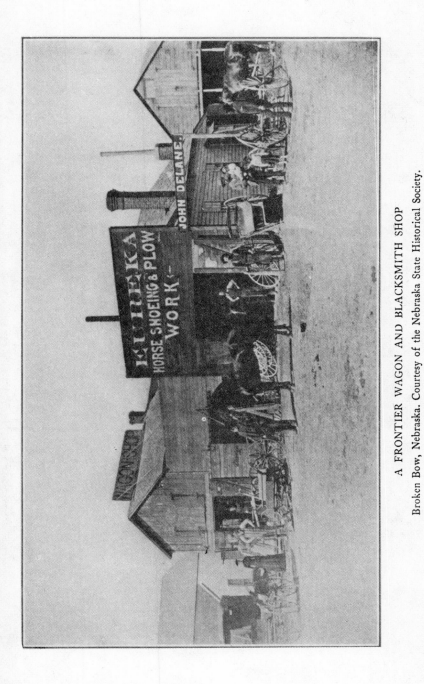

A FRONTIER WAGON AND BLACKSMITH SHOP

Broken Bow, Nebraska. Courtesy of the Nebraska State Historical Society.

In 1860 the merchants of Nebraska City advertised salt from the deposits west of the city. It was stated that there were ten furnaces at the salt basin. Later large interests started litigation over the control of the basin. Horace Smith, of the firm of Smith and Wesson, fire-arms company of Springfield, Massachusetts, invested a considerable sum of money in the business but withdrew it when he was sued by J. Sterling Morton, the founder of the Morton Salt Company. In time the salt springs seem to have lost their strength and salt manufacturing died out.

Probably most of the salt was made by settlers coming from far and near seeking this valuable commodity. During the Civil War when salt was extremely expensive, people came from the settled sections of Kansas and Nebraska, in large numbers from Missouri, and from central Iowa. As one old timer said, going for salt was like going fishing, success was due to luck. If the weather was perfectly dry they could scrape it up by the wagon-load. A few minutes' rain, however, ended this. Sometimes men came a hundred miles only to see a little rain clear the crystal incrustation off the basin in a few minutes; they were left literally holding the empty sack. After the rain the basin which had been crusted over with a quarter of an inch of crystalline salt looked as black as ink. Many farmers brought their sorghum pans to boil salt and when they had enough or were tired, they would trade their pans for salt. When the weather was dry, many would scrape more than they could haul home and they would trade the scrapings at twenty-five cents a hundredweight, receiving in return boiled salt at two dollars a hundredweight. As soon as the first rain came, scrapings rose in value from fifty cents to one dollar a hundred. Those from a distance would snatch it at those rates. All manner of products were traded for salt: Meat, flour, butter, eggs, fruit, chickens, potatoes. Others hauled wood to trade. Frequently settlers would haul a pile of wood, rent furnaces, and work all night, thus getting a supply of the valued article. Those who remained permanently at the basin had salt and scrapings to sell, furnaces to rent, and usually sold provisions. Some of the pilgrims even traded clothes for salt. One group from Winterset, Iowa, brought two four-horse wagon-loads of flour, in all five thousand pounds, for which they received an even exchange of five thousand pounds of salt. The salt basin was a lively scene with hundreds going and coming continually during the late summer and early fall. Naturally this center of trade and traffic resulted in the building of a city nearby. In the eighties salt refining of a more permanent character began in western Kansas.

In the sixties and seventies stoneware was manufactured in at least two points in Nebraska, Dakota City and Louisville. The *Dakota City Herald* stated in March, 1860, that the local pottery plant had on hand sixty thousand gallons of stoneware and at another time that about an acre was covered with jugs, crocks, jars, pots, and so forth, and that in some places they were piled on the levee in tiers three deep ready for the next boat to take them down the river. In 1878 the Louisville Stoneware Company had buildings and kilns with a capacity of twelve to fifteen thousand gallons per month.[5] These figures although apparently large may be explained by the fact that stoneware of every description was in great demand at that time; glass and tin has now been substituted for much of the earthenware. Jugs were used for carrying molasses, liquor, and medicine across the plains to the mines and were no doubt in demand at such places as Nebraska City, St. Joseph, and Leavenworth. Then, too, everyone who handled milk and butter used crocks and jars. Many frontier homes used earthenware dishes.

One industry of local importance was that of storing ice for summer use in the prairie town. The ordinary ice house consisted of a frame built of posts planted in the ground and braced. Rough boards were nailed on the inner and outer sides and the space between was filled with sawdust. This simple structure was covered with a board or shingle roof. On the farm it was possible to dig

[5] A. T. Andreas, *History of the State of Nebraska*, Vol. I, p. 514.

into the ground on a well-drained hillside, line the hole with clay, and cover it with a sloping roof made of long slough grass. In Lawrence, Kansas, during the city's warfare over the slavery struggle, the inhabitants were busy in February cutting ice for the next summer. In 1873 in the little town of Beatrice, one firm stored four hundred tons, another harvested two hundred tons, while others stored lesser amounts.

Creameries were established in the seventies and eighties. They gathered milk or cream and churned it at points along the railroad.

When slaughter houses increased their output, a natural byproduct was soap production. There were two soap and candle manufacturing concerns in Kansas in 1860 employing five men. In 1882 one factory produced two hundred thousand pounds of laundry and toilet soap annually, and another valued its annual production of laundry soap at twenty thousand dollars.

Kansas is blessed with considerable wealth of mineral deposits; Nebraska and the eastern Dakotas are almost devoid of minerals. As early as 1863 shaft mining was begun in Leavenworth and by 1882 during the rush season, the Leavenworth Coal Mining Company employed from three hundred to three hundred and fifty men; the machinery had a capacity of seventy-five thousand bushels of coal per day. In parts of southeastern Kansas thin veins of coal lie buried under only a few feet of earth. The homesteaders with pick and shovel scraped off the dirt along the creeks where the mineral lay closest to the surface and, loading the fuel in their wagons, hauled it to the nearest market where its buying power relieved the pinched economic situation in early homestead years.[6] Artificial gas was introduced into the river cities about 1870. Gas, thus produced, displaced candles in the stores and other business houses.

In addition to industries which seemed feasible and offered a

[6] With later developments along the same line by means of gigantic shovels as much as twenty or thirty feet of earth is being scraped off in present day "strip mining" in southeastern Kansas.

reasonable prospect for success and permanency, a number were attempted which were not founded on business principles as to power, raw material, or market needs, and hence were little more than optimistic, hare-brained trials at the impossible. Some, although temporarily successful, died out. Among them was cigar manufacturing. In 1858 a man from Louisville, Kentucky, set up the business at Brownville, Nebraska. During the seventies the annual sales from one plant alone in Nebraska City reached five hundred thousand cigars. In 1870 there were twelve cigar and tobacco manufacturing concerns in Nebraska. Yankton, South Dakota, had a cigar factory which sold at wholesale as early as 1874.

It was thought that cotton would be an outstanding crop in Kansas, and in 1873 Parsons rejoiced at having the first cotton-gin in the state. Several bales had been ginned. One man in Cowley County raised eighteen hundred pounds of cotton in 1873, it was announced.

In 1882 Blue Rapids, Kansas, had a woolen mill which was reported to be employing one hundred hands. The most amazing experiment of all, however, was that of silk raising and manufacture in eastern Kansas. A Frenchman, Valeton Boissiere, began to weave silk ribbon in 1869 and was enthusiastic and enterprising in the business until the Centennial Exposition in 1876. He had three looms plying constantly with a capacity of two hundred and twenty-four yards of ribbon a day. He began weaving broad goods in 1870 but the market was not profitable. In 1870 he took steps to produce his own silk. Eggs were imported from California and Japan. His display at the Centennial Exposition attracted a great deal of attention. He sold his product in New York where it commanded the highest prices. He said there was a profit for the commission man but not for him. Boissiere had hoped to demonstrate that silk could be produced in Kansas with profit; he had planted seventy acres with mulberry trees, and had induced over forty French immigrants to come to Kansas to establish a coöperative community in which each person should perform the work he was best fitted to do. Some of these immigrants were experts in silk culture and manufacturing. The value of the work performed was to be carefully graded and each person was to secure the profits of his individual labor. He planned to establish other industries operating on the same plan. The program failed because when the Frenchmen mingled with others and learned the English language, they found that they could earn much higher wages as farm laborers or mechanics than they could hope to receive on their profits from an infant industry.

In 1862 at Desoto, Nebraska, a hat factory was established. At Fort Scott, Kansas, in 1882 a castor oil pressing concern turned out eighty gallons of that prized medicine a day; at Atchison, Kansas, one hundred and forty thousand gallons of linseed oil were produced annually; sugar mills turned out quantities of cane and corn syrup; match factories were operating at various points; and there was talk of starting a corset factory in Ordway, Dakota Territory. In 1877 a gypsum mill in Central Kansas produced eighty barrels of plaster of Paris per day. Lawrence, Kansas, used the cable system to transfer power. In 1882 approximately fifteen hundred horse-power was harnessed there at the dam on the Kaw River, three hundred and fifty of which was transmitted from the river by cables and was used daily in various parts of the town. Power was carried more than one-half mile by this system. Among other concerns there were at that time four wire fence factories, a paper mill, and a chemical and patent medicine firm.

In the eighties several plants manufacturing windmills and barbed wire were opened in Kansas and Nebraska. Among the other plants in Kansas in 1882 were wagon, carriage, and agricultural implement factories, a straw lumber concern which made lumber from straw, canning works, cracker factories, flax and hemp bagging works, a stove company employing one hundred and fifty men, a wagon manufacturing company employing two hundred men and putting a wagon on the market every twenty-five minutes, and sash and door companies.

CHAPTER XXXV

CRUDE FRONTIER CUSTOMS

A WRITER in the *Forum* in 1854 asserted that there was a social equality in western country towns that prevailed nowhere else and that the daughters of the blacksmith were quite as prominent as the daughters of the banker, provided they behaved discreetly; they were likely to do this for all grew up together and attended the same schools. The only social test in the West was good conduct, he said. In the West equality was the supreme law and the foundation of the infant society. In view of this outstanding basic principle the editor or doctor who desired to give a ball was compelled to invite the farmer, the barber, the butcher, and all others. To invite a lawyer and refuse a drayman would have been considered a breach of good taste of the first water. Should one dare to issue special invitations to a particular group, he was considered an aristocrat of the highest degree. He risked incurring the enmity of the entire community or, escaping that, he found dozens of uninvited guests on his hands. It was impractical to expel this group. Private or exclusive affairs did not flourish on the frontier. The select groups, such as the "five hundred" or "upper ten," were crushed by public opinion.

The West was no place for an aristocrat. Any person who felt himself better than another quickly lost the respect of the community. There was no title nor term of respectful address. All were free and equal. No one could feel too proud to do his own work. A minister could not be ashamed to hitch up his own horse, haul his own coal, or black his own boots. There was no respect of persons, for all were respected alike if they behaved well. A storekeeper who would discriminate between a poor and a well-to-do customer, or wait on a business man before the boy belonging to the poverty-stricken homesteader, was considered a small man indeed.

In the association of the sexes there was a well-meaning laxness which the better class of society in the East considered as liberty. One writer noticed that engagements were lightly entered into and were accepted as pretexts for liberties. It was the rule for a young man to call on his affianced in the evening and remain alone with her until long after midnight. Should the home of the young lady have two or more rooms, it was thought to be an impertinence for the young lady's parents to frequent the room where the two lovers sat. This, of course, was entirely out of harmony with the code of the East in the mid-Victorian era.

There had always been a rage for military titles throughout the West. This assumed such alarming proportions after the Civil War that the rank and file almost ceased to exist.

The very nature of the frontier created a close coöperative community spirit. When the first wedding occurred the whole community looked upon it as a family affair in which all were interested and concerned. When the first white baby was born the whole settlement considered it a happy neighborhood event. When death snatched one of their number the entire neighborhood was there to weep and sympathize with the bereaved family.

The frontier supported a spirit of curiosity and tended to produce a race of people who inquired and found out all about their neighbors. When the lonely dwellers of the plain saw the white cover of the prairie schooner camped nearby, they quickly finished their work and visited the camp inquiring of the travelers their names, where they came from, and where they were going. Scores of intimate questions were asked and answered by people hungry to see new faces. Families, visiting one another for the first time, told each other personal matters which would never be mentioned between neighbors in the conservative East. Everyone knew all about his neighbor's business. It was common knowledge that a certain couple had eloped and come West against the wishes of the parents of the young lady; that a particular bachelor had come because his sweetheart had jilted him; that another man had a dark past in the old home; that a man and his wife were not happy in their marital state; that a certain man had mortgaged his place the maximum amount and intended to leave the mortgage company in the lurch; and that another was thinking more about spiritual things than in the past. An interesting example of the latter appeared in a column headed "Local Matters" in the *Beatrice Express*:[1] "We are glad to see that the efforts of one of our Methodist friends to induce two of our citizens who have been heretofore considered rather hopeless cases, to attend class meeting, have been rewarded with success."

One of the most marked peculiarities of frontier society was the versatility of the people. Many men had been employed in various occupations before they came to the West. Many worked at several vocations after their arrival in the frontier village. Governor Charles Robinson, a physician, received post-graduate training on the California and Kansas frontiers as editor, restaurant keeper, military official, member of a legislature, and governor. Many professional men worked at humble tasks, exhibiting the most striking examples of versatility to be found anywhere.

In Dakota Territory during the early years the following examples were to be found. A lawyer from New York took a subcontract for carrying the mail between two Dakota points. The district attorney of Potter County ran a milk wagon when not engaged in legal work. A young man who spent four years at West Point Military Academy was runner and night clerk at a hotel. Four traveling salesmen held homestead claims. They spent the seed and harvest seasons on their land as farmers and then, after shaving, they resumed their work as drummers. A drayman in one town had been a dry goods merchant, a farmer, and a druggist. A preacher of the Methodist Episcopal church built a skating rink, sold patent

[1] *Beatrice Express*, Beatrice, Nebraska, January 30, 1873.

rights, ran a barber shop, a meat market, a dray line, and later went on a circuit. A preacher of the Christian church ran a restaurant and boarding-house and later became president of a college founded by his sect in a frontier town.

One man who came to Nebraska in the seventies, recalled that the morning after his arrival he felt the need of visiting a barber shop and asked the doctor if there was such a shop in town. He replied: "We have a good barber in town, but I will go with you." He led the way to a saloon where the bartender said: "Why, he has gone south of town to plaster a house."

The first drug store in Osceola, Nebraska, was opened by a country blacksmith who blossomed out into a full-fledged pharmacist. The doctor mixed the important prescriptions while the budding pharmacist served his apprenticeship.

On the plains as in most new countries, marriage was entered into lightly and divorce was readily secured. At first, of course, there were no laws regulating these matters and there was little uniformity of procedure. In January, 1857, nearly three years after the organization of Kansas as a territory, the legislature voted down a bill to license marriages on the ground that it would not be well to place any obstacles in the way of marriage when the women were so hard to get.

The divorce proceedings in the Dakota Territory illustrate the ease with which the marriage contract was annulled. The third bill introduced in the territory was one granting a divorce to a lady. There is no record that the husband even knew of the action. The divorce was consummated within ten days after the introduction of the bill. The same session of the legislature granted General William Tripp a divorce from his wife on short notice. The divorce was final eighteen hours after the general appeared to request the favor. Sarah Tripp, his wife, had never been in Dakota. At her home in Maine she had no idea that her husband in Yankton was securing a divorce in order to marry his housekeeper which he did immediately after the granting of his divorce.

This does not seem to have been extraordinary. There was no mention of it in the newspapers nor did the correspondent deem it worthy of mention in his letters.[2] It is interesting to note that in the second session of the legislature a divorce bill introduced in the council was referred to the committee on public buildings. It was favorably reported on the next legislative day and passed. When it was sent to the house it was referred to the committee upon internal improvements.

Albert D. Richardson, the noted correspondent, observed that the Kansas Territorial Legislature had passed scores of divorce bills. Practically anyone asking for a divorce could obtain it, he said, and in every case both parties were authorized to marry again.[3] A Massachusetts woman whose conduct was not above reproach and who had incurred her husband's displeasure, came to Kansas and prayed the legislature for a divorce. The rules were suspended in her case; in four or five hours a bill had passed both branches of the legislature, was signed by the governor, and became a law. A man in the East inquired of a friend in the West whether his estranged wife passed by her maiden name or her wedded name and whether she had applied for a divorce. Upon examining the statutes the correspondent found she had been divorced for more than six months.[4]

The crudeness of the ways of the frontier is perhaps best illustrated in official circles. In those places where one would expect to find decorum and formality, the greatest informality existed. The newspaper correspondent at the capital of Dakota Territory made the following report of proceedings in the legislature:

I happened to drop into the representative hall a few mornings since, during their session, and there I saw the "man of waterfalls" making a loud and long speech on the university bill, in reply to the spread-eagle

---

[2] Doane Robinson, "Divorce in Dakota," South Dakota Historical *Collections*, Vol. XII, p. 269.

[3] This was indeed a shocking situation judged by the standards of the East in the fifties.

[4] A. D. Richardson, *Beyond the Mississippi*, pp. 147–148.

orator from Bonhomme. Off on one side sat the "cool, round-headed member from Yankton," eating boiled eggs with a jack knife, and carelessly resting his brain during the attacks eminating from his Sioux Falls and Bonhomme adversaries.[5]

A correspondent of the *New York Times*, in 1856, gave the following description of the Nebraska legislature:

It is a decidedly rich treat to visit the general assembly of Nebraska. You see a motley group inside of a railing in a small room, crowded to overflowing, some behind their little school-boy desks, some seated on the top of desks, some with their feet perched on the top of their neighbor's chair or desk, some whittling—half a dozen walking about in what little space there is left. The fireman, door keeper, sergeant-at-arms, last year's members, and almost anyone else become principal characters inside the bar, selecting good seats, and making themselves generally at home, no matter how much they may discommode the members. A lobby member stalks inside the bar, and from one to the other he goes talking the advantages of his bill. A row starts up in the secretary's room, or somewhere about the building, and away goes the honorable body to see the fun . . . ; then a thirsty member moves an adjournment and in a few minutes the drinking saloons are well patronized.[6]

The first territorial legislature of Nebraska was such a wild pugnacious body that according to the correspondent of the *Missouri Republican*

at one time it was feared that organization was impossible. But that was not the worst of it, for if the row had broken out, there would have been bloodshed; "as probably there was not a man in either House who was not provided with a brace of Colt's revolvers, and a bowie knife. Of course the outsiders were not unprovided." [7]

The governor's mansion in Kansas in 1855 was located at Shawnee mission and was interesting because of its bachelor as-

[5] Moses K. Armstrong, *The Early Empire Builders of the Great West* (St. Paul, 1901), p. 67.
[6] J. Sterling Morton and Albert Watkins, *History of Nebraska* (Lincoln, 1905), Vol. I, p. 287.
[7] Correspondent "Fontanell," Omaha, January 19, 1855, *Missouri Republican*, February 4, 1855, *Collections*, Nebraska State Historical Society, Vol. XX, p. 264.

pects. The corners and sides of the room were piled with books. The territorial seal, a half gallon of ink, and an old pair of breeches occupied a box at the foot of the bed. The apartment was about twenty feet square with uncarpeted floor and dilapidated walls. A double curled-maple four-poster bed provided a place for the governor and his secretary to sleep. Opposite the bed was a washstand and in another part of the room there was a crooked looking-glass, an old rusty stove, and a pile of law books. In the center of the room stood a table littered with piles of public documents, newspapers, and writing materials, covered with a blue mackinaw blanket. The Nebraska legislative rooms were curtained with two folds of plain calico, one green and the other red.

The inaugural ball which the Nebraskans gave for Governor Izard in 1855 is of interest to posterity in its portrayal of border conditions. The room in which the ceremony was held had been plastered with mud. The floor was made of rough unplaned native lumber, and rough cottonwood board benches on each side of the room served as chairs. The night was intensely cold. The floor had been scrubbed but the heating apparatus, failing to warm the room, allowed the water to freeze upon the floor. This icy dancing floor was the cause for numerous minor accidents during the evening when a number of the society leaders slipped and fell. Supper was served at midnight and consisted of coffee with brown sugar, peculiar sandwiches made of thick slices of bread and bacon, and dried apple pie.

A witness was astonished at the uncouth dress of the governor of Kansas and his party in 1855. The governor's hat was ill-kept. He wore rusty footwear which looked as though it had not known blacking for a week. He wore a red worsted comforter with the ends tucked in at the breast and a pair of buckskin riding gloves. Another member of the party wore a pair of gray trousers turned up over his boots. From one side pocket there protruded a six-shooter, and the nozzle of a whiskey flask peered out suspiciously from the other.

A PIONEER LEGISLATURE OF DAKOTA TERRITORY

In the session that located the capital in 1862. Moses K. Armstrong, *The Early Empire Builders of the Great West.*

In May, 1862, in a hotel, Governor Jayne of Dakota Territory had a disagreement with the former receiver of the land office, Judge Jesse Wherry, over the question of giving half-breeds the rights of citizenship. The difference of opinion finally led to a personal encounter. According to the newspaper correspondent the Governor and the Judge engaged in hair-pulling, choking, striking, bloodspitting, and other pugilistic exercises which were performed with grit and relish. The Dakota legislature was so quarrelsome and turbulent that in April, 1862, the Governor had to send an armed detachment of twenty men of the Dakota cavalry with fixed bayonets into the House of Representatives with instructions to preserve order and protect the House in the peaceful performance of its duties.

The early elections were equally turbulent. There were "hot times" indeed. In Dakota Territory the candidates assembled in Sioux City, Iowa, the campaign headquarters of the Sioux Valley and southern counties of Dakota,

to load up with patriotism and fire water, and charge across the Sioux to attack the bewildered voters with spread-eagle speeches, torch light parades, fife and drum, and bottles labeled "fire water." These campaign parties traveled in cavalcades made up of men on foot, on horseback, and with band wagon. The musicians furnish the music and do the fighting at the meetings, the lawyers were to make the speeches and do the lying, the voters were to furnish the cheers and do the drinking, while the candidates were to do their bragging during the campaign and to pay the bills and do the swearing after election.[8]

Old settlers reported a political meeting held in 1862 at which the speaker, a candidate for Congress, stood on a heap of barnyard refuse near a straw-covered barn. The speaker was Captain J. B. S. Todd, a relative of Mrs. Abraham Lincoln. A visitor in Kansas observed a man vote five times. In clearing his conscience he said he voted once for himself and cast four other votes as a proxy for his particular friends who would have voted for his candidate had

[8] Moses K. Armstrong, *The Early Empire Builders of the Great West*, p. 55.

they been in the territory, but unfortunately they were not, and he was favoring them in this manner.

Men were hospitable and neighborly on the plains. As the isolated settlers battled against savage men, heat, drought, devouring insects, the continual wind, and loneliness, they were drawn together in a fellowship that was akin to brotherhood. A man could ride across the prairies for days hunting stray cattle or horses and never be asked to pay for his board and lodging or his horse's provender. Often men offered to pay but almost invariably the reply was: "That's all right, stranger, just you do the same for me when I'm in your parts." And when the stranger left, the host would say: "Whenever you're this way again, don't forget to call," no matter if the guest was a perfect stranger. If a land agent, loan company representative, or other commercial man was out on the prairie it was customary for him to leave a silver half-dollar on the table although he was never charged anything.

When a stranger happened in at meal time there was invariably a command from the head of the house: "Now bring up your chair." This was followed, when the group had surrounded the table by, "Pitch right in!" If a woman headed the household, she said, "Now you just make yourself perfectly at home, and help yourself to anything you see!"

It was the custom when one farmer came along where another was at work to stop the plow and talk as long as the passer-by cared to linger; or if he happened by the house at meal time, he was expected to stay. A Kansan remembered going to the mill with his father in 1855. Their horses gave out within a mile of a settler's house. Unhitching the team and making their way to the cabin, the travelers asked to stay overnight. The permission was granted. The cabin, consisting of a single room, twelve by fourteen feet, contained the mother, two grown-up daughters, and several smaller children in addition to the guests. During the evening the oldest girl entertained her beau. That night the whole group slept in that one room. In the morning when the guests offered to pay for the meal, the hostess refused to accept anything. This custom of crowding was common on the frontier. Even though the little cabin was full of adults and children, there was always room to take in a couple with their children.

As a rule the settlers were very agreeable and obliging. Neighbors were ready to lend anything they possessed. No man driving along with an empty wagon on a good road would pass another on foot without inviting him to ride. If he had a loaded wagon and happened to overtake a lady pedestrian he would ask her to ride even if he, himself, had to walk.

If a man drove up to a cabin, the woman might go into the house and shut the door. This was not unusual and was a sign that isolation had made her timid. It was not good taste to walk directly up to the door and knock but to shout a greeting. After getting over the shock, the lady soon came out. This custom of remaining in the vehicle or on horseback while the inmates of a cabin appraised the newcomers and returned the greeting was universal. The greeting was usually: "Hello!" or "Hello! the house!" The reply was: "Come in, stranger."

A new arrival in the West wrote to his eastern friends that the language was strong and peculiar. A well-dressed individual, he said, would express his belief that he could thrash another: "I 'low that I could clean you out quicker'n greased lightnin' would pass a funeral." Nebraska was widely pronounced "Newbrasky." People from the South and New England, of course, brought their distinctive idioms and provincialisms. A large number of the Kansans came from Indiana, Ohio, and Illinois, bringing with them certain colloquialisms peculiar to that and neighboring sections—such expressions as "mighty weak," "powerful bad," "tolerable fair," and "right smart chance." [9] With the frontiersmen a pail was a "bucket," afternoon was "evenin'," sunrise was "sunup," bread was "light bread," hot biscuits were "bread," corn-bread was "Johnny cake,"

---

[9] Considerable or a large quantity. For example: He gave his horses a right smart chance of hay.

a fish spear was a "gig," a spider was a "skillet," a ramrod was a "gun stick," fifty cents was "four bits," whiskey was called "strychnine," "nux vomica," or "tanglefoot," fever and ague was called "fevernager," or in referring to this the afflicted was said to be "yaller behind the gills." A newcomer, even as early as the sixties, was known as a tenderfoot." The word tedious was pronounced "tejus." A funeral was called "a buryin'." Sociables were called "soshybles," dare goal was "dare gule," and gums were "gooms."

The chronic frontiersman, the squatter who advanced from border to border holding a piece of land until he could sell at a profit, was different from the true agrarian pioneer. He loved the wild life and felt the lack of elbow room when the country became settled. He loved the gun and rod and felt little inclination to spoil the hunter's paradise with the plow. From the viewpoint of the hustling farmer of the eastern states, they were shiftless and lazy. About 1860 Ingalls wrote that the population had not produced enough to pay for the whiskey which they had consumed. A pioneer of Ottawa County, Kansas, well illustrated this shiftlessness. He knocked a stone out of the back of the fireplace chimney and thrust a log through into the fire. When the end was burnt off he went out and pushed the log farther into the opening. The chimney was capacious and a crane hung on it supporting a haunch of venison or a huge piece of buffalo meat. When a meal was needed, the crane was swung so that the meat was over the fire. When the lowest or exposed surface was cooked a slice was cut off and the meat swung off to cool again.

This type of frontiersman was careless in dress and lacking in cleanliness. The earlier frontiersman particularly lived amid rude surroundings and spent little time on such frivolous matters as dressing and washing. The frontier habit was to go to meals in shirt sleeves and eat in comfort. The pioneer returning East was stopped on the river steamboat by the colored man in charge of the dining room and asked to put on his coat. Horace Greeley noticed the characteristic lack of cleanliness in the sixties. He said that although water was scarce on the plains it was used

for purposes of ablution with a frugality not fully justified by its scarcity. A "biled" shirt lasts a good while. I noted some in use which the dry, fine dust of that region must have been weeks in bringing to the rigidity and clayey yellow, or tobbaco stain hue which they unchangeably wore during the days that I enjoyed the society of the wearers.

An Englishman, in commenting on the efficiency of the American pioneer as a conqueror of the wilderness, said, "An ordinary American can do about as much with his axe as many Englishmen can do with a whole tool chest."

Although the bulk of the frontier population was honest, many rogues came in the boom days of heavy migration. Some had left the more civilized land of law and order because of misdemeanors and had found a haven of refuge in a land where there was little or no law. There were schemers, deceitful land agents, crooked boomers, and quacks who pretended to be doctors. There were swindlers and confidence men who, with the idea of leaving the country suddenly, dealt sharply or cheated people under the cloak of religion. Possession was nine points in the law, in fact ten points, before legal machinery began to function. There were contests, antagonisms, unfair advantages, and outright wrongs followed by quick departures or stubborn resistance. Murder and other lawlessness was common. In Nebraska, Judge Gaslin was elected in 1875 to the district in which Custer County was located. During his sixteen years of service he had sixty-eight murder trials, twenty-six of which fell within the first three years. Many homicides never came to trial on the frontier and, no doubt, this figure does not tell the whole story.[10]

There is little reason to believe that morality, so far as it pertains to married couples and fidelity in the family life, was less

[10] There were many cattlemen in that part of the state at that time; hence this does not represent a true picture of the agrarian frontier unmixed with cowboy influences.

pure than in other parts of the country during the Victorian period. Among the single men morality was probably less strict. A large male population with few good virtuous women to uphold the standard, brought lax morals. Numerous houses of ill-repute soon found a place in a segregated district of the small boom town. A good woman, however, was held in high esteem and was never insulted or embarrassed. No matter how drunk or how hilarious frontiersmen became, they showed every respect for a virtuous woman. It was almost entirely unknown for a young woman to become an unmarried mother.

Eye-glasses never found favor on the frontier. The wearer of these new fangled things was considered a "dude." Cowboys would laugh a bespectacled tenderfoot out of camp; the same spirit existed in the early farming communities. The man who carried an umbrella was decidedly unpopular, and a silk hat would have been unthinkable.

Little caresses or terms of endearment even between parents and their children were very seldom used. People who made an outward show of affection, calling each other by such terms as "Daddy dear" or "Helen dear," were under suspicion. The neighbors felt that such a family was hypocritical and comment on such a family was universally dismissed with the statement: "I'll bet they fight like cats and dogs when no one else is around." Naturally, for a lad to speak of love for a girl was strictly taboo.

One stranger in the West about 1870, noticed that the people were always "guessing" about things. They "guessed" about things which they knew perfectly well: Furthermore he was struck with the tendency of the pioneers to "gas," boast, "blow," and exaggerate. No one, he stated, saw any harm in telling a "whopper"; that is, a lie that no one would believe. Many, he observed, would have felt it not worth while to speak if they could not stretch the truth a bit. There was little difference, the observer found, between one thousand and ten thousand to the Westerner. A few dozen snakes would as readily be called one as the other. A few more flies than were agreeable would be called "wagon loads." The visitor concluded with the observation that the pioneers had a light lively way of speaking and that they delighted in dry jokes. Artemus Ward's writings, he said, were very popular with them and represented their manner of speaking very correctly.[11]

The traveling missionary from the East was shocked to find that almost without exception the masculine members of the raw frontier drank and played cards. A minister observed that a young man laid himself open to the charge of putting on airs by neglecting to greet the company, either by the customary "good evenin', gentlemen," or the yet more western polite invitation of asking "the crowd" to "step up and liquor" at "my expense." Saloons were probably more numerous than any other class of business houses. As late as 1886 Fargo, Dakota Territory, had sixty saloons and four low variety theaters.[12] At a hotel the bar was always crowded and the rule in military parlance was "fire and fall back" to make room for others to step up on the lines and take a "shot."

An early resident of Omaha characterized the activity of the early inhabitants as a continual spree. On one occasion two government officials invited him to accompany them to Council Bluffs. They took a "nip" at the bar before leaving the hotel and, once the company was settled in the carriage, a member of the company ordered the bar assistant to bring out the drinks. Going a block, the party halted for another instalment. At every opportunity this was repeated. They stopped for drinks at the half-way house, at "The Last Chance," at the ferry, and when across, at "The First Chance," then at another half-way house, and at place after place which dispensed liquor in Council Bluffs. The observer, becoming tired of this sport, left to spend the night elsewhere. The next morning he found his governmental friends still having a

[11] W. M. Stewart, *Eleven Years Experience in the Western States of America, with an Analysis of the Prairie Soil by Dr. Stevenson Macadam* (London, 1870), pp. 94–95.
[12] Charles H. Phillips, "Early Religious Activities," *Quarterly Journal*, University of North Dakota, Vol. XIII, p. 309.

"good time." The general was on a high table playing a violin to a half-drunken crowd. The party had made its way from saloon to saloon all night long. When he was asked to return home, the general cried "Not yet, my lad! We are going to make a night of it." For two years, our informant said, the Omaha boys were on an almost constant celebration.

Few, even of the elderly residents in the country in frontier days, carried watches every day. It was customary to determine the time by the sun. This practice developed into a fine art. There were no whistles compelling people to be on time to the minute, no cars to catch, and wearing a watch was looked upon as a more or less ornamental procedure. It was part of the dress-up costume to be worn to town, to the county fair, or to church. Many never even wound their watches since this was a matter of some detail and could not be executed simply by the stem.[13] The showy chain amply compensated for the neglect to utilize the watch as a time-piece.

It was a general custom for a young man to secure a watch when he was twenty-one. "Coming of age" at that time was an event of more importance than it is today.[14] A young man worked for his father until he was of age, when "his time was his own." If the father was able, he ordinarily gave the young man a team or team and wagon to begin life for himself.

Although the earlier frontiersmen were not lovers of hard work, yet they possessed a certain go-ahead spirit and hoped to make money by speculative enterprises. They tried a great many things, first at one trade and then at another. They moved about from place to place giving the country fluidity.

Women were called ladies, and school-girls of ten to fourteen were called ladies, but when they hired out they were only "hired

[13] Watches were wound with a key and the crystal had to be removed to set the hands. The first stem wind watches were so wonderful that they gave rise to the slang term "stem winder" which is still used to characterize something or some-one extraordinary.
[14] Harry P. Simmons, *Under the Kerosene Lamp*, pp. 158–160.

girls" no matter what the age. No one on the frontier would have allowed anyone to call him by such an odious epithet as servant. Hired help, degraded by such a title, would have left immediately. It was hard to keep help under any conditions. A family brought a servant girl along from St. Louis under contract to stay with her employer a year, but she married in less than three weeks after reaching the upper Missouri.

Although externally all were alike socially, it was not uncommon to find a college graduate driving an ox team in the street, chopping wood by the river, or living in a sod shanty far out on the prairie. At the loneliest cabin one might find a man who could talk intelligently on the state of affairs in the world, the latest scientific theory, or discuss a recent novel. On a table made of a dry goods box one of the best eastern papers or magazines sometimes was found. A person with very little money was considered rich. A widow who came West with three hundred dollars was considered a lucky prize for a bachelor because she was a rich widow.

BIBLIOGRAPHY

DOCUMENTS

Annual Report, County Superintendent, Seward County, Nebraska, year ending April 1, 1871.

Annual Report of J. H. Noteware, State Superintendent of Immigration, Nebraska, *Blue Valley Record*, June 6, 1872.

Constitution and By-Laws, Kansas State Grange.

First Report of the State Board of Agriculture (Kansas, 1864).

Methodist Episcopal Church Reports, Second Session, Nebraska Conference, March 26, 1862.

Minutes of the Nebraska Conference of the Methodist Episcopal Church, Ninth, Tenth, and Eleventh Sessions, Ms., Nebraska Wesleyan University.

Nebraska Council Journal, First Session.

Report of the State Board of Agriculture to the Legislature of Kansas for the Year 1873 (Topeka, 1874).

Session Laws of Nebraska, 1855–1865.

United States Census Report for the Year 1860.

United States Census Report for the Year 1870.

United States Census Report for the Year 1880.

United States Executive Documents, 1875, Vol. I, pp. 33–35.

United States Public Statutes at Large, 27th Congress, Vol. V.

United States Public Statutes at Large, 28th Congress, First Session, Vol. V.

CONTEMPORARY BOOKS AND PAMPHLETS

ARMSTRONG, MOSES K., *The Early Empire Builders of the Great West* (St. Paul, Minnesota, 1901).

BEADLE, J. H., *Western Wilds and the Men Who Redeemed Them* (Cincinnati, Ohio, 1882).

BODDAM, WHETHANI J. W., *Western Wanderings* (London, 1874).

COLT, MIRIAM DAVIS, *I Went to Kansas* (Watertown, New York, 1862).

EBBUTT, PERCY, *Emigrant Life in Kansas* (London, 1886).

FULTON, FRANCIS, and SIMS, I., *To and Through Nebraska* (Lincoln, 1884).

GREELEY, HORACE, *An Overland Journey from New York to San Francisco in the Summer of 1859* (New York, 1860).

Kansas Grange Bulletin, May 10, 1872.

Kansas Grange Program for 1889, Leaflet in Kansas State Historical Society Library.

MCNAMARA, JOHN, *Three Years on the Kansas Border* (New York, 1856).

MARTIN, EDWARD WINSLOW, *History of the Grange Movement* (Chicago, 1874).

RICHARDSON, ALBERT D., *Beyond the Mississippi* (Hartford, Connecticut, 1869).

ROBINSON, SARA T. D., *Kansas, Its Interior and Exterior Life* (Boston, 1856).

ROPES, H. A., *Six Months in Kansas*. By a lady (Boston, 1856).

STEWART, W. M., *Eleven Years' Experience in the Western States of America with an Analysis of the Prairie Soil*, by Dr. Stevenson Macadam (London, 1870).

SWEAT, LEVI G., *Sweat's Sectional Map and Settlers' Hand Book*. U. S. Court Commissioner, Chadron, Nebraska (Fremont, Nebraska, 1855).

CONTEMPORARY PERIODICALS AND NEWSPAPERS

Ainsworth Journal (Ainsworth, Nebraska), June 11, 1874–Sept. 11, 1884.

Beatrice Express (Beatrice, Nebraska), July 5, 1871–Mar. 13, 1873.

Blue Valley Record (Milford, Nebraska), Dec. 29, 1870–Apr. 30, 1873.

Canton Advocate, The (Canton, Dakota Territory), May 7, 1878–Nov. 7, 1878.

Cheyenne County Rustler (Wano, Kansas), July 10, 1885–Oct. 30, 1885.

Clay County Register (Vermilion, Dakota Territory), Sept. 7, 1872–Mar. 13, 1873.

Cold Water Review (Cold Water, Kansas), Nov. 29, 1884–Feb. 10, 1885.

Dakota Huronite (Huron, Dakota Territory), Jan. 5, 1882–May 25, 1882.

DeSoto Pilot (DeSoto, Nebraska), 1857.

Frontier, The (O'Neill City, Nebraska), Sept. 30, 1880–July 27, 1882.

Frontiersman, The (Bird City, Kansas), Oct. 13, 1885–Dec. 29, 1886.

Hays City Railway Advance (Hays, Kansas), June 23, 1868.

Herald of Freedom, The (Lawrence, Kansas), Oct. 21, 1854–July 21, 1855.

Huntsman's Echo, The (Wood River, Nebraska), June 14, 1860–July 26, 1860.

Huron Tribune (Huron, Dakota Territory), June 2, 1881–Dec. 29, 1881.

Kansas Chief, The (White Cloud, Kansas), June 4, 1857–Dec. 30, 1858.

Kansas Educational Journal (Topeka, Kansas), Jan. 1864–Apr., 1867.

Kansas Farmer (Topeka, Kansas), May 1, 1863–June 15, 1872.

Kansas Free State (Lawrence, Kansas), Jan. 3, 1855–Dec. 3, 1855.

Kansas Weekly Herald (Leavenworth, Kansas Territory), Sept. 15, 1854–Sept. 8, 1855.

Lawrence Republican (Lawrence, Kansas), May 28, 1857–Jan. 7, 1858.

Manhattan Express (Manhattan, Kansas), Aug. 29, 1859–July 28, 1860.

Nebraska Advertiser (Brownville, Nebraska), June 7, 1856–Mar. 3, 1859.

Nebraska City News (Nebraska City, Nebraska), Jan. 17, 1847–Dec. 25, 1858; Jan. 14, 1860–Sept. 14, 1861; Jan. 4, 1862–July 21, 1865.

Nebraska Farmer (Brownville, Nebraska, and Lincoln, Nebraska), 1850–1862; Jan., 1877–Dec., 1880; Jan., 1882–Dec., 1882.

Nebraska Herald, The (Nemaha City, Nebraska), Nov. 24, 1859–Nov. 22, 1860.

Nebraska Palladium (Bellevue, Nebraska), July 15, 1854–Oct. 11, 1854.

Newton Kansan (Newton, Kansas), Jan. 6, 1876–June 1, 1876.
Niobrara Pioneer (Niobrara, Nebraska), Sept. 22, 1874–Apr. 27, 1882.
Oakdale Journal (Oakdale, Nebraska), Sept. 23, 1873–Oct. 5, 1875.
Oakdale Pen and Plow (Oakdale, Nebraska), Oct. 5, 1875–June 5, 1879.
Omaha Arrow (Omaha, Nebraska), July 28, 1854–Dec. 29, 1854.
Omaha City Times (Omaha, Nebraska), June 11, 1857–July, 1858.
Omaha Nebraskian (Omaha, Nebraska), Jan. 7, 1860–Apr. 28, 1860.
Paxico Courier (Paxico, Kansas), Sept. 20, 1888–Nov. 1, 1888.
People's Press, The (Nebraska City, Nebraska), Nov. 17, 1859–Nov. 21, 1860.
Pierre Free Press (Pierre, Dakota Territory), Dec., 1883–Apr. 10, 1884.
Pioneer, The (O'Neill, Nebraska), Aug. 18, 1881–Apr. 2, 1882.
Republican Valley Empire (Clyde, Kansas, and Concordia, Kansas), May 31, 1870–Dec. 31, 1871.
Standard, The (Ellis, Kansas), Sept. 22, 1877–Oct. 27, 1877.
Sumner Gazette (Sumner, Kansas), Sept. 12, 1857–Jan. 16, 1858.
Topeka Daily Capital (Topeka, Kansas), Feb. 8, 1882–Aug. 19, 1882.
Warner Weekly Sun (Warner, Dakota Territory), Aug. 18, 1883–Nov. 3, 1883.
Western Star (Cold Water, Kansas), Sept. 20, 1884–Aug. 8, 1885.
Wichita Eagle (Wichita, Kansas), Apr. 12, 1872–Aug. 8, 1885.
Wichita Vidette (Wichita, Kansas), Aug. 13, 1870–Mar. 11, 1871.
Winfield Courier, The (Winfield, Kansas), Feb. 1, 1873–June 26, 1874.

COLLECTIONS

Collections, Nebraska State Historical Society, Vols. I–XXII (Lincoln, Nebraska, 1885–1936).
Collections, State Historical Society, of North Dakota, Vols. I–VII (Bismarck, North Dakota, 1905–1925).
Kansas State Historical Society *Collections,* Vols. I–XIX (Topeka, Kansas, 1881–1934).
Monthly South Dakotan, Vols. I–IV (Yankton and Aberdeen, South Dakota, 1898–1902).
Nebraska Pioneer Reminiscences (Cedar Rapids, Iowa, 1916).
North Dakota Historical Quarterly, Vols. I–VII (Bismarck, North Dakota, 1926–1933).
Quarterly Journal, 11 vols (Grand Forks, North Dakota, 1910–1921).
Quarterly Journal, University of North Dakota, Vols. XII–XXIII (Grand Forks, North Dakota, 1921–1933).
South Dakota Historical *Collections,* Vols. I–XVI (Aberdeen and Pierre, South Dakota, 1902–1932).

DIARIES

BEADLE, ERASTUS, *To Nebraska in Fifty-Seven* (New York, 1923).
GUTHRIE, ABELARD, "Diary of Abelard Guthrie," *Transactions and Reports,* Nebraska State Historical Society, Series II, Vol. III.

TAYLOR, NATHAN, *Diary of Nathan Taylor for Parts of the Year 1858 to 1859*, Ms., Kansas State Historical Society.

WALKER, WILLIAM, "The Journals of Governor Walker," *Transactions and Reports*, Nebraska State Historical Society, Series II, Vol. III.

NEWSPAPER REMINISCENCES

Aberdeen American News (Aberdeen, South Dakota), June 1, 2, 1931.

Beaver City Tribune (Beaver City, Nebraska), March and April, 1913.

Broken Bow Chief (Broken Bow, Nebraska), Nov. 10, 1932.

Fairbury News (Fairbury, Nebraska), March 14, 1912.

Gibbon Reporter (Gibbon, Nebraska), 1908, 1909.

Gregory Express (Gregory, Nebraska), Dec. 11, 1930.

Hastings Daily Tribune (Hastings, Nebraska), Oct. 20, 1921.

Kansas City Star (Kansas City, Missouri), Nov. 11, 1911.

Lawrence Journal-World (Lawrence, Kansas), Oct. 10, 1929.

Lennox Independent (Lennox, South Dakota), Oct. 25, 1934.

McPherson County Herald (Leola, South Dakota), June 14, 1934.

Marshall County News (Marysville, Kansas), Feb. 27, 1931.

Minden Courier (Minden, Nebraska), March 27, 1931.

North Loup Seventh-day Baptist Church Bulletin, North Loup, Nebraska. Vol. II, No. 4.

Omaha World-Herald (Omaha, Nebraska), Feb. 21, 1923; June 11, 1933.

Ord Quizz (Ord, Nebraska), June 21, 1923.

Ravenna News (Ravenna, Nebraska), July 1, 1910.

Superior Express (Superior, Nebraska), June 22, 1923, June 29, 1933.

Tecumseh Chieftain (Tecumseh, Nebraska), July 2, 1931.

Topeka Daily Capital (Topeka, Kansas), May 9, 1923.

Topeka Journal (Topeka, Kansas), May 24, 1916.

MANUSCRIPTS

ABBOTT, N. C., *Territorial Counties*, Nebraska State Historical Society Library.

BARE, IRA L., *The Live Stock Industry*, Nebraska State Historical Society Library.

BASSETT, RUTH, *The First School at Adams*, Nebraska State Historical Society Library.

BASSETT, SAMUEL C., *The Free Homestead Colony of Buffalo County*, Nebraska State Historical Society Library.

BELL, JOHN T., *Reminiscences of John T. Bell*, Nebraska State Historical Society Library.

DUNN, BELLE J., *History and Development of Blaine County*, Nebraska State Historical Society Library.

GALE, GEORGE, *History of Old Clay County*, County Scrapbook, Nebraska State Historical Society Library.

HAUMONT, JULES, "A Talk by an Old Settler to the Broken Bow D. A. R." (1929), Nebraska State Historical Society Library.

JOHNSON, L. GRACE, *Pioneering in Box Butte County*, Nebraska State Historical Society Library.

Kansas Reminiscences, Vols. III, IV, Kansas State Historical Society Library.

KENNEDY, JAMES. A letter by James Kennedy, steamboat captain on the Missouri River, giving certain information on steam boating. Nebraska State Historical Society Library.

Negro Clippings, Vols. V, VI, Kansas State Historical Society Library.

STOLLEY, W. M., *Historic Sketches of Hall County*, Nebraska State Historical Society clipping collection.

UNDERHILL, NANNIE BLAINE, *Covered Wagon Tales*, Kansas State Historical Social Library.

WALDEN, ARNOLD, *Reminiscences*, Kansas State Historical Society Library.

WATKINS, FLORENCE, *Early History of Red Willow County*, Nebraska State Historical Society Library.

PERSONAL INTERVIEWS

ARD, NOAH. January 2, 1934. Mr. Ard was born July 3, 1845, at Versailles, Missouri. His parents moved to Allen County, Kansas, in 1861. He squatted in 1866. It was later discovered that his claim lay within the railroad grant. He was one of the leaders in the Kansas Settlers Protective Association which fought the railroads for years. In time nearly all of the claimants lost their land to the railroad. Mr. Ard, after years of litigation, finally secured a clear title to his homestead. He lives today on the old claim which he took during the Civil War period.

KAISER, PETER. December 28, 1933. Mr. Kaiser was born April 11, 1844, at Belleville, Illinois. He settled in Ottawa, Kansas, in the seventies and had a knowledge of the town's institutions during homestead days.

NELSON, W. E. August 5 and November 10, 1935. Mr. Nelson was born and reared in Turner County, South Dakota. As a small boy he experienced the hardships incident to the conquest of the prairie.

NORTON, J. CLARENCE. December 29, 1933. Mr. Norton was born December 28, 1856, in Montville, Maine. His father, Joseph G. Norton, was sent out as one of the representatives to locate a place for the Ohio Soldiers Colony in 1871. The family came out to Kansas in 1872, and they located in Allen County where young Norton grew up on the homestead frontier.

TRAVIS, S. A. July 10, 1935. Mr. Travis was born in Indiana in 1860, and migrated to Huron, Dakota Territory, in 1883. He spent a short time in Aberdeen and a few months later took a claim in Sully County. He started the *Okobojo Times*, and was in a position to know the "in and outs" of the frontier newspaper business in the eighties.

WHEELER, GEORGE L. November 25, 1935. Mr. Wheeler was born in Iowa, December 8, 1855. He went to Kansas in the early seventies and as a young man traveled about on the plains selling patent medicines, spectacles, and other things.

WHEELER, MRS. J. W. October 20, 1931. Mrs. Wheeler was born at Bloomfield, Iowa, April 1, 1864. Her parents migrated to Wabaunsee County, Kansas, in 1875, where she grew up amid frontier conditions.

BIOGRAPHY AND AUTOBIOGRAPHY

ABBOTT, OTHMAN A., *Recollections of a Pioneer Lawyer* (Lincoln, 1929).

BARNS, CASS G., *The Sod House* (Lincoln, 1930).

BENGSTON, B. E., *Pen Pictures of Pioneers* (Holdrege, Nebraska, 1916).

———, *Pen Pictures of Pioneers*, Vol. II (Holdrege, Nebraska, 1931).

CRAWFORD, LEWIS F., *Rekindling Campfires* (Bismarck, North Dakota, 1926).

DAVIS, REV. HENRY T., *Solitary Places Made Glad* (Cincinnati, 1890).

DILLMAN, son of JACOB DILLMAN, *A Human Life* (Excelsior, Minnesota, 1934).

FISHER, REV. H. D., *The Gun and the Gospel* (Chicago, 1896).

GARLAND, HAMLIN, *Boy Life on the Prairie* (New York, 1899).

———, *A Son of the Middle Border* (New York, 1917).

GAYLORD, MRS. MARY M., *Life and Labors of Rev. Reuben Gaylord* (Omaha, 1889).

GOODLANDER, C. W., *Memoirs and Recollections of the Early Days of Fort Scott* (Fort Scott, Kansas, 1900).

GRIFFITH, G. W. E., *My 96 Years in the Great West, Indiana, Kansas, and California* (Los Angeles, 1929).

HUMPHREY, SETH K., *Following the Prairie Frontier* (Minneapolis, 1931).

McKEITH, G. R., *Pioneer Stories of the Pioneers of Fillmore and Adjoining Counties* (Exeter, Nebraska, 1915).

MANNING, EDWIN CASSANDER, *Biographical Historical and Miscellaneous Selections* (Cedar Rapids, Iowa, 1911).

MEYERS, AUGUSTUS, *Ten Years in the Ranks U. S. Army* (New York, 1914).

SHAW, REV. JAMES, *Early Reminiscences of Pioneer Life in Kansas* (Atchison, Kansas, 1886).

SIMMONS, HARRY P., *Under the Kerosene Lamp* (York, Nebraska, 1922).

TABER, CLARENCE WILBUR, *Breaking Sod on the Prairies* (Yonkers-on-Hudson, 1924).

TURNER, JOHN, *Pioneers of the West* (Cincinnati, 1903).

WELLS, REV. CHARLES WESLEY, *A Frontier Life* (Cincinnati, 1902).

HISTORIES AND REMINISCENT BOOKS

BAKER, MRS. NORA COX, *Recollections of Childhood* (Scottsbluff, Nebraska).

BENGSTON, B. E., *Fifty Years of Fridhem, Hardville, Nebraska* (Central City, 1930).

BRAINERD, HENRY ALLEN, *History of Nebraska Press Association*, Book I (Lincoln, June 1, 1923); Book II (July 1, 1923).

CHILD, DR. A. L., *Centennial History of Plattsmouth and Cass County, Nebraska* (Plattsmouth, Nebraska, 1877).

CORDLEY, RICHARD, *Pioneer Days in Kansas* (Boston, 1903).

CRAWFORD, SAMUEL J., *Kansas in the Sixties* (Chicago, 1911).

DILLMAN, son of JACOB DILLMAN, *A Human Life* (Excelsior, Minnesota, 1934).

GOODLANDER, C. W., *Memoirs and Recollections of the Early Days of Fort Scott* (Fort Scott, Kansas, 1900).

GREEN, C. R., *Early Days in Kansas*, Green's Historical Series, Vols. I, III, IV (Olathe, Kansas, 1913).

HARVEY, AUGUSTUS E., *Sketches of the Early Days of Nebraska City* (St. Louis, 1871).

HENRY, STUART, *Conquering Our Great American Plains* (New York, 1930).

LEACH, A. J., *History of Antelope County, 1868–1883* (Chicago, December, 1909).

McKEITH, G. R., *Pioneer Stories of the Pioneers of Fillmore and Adjoining Counties, Nebraska* (Exeter, Nebraska, 1915).

McNEAL, T. A., *When Kansas Was Young* (New York, 1922).

RHODES, WILLIAM, *Recollections of Dakota Territory* (Fort Pierre, South Dakota, 1931).

REESE, JOHN B., *Some Pioneers and Pilgrims on the Prairies of Dakota* (Mitchell, South Dakota, 1920).

REMY, DR. G. O., *Pioneer Doctors of Brown County, Nebraska*, Nebraska State Historical Society.

ROENICK, ADOLPH, *Pioneer History of Kansas* (Lincoln, Kansas, 1933), Kansas State Historical Society.

ROOT, F. A., and CONNELLEY, W. E., *The Overland Stage to California* (Topeka, 1901).

SORENSON, ALFRED, *Early History of Omaha* (Omaha, 1876).

STOKES, WILL E., *Episodes of Early Days in Central and Western Kansas* (Great Bend, 1925).

STRALEY, W., *Pioneer Sketches, Nebraska and Texas* (Hico, Texas, 1915).

TORREY, EDWIN C., *Early Days in Dakota* (Minneapolis, 1925).

WIGGIN, ELIZA JOHNSTON, *Impressions of Early Kansas* (Wichita, 1915).

GENERAL HISTORIES

ANDREAS, ALFRED THEODORE, *History of the State of Kansas* (Chicago, 1883).

———, *History of the State of Nebraska*, Vol. I (Chicago, 1882).

KINGSBURY, GEORGE W., *History of Dakota Territory* (Chicago, 1915).

MORTON, J. STERLING, and WATKINS, ALBERT, *History of Nebraska* (Lincoln, 1905).

PAXSON, FREDERIC L., *History of the American Frontier* (Cambridge, 1924).

PUTNEY, EFFIE FLORENCE, *In the South Dakota Country* (Mitchell, South Dakota, 1928).

ROBINSON, DOANE, *History of South Dakota* (Indianapolis, Indiana, 1904).

SMITH, GEORGE MARTIN, *South Dakota, Its History and Its People* (Chicago, 1915).

MISCELLANEOUS

FLANDREAU, GRACE, *Red River Trails*, A pamphlet published by the Great Northern Railway. No date given.

FOWLER, WILLIAM W., *Woman on the Frontier* (Hartford, 1876).

COUNTY AND SECTIONAL HISTORIES

ADAMSON, ARCHIBALD, *North Platte and Its Associations* (North Platte, Nebraska, 1910).

Arnold's Complete Directory of Phelps County (Holdrege, Nebraska, 1909).

BARE, IRA L., *History of Lincoln County* (Chicago, 1920).

BLANCHARD, LEOLA HOWARD, *Conquest of Southwest Kansas* (Wichita, Kansas, 1931).

Brief Historic Sketch, Waverly and the Community, A, Compiled by Parent Teachers' Association.

BRIGHAM, LALLA MALOY, *The Story of Council Grove on the Sante Fe Trail*, 1921, Kansas State Historical Society.

BROWN, GEORGE L., *Centennial History of Butler County, Nebraska* (Lincoln, 1876).

BUECHLER, A. S., and BARR, R. J., *History of Hall County, Nebraska* (Lincoln, Nebraska, 1920).

Buffalo County History, Published and Copyrighted by the Lady Helpers of the First Congregational Church (Gann Valley, South Dakota, 1934).

BULLOCK, MOTIER A., *Congregational Nebraska* (Lincoln, Nebraska, 1905).

BURTON, S. D., *Pioneer History of Custer County* (Broken Bow, Nebraska, 1910).

Community History of Beaver Crossing, 1872–1932 (Beaver Crossing, Nebraska).

CORDLEY, RICHARD, *History of Lawrence* (Lawrence, Kansas, 1895).

DOBBS, HUGH J., *History Gage County, Nebraska* (Lincoln, 1918).

DUNHAM, N. J., *History of Jerauld County, South Dakota* (Wessington Springs, South Dakota, 1909).

DUNN, BELLE J., *History and Development of Blaine County, Nebraska*, Ms. (Lincoln, 1927).

ELLIS, CAPTAIN C. H., *History of Faulk County, South Dakota* (Faulkton, South Dakota, 1909).

FATE, W. H. H., *Historical Glimpse of the Early Settlement of Union County* (Sioux City, Iowa, 1924).

FRENCH, LAURA M., *History of Emporia and Lyon County* (Emporia, Kansas, 1929).

HAYNES, REV. JAMES, *History of the Methodist Episcopal Church in Omaha and Suburbs* (Omaha, 1895).

HICKMAN, GEORGE, *History of Marshall County, Dakota* (Britton, Dakota, 1886).

History of Johnson County (Western Historical Company, 1882).

HUSE, WILLIAM, *History of Dixon County* (Ponca, Nebraska, 1896).

JONES, HORACE, *The Story of Rice County* (Wichita, Kansas, 1928).

JONES, LEWIS E., *Brief History of Cedar County, Nebraska* (St. Helena, Nebraska, 1876).

LEACH, A. J., *History of Antelope County* (Chicago, 1909).

LOCKARD, FRANCES MARION, *History of the Early Settlement of Norton County, Kansas* (Norton, Kansas, 1894).

MOORE, H. MILES, *Early History of Leavenworth* (Leavenworth, Kansas, 1906).

NYQUIST, EDNA, *Pioneer Life and Lore* (McPherson, Kansas, 1932).

OCHSENREITER, L. G., *History of Day County* (Mitchell, South Dakota, 1926).

PERKINS, JOHN B., *History of Hyde County, South Dakota* (1908).

PETERSON, LLOYD, *History of Nebraska City Schools*, Ms., Nebraska Historical Society.

SCOTT, CHARLES F., and DUNCAN, L. WALLACE, *History of Allen and Woodson Counties, Kansas* (Iola, Kansas, 1901).

SPOKESFIELD, WALTER E., *The History of Wells County, North Dakota, and Its Pioneers* (Jamestown, North Dakota, 1929).

STODDARD, W. H., *Turner County Pioneer History* (Sioux Falls, South Dakota, 1931).

STOKE, WILL E., *Episodes of Early Days in Central and Western Kansas*, Vol. I (Great Bend, Kansas, 1926).

SWEET, E. N., *History of Cuming County* (Lincoln, Nebraska, 1876).

WAKELEY, ARTHUR C., Ed., *Omaha, Gate City, Douglas County, Nebraska*, 2 vols. (Chicago, 1917).

Warner's History of Dakota County, Nebraska (Dakota City, 1893).

WESTENIUS, CHATTIE COLEMAN, *The Story of Stromsburg* (Stromsburg, Nebraska, 1931).

MONOGRAPHS

ALBRECHT, ABRAHAM, *Mennonite Settlement in Kansas*, Ms., Master's Thesis, 1925, Kansas University.

BENTLEY, ARTHUR T., *Condition of the Western Farmer*, Johns Hopkins Studies in Historical and Political Science, Eleventh Series, VII–VIII (Baltimore, 1893).

BUCK, SOLON JUSTUS, *The Granger Movement* (Cambridge, 1913).

FLINT, HERBERT, *Journalism in Territorial Kansas*, Ms., 2 parts, Master's Thesis, Kansas University.

MACY, JESSE, *Institutional Beginnings in a Western State*, Johns Hopkins University Studies, Vol. II, No. 7.

MARTIN, EDWARD WINSLOW, *History of the Grange Movement* (Chicago, 1874).

PAINE, A. E., *The Granger Movement in Illinois* (Urbana, 1904).

"The Settlement and Economic Development of the Territory of Dakota," an excerpt from the University of Iowa Studies in Social Science, Vol. X, No. 2.

MAGAZINE ARTICLES

BRIGGS, HAROLD E., "The Development of Agriculture in Territorial Dakota," *The Culver Stockton Quarterly*, Canton, Missouri, Jan., 1931.

COLE, ARTHUR C., "The Passing of the Frontier," *Mississippi Valley Historical Review*, Vol. V.

CRANDALL, HORACE B., "A Sketch of Richland County," *North Dakota Magazine*, Vol. II, No. 4.

FARMER, HALLIE, "Economic Background of Frontier Populism," *Mississippi Valley Historical Review*, Vol. X.

HARGAR, CHARLES MOREAU, "The Prairie Woman: Yesterday and Today," *The Outlook*, April 26, 1902.

HOUGH, EMERSON, "The Settlement of the West," *Century Magazine*, Nov., 1901.

LOUNSBERRY, CLEMENT, "Popular History of North Dakota," *North Dakota Magazine*, Vol. II, No. 4.

SYLVESTER, B. F., "Hoss Tradin'," *Saturday Evening Post*, Jan. 6, 1934.

INDEX

529